VIOLENCE in AMERICA

VIOLENCE

n AMERICA

HISTORICAL and CONTEMPORARY READER

Edited by Thomas Rose

FOREWORD BY PAUL JACOBS

ANDOM HOUSE · NEW YORK

Grateful acknowledgment is made to the following for permission to reprint from their works:

Ballantine Books: *Student*, by David Horowitz. Copyright © 1962 by David Horowitz.

Children, a publication of the U.S. Department of Health, Education, and Welfare: "An Impossible Situation," by Robert Coles (May–June, 1967), from an article entitled "Violence in Ghetto Children."

Commonweal: "America's Malady Is Not Violence But Savagery," by John Lukacs.

Doubleday & Company, Inc.: *From Race Riot to Sit-In*, by Arthur Waskow. Copyright © 1966 by Doubleday & Company, Inc.

Freedomways magazine, a Quarterly Review of the Freedom Movement: "The July Rebellions and the 'Military State,'" by J. H. O'Dell.

Harper & Row, Publishers: "The Homestead Strike" and "Violence in the West," from *Dynamite: The Story of Class Violence in America*, revised edition, by Louis Adamic. Copyright 1931, 1934, by Louis Adamic; renewed 1959 by Stella Adamic. "Invasion and Counterattack," from *Forbidden Neighbors*, by Charles Abrams. Copyright © 1955 by Harper & Brothers.

Mayday: "Sabotage: 'This Is Number One and the Fun Has Just Begun,'" by Andrew Kopkind. Copyright © 1968 by The New Weekly Project, Inc. "Hayden on Walker on Daley," by Tom Hayden.

The New Republic: "Appalachia: Hunger in the Hollows," by Robert Coles (November 9, 1968), "Stripped Bare at the Follies" (January 20, 1968), "Journey into the Mind of the Lower Depths" (February 15, 1964). Copyright © 1964, 1968, by Harrison-Blaine of New Jersey, Inc.

The New York Times: "A Radical Speaks in Defense of SNCC," by Staughton Lynd, September 10, 1967. Copyright © 1967 by The New York Times Company.

W.W. Norton & Company, Inc.: "Born Out of Violence," from *Thaddeus Stevens: Scourge of the South*, by Fawn M. Brodie. Copyright © 1959 by Fawn M. Brodie.

Ramparts: "Requiem for Nonviolence," by Eldridge Cleaver, May, 1968.

The Village Voice: "Visit to Chicago: Blood, Sweat, and Tears," by Steve Lerner, September 5, 1968. Copyright © 1968 by The Village Voice, Inc.

For Ruta

FOREWORD

By PAUL JACOBS

In April, 1937, seven prominent Bostonians, including the president emeritus of Harvard University, sent a telegram to the United States Senate, stating that "Armed insurrection—defiance of law and order and duly elected authority—is spreading like wildfire. . . . It is the obligation of Congress and the State Legislatures, of the President and the Governors, in their Constitutional fields, to enact and enforce legislation that will put an end to this type of defiant insurrection."

The "armed insurrection" to which the Bostonians were referring was the sit-down strike in which thousands of General Motors employees took over the GM plants in Michigan.

Today, as in 1937, it is difficult to find phrases more commonly used and less commonly understood than "law and order," "armed insurrection," or "violence." Politicians vie for public favor as they keep escalating their promises to restore or maintain "law and order"; paramilitary police departments move more quickly with massive movements of force whenever a breakdown of "law and order" appears imminent and even the distinguished head of the American Bar Association discusses "law and order" in the most general and meaningless way.

The extraordinary amount of public attention given today to "law and order," "violence," and "mobbism" is a direct result of the racial crises in America which have so seriously disrupted the public calm. Racial disorders always carry the potential of violence—of spreading over large physical areas, plus the physical destruction and widespread theft of property.

So, too, public discussions of "law and order" and "violence" associated with racial tensions always tend to be very heated, reflecting feelings of either fear or guilt or both on the part of the majority population, while fear and hate underlie the minority's reaction. In such an atmosphere of terrible tension, essential differentiations disappear into unspecific generalizations.

In 1968, just as in 1937, discussions about law and order in America begin as if there were certain commonly accepted propositions about law and order and violence. One such proposition is that *all* violence is illegal, while another is that a common view exists about the destructiveness of violence, directed either against persons or property. A third proposition is that all Americans know that fixed rules exist for the preservation of law and order, and accept those rules as being valid. Thus the "lawbreaker" is seen as a deviant whose illegal behavior stems from some personality defect or a failure in his environment.

But these propositions do not take into account either the fact that within American society there exist sharply differentiated views concerning violence and the meaning of law and order, or that certain forms of collective violence are tolerated as the political power of the protesting groups increases.

The sit-down strikes of 1937 provide a case in point: no one doubted that the strikers were violating the law. It was clear that they were occupying property that did not belong to them and were, in addition, prepared to defend their "right" to carry on this illegal activity. Yet the state made no attempt to employ force in order to remove them from the property, nor was there any prosecution of the sit-down strikers after the strike had ended. In this case, political power and economic pressure outweighed the purely legal considerations.

In general, violence during the course of a strike is likely to be judged by a different set of standards than if the same acts took place under conditions of less stress and tension. Thus even when economic pressure or political power was not enough to prevent prosecution of strikers for acts of violence, the courts tended to be more lenient toward the strikers because of the assumption that they had been engaged in defending either psychic or property interests they held in their jobs.

In Europe there has been, until recently, another form of tolerated collective violence, and that is the riot. In the past, European riots have been distinct in very important ways from the riots which have taken place in America. European riots have tended to be limited, directed at bringing about specific purposes or reforms *within* the context of the system as it is, not its transformation or overthrow. Generally, in such riots, the police do not kill anybody, shots are not exchanged, and there is little or no looting. The rioters may tear up the streets to build barricades, may overturn cars, may even burn the cars, but these acts have, in the past at least, been part of an effort either to defend their territory or achieve specific objectives within the confines of the system.

But today in America some groups engaged in collective illegal acts are making generalized, nonspecific demands upon the society, demands that cannot or will not be met. The question that is always asked of the people who participate in these illegal acts is, "What do you want?" And the answer that always comes back is, "I want what you want." But this generalized, nonspecific response is not understood because those who ask the question have a different perception about the nature of American society than those who answer the query.

One difference in perception is that most whites believe our political and legal system is based on order and embodies a shared system of values, a consensus on how changes take place. We also assume that no fundamental differences exist in our society about the view of property rights and violence. I suggest that such assumptions are incorrect and that no such wide consensus exists, especially among the nonwhite population. For example: the American Indian's perception of land and its use was, and in some cases still is, totally different from that of the white man. The most significant initial conflict that took place in this country between Indians and Europeans was over the concept of land as private property. The Indian perception of

land endowed it with a magical quality which involved a
relationship between the sun and the water and the earth,
intended for the collective use of all. The notion of a fence
to separate portions of the land was unknown to Indians,
who believed that a fence defaced the land. The Indians
could not understand the concept of converting land into
private property and consequently of giving its "owners"
the right to forbid people to go on the land: to the Indian,
land was for the communal use of all men, and all animals,
too. "We suffer the little mouse to play," said the Indian,
meaning that the mouse as well as man had a right to use
the land. And so the bloody conflict developed because the
white Europeans "bought" what the Indians did not understand they were "selling."

Another example of conflict and violence growing from
differing views of land as property is the one between the
State of New Mexico and Reies Lopez Tijerina and the
Alianza. Here a group of New Mexicans are challenging
the government on a basic question of land ownership. If
the Alianza wins, the entire State of New Mexico will belong to its members. Even now Tijerina acts on his different
vision, his different understanding of land ownership; in the
name of the Alianza he arrests police officers! He and his
group marched into the county courthouse armed with rifles
and arrested law-enforcement officials whom he accused of
violating the Alianza's rights to the land.

The case of looting, a term without legal definition, is
also based on the difference between the looters' perception
of property and that of the lootees. Looting in the racial disturbances has a number of special characteristics. First,
many of the people who participate in racial looting seem
to conceive of it as a kind of collective "taking" rather than
stealing. The notion of "taking" is ancient in black-white relations in America: a slave "took" from the master with the
approval of his fellow slaves; stealing was theft from fellow
slaves and was disapproved of in the slave community. To
"take" from the master was one of the ways which the slaves
found enabled them to survive physically and psychically.
Thus looting, like "taking," assumes the quality of a political
act, made more legitimate as it becomes a collective action.

It is also justified as a redistribution of goods, a forced

redistribution of goods; nor is it too important what the goods are, for either the looters are poor or the looting is a symbolic act, one marking identity and participation in a collective action. This perception of looting as a symbolic act is certainly prevalent in the ghettos today and indeed is so important that after the 1965 outbreak in Los Angeles, some of the black hustlers in the ghetto purchased, legitimately, all kinds of cheap merchandise to be sold in the ghetto. People bought such merchandise because one of its sales appeals was the value attached to it as allegedly having been "taken" during the outbreak.

So, too, because it meant a defiance of authority, the burning of stores was also conceived of as an act of identity.

Eldridge Cleaver, for example, describes in *Soul on Ice* how after the Watts rebellion, those prisoners in jail who came from that area suddenly spoke up and said proudly, "I'm from Watts. I'm from Watts." So, too, I saw sweat shirts with I'M FROM WATTS printed on them being worn defiantly by young men and women all over Los Angeles. For them, to have participated even vicariously in that violence brought a collective identity of which they could be proud to people who did not have an identity before.

But how, most of us ask, can people be proud of an identity achieved through violence, looting, and burning? And once again the difference between the questioner and those who might respond is one based on a different perception of the macro- and micro-worlds in which we live.

For example, the worlds of most nonwhites do not include the concept that there exists a cause-and-effect relationship in politics or that the political system is in any way responsive to their daily needs. Thus in Washington, D. C., there are black people living almost in the shadow of the Capitol who when asked if they know what the white building up across the hill is would answer no. Nor do they know what happens in the building, and why should they? The fact is there *is* no visible connection between what happens in that building and their lives. Thus the daily micro-world of many people does not include what *we* think of as "normal" politics of the "normal" political system. Indeed, the micro-world does not encompass the direct seeking of power or seeking the relief and redress of grievances through institutions. Instead, getting power or getting redress is conceived as taking place through individuals rather than through institutions. And implicit in this view of government is a lack of knowledge of or confidence in the legal system as an instrumentality that has any consequences for their lives, except bad ones.

And so the generalized, nonspecific demands—which are so often demands for identity, for humanness—become expressed through outbreaks of violence, frequently triggered by police action. The relationship of the police to the minority communities is one of especial stress, for here again a basic difference in viewpoint separates the majority group from those in the minority.

Most of us assume that the authorized representatives of society, especially the police, act with a minimum of bias in the overall interests of society. We also believe that if they are not acting "properly," if they do display bias, we can utilize better training techniques, community and human relations programs, more professional training, and better salaries to reform the police.

But this view leaves us without knowledge of the sense of basic apprehension felt by a large number of black people and brown people. When white people walk down the street and see a police officer, they do not have an apprehension that he is going to shoot or beat them. Instead, they have the expectation, based on past behavior, that he will be polite even when he gives them a ticket, and that when needed he will behave in a supportive fashion.

But a wide chasm separates that view of the police from the one acquired by so many nonwhites either through direct experience or racial memory. Thus at the level of both the assumptions concerning the basic total nature of American society and of its specific institutions, such as the police, fundamental differences are to be found whose existence is not even recognized.

This condition means that the political structure is dysfunctional. As a consequence, when a political crisis occurs, no other mode of political expression can exist except violence. (Nonviolence as a technique for achieving political change can only function when a commonly shared view exists concerning the ultimate possibility of change *within* a system.)

But since the majority of people in the society are unable or unwilling to accept its dysfunctional nature, a set of other explanations is developed to explain the phenomenon: in this case, the racial violence is attributed, completely incorrectly, to the so-called "blacks," and there is a refusal to acknowledge that a great many middle-class, educated Negroes either participate in the disturbances or sympathize with those who do, even if they remain outside the conflicts.

Such explanations for disorder and violence are extraordinarily dangerous. In this book, Thomas Rose has chosen a wide variety of other explanations and analyses of violence. Perhaps if we learn to better understand violence, we will be able to better understand its political nature; the depoliticalization of illegal acts ensures the use of massive repression as an answer to the acts. In turn, this massive repression will bring on an escalation of the illegal acts and so the country will become caught up in an ever-increasing order of violence which ultimately will end in civil warfare.

Contents

·III· VIOLENCE IN THE SIXTIES

·IV· LOOKING AT OURSELVES

INTRODUCTION

By THOMAS ROSE

Violence is integral and central to politics, society, and culture, especially in urban America, because people and institutions are committed to it as a logical and useful style of life. The impact of violence in American life is most often clouded over by the jargon that we are a "peaceful" nation dedicated to "peaceful change." Violence is a reflection of our social reality, and it is tolerated as a solution to personal and social problems. An excessive display of violence is obvious in American society and exists against a giant system of defense arguments, alibis, and rationalizations.

American culture, as this reader illustrates, tolerates, approves, propagates, and rewards violence. The glamour of violent acts and the glorification of violent men create an idealization of violence in America. It is generic and fundamental to the substance of American life, a major theme ingrained in our life styles, and is part of the individual character, as well as institutionalized in the socio-economic-political structure. We have so interiorized our own violence that it has engulfed many of us. This is why it is so important for us as individuals and as a society to understand violence. Bruno Bettelheim points out that "we cannot say that because violence *should* not exist, we might as well proceed as if it did not."

Many historians and social scientists assume that Ameri-

can life can only be understood by using models of consensus and accommodation (politics by agreement of a
few men who make and control policy at the top) because
they are so enamored of and wedded to these kinds of politics. They are hooked on the consensual model of harmony,
adjustment, and equilibrium, and most often ignore conflict
and violence or consider them marginal. Howard Zinn
points out that "a relentless commitment to his own country may cause an American to glide over the elements of
brutality of American history."

Because most of our teachers, texts, and the media have
insisted that we are a "peaceful" nation that is generally
affluent, they have been unable to describe society as it
really is, and instead give a distorted view based on how
they want it to be and how they want others to see us. One
indicator of this is the tragic lack of information about the
operation of conflict and violence in American life. When
violence and conflict are portrayed, they are skewed in a
direction of being marginal rather than integral to an understanding of American politics, society, and culture. Conflict and violence are not transitory, but have consequences
of lasting duration. Dissent, conflict, and violence cannot
be resolved within a consensual or systems model, where
everything is adjusted and patched up and left smoldering
like social and political dynamite just below the surface.

Violence is omnipresent in American history. From the
earliest beginnings of this nation until the present there
has been no period without considerable violence. William
Appleman Williams points out, in *The Contours of American History,* that the major feature of American history is
that Americans force others to be the way they want them
to be: a governing minority has always imposed its will on
the majority by force and violence, saying that "what is
good for us is good for you." The governing minority, the
"consensus," has been violent and has violated those who
continually express their disagreement, often peacefully,
with the status quo. In the political policies of social control, organized violent control is the might, the cannon, that
sanctions and upholds authority and tradition. Tristram Coffin summarizes some of our violent policies in *The Armed
Society*:

The American missionary spirit is not exclusively peaceful. There is no evidence that we are peace-loving or ever have been. We have taken what we wanted by force if need be, sometimes muttering a proper prayer over the vanquished. We shoved the Indians off their lands without a how-do-you-do; drove out the Dutch, British, French, and Spanish; fought Mexico and seized California with as little ceremony as the Russians grabbing the Baltic states; engaged in a savage Civil War; fought in Cuba and the Philippines; staged our own "revolution" in Hawaii against the native Queen; kept gunboats and Marines in China, and invented and used the great horror weapon, the nuclear bomb, in World War II. Through it all we have maintained a righteous air, contending that we have committed mayhem and felony with the purest motives. This is a result of our Puritan inheritance, which requires proof that God is on our side in every expedition and sanguinary action.

We need to distinguish between individual crimes of violence and collective violence, including riots and rebellions. This reader is not about individual crimes, although it is possible to argue that both individual crimes and rebellions occur for the same basic reason: to get a piece of the affluence or system. This happens when people feel there is no other way available to get in on the affluence and power, or when they wish to change the system. The critical difference between an individual crime and a rebellion or revolution is that of *organization.* Sorel pointed out, in *Reflections on Violence,* that there is a thin line between individual crimes and riots or rebellions because sometimes individual crimes of sabotage are acts which have a vague organization. If those who commit them are organized, their organization would more likely be found out. What makes these acts similar is that those who commit them have the same goals.

Eugene Genovese, in the "Legacy of Slavery and Roots of Black Nationalism," argues that when violence is collective and disciplined, it is political. The collective effort, not the violence, makes it political and creates a kind of bond and brings about change. This kind of violence may be termed rebellion, whereas riots are a form of unorganized protest. Rebellions are organized protest and occur only when there is a collective effort, whereas riots, although they may be protest politics, are frequently undirected, misdirected, or naively directed. Throughout American history collective violence has been counteracted with a greater violence. Rebellion has been crushed. People have rioted in this nation either because they were unorganized or because they knew collective violence was not an effective tool since it could not succeed against the violence of the government.

Albert Camus wrote that we are able to "find all direct violence inexcusable and then to sanction that diffuse form of violence which takes place on the scale of world history." We are horrified when a teenager tosses a brick, but not when a corporation steals millions of dollars. Many people take the position that when the state acts violently, it is only doing so to defend its citizens, that it is even sacrosanct, but that most individual and group violence is absolutely wrong, and even evil. Often those who cry most about violence in the streets, whether in the Revolutionary era, during the Draft Riots, or in 1968, are themselves willing to resort to violence on an institutional level. The interrelationship and interconnections between individual and institutional violence are brilliantly explored by Richard Drinnon, writing about Emma Goldman and the nineteenth-century anarchists, in his book, *Rebel in Paradise*:

> A defensible philosophical argument might be advanced that individual violence is at least as justifiable as the organized national violence called wars. Everyone is to a large extent shut up in his own consciousness—everyone, whether he likes it or not is in . . . "The Ego-Centric Predicament." The implications of this predicament are debatable—indeed debate on this subject between idealists and realists has been a basic philosophical preoccupation. It is safe to say, however, that this dilemma makes it difficult if not impossible to prove demonstrably false the argument of the anarchists that the individual—the I—is the basic reality; the state is merely an abstraction. From this point of view it is defensible to argue that it is more justifiable for individuals to use violence for their own ends than it is for them to participate in the large-scale violence of abstractions such as the state, which is composed of collectivities of individuality-denying persons.

There is also certain validity in the contention of Emma and Berkman that "force begets force"—more precisely stated as violence begets violence. Only a mind closed to a frank discussion of the problem of violence would refuse to recognize an element of truth in this claim of Berkman: "The bomb is the echo of your cannon, trained upon our starving brother; it is the cry of the wounded striker . . . the bomb is the ghost of your past crimes." Are warships built for "educational purposes"; is the army a "Sunday School"; is the gallows a "symbol of brotherhood"? Berkman asked. One necessarily must answer no and therewith recognize that the large-scale violence exercised by the state sets a pattern for and dwarfs acts of individual violence. The symbol of violence nowadays is not the anarchist's puny bomb, but the state's magnificent hydrogen horror.

Thomas Jefferson noted that an aristocracy of wealth did great harm and was a danger to American society because it gave immense political and economic power to a few who became a power elite. An institutionalized process of inequality and poverty is a basic cause of a pattern of violence with frequent outbursts. The cause of much violence in America lies within the process of allowing and keeping one third of a nation poor. This is obviously linked to the institutionalization of social, economic, and political inequality. Wealth and power are linked and seem to be a function of making sure some people are poor and kept that way, or are killed off or sent away, e.g., Indians or political radicals. Jefferson wrote: "Seldom do the victims of a social order have sufficient cohesion and political insight to attack their worst enemies."

However, the poor in America have always been both frustrated and provoked by the arrogance of wealth. They have either organized against it or tried to become a part of it. In either case violence has often taken place between the rich and poor: draft riots, slavery, labor violence, race riots, the civil rights movement. The rich have the power to be violent because of their wealth and ties to the military and government. The rich—for example, mine owners and grape growers—have had their own private police or armies at their disposal plus the local police, the militia, the National Guard, and other coercive instruments of the state. When the poor have reacted violently to their conditions on the bottom (the bottom of American society is a violent state of life), they have almost always been suppressed. Only rarely has the so-called legitimate force of the state taken the side of the oppressed. In his essay "Thoughts on Violence and Democracy," Barrington Moore points out that "The violence of the oppressor has generally been far more effective than the violence of the weak and oppressed. This is a violence that the powerful exercise against the weak in the name of freedom and order, a time-honored practice in Western Culture."

Violence is often caused by the lack of economic equality and the lack of economic democracy. Michael Harrington, writing in 1962 in *The Other America,* indicated that "if there is technological advance without social advance, there is, almost automatically, an increase in human misery, in impoverishment." Those who are denied minimal levels of health, housing, food, and education almost always explode as a result of their oppression, and the explosion is usually violent.

In *Wealth and Power in America,* Gabriel Kolko, an economic historian, points out that "the richest tenth receives 30 percent of the annual money income, as in 1961; or 14 percent of the nation owns 68 percent of the new wealth, as in 1962." The poorer half of the United States population receives only one quarter of the national personal income. One third of the population lives under the poverty level of approximately 4,000 dollars for a family of four. Even more important, Kolko points out that "the basic distribution of income and wealth in the United States is essentially the same now as it was in 1939, or even 1910." He believes that government and scholars have overlooked many chronic economic problems and challenges the idea of a predominantly prosperous middle-class society. It is a myth. The causes of poverty and their consequences are most often economic. Constant fear and anxiety about economic security, oppression, and lack of decency are bound to kindle the atmosphere with violence.

Law and order was the feature issue in the 1968 political campaign, but little was said about justice or the real causes of violence because many citizens want a policy of violent control and order to stop rebellion. Just after the 1968 election former Governor Thomas E. Dewey suggested a repeal of the Fifth Amendment—the self-incrimination clause. Howard Zinn's book, *Disobedience and Democracy: Nine Fallacies on Law and Order,* came out just before the election. He comments:

> The degree of civil disobedience should not be weighted against a false "peace" presumed to exist in the status quo, but against the real disorder and violence that are part of daily life, overtly expressed internationally in wars, but hidden locally under that facade of "order" which obscures the injustice of contemporary society.

There is a growing resistance to the draft, the war in Vietnam, and the violent conditions in our cities. Zinn adds: "Indeed, those outbreaks of either civil disobedience or disorder we have had in the United States have been not the *cause* of our troubles, but the result of them." Policy makers most often do not understand this critical difference.

Historically, violence has only been tolerated if the national interest, as defined by those in power, felt it would strengthen the consensus. The national interest respects the argument for the necessity of large-scale violence in Vietnam, and rejects the right of an oppressed minority to use violence, even if that is the only method of gaining justice. Barrington Moore, in *A Critique of Pure Tolerance,* comments on this problem:

> Before the resort to revolution is justifiable, there has to be good reason to believe that the costs in human suffering and degradation inherent in the continuation of the status quo really outweigh those to be incurred in the revolution and its aftermath. To put the point with appalling crudeness, one has to weigh the casualties of a reign of terror against those of allowing the prevailing situation to continue, which may include a high death rate due to disease, ignorance—or at the other end of the scale, failure to control the use of powerful technical devices.

A growing, steady stream of violent control may dissipate the strength of violent revolt and dissent.

Americans only become interested in violence when they see it as an attack upon the majority; otherwise it is someone else's problem. The surge of nonviolent protest in the 1960's almost always created a violent reaction. Many citizens became concerned, but almost always spoke out after the fact. This violence came from the consensus, and only seldom did the federal government use its power and say that this violence was *not* the will of the majority, the consensus. Often the national government worked seriously on civil rights legislation, but was weak when it came to enforcement. Traditionally local custom has prevailed and been more important than either basic human rights or federal law. Again Barrington Moore poses an important question, in his article, "Thoughts on Violence and Democracy":

. . . the prevailing conception of violence . . . fails to draw the crucial moral and political distinctions between the violence of the oppressors and those who resist oppression. By itself, however, this important distinction remains rather abstract. We need to inquire whether the violence of the oppressed has made important contributions to human freedom in the past and whether it may continue to make such contributions today.

The Civil War officially struck down slavery. Violence and the threat of violence during the New Deal helped to dramatize the issues. The radical left today does the same. "Had it not been for the riots it is highly unlikely that the problems of the black ghetto would have become a major political issue." The only real answer Moore gives is that "when violence results in even greater tragedy, there does not seem to be anything to be said for it." This really begs the question, because the military-industrial complex will almost always say that it will be tragic and that it must be stopped to keep the peace.

There has been no period in our history without violence. There has been a continual and recurrent, regular and irregular pattern of violence with frequent bursts: people often get tired, blow off steam, and violence quiets down both as control and as revolt. But more often outbursts are indicators of growing unrest in certain sectors of society, and they are most often squashed by the violent force of industry and government; that is the reason why, within the recurrent cycle, things simmer down but never die. In an essay entitled "Urban Violence and American Social Movements," * St. Clare Drake, a black sociologist, argues that "the incidence and intensity of urban violence . . . has fluctuated widely since the end of the Civil War." He notes a decrease in labor violence during the twenties followed by an escalation during the Depression. Lynching was common during the 1880's, but almost disappeared after the First World War, although there were always other forms of violence that replaced lynching, e.g., race riots in 1919. Harvard sociologist Gary Marx, in a speech to the American Political Science Convention in September, 1968, pointed out:

> The four largest race riots before the Vietnamese war were during war periods. The Civil War saw the New York Draft Riots where perhaps 2000 people were killed (no one bothered much to count and there are instances where police responded to rioters by simply throwing them off buildings). World War One witnessed the very brutal East St. Louis, Illinois, disturbance in which 48 people were killed. After whites set fire to several hundred black homes, white snipers fired at Negroes as they fled the flames. A white mob battled the firemen. The end of World War One saw the 1919 Chicago riot in which 38 died. . . . An incident at an amusement park triggered the 1943 Detroit riot which left 33 people dead and almost a thousand injured.

This book is composed primarily of accounts of regular and irregular, recurrent outbursts every twenty years, although the periods between peaks are not ignored. Not only is there a cyclical pattern of violence, but there are striking similarities between violence in the mid-1840's, mid-1860's, and mid-1960's. In these periods violence in large measure concerned race and a combination of war and politics. Not only were the actual incidents similar, but even the langu-

---

* This essay and Barrington Moore's "Thoughts on Violence and Democracy" are part of a collection of essays, *Urban Riots: Violence and Social Change,* put out by The Academy of Political Science in July 1968, and now available in a 1969 Vintage edition, under the same tit'

age sounded the same; however, only if it was reported in the mass media was it widely known and discussed.

Some readers may wonder at what point violence becomes counterproductive. There is no simple answer, but protest against injustice is as likely to be met with violence in the 1960's as it was in the past. St. Clare Drake points out that "violence may sometimes merely escalate the level of conflict and inflame the atmosphere, without changing the political realities of the situation." Violence often becomes counterproductive because the system insists that it is totally dysfunctional and attempts to crush it. (A theory of consensus indicates that violent revolt is always dysfunctional). Drake asks, "When does it cease to be a signaling device or a catalyst and become disastrous?" There is no simple rule to use here, but it is important to ask who makes the decision about toleration, and what strategy can be taken when signals are not understood or are violated. Our violent past suggests some answers.

ONE

THEORY
AND
DEFINITION

INTRODUCTION

The first two articles in Part One attempt to clarify the meanings of violence, violation, force, nonviolence, and conflict, and the third proposes a theory about how violence occurs. They bring together an overview or portrait, a number of interpretations and points of view, about the multiple forms and situations in which violence has both positive and negative functions and consequences.

Newton Garver, a professor of philosophy at the State University of New York in Buffalo, a Quaker, and chairman of the Peace and Social Action Program of the New York Yearly Meeting, argues that violence almost always involves the violation of persons or their personhood. Some violence is personal and overt; some is personal and covert; some is institutional and overt; and much is institutional and covert. He urges us to recognize as violent these covert acts, and to be aware of psychological violation of personhood.*

Howard Zinn is a professor of government at Boston University, a scholar and political activist, and a well-known crusader to end the war in Vietnam. He is the author of many articles and books, including *S.N.C.C.: The New Abolitionists, The Southern Mystique,* and *Disobedience and Democracy: Nine Fallacies on Law and Order.* Zinn discusses the peculiar kind of violence that is easily directed toward symbols, which are different from the immediate reality of persons or objects at which the

* His article was originally published in *The Nation,* June 24, 1968.

violence is directed. He argues that violence is blunt and unfocused on specific targets, but that nonviolence is sharp and focused. Zinn is concerned with the relationship between violence and nonviolence, and with weighing the degree of violence used against the importance of the injustice involved. When Professor Zinn looks at the relationship between violence, nonviolence, and passivity, he is concerned with the crucial distinction between violence to people and violence to things.*

In the final article in Part One, I will review a number of theories and philosophical arguments about violence in America, and discuss a tentative cyclical theory which will, hopefully, help the reader to analyze the pattern and events recounted in this book. I am especially concerned with the role of violence as political revolt and control in the process of escalation throughout an American past saturated with violence. It is the precarious balance, the constant interaction between violence as revolt and as control, violence by the oppressors and by the oppressed, which needs to be understood so that totalitarianism, a police state, or even worse, can be guarded against.

* Zinn's article originally appeared in *The Nation*, March 17, 1962.

WHAT VIOLENCE IS

By NEWTON GARVER

Most people deplore violence, some people embrace violence (perhaps reluctantly), and a few people renounce violence. But through all these postures there runs a certain obscurity: it is never entirely clear just what violence is. Those who deplore violence loudest and most publicly are usually pillars of the status quo—school principals, businessmen, politicians, ministers. What they inveigh against most often is overt attack on property or against the "good order of society." They rarely see violence in defense of the status quo in the same light as violence directed against it. At the time of the Watts riots in 1965 Mr. Johnson urged Negroes to realize that nothing of value can be won through violent means—a proposition which may be true but which the President did not apply to the escalation in Vietnam he was just then embarked upon, and which it would never have occurred to him to apply to the actions of the Los Angeles police department. Since the President is not the only leader who deplores violence while at the same time perpetrating it, a little more clarity about what exactly we deplore might help all around.

Violence often involves physical force, and the association of force with violence is very close: in many contexts the words become synonyms. An obvious instance is the reference to a violent storm, a storm of great force. But in human affairs violence and force cannot be equated. Force without violence is often used on a person's body.

If a man is in the throes of drowning, the standard Red Cross life-saving techniques specify force which is certainly not violence. To equate an act of rescue with an act of violence would be to lose sight entirely of the significance of the concept. Similarly, surgeons and dentists use force without doing violence.

Violence in human affairs is much more closely connected with the idea of violation than with the idea of force. What is fundamental about violence is that a person is violated. And if one immediately senses the truth of that statement, it must be because a person has certain rights which are undeniably, indissolubly, connected with his being a person. One of these is a right to his body, to determine what his body does and what is done to his body—inalienable because without his body he would cease to be a person. Apart from a body, what is essential to one's being a person is dignity. The dignity of a person does not consist in his remaining dignified, but rather in his ability to make his own decisions. In this respect what is fundamental about a person is radically different from what is fundamental about a dog. The way I treat my dog, which seems to be a good way to treat a dog, is to train him to respond in a more or less mechanical way to certain commands. However, to treat a human being in that way is an affront to his dignity, because a minimum of autonomy is essential to a human being.

The right to one's body and the right to autonomy are undoubtedly the most fundamental natural rights of persons. A subsidiary one stems from the right to autonomy. It is characteristic of human action to be purposive and to have results and consequences; freedom therefore is normally conceived as involving not only the right to decide what to do but also the right to dispose of or cope with the consequences of one's action. One aspect of this is the right to the product of one's labor, which has played an important role in the theory of both capitalism and communism. If this line of thought is extended to the point of considering one's property an extension of his person, the scope of the concept of violence becomes greatly enlarged—perhaps in harmony with popular thought on the subject, at least on the part of propertied persons (however, one should always bear in mind that even a propertied person can reconcile himself much more readily to loss of possessions than he can to loss of life). The right to cope with one's own problems and to face the consequences of one's acts (which I do not accord my dog) is typically abrogated by paternalism.

So violence in human affairs amounts to violating persons. It occurs in several markedly different forms, and can usually be classified into four different kinds, based on two criteria: whether the violence is personal or institutionalized, and whether the violence is overt or covert and quiet.

Overt physical assault of one person on the body of another is the most obvious form of violence. Mugging, rape and murder are the flagrant "crimes of violence," and when people speak of violence in the streets it is usually those acts that cross their minds. I share the general concern over the rising rate of these crimes, but deplore the tendency to limit the image of violence to just these three assaults. These are cases where an attack on a human body is also both clearly an attack on a person and clearly illegal. But even here we must not tie these characteristics in too tight a package, for some acts of violence are intended as a defense of law or a benefit to the person whose body is beaten—e.g., ordinary police activity (not "police brutality") and the corporal punishment of children by parents and teachers. The fact that policemen, parents and teachers invoke socially defined roles when they resort to violence indicates that these cases have institutional aspects that overshadow the purely personal ones; but that fact cannot erase the violence done. Of course not all cases are so clear (I leave to the reader to ponder just how, in sex acts, we distinguish on practical grounds between those that are violent and those that are not). But whenever you employ force on another person's body without his consent, you are attacking not just a physical entity but a person— and that is personal overt violence.

In war, what one army tries to inflict on another is what happens to individuals in cases of mugging and murder. The soldiers are responsible for acts of violence against "the enemy," at least in the logical sense that the violence would not have occurred if the soldiers had refused to act. The Nuremberg trials attempted to establish that individual soldiers are responsible morally and legally too, but this overlooked the extent to which the institutionalization of violence makes ambiguous its moral dimension. On the one hand, an individual soldier is not acting on his own initiative and responsibility; on the other, a group does not have a soul and cannot act except through the agency of individual men. Thus there is a real difficulty in assigning responsibility for such institutional violence. The other side of the violence, its object, is equally ambiguous, for "the enemy" is being attacked as an organized political force, and yet the bodies of individual men (and women and children) receive the blows. Warfare, therefore, because it is an institutionalized form of violence, differs from murder in certain fundamental respects.

Riots are another form of institutionalized violence, although their warlike character was not widely recognized until the publication of the report of the President's National Advisory Commission on Civil Disorders. Some persons maintain that a riot is basically a massive crime wave, but it also can take on a warlike character. One of the characteristics of the Watts riot, as readers of Robert Conot's *Rivers of Blood, Years of Darkness* know, was that the people who were supposed to be controlling the situation, the Los Angeles police and their various reinforcements, simply did not possess basic facts about the community. In particular, they did not know what persons could exercise a sort of leadership if the group were left alone.

So the Los Angeles police force and its various allies conducted what amounted to a war campaign. They acted like an army that seizes foreign territory, and their actions had the effect of breaking down whatever social structure there might have been—which in turn had the effect of releasing more overt violence. The military flavor of urban disturbances has increased over the years, and in 1967 the authorities of Newark and Detroit employed not only machine guns and automatic rifles but also tanks and armored personnel carriers, in what the Kerner Commission characterized as "indiscriminate and excessive use of force." For that reason the urban disorders of recent summers are quite different from criminal situations in which police act against individual miscreants.

The overt forms of violence are, on the whole, easier to recognize than quiet or covert violence, which does not necessarily involve direct physical assault on anybody's person or property. There are both personal and institutional forms of quiet violence. Consider first a case of what we might call psychological violence, involving individuals. The following item appeared in *The New York Times*:

> PHOENIX, Ariz., Feb. 6 (AP)—Linda Marie Ault killed herself, policemen said today, rather than make her dog Beauty pay for her night with a married man.
>
> The police quoted her parents, Mr. and Mrs. Joseph Ault, as giving this account:
>
> Linda failed to return home from a dance in Tempe Friday night. On Saturday she admitted she had spent the night with an Air Force lieutenant.
>
> The Aults decided on a punishment that would "wake Linda up." They ordered her to shoot the dog she had owned about two years.
>
> On Sunday, the Aults and Linda took the dog into the desert near their home. They had the girl dig a shallow grave. Then Mrs. Ault grasped the dog between her hands, and Mr. Ault gave his daughter a .22-caliber pistol and told her to shoot the dog.
>
> Instead, the girl put the pistol to her right temple and shot herself.
>
> The police said there were no charges that could be filed against the parents except possible cruelty to animals.

The reason there can be no charges is that the parents did no physical damage to Linda. But that they did terrible violence to the girl the father himself recognized when he said to a detective, "I killed her; I killed her. It's just like I killed her myself." If we fail to recognize that a real psychological violence can be perpetrated on people, a violation of their autonomy, their dignity, their right to determine things for themselves, to be men rather than dogs, then we fail to realize the full dimension of what it is to do violence.

One of the obvious transition cases between overt personal violence and quiet personal violence is the threat. A person who does something under threat of being shot is degraded by losing his autonomy. We recognize that in law and morals: if a person so threatened takes money out of a safe and hands it to a robber, we say that that person acted under compulsion, and the responsibility for what is done lies only with the robber.

Of course, the person coerced with the threat of injury or death needn't surrender his autonomy; he *could* just refuse to hand over the loot. There can be a great deal of dignity in such a refusal, and one of the messages of Sartre's moral philosophy is that whenever one acts other than with full responsibility for his own actions, he is acting in bad faith. That very demanding philosophy puts great emphasis upon autonomy and dignity, and is not to be lightly dismissed. Nevertheless one cannot expect that people will act with such uncompromising strength and dignity. To recognize that they can be broken down by threats and other psychological pressures as well as by physical attack, and that to have acted under threat or duress is as good an excuse before the law as physical restraint, establishes for the community the concept of psychological violence.

Another insidious form of psychological violence is what might be called the "Freudian rebuff." It works like this: A person makes a comment on the Vietnamese war or on civil rights or on some other current topic. The person he is talking to then says: "Well, you're just saying that because of your relations with your father." The original speaker naturally objects: "Of course I had a father, but look at the facts." And he starts bringing out the journals and newspapers and presents facts and statistics from them. "You must have a terrible Oedipus complex; you're getting so excited about this." And the person then says: "Look, I've had some fights with my father, but I've read the paper and I have an independent interest in the civil rights question. It has nothing to do with my father." To which the response is: "Well, your denial just proves how deep your Oedipus complex is."

This type of Freudian rebuff has the effect of what John

Henry Newman called "poisoning the wells." It gives its victim no ground to stand on. If he tries to advance facts and statistics, they are discounted and his involvement is attributed to Freudian factors. If he attempts to prove himself free of the aberration in question, his very protest is used as evidence against him. To structure a situation against a person in such a manner does violence to him by depriving him of his dignity: no matter what he does there is no way at all, so long as he accepts the problem in the terms in which it is presented, for him to make a response that will allow him to emerge with honor.

Although this sort of cocktail-party Freudianism is not very serious in casual conversations, there are many forms of this ploy where the whole life and character of a person may be involved. A classic literary and religious version is the dispute between Charles Kingsley and John Henry Newman in the nineteenth century, in which Kingsley challenged Newman's integrity and ended up losing his stature as a Protestant spokesman, and which is written up in fascinating detail in Newman's *Apologia*. A political variation is the Marxian rebuff where, of course, it is because of your class standing that you have such and such a view, and if you deny that the class standing is influencing you in that way, your very denial shows how deeply you are imbued with the obfuscating ideology. Between parent and child, as between husband and wife, there are variations which turn upon the identification (by one insistent party) of love with some particular action, so that the other party must either surrender his autonomy or acknowledge his faithlessness.

This sort of psychological violence is most damaging when the person structuring the situation is in some position of special authority, e.g., in schools. An imaginative child does something out of the ordinary, and the teacher's response is that he is a discipline problem. It now becomes impossible for the child to get out of being a problem. If he tries to do something creative, he will be stepping out of line again and thereby "confirming" that he is a discipline problem. If he stays in line, he will become a scholastic problem, thereby "confirming" that he did not have potential for anything but mischief. The result is a kind of stunted person typical of schools operating in large urban areas.

This last variation of the psychological rebuff leads to the fourth general category of violence, institutionalized quiet violence. The schools are an institution, and teachers are hired not so much to act on their own as to fulfill a predetermined classroom role. Violence done by the teacher may therefore not be personal but institutional: perpetrated while acting as a faithful agent of the educational system.

The idea of such institutional violence is very important. A clearer example may be a well-established system of slavery or colonial oppression, or the life in contemporary American ghettos. Once established, such a system may require relatively little overt violence to maintain it. It is legendary that Southerners used to boast, "We understand our nigras; they are happy here and wouldn't want any other kind of life"—and there is no reason to doubt that many a Southerner, raised in the system and sheltered from the recurrent lynchings, believed it. In that setup it is possible for an institution to go along placidly, with no overt disturbances, and yet to be terribly brutal.

There is more violence in the black ghettos than anywhere else in America—even when the ghettos are quiet. At the time of the Harlem riots in 1964 the Negro psychologist Kenneth Clark said that there was more day-to-day violence in the life of the ghettos than there was in any day of those disturbances. I'm not sure exactly what he meant. There is a good deal of overt personal violence in the black ghettos, for reasons Fanon has explained in *The Wretched of the Earth*. But we must also recognize the quiet violence in the very operation of the system. Bernard Lafayette of SCLC speaks angrily of the violence of the status quo: "The real issue is that part of the 'good order of society' is the routine oppression and racism committed against millions of Americans every day. That is where the real violence is." A black ghetto in most American cities operates very like any system of slavery. Relatively little overt violence is needed to keep the institution going, and yet the institution violates the human beings involved because they are systematically denied the options which are open to the vast majority in the society. A systematic denial of options is one way to deprive men of autonomy.

Perhaps denying options would not do violence to people if each individual person were an island unto himself and individuality were the full truth about human life. But it is not. We are social beings; our whole sense of what we are is dependent on the fact that we live in society, and have open to us socially determined options. What access we have to the socially defined options is much more important than what language or what system of property rights we inherit at birth. The institutional form of quiet violence operates when people are deprived of choices in a systematic way by the very manner in which transactions normally take place. It is as real, and as wicked, as the thief with a knife.

THE FORCE OF NONVIOLENCE

By HOWARD ZINN

Four instances of violence come to my mind. One I read about in the newspapers; another I witnessed; in a third I was on the receiving end; in the fourth, the most brutal of them all, I was a perpetrator.

The first took place an hour's drive from my home in Atlanta, Georgia, when a mob in Athens, screaming epithets and hurling rocks, attacked the dormitory occupied by the first Negro girl to enter the University of Georgia.

The second I saw years ago as I walked through a slum area of the Lower East Side of New York: a little old Jew with a beard, pulling his pushcart, was arguing with a Negro who was demanding payment for his work. The bearded man said he didn't have the money and the Negro said he needed it and the argument grew, and the Negro picked up a stick of wood and hit the old man on the side of the head. The old man continued pushing the cart down the street, blood running down his face, and the Negro walked away.

In the third instance, I took my wife and two-year-old daughter to a concert given in an outdoor area near the town of Peekskill, New York. The concert artist was Paul Robeson. As he sang under the open sky to an audience of thousands, a shouting, angry crowd gathered around the field. When the concert was over and we drove off the grounds, the cars moving in a long slow line, we saw the sides of the road filled with cursing, jeering men and women. Then the rocks began to fly. My wife was pregnant at the time. She ducked and pushed our daughter down near the floor of our car. All four side windows and the rear window were smashed by rocks. Sitting in the back seat was a young woman, a stranger, to whom we had given a lift. A flying rock fractured her skull. There were dozens of casualties that day.

The fourth incident occurred in World War II when I was a bombardier with the Eighth Air Force in Europe. The war was almost over. German territory was shrinking, and the Air Force was running out of targets. In France, long since reoccupied by our troops, there was still a tiny pocket of Nazi soldiers in a protected encampment near the city of Bordeaux. Someone in the higher echelons decided, though the end of the war was obviously weeks away, that this area should be bombed. Hundreds of Flying Fortresses went. In each bomb bay there were twenty-four one-hundred-pound fire-bombs, containing a new type of jellied gasoline. We set the whole area aflame and obliterated the encampment. Nearby was the ancient town of Royan; that, too, was almost totally destroyed. The Norden bombsight was not that accurate.

These four instances of violence possess something in common. None of them could have been committed by any animal other than man. The reason for this does not lie alone in man's superior ability to manipulate his environment. It lies in his ability to conceptualize his hatreds. A beast commits violence against specific things for immediate and visible purposes. It needs to eat. It needs a mate. It needs to defend its life. Man has these biological needs plus many more which are culturally created. Man will do violence not only against a specific something which gets in the way of one of his needs; he will do violence against a symbol which stands for, or which he believes stands for, that which prevents him from satisfying his needs. (Guilt by association is high-level thinking.)

With symbolic violence, the object of attack is deprived of its particularity. Only in this way can man overcome what I believe is his natural spontaneous feeling of oneness with other human beings. He must, by the substitution of symbol for reality, destroy in his consciousness the humanness of that being. To the angry crowds outside the dormitory in Athens, Georgia, their target was not Charlayne Hunter, an extremely attractive and intelligent young woman, sitting, brave and afraid, in her room. She was a "dirty nigger"—a symbol abstracted from life. To the Negro who committed violence on the streets of New York, this was not a pathetic old Jewish immigrant, forced in the last years of his life to peddle vegetables from a pushcart, but a dehumanized symbol of the historic white exploiter who used the Negro's labor and refused to pay him a just wage. To the screaming rock-throwers of Peekskill who fractured the skull of a young woman returning from a concert, the people in the car they attacked were not a family on an outing; in this car were people who had gone to hear a black-skinned communistic singer and who therefore were all congealed into a symbol representing nigger-loving communism. And as I set my intervalometer and toggled off my bombs over the city of Royan, I was not setting fire to people's homes, crushing and burning individual men, women and newborn babies. We were at war, we always dropped bombs on the enemy, and down there was the enemy.

The human ability to abstract, to create symbols standing for reality, has enabled man to compound his material possessions, to split the atom and orbit the earth. It also enables him to compound his hatreds, and expands his capacity for violence. But while there is no incentive to distort in the scientific process which changes reality to symbol for purposes of manipulation, and back to reality for purposes of realization, there *is* incentive, in social relations, for distorting the symbols of communication. With man's use of symbols, the potentiality for hatred and therefore for violence is enormously, logarithmically, magnified. And with word-symbols the possibility for distortion is infinite. In fact, distortion is inherent here, for while particles of light are sufficiently similar so that we can express the speed of all of them in a useful mathematical equation, human beings are so complex and particular, and their relationships so varied, that no generalized word can do justice to reality.

War is symbolic violence, with all people who happen to reside within the geographical boundaries of a nation-state constituting "the enemy." Race persecution is symbolic violence directed against all individuals, regardless of their specific characteristics, who can be identified with an abstracted physical type. In the execution chamber, the state puts to death anyone, regardless of individual circumstance, who fits the legal symbol: murderer. The law forcibly deprives of freedom everyone who falls within the symbolic definition of a criminal; sentences are sometimes meted out to individuals, but mostly to dehumanized lawbreakers whose acts match an abstract list of punishments.

There is symbolism also in the use of violence to effectuate desirable social change, whether through revolution, labor struggle, "just" wars or desegregation. This creates the probability that there will be only a partial correspondence between the specific obstacle to progress and the generalized, symbolized object of violence (the head of Marie Antoinette, the fifty-dollar-a-week scab, the civilian population of Dresden, the poor white in Mississippi). It may hurt the revolutionary reformer to think so, but the fact of symbolization in human violence creates a common problem for *all* users of violence, regardless of their ends. And it may displease the pacifist to say so, but these different ends do matter in deciding how much violence we should countenance in the rearrangement of the social structure.

Symbolism, with its inevitable distortions, complicates an already tough problem: developing an approach to nonviolence that is both realistic and moral. We need a rational approach that avoids both the blurred thinking shown by some advocates of nonviolence and the easy paths to brutality constructed by the "realists." I infinitely prefer the absolute pacifist to the sharp, cool *realpolitik* character who is found so often these days in academia, journalism and the government, but the same absolutism sometimes infects the nonviolence people, who emerged only recently out of the American desegregation battles and whose theories are less developed than their actions. The nonviolence people in America have been saved the consequences of a muddy theory by the favorable circumstances attending Southern desegregation, and because their technique has not been tested on more difficult problems.

The absolutism of some nonviolence spokesmen weakens their position, I believe, because people know, deep inside, even if they can't articulate the reasons, that there are times when violence is justifiable. For nonviolence seen as absolute pacifism is only one of a pair of linked values which humanitarian people share—peace and social justice. The desirability of the one must constantly be weighed against the need for the other. Also, the problem is subject to internal contradiction: sometimes the failure to use a measure of violence may make inevitable a far greater violence. Would it have been wrong to assassinate Hitler at that moment in the war when this might have brought a halt to general hostilities and the extermination of the Jews?

It is not true, as some say, that bad means always corrupt the ends. If the amount of evil embodied in the means is tiny and the amount of good created by the end is huge, then the end is not corrupted—either objectively in the result or subjectively in the conscience of the doer. This matter of conscience is often pointed to by the absolutist pacifist. Certainly, if a man sees a neighbor stealing his son's bicycle and knocks him unconcious with a baseball bat, the wielder of the bat may recover from his anger and say, "What a terrible thing I have done to save a bicycle!" But if he should see his neighbor—whom he knows to have a violent temper—pointing a shotgun at his wife and children, and does the same thing, will his conscience bother him then? Is the end corrupted by the means?

The Freedom Riders behaved nonviolently. But their action did bring violence against themselves, and against others. Nonviolence theorists will insist that the responsibility for the violence rests with those who committed it. But this dodges the question; the fact is that there was more violence in the world *after* the Freedom Riders began their rides than *before*. And for this there is only one jusification: that the amount of violence was insignificant compared to the amount of justice won.

In a world of great injustice, we need social change. Social change requires action. Action may result, either by design or by accident, in violence. The fact must be faced. And violence is an evil, along with injustice. The only way, then, to decide upon a course of action is to weigh the damage of violence against the damage of social injustice. The nonviolent absolutist, in all logic, may have to forego social change, putting himself in the contradictory position of maintaining a status quo that tolerates violence like capital punishment and police brutality against Negroes. On the other hand, people who are prepared to pursue any course of action leading to social change may find themselves in the contradictory position of using such violent and uncontrollable means that there is no society left to enjoy the benefits of the changes they seek. Our values are multiple; they sometimes clash; and we need to weigh, weigh, weigh.

Yet, I must admit that there is a powerful and humane motive impelling the absolutist position: that once you give nervous, hostile and ill-informed people a theoretical justification for using violence in certain cases, it is like a tiny hole in the dike: the rationales rush through in a torrent, and violence becomes the normal, acceptable solution for a problem.

This happened in the area of free speech. When Justice Holmes, perceptively noting that free speech is not an absolute right, came up with his famous example—should a man be allowed to shout "Fire!" in a crowded theater?—the gates were down, and the witch-hunters rushed through. The "clear and present danger" doctrine became a "fairly clear and one-of-these-days danger" doctrine. We began to persecute Communists even though their ineffectualness indicated that they were stammerers shouting fire in a foreign language to a deaf audience. Now that the absolute and unequivocal dictum of the First Amendment has been pushed aside, anything goes. This is why Justice Black insists on an absolute defense of free speech. And this may be why pacifists insist on an unequivocal rejection of violence.

I think, however, that it is in the nature of speech that the exceptions to an absolute defense of its freedom would be very few, whereas in the complex sphere of social action, there may be many situations requiring some measure of force or of pressure that produces counterforce. Moreover, in the area of free speech, most situations allow polar solutions; you either permit the speech or deny it. In the tactics of social change, however, there are countless intermediate positions beween total passivity and total violence. Still, it is terribly important to understand that our starting point should be pacifism, that the burden of proof should be placed on the arguer for violence. Just as a man should be considered innocent until proved guilty, a policy should be automatically nonviolent until the weight of reason, undistorted by symbolism, argues otherwise. And even here we need a court of appeals, because a cardinal fact about violence is that, once initiated, it tends to get out of hand. Its limits are not predictable.

The actual process of weighing violence versus injustice differs in each specific case. Symbols distort the weighing, but the amount of distortion depends on how far the symbol is from the reality. Sometimes people can refer fairly easily to the specific human situation, as was the case in the 1930's, when the epithets of "socialism" directed at the New Deal could not fool people in the presence of hunger. Such is the situation in the desegregation campaigns today, where visible and appealing Negroes push through the old stereotypes to confront white America. Desegregation is a self-propelling process, because as it proceeds it brings more and more whites into contact with human beings instead of racist symbols.

The most notable contribution of the desegregation movement to other worthy causes is as a showcase for nonviolence under conditions where the technique is shown in the best light. It indicates the possibility, heretofore not clearly enunciated by either pacifists or revolutionists, of using minimum force to achieve maximum justice. Here is nonviolence at its best—a golden mean between passivity and violence. Such techniques have been used countless times in the history of reform—in labor struggles, farmers' movements, etc.—but never yet accompanied by a theory which enables transfer to other social problems.

The weighing is easy, too, in another aspect of American life, but has here been ignored. This is in the area of legal violence against criminals and suspected criminals: capital punishment, police brutality, the murder of burglary suspects. Here, symbolism is still unassaulted by reason and humanity. Last month, in Atlanta, an eighteen-year-old boy was shot and killed while running away from the scene of a vending-machine robbery that had netted him $3.84. The policeman who shot him was not firing at a human being, but at a symbol: a thief, an enemy of society. The policeman was defending another symbol: private property. As symbols, abstracted from flesh and blood, the solution is simple: private property must be protected. As reality, it looks different: the life of an eighteen-year-old boy against the loss of $3.84.

In capital punishment, too, we are not weighing how much justice will be accomplished by the act of judicial murder. If we did, the answer would be obvious: execution of a human being—no matter how foul his deed—cannot bring more happiness, more justice, into the world. But the figure in the electric chair is not a human being, and the act is not weighed in terms of human values. He is a part of a mathematical equation in our law books which says simply that a person who has violated a certain kind of law must be murdered. Our law is symbolic, not human, so abstracted from life that it is capable of the most horrible injustice.

With regard to revolution as a means of changing the social order, the weighing of violence against injustice is more difficult, and the complexity of the problem varies from case to case. Though the American Revolution took seven years and tens of thousands of lives, we are so infatuated with the results that we don't dare question its desirability. Is it possible that methods short of all-out war might have eased Britain off the backs of the colonists? Probably not, except over a long period of time and with constant nonviolent harassment. My point here is not to pass judgment on what is a most complicated revolutionary situation, but to argue that the use of violence as a corrective is so ingrained in the human psychology that we don't even question it. The French, Russian and, more recently, the Cuban revolutions, involving shorter bursts of violence against more uncompromising and backward regimes, are easier to justify; and the fact that each brought on its own brand of Bonapartism does not vitiate the fact of long-term social transformation in a positive direction. Yet these revolutions may have shed more blood than was necessary to achieve their results. You are grateful even for an inept surgeon who removes a festering appendix, but will look next time for someone who will accomplish surgery with less damage.

It is in large-scale, international wars that the pacifist can hardly go wrong, for here the violence is so massive, so symbolic, so unfocused on specific targets, that even a tremendous turn for the better in the conditions of millions of people does not make easy a judgment for war. World War I, which caused twenty million deaths, is a classic example of mass murder for dubious gain; it was probably the most stupid war in history.

World War II assaults our emotions as we begin to weigh the results in terms of social justice against the degree of violence employed. The reality of Nazism was as close to the symbol of total evil as any phenomenon in human history. In no other war have the issues seemed as clear-cut. Because of this we were able to pass lightly over massive immorality on the part of the Allies—the killing of hundreds of thousands in indiscriminate bombing raids on cities, climaxed by the horrible deeds at Hiroshima and Nagasaki. Altogether, forty million persons' lives were wiped out. Could we have defeated Hitler at a lesser cost? With so many lives at stake, could we not have exploited every alternative, sane or wild? Could we not have used nonviolence in a thousand different ways? Perhaps we might have let Hitler take territory after territory, allowed his empire to become bloated and sick, meanwhile organizing an underground against him everywhere. I am not at all sure of this, but what I want to do is to challenge the automatic acceptance of the traditional response to evil. Not only conservatives, but liberals and social revolutionaries as well, are paralyzed by habit.

There are clearly many cases where the weighing of nonviolence against social justice is difficult. Ironically, however, in the situation today, involving rocket-propelled missiles and hundred-megaton warheads, the decision should be obvious and easy—and the peoples of the world have not made it. A fundamental reason is that it is always harder to check up on the reality behind the verbal symbol in international affairs than it is in domestic issues. And the passions of the cold war have created symbolic distortions on an unprecedented scale. This is seen in both elements of the slogan that sums up much of American thinking: that we must "fight" to save the "free world."

It should be apparent to anyone who coldly surveys the effects of multimegaton weapons—the fireball, the explosion, the fallout, the mass cremation—that the word "fight" is a monstrous euphemism, and that no possible combination of evils in the world today can balance on the scales the mammoth, irretrievable evil of a nuclear war. But we do not have an electronic mechanism to conjure up the right pictures as soon as the word "fight" is heard. Thus, whenever some political issue arises which is subject to inflammation, whether it is Berlin or Formosa or Cuba, we begin to talk of "fighting" or "making our stand here." Americans hearing the word "fight" think, perhaps, of the last war, never of annihilation, never of agony beyond the imagination. We need somehow to push aside these verbal symbols and let people confront with open eyes what Giraudoux in *Tiger at the Gates* has Hecuba describe as the face of war: the backside of a baboon, hairy and red with a fungus growth. The Russians and Chinese, their memories of death more pervading, may have less trouble than we do with symbolic obstacles. Yet Marxist terms like "struggle," which they use constantly, are loose enough to becloud a variety of dangerous actions. In every country of the world, it needs to be stated flatly now and through all present crises and possible crises: there is no piece of territory in the world, no city, no nation, no social system, whose preservation is worth a thermonuclear war.

We find ourselves at a point in history full of paradoxes: H-bombs have, by their test explosions alone, obliterated the traditional revolutionary idea of a "just war" and suggest caution to advocates of social upheaval. Yet social injustice is everywhere in the world, crying for correction. At this very moment the technique of nonviolence is brought to our attention by the sit-ins of the American South, by the sailors of the *Golden Rule,* by the demonstrators in Trafalgar Square. It is no one method, but an arsenal of methods, all of which start beyond passivity and stop short of war. It recognizes honestly that once passivity is renounced, some degree of force may enter the situation, but it is determined to keep this to a minimum, and starts always from the assumption of zero violence. Nonviolent activists win over the onlookers of the world and make things more difficult for the perpetrators of violence and injustice. They know the value of words as the tools of symbolic distortion which prevent people from perceiving reality; but they are especially concerned with human contact—interracial and international—as a way of directly smashing through the walls of symbol. While violence is blunt and undiscriminating, nonviolence is sharp, particularized, focused, flexible.

The Negro in the South has given the cue, but the nation has not taken it. That beautiful balance embodied by the sit-ins and Freedom Rides is cautiously condoned, but not emulated, by the government. And yet it is especially in the United States that the technique of nonviolence is demanded, at a time when domestic injustice and stupidity in foreign policy require assault. Ironically, our government is missing the golden mean of nonviolence on both counts, for it is passive in domestic affairs which it *can* control, and violent abroad in situations it *can't* control.

The truth is that our entire political system is geared toward a strange inversion. The antiquated structure of Congress—its committee system operating by seniority, the gerrymandered state legislatures—is only the manifestation of a basic political malaise that operates to make our legislative bodies representative of the most backward elements of the population. Our cumbersome lawmaking machinery, its controls supervised by Southern reactionaries, is not geared to the swift pace and zooming expectations of the twentieth century. This is shown in instance after instance where the President cannot get the mildest pieces of social-welfare legislation through Congress, or secure a petty amount of cash to support the United Nations. In foreign policy, on the other hand, he has a free hand. The result is that he is quicker to assault Cuba than to assault Congress.

George Kennan and others have argued convincingly that the most effective thing we can do in foreign affairs is to create a magnificent social system at home. The plain fact is that despite our superfluity of autos and television sets, we cannot really come before the world and say: here is your ideal social system, where the wealth of the nation is distributed in such a way as to eliminate poverty and insecurity, where the aged are taken care of and the sick are cured regardless of their finances, where all who want education can get it, where artists, poets, musicians and writers can achieve as much economic security as the man who designs a new Yo-Yo.

It was the feeble ineptitude of the strongest government on earth that brought on the sit-in movement. That seven hundred Negroes in Albany, Georgia, had to demonstrate in the streets to put into effect an Interstate Commerce Commission ruling that had not been enforced by the government is embarrassingly representative of the years since 1954.

What the Southern Negro has done for desegregation can also work for freedom of speech and assembly, for medical care, against capital punishment. Nonviolent techniques—the kind already used and many kinds still germinating in our imaginations—seem the only sensible answer to a world sitting in a minefield and yet needing to move. They can be effective in the swamp of representative government and within the stone walls of Communist bureaucracy. They employ humor, kindness, pressures, flexibility, attack and retreat—guerrilla warfare in time of peace. Today, when force is absolute, we may have to live, and advance, by our wits.

Man, separated from his fellow man by symbolic distortion, has been violent for most of his history. But he has also shown the ability to break through symbols, to make direct contact with other human beings and to renounce violence. He is not determined inexorably in either direction, the social psychologists and cultural anthropologists tell us. Perhaps here is our chief hope. Man is open to suggestion. And nonviolence uses neither compulsion nor silence. Calmly, powerfully, it suggests.

HOW VIOLENCE OCCURS: A THEORY AND REVIEW OF THE LITERATURE*

By THOMAS ROSE

In this essay I have developed a theory of how violence occurs as control and revolt in a continual, recurrent, regular and irregular cycle showing various peaks and outbursts and their escalation.† The American pattern of violence has never bled itself out, although it has often been controlled and channelled into isolated and local movements, because those who control America, a minority who speaks for the consensus, have always had a greater violent power and have never allowed violent revolt to prosper long without serious opposition, most often violent.‡

Violent control restrains and regulates, and is a method of social-political control. Violent revolt is dissent and strives to create change. Both violent revolt and violent control can be understood in terms of a continuum: for violent revolt, at one end is influence and persuasion, and at the other are revolution and overthrow; for violent control,

---

* I want to thank Warner Bloomberg, Jr., Edgar Litt, and H. L. Nieburg for their helpful comments and suggestions on earlier drafts. Another version of this essay is published in *The International Review of History and Political Science,* November, 1968; and in Edgar Litt (ed.), *The New Politics of American Policy,* New York, Holt, Rinehart & Winston, Inc., 1969.

† For a definition of violence, see the preceding articles by Garver and Zinn.

‡ For an example of the opposite point of view, see Richard Hofstadter, *The Progressive Historians,* New York, Alfred A. Knopf, Inc., 1968.

at one end are regulation and defensive action against revolution or the threat of revolution, and at the other are total control, overpowering totalitarianism, and fascism. Both violent control and revolt seek to influence, but because they are constantly conflicting (consensus is nearly impossible), both impose various gradations along the continuum. For control this may mean large-scale military movements in big cities or various forms of manipulation. Violent revolt thrives on conflict, and when influence is unable to create conflict and change, the threat and use of greater violence is possible.

·I· VIOLENCE AS CONTROL

Violence is one form of social-political control. Its most basic function is to support and sustain the status quo and regulate change. Gerth and Mills[1] discuss a series of intricately related social controls, including custom or folkways, which rest on conformity by expectation; fashion and convention (mores), which are enforced by community opinion; law, which is regulated by punishment; rational uniformity; ethical rules having profound influence on human action even in the absence of external sanctions; and institutional controls, which are upheld by institutions. These various forms of social control may be enforced in different ways, including violence, which can be a kind of sanction standing behind certain controls.

I would argue that many of these types of social-political control exist on a continuum with violence. Control can be used to socialize deviant groups and check potential rebellions, but it can also be used as brute force, large-scale military movement in ghettos, and in civil and world wars.

The continuum can include both direct and indirect, overt and covert, social-political control, obvious manipulation, or a more diffused and amorphous control. The degree of institutionalization relates to how deeply its effect is. Indirect influence works from afar—control is distant; whereas direct influence is more complicated. Indirect control may be termed potential threatened control, and direct control actual control. One form can be as violent as the other. Garver and Zinn pointed out that violation of personhood and symbolic violence can be equally powerful. They indicated that overt violence does not necessarily do as much permanent harm as indirect violence.

There are important differences between the kind of violent control of the military-industrial complex and that of semiprivate groups and individuals. One is officially legal and has the power of the state behind it, and the other is supra- or extragovernmental, but groups and individuals may not feel that the official law-enforcement agencies are able to control or recognize violent revolt. They may organize into groups such as the Minutemen, the American Nazi party, the Ku Klux Klan, and the Black Muslims, or they may be total institutions such as mental hospitals and prisons. They are able to exert various gradations of violent control, but often the state does not interfere with their activities which it can choose to ignore.

The problem of neutral control is an important one, and it is made especially complex by the interrelations between local, state, and national law-enforcement agencies and their political and economic relationships with the total complex. If the local police are unable or unwilling to control and protect, the state and national police may be called in because they are more neutral. The interpretation of what is violent control and whether it is needed is a complex question which is influenced by local custom, community opinion, outside influence, and other forms of control. The problem of coordination and a unity in violent control is complex in a democratically organized society because of the different levels of control, including three separate branches of government. Total control is theoretically less possible in a democratic state than in a totalitarian one, but in America one unit or branch of government can overpower another, i.e., the federal government can take over the University of Mississippi and the city of Detroit. Local police can take over Columbia and San Francisco State, but even more important, the government can systematically ignore some forms of violence, as Newton Garver and Howard Zinn pointed out. America does not have a uniform, consistent posture toward violent revolt if contrasted with Russia under Stalin. Despite American consensus, diversity persists.

VIOLENT REVOLT AS THREAT

Violence may have actual and potential use, as demonstration or threat. Lasswell discusses the expectation of violence. Fanon writes of passing from an atmosphere of violence to violent acts. The threat of potential violence can be effective before it actually erupts. H. L. Nieburg[2] points out:

> The actual demonstration of violence must occur from time to time in order to give credibility to its threatened outbreak; thereby gaining efficacy for the threat as an instrument of social and political change. The two aspects, demonstration and threat, cannot be separated. The two merge imperceptibly into each other. If the capability of actual demonstration is not present, the threat will have little effect in inducing a willingness to bargain politically. In fact, such a threat may provoke "pre-emptive" counterviolence.

How can those groups who use violence as threat have some assurance this will not provoke "pre-emptive" counterviolence? This question has often been raised by those groups using nonviolence because the state, the controllers, have assumed that nonviolent demonstrators would become violent. Seldom during the civil rights nonviolent movement of the 1960's have the nonviolent demonstrators become violent, though often the police and the public have. Can we assume that this is why the technique of nonviolence is a thing of the past, and that now most civil rights demonstrators see the failure of nonviolence? When H. Rap Brown tells black people they had better get guns, he causes the white public to become fearful and do this themselves. The threat often brings about pre-emptive violence on the part of those who are in control. The stages in the cycle we discuss next can become pre-emptive. Repression may be termed a form of pre-emptive violence by control to prevent threat and use.

VIOLENT REVOLT AS BARGAINING INFLUENCE

The threat of violent revolt should create a willingness to bargain politically in a democratic state, but all groups are not invited to the bargaining table. More specifically, are those groups who threaten and use violence as revolt given the same rights and means of bargaining power or influence as those who use violence as control? There is always a highly skewed power relation between the controllers and the revolters. This basic inequality of power in the bargaining process may itself produce violence as revolt. Often, as Nieburg points out, potentially violent groups are somewhat accommodated to avoid violence and retain stability, but they do not want to be accommodated.

Jesse Lemisch points out that poor colonial seamen resisted the Royal Navy before the American Revolution. "The seamen were fighting, literally, for their life, liberty, and property, and their violence was all the politics they could have." [3] Violence is a political resource when the bargaining process provides no other alternatives, or at least when some groups perceive no other alternatives. Political violence is an intelligible pattern of interaction that exists in America, but we refuse to understand and confront it as integral in our life.

Violence becomes bargaining power. Sometimes it represents success. Traditionally social scientists and others have argued that violence was not a political resource, that it could never mean success, but rather that it signified despair and defeat for those using it. But on the other hand, violence used to control has brought minorities in America despair and defeat, powerlessness and alienation.* It is because revolt was forbidden and control was so successful that we have black power today. Black power is political, and it simply states that the traditional bargaining process will not

---

* See John Higham, *Strangers in the Land: Patterns of American Nativism 1860–1925*, New York, Atheneum Publishers, 1967; and Paul Jacobs' and Saul Landau's forthcoming book on California, *In the Service of the Devil*, to be published by Random House in the fall of 1969.

work for those who are poor and black. The solution, a way to stop despair and defeat, powerlessness and aliena- tion, is by using the threat and demonstration of violent re- volt.

In larger perspective, minorities and dissenting groups have always used violent revolt as threat and demonstra- tion to gain power, influence, and status in the larger society since they have never really been a part of the democratic bargaining process. Violent revolt has often been the only alternative, the only available form of power. Most social scientists have discussed the accommodation process, and not the equal participation as bargaining agents of minor- ities. It was impossible for them to discuss violent revolt as a potential source of influence because they have been enamored of the "peaceful change" and accommodation theories.

The threat of violent revolt can be used successfully as a political bargaining instrument, as a method of developing policies. Roosevelt created a Fair Employment Practices Commission and Truman desegregated the armed forces because in both instances A. Philip Randolph threatened mass demonstrations and marches if they didn't. The march on Washington in 1963, backed up by constant civil rights demonstrations during the previous three years, forced Congress to pass a Civil Rights Act. During the past few years rebellions in large cities have forced the government into some reallocation of resources, a number of studies, much talk about law and order, and a good deal of coun- terviolence against revolt. Vast amounts of money are now being used for control, often erupting in violent conflict between control and revolt. Continual stories during 1967– 68 in the *Milwaukee Journal* indicate that the threat of violence by the NAACP Youth Council and Father James Groppi, as bargaining agents in absentia from the bar- gaining table, has caused the city of Milwaukee to spend vast sums of money to create the feeling of stability for the larger white community. Stokely Carmichael has pointed out that at least those blacks jailed in big-city uprisings will not be going to Vietnam. Violent revolt may be termed successful when the creation of lasting disruptions and con- flict in the system is also able to help create policies and the demand for policies which get at the causes of revolt rather than exacerbate them.

SOCIO-POLITICAL CONTROL

Violence is social control and authority, and a technique, or tool, of social control. Violence can mean physical assaults and other methods of inflicting harm or gaining power by mental or emotional means, or it can mean sabotage, economic disruption, etc. In his article, "The Garrison State," Harold Lasswell explains that violence may become total control over the entire mass and over each individual's life, "in order to control, atomize, terrorize them (and) . . . capture them ideologically."

Absolute violence may be defined as terror: concentration camps, totalitarian regimes, and some forms of overpowering. Terror depends on the techniques of social control, or in the case of a terroristic regime, social organization. E. V. Walter[4] clarifies terror by talking about the process of terror, which involves a combination of "the actual threat of violence, the emotional reaction, and the social effects." He restricts his discussion to terror as an emotional state "caused by specific violent acts or threats," and distinguishes this from a system of terror, a zone of terror, a siege of terror, and a regime of terror.

The process of terror should be separated from power, force, and coercion, i.e., power is all forms of influence and compulsion; force is an agency that compels a person to do something he does not want to do; and coercion is social compulsion or institutionalized force. Finally he calls violence—differentiating it from the process of terror—destructive harm. "Violence may occur without terror, but never terror without violence." Various forms of violence easily shift over during the process of terror—stopping disobedience and resistance, sapping their potential in advance, breaking the power to resist. Walter comments:

> Every state has the necessary conditions for terrorism, namely, a staff of men obedient to the directors of the system and equipped with instruments of violence, as well as a population capable of experiencing fear. The sufficient conditions

invite our exploration, and we must search for them. To identify controlling factors, we must construct a ladder going from actual to potential terrorism, with three levels: (1) situations in which terrorism is practiced; (2) situations in which the agents of violence are not practicing terrorism at the time, but nevertheless are disposed to initiate violence if people were to behave in a certain way; (3) situations in which terror is absent, but in which there is a threshold of stress beyond which an armed staff will be converted into a terroristic apparatus and a regime of terror established.

Totalitarian systems or states—Russia under Stalin, Nazi Germany, Haiti, South Africa—and concentration camps, including totalitarian prison camps, come closest to a process of terror in which the final stages of absolute violence coincide with the destruction of humanity. Hannah Arendt points out that a totalitarian government operates only by the law of nature or history, which is really translated as lawlessness: totalitarian domination. Total terror leaves nothing arbitrary. It creates a "band of iron" which holds people so tightly together that their plurality disappears into one gigantic mass.

Thomas Merton, writing in *The Catholic Worker,* pointed out that under these conditions, we must associate incredible brutality and inhumanity with so-called respectable people in an extraordinary situation. He believed that Auschwitz worked because

> . . . people wanted it to work. Instead of resisting it, rebelling against it, they put the best of all their energies into making genocide a success. Almost all of them committed gratuitous acts of arbitrary cruelty and violence which were forbidden even by the Gestapo's own rules. . . . there can be little doubt that many of these men tortured and killed because they thoroughly enjoyed it. (Men . . . will instinctively welcome and submit to an ideology which enables them to be violent and destructive without guilt.). . . we have no need of monsters: ordinary policemen and good citizens will take care of everything.

VIOLENCE AS A FAILURE OF POWER
AND AN EXTENSION OF POLITICS

Social scientists and social philosophers often argue that the conditions of mass society have injured or destroyed the foundations of political community. They say that a politicized mass has replaced a political community. If people do not control their social and political lives and communities, if the power of the people fails, then violence may become *the* significant force in community. A pattern of violent control may be established when political participation wanes and is coupled with absolute deprivation among various groups, but revolt and participation, in turn, often create violence. What is critical here is who determines that assumption of political obligations and participation is positive or negative. This depends on how the ruling minority, those who impose a false consensus, views the participation of others. In the case of labor struggles, black revolt, and student confrontations, it is obvious that the military-industrial-academic complex does not consider these to be forms of participation that Americans needed.

Another frequently held position is that the ultimate kind of power is violence. The power elite determines the degree of violent controls. (This tends to determine the amount of reactive revolt and therefore a cycle of violence and counterviolence is maintained.) The state has exclusive claim to the resources of violent control. Paul Tillich worries that the state is able to use its power of violent control to its ultimate limits: overpowering by punishment or liquidation.[5]

Clausewitz, the classic war theorist, argues in *On War* that war, or the militarization of society or sectors of a society, is an extension of politics. Control will not become overpowering unless the controllers can remove the revolters' ability to resist. What is important is that political policies are translated into violence and war. Clausewitz indicates that "war is a mere *continuation* of policy by other means." He writes:

War is a political instrument carrying out political transac-

tions by violent means, and is an act of violence practiced
without limits. The aim of all action in war is to disarm the
enemy and remove his ability to resist, and victory in battle
consists in nothing less than the physical and moral destruction of the enemy's armed forces.

War is not the action of a living force on a lifeless mass,
but . . . always the shock of two living forces colliding.

FORCE

John Dewey wrote that Americans are given to "moraliz-
ing" force, and that no ends are accomplished without the
use of force. Force is most often used unwisely and ineffec-
tively. He defines the organization of force as efficiency, and
distinguishes between power or energy, coercive force such
as prisons, and violence. Power "denotes effective means of
operation; ability or capacity to execute, to realize ends.
Granted an end which is worthwhile, and power or energy
becomes a eulogistic term. . . . Not to depend upon and
utilize force is simply to be without a foothold in the real
world." Coercive force is the middle ground between power
as energy and power as violence, according to Dewey. He
argues:

> There remains a difference between narrow and partial ends
> and full and far-reaching ends; between the success of the few
> for the moment and the happiness of the many for an endur-
> ing time; a difference between identifying happiness with the
> elements of a meager and hard life and those of a varied and
> free life.[6]

Hannah Arendt comments that "Just as the rule of law,
although devised to eliminate violence and war of all against
all, always stands in need of the instruments of violence in
order to assure its own existence, so a government may
find itself compelled to commit actions that are generally
regarded as crimes in order to assure its own survival and
the survival of lawfulness." [7] Reinhold Niebuhr argues that
the risk of violence is often necessary in preserving national
societies. "The law tends always to become to some extent
the instrument of the status quo and an instrument for resisting change." This should have different meanings for

people who live in democratic representative nations and for those in countries where the people have no access to means of affecting the status quo.

For Sorel, writing at the turn of the century, Marxism becomes a theory of revolutionary syndicalism or a philosophy of history where the essential factor is violence. Sorel's most significant contribution is the distinction between force and violence—acts of authority and acts of revolt. Too often, he warned, we believe violence and force are one. Because of this ambiguity, he argues, "the term violence should be employed for acts of revolt; we should say, therefore, that the object of force is to impose a certain social order in which the minority governs, while violence tends to the destruction of that order."

His argument is all the more important because he feels that the orthodox Marxists did not make this distinction. Sorel feels they made a grave error in thinking the proletariat must acquire force like the middle class. "The mass of the producers would merely change masters." He comments further:

> Whether force manifests itself under the aspect of historical acts of coercion, of fiscal oppression, or of conquest, or labor legislation, or whether it is wholly bound up with the economic system, it is always middle-class force labouring with more or less skill to bring about the capitalist order of society.[8]

Proletarian violence for Sorel is the general strike, which he compares to Napoleonic battles: both crush the adversary. Revolutionary syndicalism and the general strike are the crucial elements in a Marxist revolution. They keep the minds of the workers alive and ready to strike, but only when accompanied by violence.

CONTROL BY FEAR

Control is maintained by encouraging the public to be fearful and anxious about violence. The institutionalized symbols of violence are "those" people and groups that are violent. "We" fear the ghetto, the hippy, the Indian, and the Mexican because "we" are socialized to believe "they" are violent. Of course Communists are very violent and most Americans have an almost psychotic fear of "them." As long as "we" believe this, then "we" will use all our power, influence, and resources to control "them." Control is maintained by fear. Ronald Laing, a British psychoanalyst, points out:

> The invention of Them creates Us, and We may require to invent Them to reinvent Ourselves.
> Violence attempts to constrain the other's freedom, to force him to act in the way we desire, but with the ultimate lack of concern, with indifference to the other's own existence or destiny.[9]

This is a classical psychological pattern: projection of ourselves as good and others as evil. We are warped, fearful, hate-ridden, frustrated, but more specifically, we suffer status anxiety. Perhaps the dialectic has turned full circle. "We" feel that only "they" are violent. "We" insist, often with anger, that "they" be kept in "their" place and that "they" are the cause of all the trouble: violence in the streets, anti-war protesters, and others who do not know "their" place. We are unable to look at ourselves in the mirror and see ourselves as we really are. Jean-Paul Sartre has written that as the dialectic unfolds, "they" will look in the mirror at "our" violent reflection and meet "us" with all the violence "they" can muster.

·2· VIOLENCE AS REVOLT

The Declaration of Independence states:

> When in the course of human events it becomes necessary for one people to dissolve the political bands which have connected them with another, and to assume among the powers of the earth, the separate and equal station to which the laws of nature and of nature's God entitle them, a decent respect to the opinions of mankind requires that they should declare the causes which impel them to the separation. . . . whenever any form of government becomes destructive of these ends, it is the right of the people to alter or to abolish it, and to institute new government, laying its foundation on such

principles, and organizing its powers in such form, as to them
shall seem most likely to effect their safety and happiness.*

Violent revolt is characteristic of the American political
process and should not be considered as outside socio-politi-
cal life. It can be explained as gradations on a continuum:
on the one end of the continuum, violent revolt can mean a
reaffirmation of life, and on the other, suicide because conditions are intolerable. Most often violent revolt is directed
against the state in general, of course, the status quo, or
a combination which we now call the military-industrial-
academic complex. The basic cause of most violent revolt
is injustice and inequality, violation of personhood, and
symbolic violence. Violent revolt, such as rebellions in big
cities in the 1960's, often has deeper roots, causes which
may lead to revolution. One episode often leaves a cumulative tradition, helps build a tradition of successful revolt.
American race relations, labor struggles, and draft resistance
are evidence of this tradition. Speaking about conscription
today in *Vietnam: The Logic of Withdrawal,* Howard Zinn
comments that "Modern warfare . . . violated the principle of free choice on two counts, because it is fought by
conscripts and against people who did not decide to be involved (civilians)."

Barrington Moore observes that violence often fails to
work, results in greater tragedy, "when revolutionary rhetoric outruns the real possibilities inherent in a given historical situation." We can talk of revolt that is aimed
at influencing the government or those who rule. This kind
of revolt and protest usually focuses on specific issues. It
seeks to dramatically alter the system, but not to overthrow
it. It is this kind of revolt that is less violent and bloody than
the K.K.K., anarchists murdered by capitalists, the use of
troops in labor struggles, slavery and institutional racism.
More specifically, revolt aimed at influencing includes most
recent civil rights history in the 1960's, from marches in
Selma to big-city rebellions, and most antiwar revolt and
resistance in the past few years.

At the other end of the continuum is violent overthrow of

---

* For an interesting interpretation, see Truman Nelson, *The Right
of Revolution,* Boston, Beacon Press, 1968.

the government by wholesale revolutionary activity. The American Revolution and the Civil War are the most obvious examples, but Door's Rebellion in the mid-nineteenth century is another less known example of an attempt made to overturn the government. Obviously attempts at overthrowing the American government have been rare, but the threat has more often existed. The threat, in theory, is advocated in the literature of some groups who desire revolt, such as abolitionists, anarchists, socialists, and today Students for a Democratic Society, black power organizations, and the Minutemen, but that threat is not the same as an overt advocacy of violent revolt. Albert Camus argues that rebellion is a reaffirming of existence. "I rebel, therefore we exist."

JUSTIFICATION OF VIOLENT REVOLT

Sidney Hook argues that the real issue concerning violent revolt is its justification by subordinate groups who want to capture power, influence, and the ability to bargain. He points to the moral issues:

> . . . devotion to the values of peace and serenity is higher than devotion to life itself. . . . the use of violence against violence cannot be sanctioned; but where other values are considered as intrinsically desirable as serenity or blessedness, the use of violence may be extenuated as the necessary, even if painful, means of achieving them.[10]

Hook indicates further that humanity, love, and reason have always provided justification for violence.

Reinhold Niebuhr explains the ethical consequences of violence. He considers the influence of violence as a *moral* instrument of social change, and argues that nothing is intrinsically immoral or moral, nor natural and inevitable. Violent revolt must be situationally understood. This, Americans have been unable to do, and have insisted that all violence is bad. Niebuhr, taking the position that it is possible to establish justice through violence, concludes:

> A distinction must be made, and is naturally made, between propaganda which a privileged group uses to main-

tain its privileges and the agitation for freedom and equality carried on by a disinherited group.

Equal justice is the most rational ultimate objective for society. . . . Violence may tend to perpetuate injustice, even when its aim is justice. . . . A social conflict which aims at the elimination of these injustices is in a different category from one which is carried on without reference to the problem of justice.[11]

Individuals and groups have a "higher moral right" to challenge their oppressors than the oppressors have a right to maintain a system by violent control. Niebuhr points out that there is no impartial tribunal that can judge the claims of either group. There is, for example, no neutral community within America, although he points out that oppressed nationalities in other nations "have always elicited a special measure of sympathy and moral approbation from the neutral communities." One might argue that the U.S. Supreme Court is a neutral community or body, but one must have money or power (or monied or powerful advocates) to reach that level of justice.

SOCIAL CHANGE

There is little agreement among social scientists as to whether violence brings about social change, or whether social change heightens the possibilities of violent revolt. It seems likely that there is some truth in both remarks: *change is not undimensional.* Under "normal" conditions of social change, there is primarily what H. L. Nieburg calls "frictional" violence: grievances are adjusted through debate, legislation, public policy, and contact. There is little violent revolt. As social change increases, as conflict between white and black (or between oppressed and oppressors) increases, and the normal frictional methods of control are unsuccessful, violence becomes "political."

According to Nieburg, political violence "addresses itself to changing the very system of social norms which the police power is designed to protect." Spontaneous acts of violent revolt are encouraged when it becomes obvious that the "peaceful procedures" of social and political process are closed. Nieburg concludes that "To understand the role of political violence, we must see it as part of the continuum of the total (formal and informal) polity."

As social change increases at a faster rate, there will be more violent revolt. There are three assumptions in this statement: under normal conditions, violence is spasmodic; as abundance rises for the majority, violent revolt increases among the less affluent; and finally, violent revolt is caused by an imperfect coordination of culturally prescribed aspirations and socially structured avenues for reaching these aspirations.[12]

The preconditions of violent revolt as influence and revolution are similar. Brinton lists three preconditions of revolution: the fruits of progress are not distributed evenly; government is corrupt or ineffective in trying to institute reforms; and the intellectuals are developing a social consciousness.[13] Certainly all three existed (with some question about the third) before the Revolution and Civil War, and one has only to stretch the imagination a little to see that these prodromal symptoms have had an important effect on the civil rights movement and big-city rebellions of the 1960's. Some of the more resistive revolt against the war in Vietnam originating from the universities has had all three preconditions. These symptoms also apply in some of the more violent union revolts, and some where violence has only been threatened.

Violent revolt can be an agent of social change. When some groups and individuals are oppressed—for example, "the other America"—they begin to understand, and believe, that social change will only take place if they revolt.

This was the position of Emma Goldman, the American anarchist, who felt the oppressed were caught in a tight net of forces which finally made them lash out violently. She had Kropotkin's dream that anarchism would offer more than a mystique of violence: "it would be an inevitable concomitant of significant social change." Even when she did not agree with violent acts, she understood the impelling motives behind them. Although she rejected the ethic of individual acts of violence, "she still had not, at the end of her life, discarded the illusion that large scale violence . . . could bring about her ultimate ends of peace, freedom, and justice." [14] In sum, her realism was change through revolt as influence. Her dream, her vision of utopia, was a violent revolution leading to a new life without oppression.

SOCIAL MOVEMENTS AND VIOLENT REVOLT

Most political, ethnic, racial, and religious groups whose interests have been flagrantly violated, abused, or ignored are potential sources of violent revolt and unrest. The number of social movements and their influence grows or ebbs in proportion to the recognition and resolution of their dissatisfaction and demands.

The successful use of violent revolt is discussed by Ernest Kaiser from a Marxist perspective.[15] He argues that works advocating indiscriminate guerrilla war and spontaneous individual violent revolt against the system are what Lenin called "revolutionary phrasemongering and an extreme, left-wing infantile disorder with programs doomed for defeat." Kaiser further indicates that there is a need to organize people, form alliances and coalitions, even if they are temporary and wavering. Power and influence do not come out of the barrel of a gun.

Andrew Kopkind argues that recent big-city rebellions produce a new kind of ghetto with more organization. He argues that a primitive new politics has emerged out of the summer of 1967 in the ghettos. Tough black street leaders have become "new" political leaders. "They are half guerrilla, half ward healer. They work between organization and revolution, groping for a way in which a bitter and mobilized minority can change a system they know will never accept them as they are." Tom Hayden, writing about Newark, said that seeing violence, our friends and kin being hurt, makes you become a part of their lives. "It touches people personally and springs a commitment to fight back." Tom Parmenter wrote that some experts involved in community organization see the rebellions as an "opportunity to assert leadership in building a community. They see more value in organization than in looting. They view organization as a constructive solution. Riots may run out of gas in a week, but if organization can begin, it can keep going."

Sidney Hook points out that the Christians and the

Jacobins were propelled to use violence. He shows that violence has been "an invariable concomitant of all mass movements of social reform." Hook is aware that the threat or shadow of violent action has played a powerful part in social movements aimed at both influence and overthrow, from one end of the continuum to the other.

VIOLENT REVOLT AND THE ETHIC OF CRISIS

Crisis and drama help create change, develop mass movements, and instill fear in those at whom the revolt is aimed. In *Reflections on Violence* Georges Sorel advocated an ethic of crisis, accentuating dramatic social change. For Sorel, crisis and drama were a technique of keeping the middle class in a state of fear, and illuminating the conflict of ethical values. Even a few violent acts would suffice. Small violent insurrectionary acts in defiance of all authority dramatize the spirit of violent revolt, but for Sorel, they have historical value only if they are a "clear and brutal expression of the class war; middle classes must not be allowed to imagine that, aided by cleverness, social science, or high-flown sentiments, they might find a better welcome at the hands of the proletariat."

This basic ideology has threads throughout American history. The Student Nonviolent Coordinating Committee, and other groups in recent years, has used all sorts of violent dramatic threat and action which have made the middle class fearful, but more important, often united the black community. Crisis and drama are organizing devices around which a movement for violent revolt can be built. Citizens can read and see material on violence in the same way that adolescents read "marriage manuals" as pornography, and that others are tied nightly to violent westerns on television. Certainly films and novels about urban gangsterism, violence in the streets, and war are also ways of addicting and organizing people around the crisis and drama of violence.

The use of dramatic production to show the violence of society, and control, and/or the need for violent revolt is obvious in the works of Bertolt Brecht, especially *Mother Courage,* which shows the horrors and suffering of war.

Many films place fantastic emphasis on violence. *Bonnie and Clyde,* produced in 1967 and nominated for an award as the best motion picture of that year, is a magnificent study of violence in America, showing the continual crisis-ethic of violence as a way of life, needlessly brutal, involving a kind of self-annihilation and comfy identification. It focuses on a small group of people during the Depression, when a minority imposed both unpopular and unreal laws.

Those who remember *Gone with the Wind, Patriotic Gore,* and *Let Us Now Praise Famous Men* will understand that every decade in American history is filled with films and literature about violence. An example in the early sixties was the film of Warren Miller's *The Cool World,* which attempted, by using characters who actually lived on location, to show what life was like on the bottom for a teenage gang in Harlem. In 1968 the state of Massachusetts banned a brilliant documentary film about violence in a state mental institution. Documentaries about violence that strip bare that which unnerves are shut out from the public.

The purpose of Guerrilla Theater, which uses some of Antonin Artaud's ideas, is to make Americans understand their own violence, especially the relationships of domestic and international violence. Various groups of black young people are using drama to show their anger and revolt to the white world, i.e., Youth for Service in San Francisco and the Blackstone Rangers in Chicago. Guerrilla Theater groups have sprung up on a number of university campuses, and in a number of big cities, in the past few years.

VIOLENT REVOLT IS FUNCTIONAL

Frantz Fanon argued that violent revolt makes it possible for the masses to understand social truths, that only a violent struggle will create significant revolutionary changes for black Americans whom he considered a colonial people.[16] Lewis Coser writes that violence is functional as an alternative road to achievement, as a danger signal, and as a catalyst.[17] Whereas Coser stressed the integrative functions of violence, Ralf Dahrendorf emphasizes the diverse functions of violence and the greater significance of disruption and conflict over mere integrative functions.[18] Let us conclude this section with a letter, quoted in *The Black Power Revolt,* that Frederick Douglass wrote in 1849 on the functions of revolt:

> The whole history of the progress of human liberty shows that all concessions, yet made to her august claims, have been born of earnest struggle. The conflict has been exciting, agitating, all-absorbing, and for the time being putting all other tumults to silence. It must do this or it does nothing. If there is no struggle, there is no progress. Those who profess to favor freedom, and yet depreciate agitation, are men who want crops without plowing up the ground. . . . They want the ocean without the awful roar of its many waters.
>
> . . . Power concedes nothing without a demand. It never did, and it never will. Find out just what people will submit to, and you have found out the exact amount of injustice and wrong which will be imposed upon them; and these will continue till they are resisted with either words or blows, or with both. The limits of tyrants are prescribed by the endurance of those whom they oppress. In light of these ideas, Negroes will be hunted at the North, and held and flogged at the South, so long as they submit to those devilish outrages, and make no resistance, either moral or physical. Men may not get all they pay for in this world; but they certainly pay for all they get. If we ever get free from all the oppressions and wrongs heaped upon us, we must pay for their removal. We must do this by labor, by suffering, by sacrifice, and, if needs be, by our lives, and the lives of others.

·3· THE CYCLE OF VIOLENCE

Many conflict theorists argue that conflict prevents the ossification of society by posing a constant pressure for innovation and creativity. Because conflict has diverse, integrative, and disruptive functions, it can lead to fundamental social change. A conflict model, and conflict situations, are operative at various levels or zones in society. American society is often defined by the "quality and types of conflict situations tolerated if not openly sanctioned." Conflict functions, and is a struggle, within the structure or system over status, power, laws, norms, values and resources. Conflict is not outside the system, but gives direction to change, helps produce necessary change, and contributes to the settlement of issues and problems. It is a problem-solving vehicle.

Political, social, and economic conflict are often cyclical in the United States, a nonequilibrated nation. Conflict and violence, within a cycle of control and revolt, are more likely when there is absolute deprivation in socioeconomic and political terms rather than relative deprivation. Conflict is a more intensive dynamic component and process because various groups and institutions in our society are in such severe disequilibrium. It is possible for conflict to be violent or nonviolent, and to occur at any point in the cycle, or for it to be the basis of revolt or control. Less disequilibrium, recognition of the positive factors of conflict, greater democratic organization and participation, and more effective parliamentary institutions should tend to decrease the tendency toward violent means.

Within the cyclical theory, continual violent revolt has had a formative influence on the policy response of violent control. Various policies evolve and respond within a cycle of control and revolt. I would argue that traditionally there has been a balance between revolt and control, but that America is moving in a direction where violent control, repression, and suppression are tending to become policy, and revolt is quelled. The merits of this policy were argued during the spring of 1968 when Mayor Daley of Chicago and Mayor Lindsay of New York discussed whether or not police should "shoot to kill" people involved in civil disturbances.

This essay indicates that if both control and revolt are escalating, increasing conflict is caused in part by the ruling consensus or elite, the military-industrial-academic complex, which insists that conflict and violence must be interpreted as dysfunctional. Too seldom are policy makers able to understand and cope with the causes of conflict and violence. Violence of the oppressed is directly proportionate to the violence exercised by their oppressors. Resistance or expectations of resistance increase the probability of violent control.

Tom Hayden, writing about Newark during the summer of 1967,[19] describes a particular instance which confirms this theory: 1) official violence (control) has been used for years to quell the aspirations, rights, and demands of the black community; 2) the response of the ghetto, whose cries have not been heard, was rebellion or revolt with various degrees of violence; 3) the controllers—the government local and national guard—used violent control as a destructive technique, or authority and repression; 4) and 5) each side escalated with greater violence.

STAGE ONE

Violence has become an efficient means of control. According to Lasswell, we are moving into an era where violence dominates the society. More specifically, specialists on violence (the military-industrial-academic complex) are becoming the most powerful, overpowering group in society. They dominate the instruments of violence. Marvin Wolfgang argues that the greater the participation which members of society have in its maintenance, control, and direction, the less vulnerable that society will be to the emergence of collective violence. Democratic bargaining processes break down because violent control becomes centralized. Fear of violent revolt often produces pre-emptive violence. There is an escalation or build-up of violent control in anticipation of future violent revolt.

Violent control increases in a society that is more and more one-dimensional, in which there is domination of the individual, paralysis of criticism, lack of meaningful opposition, an overriding concern with preserving the status quo, the obliteration and integration of opposites, and merging and swallowing up of alternatives.[20] Many people feel trapped. Violent control is also being created by an increase in deprivation among some groups and the lack of participatory politics: there is a need for organizations on a neighborhood and small-community level run by the residents.

STAGE TWO

Violent revolt, as Morris Janowitz points out, establishes a vague political presence. Some groups demand recognition by a kind of "defiance" politics. Retaliation against growing control is an affirmation that society is neither peaceful nor participatory. (It is also a sign that the society is not completely dead, not absolutely dead.) The factors in stage one increase the threat and demonstration of violent revolt. Throughout American history, racial, ethnic, and political minorities have felt oppressed and outside the processes of participation and bargaining. They have felt that they have had no influence in making adjustments or drastic changes. Violent revolt has appeared to be the only alternative.

Engels argued that the masses are forced to use violence.[21] As people become more aware of inconsistencies, tensions rise and violent revolt becomes a fact. P. A. B. Calvert indicates that at this stage direct forms of violent revolt, including strikes, demonstrations, and riots, which have an "overriding political purpose," occur. When the propaganda effect is highly disproportionate to the objectives of these acts, the cycle tends to be perpetuated. Less communication and more confrontation between revolters and controllers increase the probability of greater violence by both sides. Irving Louis Horowitz points out that

> . . . the use of violence to counter the force of the state wherever it occurred—in the Haymarket affair, in Coxey's Army, the American Federation of Labor Dynamiters, Centralia Steel unionization, by the Wobblies of the West—all came to a frustrating and dismal end, . . . the state unleashed a steady stream of counter-violence. . . .[22]

STAGE THREE

Control as counterviolence to knock out violent revolt and repression is increased. (The various forms here are only extensions of stage one, but in stage one they are not visible beyond the view of most Americans.) Revolt is put down or smashed. Dissent and other deviant behavior are prohibited. Violence becomes a decisive form of political power in response to conflict. If resistance on the part of those revolting increases, those in control use counter-resistance. Ultimate repression and control are overpowering. It is likely that Barrington Moore had this in mind when he wrote:

> We have also noticed the crucial part that the military forces and the police can play, that no violent transformation can possibly take place unless the insurgent elements can neutralize or gain control of the instruments of violence.[23]

As long as they cannot gain control, repressive legislation in reaction to their revolt will grow on the local, state, and national levels. The New York Civil Liberties Union said 1967 had not been a good year for individual rights and warned "that state reprisals against peaceful protest could lead to increased violence." They continued:

> If peaceful protest leads to reprisals the temptation to employ more radical means to protest is strengthened. Escalation of violence in protest demonstrations can thus become as difficult to reverse as escalation of violence in international relations. . . . the mere fact of overregulation, quite apart from the merits of any particular regulations, is destructive of individual dignity and individual liberty.

STAGES FOUR AND FIVE

Repression, suppression, and exceptional social control which turn those revolting into outlaws bring counterviolence against the state, which has firmly established control. Counterescalation occurs on both sides when adjustments between revolters and controllers are not made. Blood is spilled in a pattern of violent control versus answering revolt and vice versa. Rebellions spread from one city to another or from one strike to a series. The National Guard is called out as private police were in earlier years. The agents of control are equipped with highly technical weapons. In 1969 both armored trucks and such chemical agents as mace are being used. As a nation, perhaps we have not reached stages four and five, that is, the phases of spiraling control and revolt, but it is possible to speak of pockets of overpowering control and intervention: the National Guard moved into and took over areas of Newark; they had moved into Little Rock and the University of Mississippi; and more recently the police moved onto the campuses, in New York, Orangeburg, and San Francisco. The government has created intense fear and hatred in many of our cities and universities which may explode in a cumulative series of events, and at this juncture, a kind of overpowering totalitarian policy of control may evolve. In sum, the policy of violent control and repression has never been an anomaly. Violent revolt has traditionally been political, for when control is threatened, it retaliates with policies of violent control.

CONCLUSION

We cannot develop creative, constructive policies to deal with violence if we do not understand what it is and why it occurs. We cannot eliminate violence, but we can hope to regulate and reduce the causes and repercussions of violence by means other than control and without escalation of a policy of violent control. A theory of conflict resolution addresses itself to the causes, rather than the expressions, of social conflict. Its purpose is not the elimination of causes. Regulation will replace suppression and repression. Suppression forces and submerges conflict, though conflict will eventually erupt. Irving Louis Horowitz points out that "to plan for social change very often means to anticipate social conflict and devise programs for meeting the problems which arise out of such conflict. . . . The rejection of conflict is an invitation to violence and coercion. Conflict may often turn out to be a 'safety valve' for minimizing violence. . . ." Violent revolt will have to increase in order that the larger society learn this.

We are in a position not only to tolerate conflict, with a low yield of violence, but induce dissensus—for the purpose of avoiding all-out conflict which is unstructured. Political parties, voluntary social organization, and athletic events are examples of the safety-valve factor in such forms of conflict. By taking conflict as a social constant it may yet be possible to avoid the consequences of *maximum* conflict. There is abundant evidence that low-yield violence is at least as plausible within a world of programmed conflict as it is in in the diplomatic world of compromise.[24]

The causes of conflict and violence and their relationship to the policy of violent control must be understood, and the will to solve problems inherent in those causes must be developed. It must be made crystal clear that poor Americans, especially blacks, find that life in this nation is now unacceptable, as do many college students, minority groups, and a growing number of Americans who find our foreign policy totally unacceptable. America now has a grotesque inversion of priorities; there are incompatible demands being made upon our values and resources. Too often fear has been the basis of a policy of violent control because Americans wanted to be protected from those who are excluded from any real participation in American life rather than create a more equalitarian society. We can now make an effort to understand and alleviate the causes of violent conflict and revolt, or we can continue to be reactionary and suppress conflict and revolt.

NOTES

1. See Hans Gerth and C. Wright Mills, *Character and Social Structure: The Psychology of Social Institutions,* New York, Harcourt, Brace & World, Inc., 1963.

2. All references to H. L. Nieburg are from "Violence, Law, and the Social Process," in Louis Massotti (ed.), *Riots and Rebellions,* Los Angeles, Sage Publications, 1968; "Uses of Violence," *Journal of Conflict Resolution,* March, 1963; and a forthcoming book, *Political Violence,* New York, St. Martin's Press, Inc., 1969.

3. Jesse Lemisch, "The American Revolution Seen from the Bottom Up," in Barton J. Bernstein (ed.), *Towards a New Past: Dissenting Essays in American History,* New York, Pantheon Books, Inc., 1968.

4. All references to E. V. Walter are from "Power and Violence," *American Political Science Review*, June, 1967; "The Rise and Fall of the Zulu Power," *World Politics*, April, 1966; and "Violence and the Process of Terror," *American Sociological Review*, April, 1964. See also *Terror and Resistance*, New York, Oxford University Press, 1969.

5. Paul Tillich, *Love, Power and Justice*, New York, Oxford University Press, 1960.

6. John Dewey, "Force, Violence, and Law," *John Dewey's Philosophy*, New York, Random House Modern Library, 1939. See also Howard Zinn, *Disobedience and Democracy: Nine Fallacies on Law and Order*, New York, Vintage Books, 1968.

7. Hannah Arendt, *Eichmann in Jerusalem: A Report on the Banality of Evil*, New York, Compass Books, 1965. See also *The Origins of Totalitarianism*, New York, Meridian Books, 1966; and "Reflections on Violence," *The New York Review of Books, February 27, 1969.*

8. Georges Sorel, *Reflections on Violence*, Paris, 1905, New York, Collier, Inc., 1961.

9. R. D. Laing and D. C. Cooper, *Reason and Violence*, London, Tavistock, 1964; and R. D. Laing, *The Politics of Experience and The Bird of Paradise*, Baltimore, Penguin Books, 1967.

10. Sidney Hook, "Violence," *Encyclopedia of Social Sciences*, 1934.

11. Reinhold Niebuhr, *Moral Man and Immoral Society*, New York, Charles Scribner's Sons, 1932; and Staughton Lynd's discussion of this book in his introduction to *Nonviolence in America*, Indianapolis, The Bobbs-Merrill Company, 1966.

12. For an interesting discussion of these problems, see Thomas Merton, *Faith and Violence*, Notre Dame, Indiana, University of Notre Dame Press, 1968.

13. Crane Brinton, *Anatomy of Revolution*, New York, Vintage Books, 1956. See also Barrington Moore, "Revolution in America?" *The New York Review of Books*, January 30, 1969.

14. See the magnificent study of violence by Richard Drinnon, *Rebel in Paradise: A Biography of Emma Goldman*, Chicago, University of Chicago Press, 1961.

15. Ernest Kaiser, "Negro History: A Bibliographical Survey," *Freedomways,* Fall, 1967.

16. Frantz Fanon, *The Wretched of the Earth,* New York, Grove Press, 1966.

17. Lewis A. Coser, *Continuities in the Study of Social Conflict,* New York, Free Press, 1967.

18. Ralf Dahrendorf, *Class and Class Conflict in Industrial Society,* Stanford, California, Stanford University Press, 1960.

19. Tom Hayden, *Rebellion in Newark: Official Violence and Ghetto Response,* New York, Vintage Books, 1967.

20. Herbert Marcuse, *One Dimensional Man,* Boston, Beacon Press, 1964; and *The Critical Spirit: Essays in Honor of Herbert Marcuse,* Boston, Beacon Press, 1967.

21. Friedrich Engels, *Anti-Dühring,* Moscow, Foreign Languages Publishing House, 1962. See Part Two, "The Force Theory."

22. Irving Louis Horowitz (ed.), *The Anarchists* New York, Dell Publishing Company, 1964.

23. Barrington Moore, "Revolution in America?" *The New York Review of Books,* January 30, 1969.

24. Irving Louis Horowitz, *Three Worlds of Development,* New York, Oxford University Press, 1966. See Chapter 12, "Consensus and Dissensus."

TWO

VIOLENCE
IN
AMERICAN
HISTORY

INTRODUCTION

The purpose of Part Two is the presentation of articles which describe and analyze both the process and the fabric within which violence evolves, including a number of major outbursts. The articles include discussion about violence in the Revolutionary era, our violent attitude toward Indians, the Draft Riots, the violent institution of slavery and its aftermath, Nativism, vigilante movements, labor conflicts, race riots, and the violence of white Americans when Negroes move into neighborhoods which they claim as their own.

It is impossible within the confines of this reader to present a narrative of everything just mentioned, and to be mentioned, in this introduction and in the articles dealing with America's violent past. I had to be selective, and my selections involved five criteria: that the events be described with great clarity and involvement; that they be those which seem classic, profoundly history-making; that they occur within a patterned cycle every twenty years, beginning in the early eighteenth century, and that they be linked together; that they have a special meaning or relevance today because of striking similarities throughout history; and that they involve different groups and different forms or kinds of violence. Before introducing the chapters in Part Two, I want to describe at least in outline form, various outbursts of violence for which there is no space for an entire chapter.

Although I have included a chapter on anti-Catholic violence, I have left out waves of violence against, for example, the Chinese. John Higham points out in his book, *Strangers in the Land: Patterns of American Nativism 1860–1925*:

> No variety of anti-European sentiment has ever approached the violent extremes to which anti-Chinese agitation went in the 1870's and 1880's. Lynchings, boycotts, and mass expulsions still harassed the Chinese after the federal government yielded to the clamor for their exclusion in 1882.

The frontier town was almost always violent, as was the frontier itself, described by Francis Parkman in *A Half Century of Conflict*, and Henry Nash Smith in *Virgin Land*. Life in early American cities was not peaceful either: protest against real and felt abuses almost always produced violence and the destruction of property in the first three quarters of the seventeenth century. Before Philadelphia passed "the night watch law" in 1750, crime flourished, including petty larceny, rape, robbery, assault, felony, and homicide—and women often were the perpetrators. In 1749 a Manhattan newspaper commented, "It seems to be now become dangerous for the good People of this City to be out late at Nights without being sufficiently strong or well armed." Carl Bridenbaugh, in *Cities in Revolt*, wrote:

> One of the most portentous manifestations of the spirit of this age was the mobbish temper of the masses . . . who were far from being a mere 'rabble' seeking bread and an opportunity to release pent-up boorish boisterousness. . . . The mob always involved 'a majority of middle-class citizens and the approval of many more.' The mob was . . . the first outward and visible signs of the profound revolt of the Western World against aristocratic rule, and they convinced a few royal officers at least that England's American colonies would never remain docile.

The fear of mobs in Boston, Bridenbaugh continues, produced an act in 1751 for suppressing riots, "which provided penalties of confiscation of all personal and real property, and a whipping of thirty-nine lashes every month for three months, for anyone engaging in an unlawful assembly or in destroying property." Violence in the Revolutionary era involved more than this. Jesse Lemisch, in his article in *Towards a New Past: Dissenting Essays in American History*, discusses Bacon's Rebellion, the Whisky Rebellion, the Boston Massacre, the Stamp Act Riot, and the Battle of Golden Hill. The powerless, those on the bottom, were deeply involved in this violence because colonial America was not democratic, because disfranchisement was widespread. They were aware of the "contradictions and limitations in the thought of Revolutionary leaders. . . ." And since their influence did not reach the courts and assembly halls, they made use of a new politics: "a politics of the street was replacing the old politics—the politics of the assembly hall. . . . Unlike others, they had fewer legal channels through which to express their grievances. . . . their violence was all the politics they could have."

George Mowry has given his book, *The Twenties*, the subtitle of *Fords, Flappers, and Fanatics*. Violence occurred over "such matters as religion, marriage, and moral standards, as well as the issues over race, prohibition, and immigration. . . ." After the passage of the Volstead Act there was immediate opposition by a majority of Americans: illegal liquor traffic, overzealous enforcement, corruption, hired guns, and the growth of organized gangsterism financed by bootlegging flourished. Clarence Darrow comments that a minority of prohibitionists destroyed liberty. "It was on this foundation that they foisted upon the U.S. a reign of terror, intimidation, violence, and bigotry unprecedented in the modern world." He argues that prohibition was adopted under the cloak of war.

The violent federal suppression of aliens and radicals from the turn of the nineteenth century to the beginnings of the New Deal is brilliantly examined by William Preston, Jr., in *Aliens and Dissenters*. Discussing the Palmer raids, Preston comments:

If the Palmer raids thus were a sacrificial offering to an intense nativism by certain high priests of repression, they were also the unique convergence of the two parallel and often complementary traditions. From the 1890's on, the antialien and antiradical movements had established a series of prec-

edents for dealing with the marginal groups in society. . . .
The intensity of those raids reflected the force exerted when
the two traditions fused.

The first three decades of the twentieth century had their
roots in the Alien and Sedition Acts in the late 1790's,
described thoroughly by John C. Miller in his book, *Crisis
in Freedom*.

Violence in the South is a much larger issue than the
horrors and brutality of slavery. There is not room in this
little book to go into the origins of violence in the ante-
bellum South,* but it is well to remember what it is that
"won for the ante-bellum South the reputation of being a
land of violence." John Hope Franklin identifies and describes that reputation in his excellent book, *The Militant
South*. Franklin indicates that fighting and dueling were a
code of living:

> The prevalence of violence was due, in part at least, to the
> section's peculiar social and economic institutions and to the
> imperfect state of its political organization. The passions that
> developed in the intercourse of superiors and inferiors showed
> themselves in the intercourse with equals, for, observed
> Stirling, 'the hand of the violent man is turned against itself.'
> Far from loathing violence, the man of the South was the
> product of his experiences as a frontiersman, Indian fighter,
> slaveholder, self-sufficient yeoman, poor white, and Negro.
> He gladly fought, even if only to preserve his reputation as a
> fighter.

The period from Reconstruction to World War I was
saturated with labor violence, although much of it, and its
causes, was covert and institutionalized. What gave rise to
this terrible violence? The most well-known reason was
the demand for an eight-hour day. But the larger reason was
the brutal conditions of working people, especially women
and children, as described by Upton Sinclair in *The Jungle*.
Not only did they work long hours, but the fumes and injuries from machinery turned young women and children

* See Winthrop D. Jordan, *White Over Black: American Attitudes
Toward the Negro, 1550–1812*, Chapel Hill, University of North Carolina
Press, 1968.

into old men and women while still in their teens. Jacob A. Riis's *How the Other Half Lives*, written in 1890, and Lincoln Steffens' *Shame of the Cities*, written in 1904, describe the horrible living conditions of the poorly paid working class. Marie Van Vorse, a muckraker writing in the early twentieth century, describes conditions in the factories:

> These little particles (of cotton) are breathed into the nose, drawn into the lungs. Lung disease and pneumonia—consumption—are the constant, never-absent scourge of the mill village. The girls expectorate to such an extent that the floor is nauseous with it; the little girls practice spitting and are adept at it.*

The history of the physical, psychological, and economic violence of unemployment and poverty in America is little known. Before the Depression of the thirties, the unemployed man was not so much thought of as lacking a job or being unable to get one; instead he was looked upon in much the same light as the hobo, the alcoholic, and the criminal. A Massachusetts law of 1793 stated that the solution to the problem of unemployment was *removal* for all but the respectable poor. "Removal meant incarceration. It involved the isolation, containment, stigmatization, and exploitation of the poor." The poor were *removed* to *bad* neighborhoods where they were shunned and kept under suspicion. In 1819 Governor De Witt Clinton of New York declared that there were *deserving* and *undeserving* unemployed and poor. The deserving were employable and virtuous; the rest were otherwise.

During the national depression beginning in 1873, it was difficult to ignore the unemployed and poor. A book by Robert V. Bruce, *1877: Year of Violence*, sounds very similar to reports from the 1930's, and in many ways gives the feeling or tone of life of many unemployed and poor today:

> His daily wage fell at least 25 percent in the same time —50 or 60 percent by some estimates. As layoffs became

* "The Woman Who Toils," in Harvey Swados (ed.), *Years of Conscience: The Muckrakers*, New York, Meridian Books, 1962.

longer and more frequent, total yearly earnings fell off even more. This cruel reduction of living standards probably caused a greater sum of misery than did out-and-out employment. It was the great cities that bore the brunt of hard times. In every city soup kitchens ladled out watery stew by the tankful. Police-station basements filled up with huddled masses, doubtless yearning to breathe free but settling for a plank to lie on and a refuge from the cold and wet of the night. Everywhere men drifted aimlessly, hopelessly.

These kinds of conditions provided the fabric for a labor movement, and labor struggles that were often violent, beginning in the 1870's and continuing daily for fifty years. This included Coxey's jobless Bonus Army, which was run out of Washington, D.C., in 1932 by United States troops under MacArthur. The tents and shacks sheltering the poor and hungry were burned, and the unemployed were gassed, shot, and beaten before being routed as ordered by President Hoover.*

Most Americans think that anarchists and the I.W.W. (Industrial Workers of the World) believed in violence, but as Richard Drinnon points out in his biography of Emma Goldman, *Rebel in Paradise*, most anarchists did not really approve of violence. Drinnon comments on Goldman:

> Much of the popular indignation against Emma was the result of this theory of the inevitability of violence and this sympathy for overly sensitive individuals. A popular outcry was raised not because she committed violent acts herself, but because she refused to join in the condemnation of individual violence. Although after 1892 "never again had I anything directly to do with an act of violence," she pointed out, "I have always taken my stand on the side of those who did. I have fought shy, all my life, from joining the cry of Crucify! Even if I did not agree with the act(s) I understood the impelling motives of them." To the authorities and to the public generally such an attitude seemed conclusive proof that she abetted acts of violence.

Carey McWilliams describes decades of violence and brutality on the part of growers against the Chinese, Japanese,

* See Irving Bernstein, *The Lean Years*, Boston, Houghton Mifflin Company, 1960.

Filipinos, and Mexicans in his book, *Factories in the Field.*† It wasn't until the 1960's that Cesar Chavez was finally able to successfully organize farm workers for the first time, but violence and repression have a long, long history in California and continue today to operate against unorganized and organized farm workers. Many of John Steinbeck's books give great insight into violence in the fields during the 1930's.

In 1969 many leaders of antiwar and black power groups are worried about the possibility of being rounded up and heaved into a stockade or concentration camp. This kind of violent internment is nothing new in America. During the war with Japan, more than 110,000 Japanese-Americans were imprisoned without trial behind barbed wire in what were called detention centers, and were told that if they appeared on the West Coast they would be slaughtered wholesale. That didn't happen, but within the concentration camp they were surrounded by barbed-wire fences, roving searchlights, and armed guards, and had to endure mess-hall feeding, severe overcrowding, and shortages of food and medical supplies. All men of draft age, over seventeen, were asked to swear "unqualified allegiance to the United States" or be classified as disloyal. Six thousand would not swear allegiance and three thousand more qualified their answers. Morton Grodzins, in *The Loyal and the Disloyal*, gives four reasons for declarations of disloyalty:

> A substantial group declared themselves disloyal as a protest against their wartime treatment. . . . Loyalty to nation meant disloyalty to family. . . . Loyalty meant the threat of being forcibly moved from relocation centers, the necessity of facing an uncertain, immediate future without economic resources and under threats of social ostracism, if not actual physical violence. . . . A fourth definition of disloyalty was an expression of preference for Japanese life-ways and a preparation for living in Japan in the event of Japanese victory.

The pathology of this impossible so-called choice between being unthinkingly loyal to America (wearing a uniform

† Reprinted in 1969 by Archon Books.

and perhaps killing your family and friends) or being termed disloyal because of positive identification with ancestry, nation of origin, and family seems in many ways strikingly similar to the situation of those who resist the war today, and especially those who believe that it is more important to be loyal to your black brothers than to any government policy.

The first and third essays in Part Two are general introductions or overviews. The other nine are concerned with outbursts within the recurrent, continual patterned cycle of a peak every twenty years.

Howard Zinn has written an original essay entitled "Violence and Social Change in American History." In his analytical and descriptive article he insists that we have a double standard for the judgment of violence. Zinn explains the relationship of social change and violence and then discusses a number of important violent events, among them the massacre of the Indians, the Civil War, slavery, depressions and labor violence. Finally, Zinn suggests what a standard ethic of violence might be.

Following Zinn's introductory essay are two selections from *Chief Flying Hawk's Tales: The True Story of Custer's Last Fight*, as told by Chief Flying Hawk to M. I. McCreight. These give a little more feeling, a sense of what happened, from an Indian's point of view. Much is known about Custer (1839–1876), the soldier and famous Indian fighter, but the short selections included here are especially important because they are in the words of Indians whose lives, and way of living, were often violently crushed as the new nation grew and developed. Red Cloud's speech and the brief selection on New Amsterdam (early urban violence) give tremendous insight into early American confrontation politics over independence, land rights, the crushing of a way of life, the meaninglessness of treaties, the lack of a vehicle to make one's views widely known, starvation, fear, economic exploitation, and physical butchery.*

* See also Dale Van Every, *The Disinherited*, New York, Avon Books, 1966; and Helen Hunt Jackson, *A Century of Dishonor*, Harper Torchbooks, 1969 (reprint of the 1881 Harper and Brothers edition).

Richard Maxwell Brown, a professor of history at the College of William and Mary, has written an important article about the history of vigilante groups which is from his testimony in October, 1968, before the National Commission on the Causes and Prevention of Violence. Professor Brown outlines the American tradition of extralegal violence in support of community values—lynch mobs, K.K.K., Whitecaps, nightriders, claims clubs—with particular emphasis on vigilantism, and concludes that these traditions still blossom. His article is an overview, and sadly there is not room to include articles about specific vigilante groups such as those in San Francisco* and in Illinois.† The violence commissioners seemed to take most of Professor Brown's remarks as a big joke, but perhaps they didn't and still don't understand violence.

The hatred of foreigners, especially those from Catholic nations, gave rise to the development of Nativism, which involved many years of anti-Catholic violence, including murder, burning, and riots. The most complete account of the origins of American Nativism is Ray Allen Billington's *The Protestant Crusade*, which traces Nativist roots from early American settlements to the 1850's. The selection included in this reader is from John Bach McMaster's monumental history of the United States, published in 1914. McMaster's description of the Philadelphia Riot of 1844 is interesting, but even more important is his reporting of events beginning in 1837 in which he describes the evolution of Nativism and its effect on people and politics. McMaster was a professor of history at the University of Pennsylvania and his book, like many histories in the late nineteenth and early twentieth centuries, is based primarily on newspaper and magazine accounts. Nativism did not end in the 1850's, and its development after that decade is best described in John Higham's *Strangers in the Land: Patterns of American Nativism 1860–1925*.

The three most interesting accounts of the Draft Riots

* See John M. Myers, *San Francisco's Reign of Terror,* New York, Doubleday & Company, Inc., 1966.
† See Paul Angle, *Bloody Williamson,* New York, Alfred A. Knopf, Inc., 1952; and Morris Janowitz, "Black Legions on the March," in Daniel Aaron (ed.), *America in Crisis,* New York, Alfred A. Knopf, Inc., 1952.

which took place in the streets of New York City during a
hot week in July, 1863, are by Herbert Asbury, *The Gangs
of New York*, by James McCague, *The Second Rebellion*,
and by Joel Tyler Headley, "Draft Riots of 1863," in his
book, *The Great Riots of New York, 1712 to 1873.** During that one week nearly two thousand people were killed,
countless buildings destroyed, and more than ten thousand
troops brought into the city to join with the New York
police in trying to restore order. Headley's account, written
only ten years after the Draft Riots, includes 150 pages on
those riots alone, and descriptions of ten other riots, including the Doctors' Riot, Election Riots, Flour Riots, and
Orange Riots. Headley's account seems both more thorough
and more exciting than the others. And even more important, what he writes about is strikingly similar to the burning, sacking, and resisting that are part of the protest
against the draft today.

Headley was active in the Know-Nothing party, and in
1846 became associate editor of the *New York Tribune*.
He was a military historian and the author of many books,
including *Napoleon and His Marshals* (which went into
more than fifteen editions), *Washington and His Generals*,
Sacred Mountains, and *Sacred Heroes and Martyrs*. Although virtually unread today, by 1853 his books had
reached a total sale of 200,000 volumes. Headley's point
of view in *The Great Riots of New York, 1712 to 1873*
is made obvious in his dedication: "To the Metropolitan
Police, whose unwavering fidelity and courage in the past,
are a sure guarantee of what they will do for New York
City in the Future, this work is respectfully inscribed by the
Author."

Slavery was clearly an institutional form of violence that
has many holdovers today. It would take many volumes of
documentation to bring out what has been written by and
about slaves, of violence perpetrated against slaves, of
the violent rebellion of the slaves against their masters'
treatment, and of the institution of servitude itself. The article included here is "Born Out of Violence," by Fawn M.

* Headley's book, originally published in 1873, will be reissued in 1969
by The Bobbs-Merrill Company, with an introduction by Thomas Rose
and James Rodgers.

Brodie, a professional writer. It is from her recent biography, *Thaddeus Stevens: Scourge of the South*. Stevens was a radical, an architect of reconstruction, an associate of Lincoln's, and a leader in the battle for suffrage and schooling. Miss Brodie begins this chapter with a description of the underground railroad and those who used it to escape from slavery, and the militia who wished to destroy it. She continues with a description of the bloody Christiana Riot, violence between abolitionists and proslavery elements, and more generally the clash between Free-Soilers, Whigs, and the Know-Nothing party. Finally, Miss Brodie discusses the violent outcome of the Kansas-Nebraska Act, the beating of Sumner on the floor of the U.S. Senate, with the approval of the majority, and his subsequent death from that violence a few years later.

Labor violence resulted directly from poor working conditions and oppressive control by the owners of factories and industry. There is also a great similarity between labor struggles and the conditions in cities today. Brutality and violence most always beget brutality and violence, but the question is why must similar conditions always create escalation of the cycle. The problem of police brutality in labor struggles often sounds like the problem of police in cities in the sixties.

The first giant outbreak of labor violence began in the late 1870's, with world-wide attention focused on violent railroad uprisings in 1877.* The violent clash of labor and industry-management continued through the 1880's, into the 1890's, and for most of the first three decades of the twentieth century.† This period was described by Drinnon:

> This was a period when many disputes were settled by violent means. It was, as Charles Beard wrote, "a baronial epoch when physical force was a normal part of high business procedure." Somehow the same people who were horrified by the Molly Maguires and such sporadic acts of violence as

---

* See Robert V. Bruce, *1877: Year of Violence,* Indianapolis, The Bobbs-Merrill Company, 1959; and Samuel Yellen, *American Labor Struggles,* New York, Russell & Russell Publishers, 1936.

† See Henry David, *History of the Haymarket Affair*, New York, Russell & Russell Publishers, 1936 (second edition).

Berkman's were undisturbed by the frequent outrages committed by Pinkerton armies of strikebreakers.

Louis Adamic was an important essayist, born in Slovenia, who came to the United States as a teenager. *Dynamite: The Story of Class Violence in America* was his second book, written in 1931, the first being a study of a return trip to his native Yugoslavia. I have included two of his narrative essays on violent strikes, one on the Homestead Strike in Pennsylvania, the other on Coeur d'Alene, in Idaho. The third essay on labor violence is taken from Mary Heaton Vorse's book, *Labor's New Millions*. Marquis W. Childs wrote a foreword to that book, in which he commented on Mrs. Vorse's keen understanding of labor struggles and victories. "She has lived through, often as an active participant, almost every important labor conflict in America during the past two decades." During the Republic Steel Strike, one of the bloodiest, when she was walking toward the picket line with a friend, they were hit by gunfire; Mrs. Vorse was felled by a bullet, but survived. Her chapter included here, "Violence—The Chicago Massacre," is a description of a horror in 1936 which was finally investigated by the La Follette Civil Liberties Committee Congressional hearings, which provided a huge library about violence and American labor. Few books have been written about those hearings. Vorse's is an exception and so is Leo Huberman's, *The Labor Spy Racket*.

Major racial violence occurred in big cities in 1919 and 1943. Always started by marauding whites, the rioting inflicted incalculable suffering on the black community. Arthur Waskow, active in District of Columbia politics and an expert on police-community relations, is a historian at the Institute for Policy Studies in Washington, D.C., and has written the definitive history of these incidents—*From Race Riot to Sit-in: 1919 and the 1960's*, published in 1966. The chapter included here, "Public and Private Violence: 1919," is an analysis of the role of violence in racial and other conflicts, and on the legitimate and illegitimate use of violence. Readers are encouraged to consult his book for thoroughly researched narratives and descriptions of specific riots in 1919 and 1943.

Among the race riots in 1943, including those in Harlem, Chicago, and Los Angeles, was one in the latter city involving Mexican-Americans and servicemen. Fanned by the newspapers, the Los Angeles Riot became one of the largest outbreaks of racial hatred and illegal violence against Mexican-Americans. Watts only followed this tradition of violence. Carey McWilliams, currently the editor of *The Nation*, is an expert on ethnic and racial violence in California. His article, "The Los Angeles Riot of 1943," is taken from his book, *North from Mexico*, published in 1948.

The final chapter in Part Two connects violence in our past to violence in the 1960's. It is from Charles Abrams' book, *Forbidden Neighbors*, published in 1955. Abrams is a professor of urban planning at Columbia University and the author of many important books on cities, including *Man's Struggle for Shelter in an Urbanizing World*. In the chapter included here, "Invasion and Counterattack," Abrams discusses the violent results of Negro migration into cities, beginning during the Depression and continuing today. He is concerned not only with the bombing and burning of homes when Negroes move in, but also with violence involving anti-Semitic, anti-Catholic, anti-Mexican, and anti-Oriental hatred. He describes one of the long series of outbursts in a nation whose culture and daily life is tightly woven with violence. It is only another chapter in the tradition of group, racial, religious, and political violence.

VIOLENCE AND SOCIAL CHANGE IN AMERICAN HISTORY

By HOWARD ZINN

There is a basic misconception about the United States, I am going to argue, which goes something like this: that the United States is a peculiarly nonviolent nation, with a special dispensation for achieving social change through peaceful parliamentary reform. My thesis is that this idea is based on two failures of vision: one is a failure to recognize how much overt violence has characterized our behavior toward nationalities and races other than our own; the other is a failure to recognize the place of violence—both overt and hidden—in American social progress. This misconception brings about a double standard: there is, on the one hand, a national tendency to absolutize the value of social change at the expense of human life when the violence required for this change is directed at other nations or other races; and on the other hand, a tendency to absolutize the value of peace at the expense of social change *within* the national framework.

With these preliminary statements, I would like to discuss violence and social change in the history of the United States, not pretending to do more than a brief, impressionistic survey. And then I want to suggest a number of propositions about violence which may be worthy of thought.

Our first great social upheaval was the expulsion of the British and their local officialdom in the establishment of an independent nation. A new privileged class was created, based on the overthrow of the royal and proprietary colonial governments and the redistribution of land after the confiscation of royal, proprietary and Loyalist estates. There were accompanying changes: the diminution of property requirements for political participation in the new state constitutions; the abolition of primogeniture and entail; the disestablishment of the Anglican Church; and the freeing of slaves in the Northern states. This was accomplished by seven years of warfare in which 25,000 in the Continental Army were killed, about one out of every eight men who served. To judge the extent of this violence, one would have to consider that the same ratio of dead in our present population would amount to a death list of 1,500,000.

The next great social change was the pacification of the continent and the creation of a vast common market, from ocean to ocean, 1,500 miles deep, through which labor, capital, raw materials, and finished goods could move freely. This was a vital prerequisite for the development of that industrial colossus which in the twentieth century would produce half the world's goods with six percent of the world's people. And the creation of this common market involved a series of violent acts which we have conveniently put out of memory.

The first of these acts was the expulsion and extermination of the Indians, who at the time of Columbus numbered 1,000,000 in what is now the United States, and who number about 400,000 today. Violence certainly is frequent *within* groups, but it seems to be invoked most easily when directed at strangers. The outsider is either physically odd, linguistically or culturally distinct, or is invested with strangeness because of distance. He becomes an invisible victim, an object of sorts, toward whom enmity can multiply without qualm. In the early nineteenth century, a French traveler noted this in American treatment of the Indian:

> In the heart of this society, so policed, so prudish, so sententiously moral and virtuous, one encounters a complete insensibility, a sort of cold and implacable egoism when it's a question of the American indigines. . . . it's the same pitiless instinct which animates the European race here as everywhere else.

According to John Collier, Commissioner of Indian Affairs in the Roosevelt Administration and one of the world's leading authorities on the Indians, there were 600 distinct Indian societies at the time the white man arrived in North America, and there was not one square mile of the continent unoccupied or unused. "These societies existed in perfect ecological balance with the forest, the plain, the desert, the waters, and the animal life." Their warfare with one another was controlled, moderate, cautious; their ambitions were small.

Then the white man came, and not one white conqueror, as in the area south of the Rio Grande, but various powers: Spanish, Dutch, French, and English, battling with one another and drawing the Indians into their battles. Still, the Indian societies were kept whole, and rule was indirect, as a calculated policy of the competing European powers, and then codified by the new United States as the basic law of Indian relations.

But when the Spanish, Dutch, French, and English were gone from the continent, Collier says, "there remained only one expanding empire, race-prejudiced and with a boundless land hunger. The former policies toward Indian societies and Indianhood became reversed; a policy at first implicit and sporadic, then explicit, elaborately rationalized and complexly implemented, of the extermination of Indian societies and of every Indian trait, of the eventual liquidation of the Indians, became the formalized policy, law and practice."

The record is hard to read without flinching, because it is the shadowed underside of the most cherished events in American history. We romanticize the early Virginian adventurers, but they settled on the territory of the Powhatten Confederacy and destroyed its members in bloody warfare. We are proud of the Puritans, but that great Puritan divine, Cotton Mather, a leading intellectual of the colony, said, when disease decimated the Indians after the Mayflower landing: "The woods were almost cleared of those pernicious creatures, to make room for a better growth." When the New England settlers burned the wigwams of the Pequots and massacred them as they fled, Cotton Mather recorded it coolly: "It was supposed that no less than six hundred Pequot souls were brought down to hell that day." Andrew Jackson, often heralded as a kind of early New Dealer, sent General Winfield Scott after the Cherokees of Georgia, driving fourteen thousand of them westward in the "trail of tears," in which four thousand died on the way. After the Civil War, the Plains Indians were hunted down, harassed, and killed, the remaining ones squeezed into the Indian Territory of Oklahoma and finally driven out of there, too.

The United States Army crushed the Indian in a series of wars and battles: the Chivington Massacre of 1864 in Colorado, the Black Kettle Massacre by Custer in 1868 in Texas, the driving of the Cheyennes south in 1878, and the Massacre of Wounded Knee in 1890. There were the Cheyenne-Arapaho War and the Sioux Wars of the 1860's. In the 1870's came the Red River War, the Nez Percé War, the Apache War, and more Sioux Wars.

In the record of violence, we might note a phenomenon different than either the quick destruction of the body, or the slow destruction of the spirit, and that is the elimination of the means of life—land, shelter, clothing, food. In the case of the Plains Indian this was accomplished by the slaughter of his most essential raw material: the buffalo. First the railroads split the great herds in two parts; then professional hunters with repeating rifles made the plains a slaughterhouse; by 1870 a million a year were being killed. By 1875 the southern herd was practically exterminated, and ten years later, the northern herd.

Collier says: "It was among the Plains Indians that the policy of annihilation of the societies and then of the individual Indian personality was carried to the farthest extreme." This statement is important because it is a recognition of violence beyond the physical: the destruction of culture and personality. It sounds strangely familiar to us these days, because we have lately become aware that lynching was not the worst thing that happened to the Negro in this country. In Stanley Elkins' comparison of the Nazi concentration camps with the American slave plantations (in his book, *Slavery*), his concern is not the whippings and beatings, but the assaults on the psyche, the warping of the self, the crippling of identity. And of course this did not end with the outlawing of slavery, because the violence done to the Negro person continues on the Southern plantation, in the Southern town, and in the Northern ghettos. Again and again, the young Negro uses the term "concentration camp" or "prison" to describe the ghetto.

The evacuation of the Indian was one necessary step in the forcible clearing of that national area which would house the most productive economy in world history. Piece by piece, what is now the United States was assembled: some acquisitions were made through clever diplomacy, such as the Louisiana Purchase and the Oregon Territory; others were made through violence, such as East Florida after a campaign of harassment by Andrew Jackson, and the Southwestern states (from New Mexico to California) as a result of the Mexican War. By the time of the Civil War, the United States extended from ocean to ocean. By 1890, Frederick Jackson Turner could use the Census Bureau's finding that the frontier was gone to start a train of discussion on its meaning. That Turner saw the frontier as a benign influence on American democracy was still another sign of the national tendency to test our benevolence by how we behave toward one another, and not toward those—whether Indians, Negroes, Mexicans, or Spaniards —*beyond* the frontier.

The Civil War, with all its complexities, is very much a part of the same process described above, a violent and successful effort on the part of the national government to maintain its control over a great agrarian hinterland whose raw materials and markets were needed for the burst of economic development that would take place in the late nineteenth century. President Lincoln said plainly that the retention of the South in the Union, and not slavery, was his main concern. My point is that the presumed peaceful constitutional and economic development of this great territory of the United States required a war that took 600,000 lives. Out of a population of 33,000,000, some 2,300,000 young men went to fight, and one out of four died. If applied to our present population, it would be as if 3,500,000 died in war. Edmund Wilson, in his biting introduction to *Patriotic Gore*, takes some of the romantic nonsense out of not only the Civil War Centennials, but all adulatory treatments of American territorial growth.

In the course of the war, slavery was abolished. Whether it was the prime cause of the war or not (and we would have to distinguish between its economic-political aspects and its human aspects to discuss that), its abolition was one of the great social changes in American history, and was a consequence of the most concentrated burst of violence this nation has ever experienced. It is hard to see how slavery could have been ended when it was, without *either* a series of revolts such as those planned by John Brown, or finally a devastating war waged, ironically, two years later by the very government that condemned John Brown to death for seeking a *less* costly means of emancipating the slave.

If the position of the Negro in this country is any test of the thesis that our free institutions have developed on the basis of peaceful parliamentary change, that thesis could hardly be advanced with any seriousness. That it can be advanced is testimony to how small a part the Negro plays in the national consciousness. He is always an exception, to be noted and then shoved aside, so that the state of the nation can be calculated without his troublesome presence. (When one sixth of the nation consisted of black slaves, this was known as "the peculiar institution.") The violence done *to* the Negro in his state of slavery, beyond the physical violence, divesting him of property, of wife and children, of education, of African culture, of his own identity—the process of total alienation—was never properly counted, even by our more humane scholars, who often limited their concern to wondering how many Negroes were really whipped by the plantation owner. And the violence done to his spirit in contemporary society is only beginning to enter our consciousness.

With independence from European control secured, with the continent united and pacified (and here, as with the American Revolution, there were bonuses: a National Bank, and Tariff, Railroad, and Homestead Acts, no longer opposed by the South), the next great social change was the industrialization and urbanization of an agrarian nation. This can be considered a peaceful development only if violence is limited to overt, intense physical harm. Those who worked on the railroads, in the mines, in the factories and mills were subjected to a kind of servitude destructive of both body and spirit. The hours were long, the wages low, and often there was a serflike incarceration in company towns. George Fitzhugh, in *Cannibals All*, had, just before the Civil War, castigated Northerners who criticized slavery while holding on to their industrial system. "You, with the command over labor which your capital gives you, are a slave owner—a master, without the obligations of a master. They who work for you, who create your income, are slaves, without the rights of slaves."

The depressions of the 1870's and the 1890's brought great distress. During the first three months of 1874, for instance, about 90,000 homeless workers, many of them women, lodged in New York City's police station houses, huddled together on benches. They were turned out at daybreak, hungry, to make room for the next batch. The Granger, Greenback, and Populist Movements rose in response to the distress of farmers in those years. The depressions eased and the movements declined, but the point is that the nation's industrial progress was made at great human cost to millions of people, a cost that must be reckoned in any expanded definition of violence. Barrington Moore's new book, *Social Origins of Dictatorship and Democracy*, illustrates, in his words, "the contributions of violence to gradualism" in the chapter in which he discusses the enclosure movement in England, another country with supposedly peaceful parliamentary development.

Another of the important social changes in American history was the development of what we call the "welfare state," the establishment of acceptable living standards for two thirds of the nation, limiting poverty and distress to those parts of the population which cannot easily combine (farm and service workers) or which lack a territorial base (migrant workers) or which are set off racially from the rest of the population. The welfare state began slowly in the Progressive Era with the legislation of the Wilson Administration and reached its height with the New Deal. What is often overlooked is the part played by violence of an overt kind in bringing about what is called the Age of Reform, which started in the twentieth century.

The Progressivism of Roosevelt-Taft-Wilson followed a period of the most violent labor struggles any country has ever seen: the railroad strikes of 1877, which brought troops and workers into armed clashes; the Haymarket events of 1886; the Homestead Strike of 1892; the Lawrence Textile Strike of 1892; the Pullman Strike of 1894; the Colorado Coal Strike of 1913–14, culminating in the Ludlow Massacre. This was the period of Big Bill Haywood, Mother Jones, and the Industrial Workers of the World. As for the New Deal era, it was accompanied by violent strikes, sit-down and regular; the mayhem documented in the La Follette Committee hearings is startling to anyone who thinks that the quiet politicking and the eloquence of FDR tells the story of the New Deal reforms.

The most important social change of recent years is the *de jure*, although not the *de facto*, end of segregation in the South and the awakening of the nation to the outcry of the Negro, for the first time since Reconstruction. Whatever the inadequacies, the lack of enforcement, of the various Civil Rights Bills passed since 1957, however empty are many of the passionate statements on racial equality from the White House, it seems quite clear that ten years of turbulence in the Negro community, from the Montgomery boycott of 1955 to the Selma march of 1965, had a great deal to do with these small gains.

To turn to a quick overview, American society, I believe, does show a growing consensus over time. What we have, however, is not one long consensus, but a series of steps toward consensus, each accompanied by violence which either destroyed, expelled, or incorporated a dissident group. The Revolution established a new consensus based on independence, expelling the British and their Loyalist supporters. Those not satisfied with the new privileged classes (Shays' rebels in Massachusetts, the Whisky rebels in Pennsylvania) were suppressed by force of arms to create an outwardly peaceful consensus under the new Constitution. Those left out of the new arrangement—the black people —were repressed with the entire paraphernalia of the slave system. Organized labor, after the 1877–1939 period of violent strikes, was brought into the consensus with New Deal legislation. And recently, the middle-class Negro has been pacified with the promise of incorporation into white middle-class life, leaving his brethren (represented by the Stokely Carmichaels and others like him) outside the consensus.

More and more elements of American life have been invited into the dominant in-group of American society, usually after overt violence of various kinds; each accretion solidifies the group, which can then continue, or even increase, the violence directed toward those outside the consensus (respectable Negro leaders will be more and more welcome at the White House, while the police will be more and more used to break up Negro rebellions in the cities or on college campuses). The creation of a substantial consensus at home seems to create the possibility of using even greater amounts of violence against out-groups abroad. (I have not spoken of the rapid increase in the means of violence and the use of violence by the United States abroad in this century, because this is too well known; I would single out as dramatic points of significance the fire-bombing of Dresden, the atom-bombing of Hiroshima, and the napalm-bombing of Vietnam.)

Our much-praised peaceful constitutional development, in other words, is based on a system which keeps peace on the national level, while violating it on two other levels of human existence. That is, the system permits disturbing the inner peace of millions of Americans who are too poor, or too colored, or too different in one way or another to be treated with respect by government and society. And in the field of foreign policy it permits an absolutism in decision-making which acts against what both Hobbes and Locke recognized as a basic law of human nature—the preservation of life.

This brings me back to my thesis: that we have a double standard for the judgment of violence within and without the national-racial group, in which we place a supreme value on peace within the society that has already incorporated us, and a supreme value on violence directed at those outside the corporation. A striking example of this

is the general alarm with which the government and the
public have greeted militant Negroes' talk of self-defense,
or any departure from absolute nonviolence, along with the
general willingness of the government and the public to
use the most fearsome weapons of violence in Asia.

Let me try now to state in conclusion what some of the
elements of a single-standard ethic of violence might be:

1) All forms of pain and abuse—whether overt, concentrated, and physical, or psychological, hidden, and attenuated—should be placed on the same scale of destructive actions. This creates great problems in weighing some
forms of violence against others, but is preferable to solving
problems too easily by assigning *no* weight to types of violence beyond the standard definition. The common ingre-
dients, the molecular elements of all kinds of violence, need
to be isolated. (For instance, we need to recognize the
identity of the violence in both crime and punishment.)

2) It follows from this that we pay a price for superficial social peace which represses and hides subsurface
violence. The price is not only the maintenance of that
infraviolence, but the eventual explosion into overt violence.
The much-lauded compromises of 1820 and 1850 which
smoothed over the slavery question may have made inevitable the Civil War. The Depression of the 1930's may have
been a price paid for glossing over the distress of the
1920's. Grievances saved pay compound interest.

3) Official violence should be granted no special privileges over private violence. John Brown was hanged for
attempting, by a rather small-scale act of violence, to free
the Negro slaves; but the United States government draws
little opprobrium for a war in which 600,000 were killed
in the same cause. A police murder, however unjustified,
is privileged in a way that a private citizen's act of murder
is not.

4) Violence done by others should be weighed equally
with violence done by ourselves; we were horrified when
Hitler killed several thousand people by dropping bombs
on Rotterdam, but easily accepted the killing of over
100,000 people in the bombing of Dresden. We count the
Viet Cong killing of a village chief as more terrible than
the American bombing of the population of the village.

Pearl Harbor is infinitely more condemned than Hiroshima. We are more troubled by a rock thrown by a Negro at a white policeman than by the policeman's shooting of another Negro. We would be shocked if Negroes decided to bomb the state of Alabama to get rid of its oppressive regime—but in international affairs we accept such reasoning.

5) We should assume that all victims are created equal, that violence done to men of other races or other political beliefs is not thereby given special dispensation: a dead Communist is a dead man, as is a dead anti-Communist. George Orwell, in *Homage to Catalonia*, wrote of holding his fire in the Spanish Civil War when a Fascist soldier, running past, had trouble keeping his pants up. "How can you kill a man," he wrote, "who is having trouble holding up his pants?"

6) Violence to property should not be equated with violence to people. When I was living in Atlanta, a policeman there shot and killed a Negro teenager who was running away from a store where a vending machine had been robbed of two dollars. Such scenes can be multiplied by the hundreds; many of those killed in urban riots in recent years were doing nothing but looting stores.

7) We should be constantly aware of our disposition to accept violence on the basis of symbolic arguments: animals commit violence for immediate and visible purposes, but humans can be driven to violence by a word, a slogan, a Pavlovian conditioning process in which we are so far removed from what the symbol stands for that we cannot rationally weigh the human costs and gains of our own acts. The word "nigger" or "imperialist" or "Communist" has driven, and still drives, a rational judgment from the minds even of intellectuals.

8) Finally we should be aware of Jeremy Bentham's criterion, in his utilitarian scheme, of fecundity: that not only should we measure immediate results of actions, but that we should also consider the proliferating effects—of excessive action in the dispensation of overt violence, and of inaction in the toleration of subsurface violence. Insensitivity in either case may lead to unexpected and terrible consequences.

From Chief Flying Hawk's Tales: The True Story of Custer's Last Fight

By CHIEF FLYING HAWK AND
M. I. McCREIGHT

RED CLOUD'S SPEECH

I will tell you the reason for the trouble. When we first made treaties with the government, our old life and our old customs were about to end; the game on which we lived was disappearing; the whites were closing around us, and nothing remained for us but to adopt their ways. The government promised us all the means necessary to make our living out of the land, and to instruct us how to do it, and with abundant food to support us until we could take care of ourselves. We looked forward with hope to the time we could be as independent as the whites, and have a voice in the government.

The army officers could have helped better than anyone else but we were not left to them. An Indian Department was made with a large number of agents and other officials drawing large salaries—then came the beginning of trouble; these men took care of themselves but not of us. It was very hard to deal with the government through them—they could make more for themselves by keeping us back than by helping us forward.

We did not get the means for working our lands; the few things they gave us did little good.

Our rations began to be reduced; they said we were lazy. That is false. How does any man of sense support that so great a number of people could get work at once unless they were at once supplied with the means to work and instructors enough to teach them?

Our ponies were taken away from us under the promise that they would be replaced by oxen and large horses; it was long before we saw any, and then we got very few. We tried with the means we had, but on one pretext or another, we were shifted from one place to another, or were told that such a transfer was coming. Great efforts were made to break up our customs, but nothing was done to introduce us to the customs of the whites. Everything was done to break the power of the real chiefs.

Those old men really wished their people to improve, but little men, so-called chiefs, were made to act as disturbers and agitators. Spotted Tail wanted the ways of the whites, but an assassin was found to remove him. This was charged to the Indians because an Indian did it, but who set on the Indian? I was abused and slandered, to weaken my influence for good. This was done by men paid by the government to teach us the ways of the whites. I have visited many other tribes and found the same things were done amongst them; all was done to discourage us and nothing to encourage us. I saw men paid by the government to help us, all very busy making money for themselves, but doing nothing for us.

Now do you not suppose we saw all this? Of course we did, but what could we do? We were prisoners, not in the hands of the army but in the hands of robbers. Where was the army? Set to watch us but having no voice to set things right. They could not speak for us. Those who held us pretended to be very anxious about our welfare and said our condition was a great mystery. We tried to speak and clear up that mystery but were laughed at as children.

Other treaties were made but it was all the same. Rations were again reduced and we were starving—sufficient food not given us, and no means to get it from the land. Rations were still further reduced; a family got for two weeks what was not enough for one week. What did we eat when that was gone? The people were desperate from starvation;

they had no hope. They did not think of fighting; what good would it do—they might die like men but what would the women and children do?

Some say they saw the Son of God. I did not see Him. If He had come He would do great things, as He had done before. We doubted it for we saw neither Him nor His works. Then General Crook came. His words sounded well but how could we know that a new treaty would be kept better than the old one? For that reason we did not care to sign. He promised that his promise would be kept —he at least had never lied to us.

His words gave the people hope; they signed. They hoped. He died. Their hope died with him. Despair came again. Our rations were again reduced. The white man seized our lands; we sold them through General Crook but our pay was as distant as ever.

The men who counted (census) told all around that we were feasting and wasting food. Where did he see it? How could we waste what we did not have? We felt we were mocked in our misery; we had no newspaper and no one to speak for us. Our rations were again reduced.

You who eat three times a day and see your children well and happy around you cannot understand what a starving Indian feels. We held our dying children and felt their little bodies tremble as their soul went out and left only a dead weight in our hands. They were not very heavy but we were faint and the dead weighed us down. There was no hope on earth. God seemed to have forgotten.

Someone had been talking of the Son of God and said He had come. The people did not know; they did not care; they snatched at hope; they screamed like crazy people to Him for mercy; they caught at the promise they heard He had made.

The white men were frightened and called for soldiers. We begged for life and the white men thought we wanted theirs; we heard the soldiers were coming. We did not fear. We hoped we could tell them our suffering and could get help. The white men told us the soldiers meant to kill us; we did not believe it but some were frightened and ran away to the Bad Lands. The soldiers came. They said, "Don't be afraid—we come to make peace, not war." It was true; they brought us food. But the hunger-crazed who had taken fright at the soldiers' coming and went to the Bad Lands could not be induced to return to the horrors of reservation life. They were called Hostiles and the government sent the army to force them back to their reservation prison.

NEW AMSTERDAM

Referring to the purchase of Manhattan for a lot of fishhooks and trinkets valued at twenty-four dollars, the chief's countenance indicated that it was the best kind of argument to prove how the white men cheated the innocent red folks on every occasion. The Indians had befriended the helpless adventurers when they came among them, and for their kindness the settlers attacked them one night and killed more than a hundred and twenty men, women and children while they were asleep in their wigwams. This was about the first massacre. But it was a white-man massacre of Indians. They ran their bayonets through the stomachs of little babies and flung them out into the river. They cut off the hands of the men and cut open the women with their swords. They went among them with a torch of fire and burned their homes until no Indians were left and these all were friendly Indians who sold the white people their island for needles, awls and fishhooks, and brought the furs to them. (This was in 1642 under Kieft's regime.)

The white man's account of this affair tells us that on February 25 at midnight, Kieft sent Sergeant Rodolf with a party of soldiers to Pavonia and another party under Adriensen to Corlear's Hook where they rushed in upon the sleeping families and killed them all in the most hideous butchery that can be found in American annals.

An eyewitness records it in these words: "I remained at the Director's (Kieft) and took a seat in the kitchen near the fire. At midnight I heard loud shrieks and went out on the parapet of the fort to look—at the flash of guns. I heard no more of the cries of the Indians; they were butchered in their sleep. Sucklings were torn from their mothers' breasts, butchered before their mothers' eyes, and their mangled limbs thrown quivering into the river or the flames. Babes were hacked to pieces while fastened to the boards; others were thrown alive into the river, and when the parents rushed in to save them the soldiers prevented them from landing."

DeVries said of it: "Some came running to us from the country having their hands cut off; some lost both arms and legs; and some were supporting their entrails with their hands, and mangled in other horrid ways, too horrible to be conceived."

The white man's own history refers to this massacre in the following language: "This crime has hardly a parallel in the annals of savage atrocities, directed as it was upon a friendly village of harmless, unsuspecting Indians."

But this was merely the beginning of a series of white-man massacres that continued for nearly three centuries.

THE HISTORY OF EXTRALEGAL VIOLENCE IN SUPPORT OF COMMUNITY VALUES

By RICHARD MAXWELL BROWN

The mainstream of extralegal violence in support of community values has been *vigilantism*. By vigilantism, I refer to the tradition in which organized, extralegal movements take the law into their own hands. This is the classic definition of vigilantism. In quantitative terms vigilantism has embraced by far the greatest amount of extralegal violence in American history, and in my opinion, vigilantism reveals extralegal violence in support of community values in its purest form. By examining the history of vigilantism we can best get at the significance of extralegal violence in support of community values, and I wish to devote the bulk of my testimony to vigilantism. But before doing so I wish to cite briefly other major forms of extralegal violence in support of community values that our country has endured:

1) *Lynch mobs.* By a lynch mob, I mean any unorganized, spontaneous, ephemeral mob which gathers quickly does its fatal work, and disperses speedily. Predominant period: from the end of Reconstruction to the 1930's Chief victims: Negroes in the South; white people in the West, North, and East. Ephemeral lynch mobs are to be distinguished from the organized, semipermanent vigilant movements.

2) *Ku Klux Klan.* There have been three Ku Klux Kla

movements. The first movement arose in the South during Reconstruction in defense of white supremacy and home rule. The second Ku Klux Klan of the 1920's spread all through the country, and outside the South directed its violence mainly against immoral and incorrigible white persons. The present K. K. K. of the 1950's and 1960's is mainly a Southern movement devoted to white supremacy.

3) *Whitecaps.* Predominant period: 1880's to the era of World War I. No overall organization. The aims of the local movements varied, but in the North, East, and West Whitecap violence generally focused on the moral regulation of white men and women. Now practically forgotten, Whitecap activity was once so pervasive that it had virtually become a generic term for local violence.

4) *Nightriders.* These bands were responsible for much of the illegal, clandestine violence that has occurred sporadically during the nineteenth and twentieth centuries. The greatest movement of organized nightrider activity occurred in western Kentucky during the 1900's when tobacco farmers as nightriders rose in violent revolt against large tobacco companies.

5) *Claims Clubs.* These appeared mainly in the trans-Missouri West in the 1840's and 1850's in defense of "squatters' rights" against land speculators.

6) *Miscellaneous* movements of extralegal violence have occurred in large numbers for immensely varied purposes. For example, Indiana and Ohio farmers in the nineteenth century banded together to destroy canals and reservoirs which they felt had baneful effects on the health and lands of their countrysides.

With apologies for the extreme brevity of my treatment of the foregoing movements, let me now return to my main concern: vigilantism. The first vigilante movement in American history occurred in 1767, just 201 years ago. From that time until about 1900 vigilante activity was an almost constant factor in American life. Far from being a phenomenon only of the far western frontier, there was as much, if not more, vigilantism in the eastern half of the United States as in the western. Although the first vigilante movement occurred in Piedmont, South Carolina, in 1767–69, most of the Atlantic seaboard states were *without* significant vigilante activity. But beyond the Appalachians there were few states that did not have one or more major vigilante movements. Altogether, in my research, I have discovered approximately 350* vigilante movements, large and small. I am confident that my research has uncovered the major vigilante movements, but I am equally confident that many lesser movements will remain undetected by historians.

Vigilantism arose as a response to a typical American problem: the absence of effective law and order in a frontier region. It was a problem that occurred again and again beyond the Appalachian Mountains. It stimulated the formation of hundreds of frontier vigilante movements.† On the frontier the normal foundations of a stable, orderly society —churches, schools, cohesive community life, etc.—were either absent or present only in rough, immature forms. The regular (and by regular, I mean legal) system of law enforcement frequently proved to be woefully inadequate for the needs of the settlers.

Fundamentally, the pioneers took the law into their own hands for the purpose of establishing order and stability in newly settled areas. In the older settled areas the prime values of person and property were dominant and secure, but the move to the frontier meant that it was necessary to start all over. Upright and ambitious frontiersmen wished to re-establish the values of a property holder's society. The hurtful presence of outlaws and marginal types in a context of weak and ineffectual law enforcement created the specter and, often, the fact of social chaos. The solution hit upon was vigilantism. A vigilante roundup of ne'er-do-wells and outlaws, followed by the flogging, expulsion, or killing of them, not only solved the problem of disorder, but had crucial symbolic value as well. Vigilante action was a clear warning to disorderly inhabitants that the newness of settlement would provide no opportunity for eroding

* Actually 341.
† There have, indeed, been urban as well as rural vigilante movements. In fact, the greatest of all American vigilante movements—the San Francisco vigilance committee of 1856—was an urban one. There were many other urban vigilante movements. Moreover, vigilantism has by no means been restricted to the frontier, although most typically it has been a frontier phenomenon.

the established values of civilization. Vigilantism was a violent sanctification of the deeply cherished values of life and property.

Because the main thrust of vigilantism was to re-establish in each newly settled area the conservative values of life, property, and law and order, vigilante movements were usually led by the frontier elite. This was true of the first vigilante movement in American history, and it was true of the greatest American vigilante movement—the San Francisco vigilance committee of 1856, which was dominated lock, stock, and barrel by the leading merchants of the city. Again and again, it was the most eminent local community leaders who headed vigilante movements. It would be easy to compile a "Who's Who of American Vigilantism," and in it would be included men who had been, were, or would become U.S. senators, governors, judges, wealthy capitalists, prominent lawyers, landed magnates, state legislators, and even clergymen. Presidents of the United States have not been immune. While serving as President, Andrew Jackson once approved the recourse of Iowa pioneers to vigilante activity, and as a young cattle rancher in North Dakota, Theodore Roosevelt begged to be admitted to a nascent vigilante movement. Roosevelt was rebuffed (because the vigilantes thought he would talk too much!), but to my knowledge, he never repented his desire.

Let me pause for a moment to sketch quickly the prototype of a vigilante movement. Vigilante movements varied in size from the smallest of a dozen or so members to the five or six thousand who belonged to the San Francisco vigilance committee of 1856. An average one might contain a hundred or two hundred members. It would be organized in some sort of command or military fashion. A highly rationalized organization, it would usually have some sort of constitution, articles, or manifesto to which the members would subscribe. Outlaws or other malefactors captured by the vigilance committee would be given a formal, though speedy, trial in which the defendant would have counsel or an opportunity to defend himself. The defendant was almost never acquitted, but the vigilantes' attention to the spirit of law and order caused them to give him, by their lights, a fair trial. In the early decades of vigilantism the punishment was usually whipping and or expulsion.* By the middle of the nineteenth century, hanging was the usual penalty. "Vigilance committee" or "committee of vigilance" was the common name of the organization, but originally —and far into the nineteenth century—vigilantes were known by the now obsolete term of "regulators." Variant names for vigilante groups were "moderators," "slickers," "stranglers," "bald knobbers," "committees of safety," and in central Texas, simply "mobs."

Vigilantism became such a pervasive feature of American life that as the nineteenth century wore on, it developed its own self-justifying ideology. There were four main elements in the ideology of vigilantism:

1) The first was the principle that *"self-preservation* is the first law of society, and the basis upon which its structure is built." To the vigilante, the threat of crime and disorder justified taking the law into one's own hands as an act of self-preservation.

2) The second element in the ideology of vigilantism was the *right of revolution.* Vigilante leaders recognized that taking the law into their own hands was, in effect, a revolutionary act against the authority of the state. Of this they made a virtue, claimed revolution as a right, and cited for their precedent the American Revolution of 1776.

3) A third element in the vigilante ideology was *popular sovereignty.* To Americans of the nineteenth century, popular sovereignty—a favorite concept—meant that the rule of the people was superior to all else. The people joined together for self-protection in a vigilante movement saw their organization as above the regular system of law and order should the latter prove incapable of protecting life and property.

4) The final element in the ideology of vigilantism was the *doctrine of vigilance* which swept America in the first half of the nineteenth century. For some reason it was the

* The duration of vigilante movements varied greatly. Movements which lasted as long as a year were long-lived. More commonly they finished their business in a period of months or weeks. The chief criterion for a vigilante movement in the classic sense (in order to distinguish it from a lynch mob) is rational organization and existence for a definite period of time, even though that period might be quite brief.

passion of Americans to be *vigilant* in all things and against all manner of threats and dangers. Vigilance committees and associations were formed in all areas of the nation, a great many of them having nothing whatsoever to do with the classic problems of crime and disorder. The widespread doctrine of vigilance was a powerful underpinning for classic vigilantism.

In addition to all other arguments for vigilantism, there existed a persuasive economic rationale. Vigilantism was much cheaper and, in gross terms, much more efficient than the regular system of law and order. The public expenses involved in a cumbersome and complex system of courts, juries, attorneys, judges, jails, prisons, law-enforcement officials, and prisoner maintenance before and after trial added up to one of the largest items in the budgets of local communities and counties. Effectual dealing with a frontier crime problem in a legal way inevitably meant heavy expenses for the afflicted municipality or county of the nineteenth century. This was onerous in two ways: 1) The frontier areas where crime was a vexing problem were what we would today call "underdeveloped areas." In many cases the slenderness of their new and underdeveloped economic resources meant that a regular system of law and order was a genuine economic burden. 2) The frontier elite which took the lead in vigilante movements was often dominated by ambitious young men scrambling toward economic success and high social status. A steep rise in taxes in order to support an effective system of law and order was a burden they frequently did not care to assume. Vigilante justice was indeed quicker and cheaper than regular justice. It was also more certain; there was no appeal from a vigilante hanging. One band of vigilantes in pre-Civil War Indiana actually paraded under a banner bearing the words *"No expense to the County."* It was a sentiment and justification voiced again and again by vigilantes. In the nineteenth century vigilantism was the lazy way, the careless way, the cheap way by which Americans often dealt with the problem of disorder.

The waning of vigilante activity came about when, at last, the regular agencies of local law enforcement began to effectively carry out their responsibilities and thus fill a void into which vigilantism had too often rushed.* This development occurred during the latter part of the nineteenth century and the early part of the twentieth. The significantly improved law enforcement stemmed from two factors. One was the technological revolution in communications and transportation—the railroad, telegraph, telephone, and automobile—which made state and local law-enforcement officers highly mobile at less expense than had been the case in the horse-and-buggy era and with a tremendous increase in effectiveness. Second, the economic rationale which saw vigilantism as an efficient and economical way of suppressing crime was undermined by the increasing material prosperity of America. The end of the frontier era saw local and regional economies emerge from their impoverished, underdeveloped state. The material means were at hand to bear more easily the high costs of regular law enforcement. Regular justice was at last economically competitive with vigilante justice, and the latter was no longer worth the trouble and danger.

A final, vital question about vigilantism remains: did it work? Momentarily putting aside moral and philosophical issues, the question is whether, pragmatically, vigilantism was a success. Was it an effectual cure for a breakdown in law and order? In purely pragmatic terms vigilantism was often successful. There are many examples of vigilante movements which dealt in restrained but decisive, orderly though illegal ways with serious problems of disorder. Having done so, these vigilante movements disbanded, leaving as their legacy a more orderly and stable society. But the model of a positive, successful vigilante movement was often eclipsed by one of another sort: a vigilante movement which slid downhill into the besetting sins of vigilantism—excess and extremism—and thereby brought into

* I have time to mention only briefly the vast Anti-Horse Thief Association movement of the nineteenth and the early twentieth centuries. An offshoot of the vigilante tradition, it extended from New England to the Southwest and at its peak in the late nineteenth century numbered hundreds of thousands of members. Local A.H.T.A. groups were often chartered by the state and sometimes given constabulary power. They ordinarily did not resort to vigilantism but instead supplemented local law-enforcement agencies in a legal, nonviolent way. They were transitional organizations between vigilante justice and regular justice.

being a powerful countermovement. The result then was the brutal "vigilante war" in which upstanding men and decent men would be found on both sides. Anarchy was the result, and it usually took the intervention of outside forces —ordinarily the state militia—to restore order. Even then the trouble was sometimes not settled, and the accursed area might suffer through a generation or more of ill feeling and low-level tumult.

Thus, in short-run terms and by the pragmatic test, vigilantism yielded mixed results: sometimes good and sometimes bad. But moral and philosophical considerations must be taken into account. Germane at this point is something I have not yet mentioned: the philosophy of anti-vigilantism. From the very beginning there was always a cogent and vigorous philosophy of antivigilantism. It held that due process of law was among the most precious jewels of the Anglo-American legal heritage, that true law and order means observing the letter of the law as well as the spirit, and finally, that the only way to get real law and order is to pour all one's energies and substance into making the regular system work. The philosophers of antivigilantism were on strong ground in their view that, in the long run, far from enhancing respect for law and order, vigilantism bred an insidious and deep-dyed disrespect for it and planted in men the arbitrary tendency to judge for themselves when they should be orderly and lawful.

When I first began my study of American vigilantism eleven years ago, I thought I was dealing with a finished chapter of American history. But as the years passed, I began to wonder. Occasionally I addressed audiences of laymen on the strictly historical subject of vigilantism; some-one would always get up and say, "That sounds like a good idea; we could use some of that today."

I fear that a new wave of vigilantism is a real prospect today. There are disquieting signs that it has already begun. The history of vigilantism shows unmistakably that in the past when the American people have been faced with a breakdown of law and order, they have resorted to vigi-lantism. The conditions which, historically, have produced vigilantism are with us today. There is no question in my mind that we are faced with a breakdown in law and order, one which actually exceeds anything in the past that I am aware of.* I am not referring, primarily, to the Negro riots that have occurred since 1964. Instead I am referring to a problem which antedates the riots: namely, the fact that for two decades or more our great cities have been slowly strangling in the grips of mounting crime. I am referring also to the immense proportions of automobile theft which have an impact deep into the rural highways and byways of America. Finally I am referring to the staggering inroads of organized crime, especially by the Cosa Nostra organizations.

Although I spoke earlier about the waning of vigilante activity around 1900, the vigilante tradition itself lives on. It has become a permanent part of the American intellectual heritage. The memory of vigilantism is kept green in our movies and television plays, in our novels and stories. The ideology of vigilantism is not dead (except for the doctrine of vigilance) but is waiting to be used by the mischievous and the misguided. Since 1964 (at the latest) we have seen the emergence of a series of quasi-vigilante movements. I refer to the neighborhood patrol movement of Crown Heights in Brooklyn (1964), to the People's Civic Association of the East New York, Brownsville, and Flatbush areas of Brooklyn (1967), to the North Ward Citizens Committee of Newark (1967–68), and to the self-styled "vigilantes" of West Hollywood, Florida (1968). Similar in character has been the Negro movement of Deacons for Defense and Justice in Bogalusa, Louisiana (1965), and other Southern localities. None of these movements has, to my knowledge, taken the law into its own hands, but officials are rightly concerned that that will be the next step. The police and other concerned officials look upon those organizations as vigilantes and so refer to them.

I am strongly opposed to the vigilante solution, but unless our country receives some real and honest leadership on this

---

* I am well aware that there is today a lively controversy as to whether our basic problem is really a steeply rising crime rate, or rather, rapid demographic changes. In either case, the effect has been virtually traumatic. All things considered, I stand on my statement.
—R. M. B., Nov. 13, 1968

issue, my reading of American history warns me that the people, in their desperation and confusion, will turn to vigilantism on a grand scale. On the basis of a vast body of expertise, we know how to deal with our crime problem of today and thus avoid the enormous pitfall of vigilantism. Our expert knowledge is best exemplified by the monumental 1967 report of the President's Commission on Law Enforcement and Administration of Justice. Doubtless the members of the present commission are familiar with that report. It shows that we have the know-how to deal with the problem, but it also frankly tells us that we are not spending the money needed to cope with it. The Law Enforcement Commission in its report called for a "Federal program totaling hundreds of millions of dollars a year during the next decade" and also asked "the States, the cities, and the counties . . . to make substantial increases in their contributions to the system of criminal justice." Only by massive expenditures of this sort will we approach a solution to the current breakdown and avoid the outbreak of vigilantism for which, otherwise, I fear we are inevitably headed. And only by similar massive expenditures for rooting out the sociological and psychological causes of remedial crime and violence will we at last be able to reduce the problem below crisis proportions.

The American vigilantes of the nineteenth century were not willing to spend the money and energy to make the regular system of law and order work. If we truly want real law and order, we will spend the money and the effort needed to gain it. But if we and our leaders merely wish to pay lip service to law and order as an empty ideal, we shall probably, in the end, turn to the easy way, the cheap way, the ultimately disastrous way of vigilantism.

THE RISE OF NATIVISM AND ANTI-CATHOLIC VIOLENCE

By JOHN BACH McMASTER

From the opening of the year no little anxiety was caused the Democrats by the growing strength of the Native Americans, and by their fusion with the Whigs in New York and Philadelphia. The formation of the Native American Association of the United States at Washington in 1837 was followed by the rise of like associations elsewhere. As yet the movement was non-partisan, and the demands an amendment or repeal of the Naturalization Law and restrictions on immigration. Thus, at Germantown, where a meeting of native citizens of all parties formed an association in 1837, the preamble and constitution set forth that the stranger, worn down by oppression at home, was welcome to come and share the blessings of our land. But his claims to vote, to have a voice in legislative halls, and be eligible to office, were vigorously denied. Is it not plain to every reflecting mind, it was asked, that the Naturalization Law is an evil, and should be repealed? Foreign influence, even now by far too powerful in our country, is rapidly growing. The day is near when most of our public offices will be filled by foreigners, and when, instead of governing ourselves, as is our native right, we shall be ruled by men who but a few years ago scarcely knew we existed. Europe is ridding herself of an excess of population that has become burdensome to her. And who does she send us? Her paupers, her criminals, her convicts, the outpourings of her almshouses and her jails. Many who came of their own choice were disgruntled malcontents at home. Greedy of power, ignorant of our customs, caring nothing for our laws, heedless of all civil restraint, they became the spreaders of anarchy, radicalism, and rebellion among our free and happy people. Nothing but a repeal of the Naturalization Law could cure these evils, already become unbearable.

When the Constitutional Convention of Pennsylvania was in session an attempt was made to secure an amendment forbidding foreigners who came to Pennsylvania after July fourth, 1841, to hold any public office in the Commonwealth.

The effect of this widespread hostility to foreign immigrants in 1837 was further shown in the memorials which reached Congress in the early months of 1838. One, sent by six hundred citizens of Sutton and Milville, in Massachusetts, asked Congress to inquire whether there was not a hidden design against the liberties of our country in the great influx of foreigners; whether the morals and social condition of the newcomers did not augur an increase in pauperism and crime; whether there were not in the country those whose allegiance to a foreign despotic prince required them to uphold his interests against ours; whether there was not a foreign conspiracy against our Republic, and whether plans for its execution had not been formed and put in operation.* Another complained that the ease with which foreigners of doubtful morals and hostile political principles acquired the right to vote was a source of real danger to the country. The petitioners saw with great concern the influx of Roman Catholics. To such persons, as men, they had no dislike. To their religion, as a religion, they had no objection. But against their political opinions, interwoven with their religious belief, they asked legislation. They asked whether this union of Church and State, this allegiance to the Pope, did not require legislation; whether there was not in operation under the Leopold Foundation a plan for the overthrow of our civil and religious liberties, and whether this was not to be affected by the emigration of Roman

---

* Executive Document No. 70, 25th Congress, 2d Session, Vol. ii.

Catholics from Europe, and their admission to our right of suffrage.*

The complaint against the Leopold Foundation was of long standing. In 1828 Frederick Schlegel, one of the greatest of German scholars, the friend and adviser of Metternich and Counsellor of Legation in the Austrian Cabinet, delivered a course of lectures. His purpose was to prove that Protestantism favored democracy, while Catholicism supported monarchy; that the political upheavals from which Europe had so long suffered were the natural outcome of the Reformation; that the great nursery of their destructive principles, the revolutionary school for France, Spain, and all of Europe, was North America, and he left his hearers to infer that democracy should be destroyed in America by founding Roman Catholic missions. When, therefore, at the close of his lectures, the Leopold Foundation was organized in Austria and spread to Hungary, Italy, Piedmont, Savoy, and France, the cry was raised that its object was to build up the power of Rome in the United States by encouraging the emigration of Roman Catholics from Europe, and by establishing missions in the various States.

A memorial from native Americans in New York City made the old complaints of influx of foreigners, paupers, and criminals, the ease with which they became voters, and the danger to the Republic, and demanded a residence of twenty-one years before naturalization.†

The Germans of Southeastern Missouri met at Cape Girardeau, and appointed a Committee of Vigilance and Correspondence "to watch the proceedings of Native Americans and of Congress," and called on all Germans living in the United States to join in an effort to defeat the aims of the natives.

The memorial which the meeting sent to Congress was referred, with others, to a Select Committee of the House, from which in time came a long report, and a bill to regulate the naturalization of foreigners.‡ As the House took no

---

* Memorial from Washington County, New York. Executive Document No. 154, 25th Congress, 2d Session, Vol. vii.

† Executive Document No. 313, 25th Congress, 2d Session, Vol. ix.

‡ Reports of Committees, Report 1040, 25th Congress, 2d Session, Vol. iv.

action, more petitions were presented. In 1839 citizens of Louisiana complained of the hordes of foreigners, cemented by social, political, and religious ties, who were daily suffered to acquire equal rights, immunities, and privileges with natives; complained of the injustice, the unfairness, of the law that deprived a native-born youth who lacked but one day of being twenty-one, of the right to vote, and gave it to a foreign-born youth the day he became twenty-one, if he happened to have been under eighteen when he came to us, knowing nothing of our laws and institutions; and asked for the entire repeal of all naturalization laws, and for protection from the indiscriminate influx of foreigners. Should the request be denied, they doubted not that erelong, in appealing to some future Congress, they would have to sue at the footstool of those whose feelings, prejudices, and aspirations would be alien to their own. They could not doubt that the mass of foreigners would soon array themselves as a distinct party under foreign leaders.*

In 1840 petitioners in Illinois declared that the further admission of foreigners to a share in the political rights of natives would be harmful to the interests of the country, and sooner or later ruin republican institutions, and asked for a repeal of the naturalization laws. In New York City in 1840 the movement of the Roman Catholics for a share of the public-school money for their parochial schools, and the continued agitation of the school question, led to a demand for an amendment of the State Constitution restricting the franchise. Strong associations of natives now existed in Lexington, in Louisville, in St. Louis, and a well-organized and active party in New Orleans. Against these the Louisville *Advertiser* cried out. The liberty we enjoy, it was said, and for which our fathers fought and bled, was not won by natives alone. We cannot think, therefore, that none but natives should enjoy political rights. With Washington were associated a Lafayette, a Steuben, a Pulaski, a De Kalb. The blood and valor of generous foreigners—French, English, Irish, Scotch, and German—insured the success of the Revolution. This attempt to repeal the naturalization laws shows a contempt for the rights of man.

---

* Petition of Citizens of the State of Louisiana, January 24, 1839. Executive Document No. 162, 25th Congress, 3d Session, Vol. iv.

In Missouri the Democrats took up the cause of the naturalized citizen, and the legislature denounced the Native Societies and called on Senators and Representatives in Congress to vote against the bill introduced by Mr. Hand.* In New York City during the spring elections a serious street fight occurred in the Sixth Ward between the Catholics and Orangemen, aided by natives. Many were hurt, several houses were damaged, and the windows of the residence of Archbishop Hughes were broken.† Grateful for the support of the "patented citizens," as the naturalized citizens were called, the chief of Tammany Hall appointed some Irishmen to petty offices. Disgusted at such truckling to foreigners, a few Democratic leaders quit their party and organized the natives. Up to Election Day it was not supposed that a thousand votes would be cast for the Native American ticket. To the surprise, it was said, of the natives themselves, nearly nine thousand votes were polled, and two strong Democratic wards were carried by them. Five-sixths of them were given, it was estimated, by Democrats bent on punishing their party.‡

When the election of a mayor came on in the spring of 1844, Democrats, Whigs, and Natives placed tickets before the people. But the Whigs, almost in a body, deserted their candidate, fused with the Natives, and twelve aldermen, eleven assistants and a Native mayor were elected by an immense majority.§

In Williamsburg, a town opposite New York, the Natives carried their entire ticket. Meantime the quarrel between them and the adopted citizens had spread to Philadelphia. In 1839 the Democrats nominated for office an Irish citizen named Hugh Clark. Many of the party took offence. Adopted citizens should, it was said, be suffered to vote, but officeholding should be limited to men born on the soil. On Election Day, accordingly, Clark, in the slang of the day, was "spotted," and though every other Democrat on the ticket was elected, he was beaten. The incident was soon

---

* Executive Document No. 37, 27th Congress, 2d Session, Vol. ii. The resolution was passed February 16, 1841.
† Anti Slavery Standard, April 21, 1842.
‡ Globe, November 9, 10, 1843.
§ American Republican, April 26, 1844.

forgotten by the Natives, but not by the Irish, who bided their time, and three years later, with Hugh Clark at their head, voted the Whig ticket, and elected Morton McMichael sheriff. Having shown their power, the adopted citizens went back to the Democratic ranks, voted the Democratic ticket in the autumn of 1843, and were thanked for their aid by a leading Democratic newspaper. While rejoicing, said the editor, over the recent election, we must not forget that we owe it to the aid of the naturalized citizens. They had been insulted in the grossest manner in the person of one of their countrymen, Hugh Clark. That they should feel the insult keenly was no more than natural. They believed he was rejected and proscribed because he was an Irishman, and have shown that such insults cannot be given with impunity. We thank our naturalized Irish citizens.*

Angry at the action of the adopted citizens in Philadelphia, and encouraged by the success of the Natives in New York, the Americans in Philadelphia now began to organize in earnest. Early in December a call was issued, and an American Republican Association formed in the Second Ward of Spring Garden. The movement spread fast; associations were started in Locust, Cedar, and North Mulberry wards, early in 1844, and before the end of March others existed in each of the four wards of Spring Garden, the five of Southwark, the five of Kensington, the four of Moyamensing, in each ward of the city proper, in Manayunk, in Roxborough, in North Penn Township, in Germantown, and in the District of Penn.†

For the time being the Native American movement became an absorbing topic of public discussion, of lectures before the various literary institutes, and of the public debates it was the custom to hold on current issues in the lecture rooms scattered over the city. On one occasion the Rev. Dr. Barnes addressed the Wilbur Fisk Literary Institute on "Popery incompatible with free institutions, and leading to the subversion of American liberty." ‡ On another, "the

---

* *Inquirer,* October 12, 1843.
† Calls for the formation of these ward associations and notices of their meetings were regularly published in the *Philadelphia Ledger* during December, 1843, and January, February, March, and April, 1844.
‡ *Philadelphia Ledger,* December 3, 1844.

citizens of the city and county opposed to fanatical persecution, and in favor of the rights of civil and personal
freedom secured by our National and State Constitution," *
discussed the subject from their point of view. "Are the principles of the American Associations just?" was the question,
on another occasion, for discussion in one of the Union
Library Company lectures.† "Ought persons of foreign
birth to enjoy the same rights and privileges as natives?"
was the theme for a prolonged debate in the lecture room
of the Museum on George Street.‡ "Are the doctrines and
principles of the Native American party such as should en-
title them to the support of the people of the United States?"
was next argued with equal warmth.

That nothing which could arouse bad feeling might be
lacking, the old issue of the Bible in the schools had by
this time been dragged forth for discussion. As far back as
1834§ the Board of Controllers of the Public Schools
noticed that in some schools religious exercises had been introduced, and books of a religious character used which had
not been authorized. Believing that such books and exercises
had a tendency to produce sectarian influence, the board,
accordingly, ordered them to be disused as contrary to law.
This rule had never been enforced, and in 1842 the Bishop
of Philadelphia complained that Catholic children were
forced to read the Protestant version of the Bible, and join
in Protestant religious exercises. The board, thereupon,
ordered that no child be required to take part in the religious
exercises, or listen to the reading of the Bible, whose parents
were conscientiously opposed thereto, and that children
whose parents preferred any particular version of the Bible,
without note or comment, be furnished with the same.‖

About a year later, while the Native excitement was rising
high, Hugh Clark, a school director in Kensington, visited a
girls' grammar school to show it to a friend. There, according to his own account of what happened, when the Bible
was about to be read, he saw some of the scholars leave the

* *Ibid.*, February 1, 1844.
† *Ibid.*, February 22, 1844.
‡ *Ibid.*, March 13, 28, 1844, April 4, 1844.
§ December 9, 1834.
‖ Resolution of January 10, 1843.

assembly room and go into a class room. On inquiring the reason he was told that they objected to the version used. Whereupon he said to the woman principal that if the reading of the Bible caused such confusion it ought not to be read. The story as told by a fellow-director was, that he entered the school, peremptorily commanded the principal, Miss Bedford, to stop the practice of reading the Bible, and was told by her that she would give up her place first. This, the director declared, was the work of "Popish influence," and he called on Protestants to resent the attempts "to kick the Bible from the schools."

All Kensington was at once aflame, and notices were posted for a meeting in the Odd Fellows Hall. But such a crowd assembled that the hall could not hold it, and the meeting was held in a Methodist church near by. There it was resolved that the rejection of the Bible from the schools would destroy morals, and put us on a level with the age before the Reformation; that Hugh Clark be requested to resign, and that Miss Bedford be thanked for her refusal to exclude the Bible from her school.*

And now the excitement spread to the city. Meetings were held in the State House Yard, to which all were invited who wished to see the Naturalization Law changed, who wished to have the Bible read in the schools, and who were opposed to the rule of foreigners.† The Catholics complained to the Board of Controllers that hymns were sung, and religious exercises held, in the schools in which Catholics could not conscientiously take part; that a sectarian version of the Scriptures was read, and children required to unite in the recital of the Commandments according to a translation not accepted by Catholics, and contrary to their consciences; that the words "without note or comment" in the board's resolution of 1843 shut the Catholic version of the Bible from the schools, and that the resolutions of 1834 and 1843 were not enforced.‡ Bishop Patrick asked that these resolutions be enforced, and the board so ordered.

A few days later, at an election in Spring Garden, the Natives were attacked and driven from the polls by the

---

* *Public Ledger*, February 29, 1844.
† *Ibid.*, March 12, 13, 1844.
‡ *Ibid.*, March 13, 14, 1844. See also *Ledger*, April 2, 1844.

Irish. The great riot, however, occurred early in May. In the latter part of April an American Republican Association was formed in the Third Ward of Kensington, and the third of May chosen for a mass-meeting on an open lot near the school house at Second and Master streets. The meeting was held, but no sooner had the publisher of the *Native American* taken the platform than a hoard of foreigners with clubs and stones scattered the crowd. Driven from the street, the Natives repaired to the George Fox Temperance Hall, and there adopted resolutions calling on their fellow-citizens at large "to visit with their indignation the outbreak of the vindictive anti-republican spirit manifested by a portion of the alien population of the Third Ward, Kensington," and invited "our fellow-citizens at large to attend the next meeting, to sustain us in the expression of our opinions." *

The next gathering was held on May sixth, in the afternoon. A gust of wind and rain drove the crowd into the Market House. There a fight was started and the disturbance spread to the street, where muskets and guns were discharged from the roofs, windows, and doors of the houses. The Natives replied with stones and bricks, the riot became general, and before they were driven from the ground one was killed, and many seriously wounded. †

News of the fight spread rapidly, and that evening a mass-meeting of Americans in the Assembly Building, on Chestnut Street, resolved that the Native American party would "attend to their graves *en masse* the bodies of those martyrs of republicanism who were slain," by a "band of savage foreigners," and offered a thousand dollars reward for the detection of the murderers. ‡

On the following day there was a great mass-meeting in the State House Yard, where speeches were made and resolutions adopted. One declared the attack, by a portion of the Irish inhabitants of Kensington, on a body of American citizens assembled to express their opinions on public issues was proof that the Naturalization Law ought to be repealed, and that foreigners could not understand the spirit of American institutions in the short space of five years. An-

* *Philadelphia Ledger*, May 4 and 6, 1844.
† *Ibid.*, May 7, 1844.
‡ *Ibid.*

other asserted that the Bible was a necessary part of instruction in the schools, and that the Natives were determined to keep it there.

After the resolutions were adopted a motion was made that the meeting proceed to Kensington. The presiding officer attempted to prevent its adoption, but it was carried, and a large crowd with a drum, and a soiled and torn flag inscribed "This is the flag that was trampled by Irish Papists," set off for the scene of the late riot. About five o'clock the Natives reached the vacant lot on Master Street, and were about to raise the flag when a volley was fired at them from the house of the Hibernia Hose Company. A rush was made for the building; another volley killed one man and wounded six others. But the Natives broke in the door, dragged out the hose carriage, and destroyed it. Firing from house-tops and windows now became general, and toward six o'clock the Natives were driven from the ground. About half-past six a score or so came back fully armed, took position before the Hibernia Hose Company, opened fire, drove their enemies to cover, and set fire to the house next to the Hose Company. Thence the flames spread rapidly till some fifty buildings, including the Market House and the quarters of the Hose Company, were destroyed.

Meantime General Cadwalader, at the request of the sheriff, came on the ground with a small body of militia, and during a few hours the fighting ceased, but not before eight Natives were killed and forty wounded.

During the morning of Wednesday, the eighth of May, quiet reigned in Kensington. A great crowd, however, gathered to view the scene of the fighting, and in it was mingled the reckless, law-defying element from all parts of the city. About noon, a report having spread that the militia were ordered not to fire on the people, the disorderly element broke loose, and a house was set on fire. Flags of red, white and blue rags, sewed, pinned, or tied together, were now hung from the windows in every direction as mute appeals for protection. But the mob was now afoot, houses were searched for arms, and at three o'clock St. Michael's Catholic Church on Second Street was given to the flames. A schoolhouse, called the Nunnery, was next set on fire; a grocery store where the Catholics were said to have bought ammunition was sacked, and the houses of Hugh Clark and his brother were looted. By that time the whole Irish population had fled from their homes with such goods as could be carried away.

After wreaking vengeance in Kensington the mob came back to the city, and gathered before St. Augustine's Church, in Fourth Street, and about ten o'clock that night set it on fire.

The whole city was now in a state of intense excitement. Councils met, and sat till dawn. The mayor announced a town meeting at the State-House. The sheriff bade the aldermen of each ward and township of the city and county assemble the citizens, and take measures to preserve the peace. The Governor hurried militia from Harrisburg and Lancaster, and ordered out all the troops in the city. The crew of the United States steam frigate *Princeton* was posted in the Girard Bank; the Bishop closed all the Catholic churches in the city; the people volunteered by hundreds to aid the police; the Catholic churches, and all the streets where disturbances had occurred or where it was feared they might occur, were strongly guarded, and business was at a standstill. The arrival at New York of Catholic clergy, and numbers of Irish driven from their homes, created such excitement that a meeting of Native Americans that was to be held in the Park was postponed. A Committee of Natives, sent to Philadelphia to find out the facts, reported that natives had been assailed and murdered while exercising their rights, and were justified in repelling such attacks; but the riots which followed were not the work of Native Americans, and were deplored by all honorable men.

The troops were soon dismissed. The citizens went back to their daily occupations, and some arrests were made, but no convictions followed. The excitement, however, did not go down. During May and June meeting after meeting was held in the woods, and before the State-House, where, on one occasion, twenty thousand people were said to have assembled. The American Republicans issued an address blaming the mayor and the sheriff and the civil authorities, and demanding a searching examination of the riots. The Grand Jury ascribed them to the wretched manner in which the law had been administered by the authorities of the city and State, and to the attempt of a party of citizens to exclude the Bible from the schools.* The Catholic citizens met at the Cathedral, and replied. They denied that the Catholics had sought to exclude the Bible from the schools, and cited the letter of Bishop Patrick. Teachers, they said, used King James's version, and this led Catholic children to regard as authoritative a version rejected by the Church. In Baltimore the School Directors had provided the Catholic children with the Catholic version. Was it too much to expect the same measure of justice in Philadelphia? They denied that they owed allegiance to any foreign power or potentate. The obedience which, as children of the Church, they yielded to the Chief Bishop had nothing to do with the things of this world. They denied, finally, that the great body of Catholics should be held responsible for the acts of a small band of men because most of them held the Catholic faith.† A Native American meeting at Southwark commended the Grand Jury, censured the School Directors for electing a foreigner Controller of the Public Schools for that district, and demanded his resignation. They were quite able to govern Southwark without the aid of foreigners, and called for the resignation of the Irish commissioner from the First Ward.‡

July fourth was made the occasion of the most remarkable parade which, up to that time, had ever been witnessed in Philadelphia. Eight-and-forty American Republican associations, with flags and banners ornamented with inscriptions and allegorical designs, marched through the streets of the city, and in a piece of woods on the outskirts celebrated the day with speeches, fireworks, and the reading of a declaration of Native American principles.

On the evening of the fifth of July rioting began again. During the afternoon a furniture car stopped in front of the Catholic Church of St. Philip de Neri, in Southwark, and the driver was seen to carry a number of muskets into the church. A report spread that the Catholics were arming, a crowd gathered about the church, the sheriff was notified, and General Patterson called on for military aid. On reaching the church the sheriff and two aldermen entered, and

* *Philadelphia Ledger*, June 17, 1844.
† *Philadelphia Ledger*, June 22, 1844.
‡ *Ibid.*, June 26, 1844.

soon reported that a dozen muskets had been found. These were delivered to a committee of citizens to carry to the watch-house. The crowd, however, was not satisfied, and demanded that a search be made by a committee. The sheriff consented, the searchers were chosen, and in the first room entered were two armed guards, and twenty-seven muskets stacked along the wall. Further search revealed eight other armed men, more guns, pistols, cartridges, caps, buckshot, and a keg of powder. The priest stated, truly, that the muskets had been in the building for over a month, and had been obtained by order of the Governor.*

It was now about two o'clock in the morning of Saturday, and the crowd dispersed. By five the people began to assemble again, and at seven the sheriff with his posse cleared the street before the church, and the militia which had come on the scene during the night were stationed so as to command all the streets in the neighborhood. In one of them the mob stoned the troops, whereupon General Cadwalader ordered them to open fire with a small cannon. But Mr. Charles Naylor, one of the posse, instantly ran into the middle of the street and countermanded the order. For this he was arrested, and confined in the church. At midnight, as all seemed quiet, and the troops were withdrawn, save the Mechanic Rifles and the Hibernia Greens, left to guard the church. Early the next day, which was Sunday, the crowd gathered again, demanded the release of Naylor, and when it was refused, broke into St. Philip de Neri and set him free.

Demand was then made that the Hibernia Greens leave the ground. It was granted; but, as they marched away, followed by a jeering crowd, one of them turned, fired, and shot a boy, whereupon they all broke ranks and fled. The report that the Greens had fired on the people produced intense excitement, and the mob again entered the church, but were persuaded by members of the American party to do no injury.

Word of these doings having reached the authorities, the militia was again called out, and as the soldiers forced their way through the crowd they fired two volleys and killed

* Report of Committee of Nineteen. *Ledger*, July 15, 1844.

and wounded a number of people. The rioters, having obtained a cannon and some muskets, came back after dark and fired on the troops. This was promptly returned, and the fight thus begun continued till early in the morning of Monday.

On that day the Commissioners of the District and the aldermen appealed to the authorities to withdraw the troops, and pledged themselves to keep order. Late in the afternoon they were marched away, leaving the church under guard of a strong body of citizens. Meantime the Governor had heard of the riot, and had called out the State troops, which came pouring into the city till some five thousand had arrived. No further rioting followed, and in time they, too, went back to their homes.*

Late in July a Native American meeting in Kensington stated the principles of the party. They were, that natives had the inalienable right to make their own laws; that a residence of twenty-one years should precede naturalization; that none but natives should be put in office; that the rule of any religious sect should be opposed, and the march of exclusive privileges resisted.†

The effect of these riots on the Presidential campaign was widespread. The Indiana State Convention of Democrats complained of the attempt to array the native against the foreign-born voter as springing from the same spirit of federalism that dictated the Alien and Sedition Acts of 1798. Every citizen, native or voluntary, was entitled to the enjoy-

---

* Many pamphlets were called forth by these riots. Among them are: The Warning of Thomas Jefferson; or, A Brief Exposition of the Dangers to be Apprehended to our Civil and Religious Liberties from Presbyterianism. By Justus E. Moore. The Crisis, An Appeal to our Countrymen on the Subject of Foreign Influence in the United States, N.Y., 1844. Address of the American Republicans of the City of Philadelphia to the Native and Naturalized Citizens of the United States, 1844. The Origin and Progress of the Native American Party in Politics, etc., by John H. Lee, Philadelphia, 1855, contains a very full account of the Philadelphia riots in 1844. Clay or Polk? by an Adopted Citizen Having Twenty-one Years' Residence in the United States, N.Y., October, 1844. A Brief View of the Origin and Object of the Native American Party, by a Native American. A Defence of our Naturalization Laws with a Friendly Warning to Members of the Native American Party. An Appeal to the Voluntary Citizens of the United States from all Nations, on the Exercise of their Elective Franchise at the Approaching Presidential Election. H. E. Riell, N.Y., 1844.

† *Philadelphia Ledger*, July 31, 1844, and August 27, 1844.

ment of the religious, political, and civil rights guaranteed by the Constitution. Democracy knew not, and did not seek to know, such distinctions as native and adopted citizens, but held out the right hand of fellowship to every foreigner who came to our shores.* The Ohio *Statesman* called on all Whigs not to aid or abet the organization of a Native American party.† Polk was denounced because some one asserted that his grandfather had been a rank Tory in 1775. Frelinghuysen was charged with opposing the attempt of Archbishop Hughes to have the literary fund divided between Protestant and Catholic schools, with membership in the Native American Association, and with instigating the Philadelphia riots.‡ The New York *Journal of Commerce* found it necessary to defend Polk against the charge that he was a Catholic;§ and Frelinghuysen, in answer to two men who inquired, declared that he had no connection with the Native Americans, had nothing to do with the division of the school funds between Catholics and Protestants in New York, and condemned the violence of the mobs in Philadelphia.|| At the dedication of a hickory pole in front of the office of the Washington *Globe* one transparency exhibited an Irishman leaning on his spade, another a German emigrant with his plough.¶ An Ithaca newspaper declared that a traveller in Tennessee, in 1836, saw forty-three slaves in manacles being driven to market, each one of them branded J. K. P., and cited Roorbach's "Travels Through the Western and Southern States." The Democrats proved that no one by the name of Roorbach existed; that the forgery was based on Featherstonhaugh's "Excursion Through the Slave States," and Roorbach became a synonym for a political lie.

After the Philadelphia election, in October, was carried by the Natives, the Democrats in several States made earnest appeals to the "voluntary citizens" for support. The Democratic State Convention in Ohio, in a long address, assured them that their countrymen, looking to this country as an asylum and a refuge from tyranny, were seriously threatened

---

* *Globe*, June 28, 1844.
† *Ibid.*
‡ *Albany Journal*, July 23, 1844.
§ *Globe*, June 28, 1844.
|| *Ibid.*, July 31, 1844.
¶ *Ibid.*, August 27, 1844.

with disfranchisement, cited the successes of the Natives in New York in April, and in Philadelphia in October, as proof that the Whigs were in the movement, and assured them that the only safety of the naturalized citizen was in the Democratic party, which boldly and openly denounced Native Americanism.* The Albany *Argus*† cried out against the union of Whigs and "Church Burners" in Philadelphia, and bade the Democrats be up and doing. Spread the news of this union, said the editor, into every hamlet from Maine to Louisiana. Go among the hundred thousand Germans, and the fifty thousand sons of Ireland in Ohio; go among the Catholics of Maryland, go among the Swiss, Germans, and Irish of Indiana, and tell them of these facts.

* *National Intelligencer,* October 29, 1844.
† *Ibid.,* October 22, 1844.

Draft Riots of 1863

By JOEL TYLER HEADLEY

COMMENCEMENT OF THE MOB

Meanwhile, events were assuming an alarming aspect in the western part of the city. Early in the morning men began to assemble here in separate groups, as if in accordance with a previous arrangement, and at last moved quietly north along the various avenues. Women, also, like camp followers, took the same direction in crowds. They were thus divided into separate gangs, apparently to take each avenue in their progress, and make a clean sweep. The factories and workshops were visited, and the men compelled to knock off work and join them, while the proprietors were threatened with the destruction of their property, if they made any opposition. The separate crowds were thus swelled at almost every step, and armed with sticks, and clubs, and every conceivable weapon they could lay hands on, they moved north toward some point which had evidently been selected as a place of rendezvous. This proved to be a vacant lot near Central Park, and soon the living streams began to flow into it, and a more wild, savage, and heterogeneous-looking mass could not be imagined. After a short consultation they again took up the line of march, and in two separate bodies, moved down Fifth and Sixth Avenues, until they reached Forty-sixth and Forty-seventh Streets, when they turned directly east.

The number composing this first mob has been so differently estimated, that it would be impossible from reports merely, to approximate the truth. A pretty accurate idea, however, can be gained of its immense size, from a statement made by Mr. King, son of President King, of Columbia College. Struck by its magnitude, he had the curiosity to get some estimate of it by timing its progress, and he found that although it filled the broad street from curbstone to curbstone, and was moving rapidly, it took between twenty and twenty-five minutes for it to pass a single point.

A ragged, coatless, heterogeneously weaponed army, it heaved tumultuously along toward Third Avenue. Tearing down the telegraph poles as it crossed the Harlem & New Haven Railroad track, it surged angrily up around the building where the drafting was going on. The small squad of police stationed there to repress disorder looked on bewildered, feeling they were powerless in the presence of such a host. Soon a stone went crashing through a window, which was the signal for a general assault on the doors. These giving way before the immense pressure, the foremost rushed in, followed by shouts and yells from those behind, and began to break up the furniture. The drafting officers, in an adjoining room, alarmed, fled precipitately through the rear of the building. The mob seized the wheel in which were the names, and what books, papers, and lists were left, and tore them up, and scattered them in every direction. A safe stood on one side, which was supposed to contain important papers, and on this they fell with clubs and stones, but in vain. Enraged at being thwarted, they set fire to the building, and hurried out of it. As the smoke began to ascend, the onlooking multitude without sent up a loud cheer. Though the upper part of the building was occupied by families, the rioters, thinking that the officers were concealed there, rained stones and brick-bats against the windows, sending terror into the hearts of the inmates. Deputy Provost Marshal Vanderpoel, who had mingled in the crowd, fearing for the lives of the women and children, boldly stepped to the front, and tried to appease the mob, telling them the papers were all destroyed, and begged them to fall back, and let others help the inmates of the building, or take hold themselves. The reply was a heavy blow in the face. Vanderpoel shoved the man who gave it aside, when he was assailed with a shower of blows and curses. Fearing for his life, he broke through the crowd, and hastened to the spot where the police were standing, wholly powerless in the midst of this vast, excited throng.

In the meantime, the flames, unarrested, made rapid way, and communicating to the adjoining building, set it on fire. The volumes of smoke, rolling heavenward, and the crackling and roaring of the flames, seemed for a moment to awe the mob, and it looked silently on the ravaging of a power more terrible and destructive than its own.

At this time Superintendent Kennedy was quietly making his way across the town toward the office of the provost marshal, Jenkins. But noticing a fire as he approached, he left his wagon at the corner of Forty-sixth Street and Lexington Avenue, and walked over toward Third Avenue. The street was blocked with people, but they seemed quiet and orderly as any gathering in presence of a fire, and differed from it only in that the countenances of all seemed to wear a pleased, gratified look. As he unsuspiciously edged his way forward toward the fire, he heard some one cry out, "There's Kennedy!" "Which is him?" asked a second; and he was pointed out.

Kennedy was dressed in ordinary citizen's clothes, and carried only a slight bamboo cane. Thinking the allusion to him was prompted only by curiosity, he kept on, when suddenly he felt himself violently pushed against. Turning around, he encountered a man in a soldier's old uniform, and sternly demanded what he meant by that. The words had hardly escaped his lips, when a heavy blow was planted full in his face. Instantly the crowd closed around him, and rained blows in rapid succession on him, until he fell over and down the graded street, some six feet, into a vacant lot. The crowd, with yells, poured after him. Kennedy, springing to his feet, started on a run across the lot toward Forty-seventh Street, distancing his pursuers. But as he reached Forty-seventh Street, and attempted to ascend the embankment, another crowd, which had witnessed the pursuit, rushed upon him, and knocked him back again in front of his pursuers. He quickly sprang up, though bleeding and stunned, for he knew his only chance for life was in keeping his feet. But the crowd closing around on both sides gave him no chance to run. One huge fellow, armed with a heavy club, endeavored to break in his skull, but Kennedy dodged his blows. Careful only for his head, he let them beat his body, while he made desperate efforts to break through the mass, whose demoniacal yells and oaths showed that they intended to take his life. In the struggle the whole crowd, swaying to and fro, slowly advanced toward Lexington Avenue, coming, as they did so, upon a wide mud-hole. "Drown him! drown him!" arose at once on every side, and the next moment a heavy blow, planted under his ear, sent him headforemost into the water.

Falling with his face amid the stones, he was kicked and trampled on, and pounded, till he was a mass of gore. Still struggling desperately for life, he managed to get to his feet again, and made a dash for the middle of the pond. The water was deep, and his murderers, disliking to get wet, did not follow him, but ran around to the other side, to meet him as he came out. But Kennedy was ahead of them, and springing up the bank into Lexington Avenue, saw a man whom he knew, and called out: "John Eagan, come here and save my life!" Mr. Eagan who was a well-known and influential resident of that vicinity, immediately rushed forward to his assistance, and arrested his pursuers. But the Superintendent was so terribly bruised and mangled, that Eagan did not recognize him. He, however, succeeded in keeping the mob back, who, seeing the horrible condition their victim was in, doubtless thought they had finished him. Other citizens now coming forward, a passing feed wagon was secured, into which Kennedy was lifted, and driven to police head-quarters. Acton, who was in the street as the wagon approached, saw the mangled body within, but did not dream who it was. The driver inquired where he should take him. "Around to the station," carelessly replied Acton. The driver hesitated, and inquired again, "Where to?" Acton, supposing it was some drunkard, bruised in a brawl, replied rather petulantly, "Around to the station." The man then told him it was Kennedy. Acton, scanning the features more closely, saw that it indeed was the Superintendent himself in this horrible condition. As the officers gathered around the bleeding, almost unconscious form, a murmur of wrath was heard, a sure premonition what work would be done when the hour of vengeance should come.

Kennedy was carried into head-quarters, and a surgeon immediately sent for. After an examination had shown that no bones were broken, he was taken to the house of a friend, and, before the week closed, was on his feet again.

THE SECOND DAY:
CONFRONTATION

Lieutenant Wood, whom General Brown had sent off, with a company of regulars, came in conflict with a mob, two thousand strong, in Pitt and Delancey Streets. Marching along Houston to the Bowery, he turned down the latter, and kept on to Grand. On reaching Pitt Street, he beheld the hooting, yelling crowd coming straight toward him. He immediately formed his little force of one hundred and fifty men in line across the street, and brought them to "shoulder arms." One of the ringleaders stepped forward to speak to him, when Lieutenant Wood waved him off. This was the signal for the attack, and immediately a shower of stones fell among the soldiers. The officer ordered the men to fire—it was said over the heads of the rioters—in order to disperse them. The result was scattering shots in return from the latter. Wood then ordered a point-blank volley, when men tumbled over right and left. The crowd did not wait for a second, but fled in every direction. Wood then marched back to head-quarters, but on the way slipped and sprained his ankle, which caused a report that he had been wounded.

A bloody conflict also took place between the police and mob in the same avenue where Colonel O'Brien fell, below Thirtieth Street. There was a wire factory here, in which several thousand carbines were stored. Of this, some of the rioters were aware, and communicated the fact to others, and a plan was formed to capture them. Having discovered from the morning's experience that the military had been called in to aid the police, arms became imperatively necessary, if they hoped to make a successful resistance. All public depositories of arms they knew were guarded, but this factory was not, and hence they resolved to capture it without delay. Swarming around it, they forced the entrance, and began to throw out the carbines to their friends. The attack, however, had been telegraphed to head-quarters, and Inspector Dilks was despatched with two hundred men to save the building, and recover any arms that might be captured. He marched rapidly up to Twenty-first Street, and down it to the avenue. Here he came suddenly upon the mob, that blocked the entire street. As the head of the force appeared, the rioters, instead of being frightened, greeted it with jeers and curses. It was two hundred against a thousand; but the inspector did not hesitate a moment on account of the inequality of numbers, but instantly formed his men and ordered a charge. The mob, instead of recoiling, closed desperately on the police, and a fierce hand-to-hand encounter took place. The clubs, however, mowed a clean swath along the street, and the compact little force pushed like a wedge into the throng, and cleared a bloody space for itself. The orders were to recapture all the arms; for this was of more vital importance than the capture of men. Wherever, therefore, a musket was seen, a man would dash for it, and, seizing it, fight his way back into line. On the pavement, the sidewalk, and in the gutters, men lay bleeding and dying, until at last, the more resolute having been knocked on the head, the vast crowd, like a herd of buffalo, broke and tore madly down the street. One of the leaders was a man of desperate courage, and led on the mob with reckless fury, though bleeding freely from the terrible punishment he received. As his comrades turned to flee, leaving him alone, a fearful blow sent him reeling and staggering toward the sidewalk. As he reached it, he fell heavily over against the iron railing, and his chin striking one of the iron pickets, the sharp point entered it and penetrated through to the roof of his mouth. No one noticed him, or if they did, paid no attention to him in the headlong flight on the one hand, and swift pursuit on the other. Thus horridly impaled, his body hanging down along the sidewalk, the wretched man was left to die. At length Captain Hedden noticed him, and lifting up the corpse, laid it down on the sidewalk. It was found, to the surprise of all, to be that of a young man of delicate features and white, fair skin. "Although dressed as a laborer, in dirty overalls and filthy shirt, underneath these were fine cassimere pants, handsome, rich vest, and fine linen shirt."* He was evidently a man in position far above the rough villains he led on, but had disguised himself so as not to be known. He never was known. The corpse, during the fight that followed, disappeared with the bodies of many others.

The street being cleared, Dilks turned his attention to the factory, which was filled with armed rioters, who were determined to defend it to the last. Detaching a portion of his force, he ordered it to take the building by storm. Dashing over all obstacles, the men won the stairway step by step, and entering the main room on the second story, felled a man at almost every blow. Those who succeeded in escaping downstairs were knocked on the head by the force in the street, and soon no rioters were left but the dead and dying. How many fell in this fight it is impossible to tell; but one physician alone dressed the wounds of twenty-one desperately wounded men. Taking what guns they could find and had captured in the street, the force marched triumphantly back, cheered on their way by the spectators.

In the meantime, Mayor Opdyke's house in Fifth Avenue had again been attacked and partially sacked. Captain Maniere, one of the provost marshals, however, assembled a small force, and drove out the rioters, who were mostly young men and boys, before the work of destruction was complete. The news of this attack had been telegraphed to head-quarters of the police, and Captain Helme, of the Twenty-seventh Precinct, despatched to its defence. At his approach the rioters dispersed. Soon after, he was ordered with his command over to the Second Avenue, accompanied by a detachment of troops under Captain Franklin. This was in the afternoon—the mob had reassembled, and reinforced by those who had been dispersed at Thirty-fourth Street, where Colonel O'Brien fell, had overcome the small body of police at the wire factory, and again taken possession of it. They had found some boxes of guns that had been overlooked by Dilks, and having armed themselves, determined to hold it. Even women joined in the defence. As the force approached, it was greeted with shouts of defiance and missiles of every kind. An immense crowd was gathered

* D. M. Barnes.

outside, while the windows of the five-story building were filled with angry, excited faces, and arms wildly gesticulating. Charging on this dense mass, and clubbing their way to the building, the police entered it, and streaming up the stairways, cleared it floor by floor, some being knocked senseless, others leaping from windows, to be killed by the fall, and others escaping downstairs, to be met by the force in the street. A thorough search was now made for arms, and the building emptied of them. Taking possession of these, the police and military took up their line of march for head-quarters. They had not proceeded far, however, before the mob that had scattered in every direction began to pour back again into the avenue, and close on the military that were bringing up the rear. Following them with hoots and yells that were unheeded, they became emboldened, and pressing nearer, began to hurl stones and bricks, and everything they could lay their hands on, against the soldiers. The latter bore it for awhile patiently; but this only made the wretches more fierce and daring. Seeing there was but one way to end this, Captain Franklin ordered his men to "about face"; and "ready, aim, fire," fell in quick succession. The yelling, shouting crowd were in point-blank range, and the volley told with deadly effect. The street was strewed with dead and dying, while the living fled down the avenue.

In the meantime, mobs had sprung up in every part of the city; some larger and some smaller; some after negroes, others firing buildings or sacking them.

Some idea of the pressure on the Police Commissioners during this forenoon, and the condition the city was in, may be gathered from the following despatches, which are only a small portion of those received and answered in two hours:

10.20. From Thirteenth. Send military here immediately.

10.22. To Seventh. Find military and send them to Thirteenth Street forthwith.

10.45. From Sixteenth. A mob has just attacked Jones' soap factory; stores all closed.

10.50. To Twenty-sixth. Tell Inspector Leonard to send one hundred men here forthwith.

10.55. To Twentieth. From General Brown. Send to arsenal and say a heavy battle is going on. Captain Wilkins and company of regulars will report to me here at once.

11.18. From Sixteenth. Mob is coming down to station-house; we have no men.

11.20. From Eighteenth. The mob is very wild, corner Twenty-second Street and Second Avenue. They have attacked the Union steam factory.

11.35. To Twenty-sixth. Send another one hundred men here forthwith.

11.35. From Twentieth. Send one hundred men to disperse mob assailing Mayor Opdyke's house.

11.38. To Twenty-first. Can you send a few men here?

11.40. From Twenty-second. The mob has gone to Mr. Higgins' factory, foot of Forty-third Street, to burn it.

11.45. From Eighteenth. What shall we do? The mob is about 4,500 strong.

Answer. Clear them down, if you can.

11.50. From Eighteenth. We must leave; the mob is here with guns.

11.50. From Twentieth. Mob tearing up track on Eleventh Avenue.

11.58. The mob have just sacked a large gun-store in Grand Street, and are armed, and are on the way to attack us.

12:10. To Fifteenth. Send your men here forthwith.

12.35. From Twentieth. Send two hundred men forthwith to Thirty-fifth Street arsenal.

12.36. From Twenty-first. The mob have just broken open a gun-store on Third Avenue, between Thirty-sixth and Thirty-seventh Streets, and are arming.

12.40. From Twenty-first. Send help—the crowd is desperate.

CLOSING SCENES

This week of horrors—a week unparalleled in the history of New York—was drawing to a close. It had been one of terror and dismay to the inhabitants, who thought only of the immediate effects on themselves of the triumph of the mob. A great city laid in ashes, given up to robbers and cut-throats, is at any time a terrible spectacle; but New York in ruins at this time was a republic gone—a nation un-crowned and left desolate; but the battle, both for the nation and city, had been nobly fought and won; and Friday, the fifth day of this protracted struggle, dawned bright and tranquil. The storm of the night before had passed away, and the streets, thoroughly washed by a drenching rain, stretched clean and quiet between the long rows of buildings, emblematic of the tranquillity that had returned to the city.

On Saturday morning it was announced that the authorities at Washington had resolved to enforce the draft. It had been repeatedly asserted during the riot that it was abandoned, and the report received very general credence. Still, the official denial of it produced no disturbance. The spirit of insurrection was effectually laid.

It is a little singular, that, in all these tremendous gatherings and movements, no prominent recognized leaders could be found. A man by the name of Andrews had been arrested and imprisoned as one, but the charge rested wholly on some exciting harangues he had made, not from any *active* leadership he had assumed.

There were, perhaps, in the city this morning not far from ten thousand troops—quite enough to preserve the peace, if the riot should break out afresh; and orders therefore were given to arrest the march of regiments hastening from various sections to the city, under the requisition of the Governor. Still, the terror that had taken possession of men could not be allayed in an hour, and although the police had resumed their patrols, and dared to be seen alone in the streets, there was constant dread of personal violence among the citizens. Especially was this true of the negro population. Although many sought their ruined homes, yet aware of the intense hatred entertained toward them by the mob, they felt unsafe, and began to organize in self-defence. But the day wore away without disturbance, and the Sabbath dawned peaceably, and order reigned from the Battery to Harlem. The military did not show themselves in the street, and thousands thronged without fear the avenues in which the fighting had taken place, to look at the ruins it had left behind.

Born out of Violence

It was conceived in violence, passed in violence, is maintained in violence, and is being executed in violence.
   —ABRAHAM LINCOLN, *on the Kansas-Nebraska Act, August 24, 1855*[1]

By FAWN M. BRODIE

Thaddeus Stevens lived in the heart of an area scattered with stations on the Underground Railroad. For years the Quakers, Scotch Presbyterians, and Negroes had quietly cooperated in aiding the fugitives from the South, and by a conspiracy of hostile silence had frustrated most of the attempts of the slavehunters who infiltrated the region continuously, searching for lost property. Under the Fugitive Slave Law of 1850, however, all that was needed to establish the identity of a slave was an affidavit made out by the slaveowner's agent, and any unfortunate Negro, unlike even the Roman slave, was presumed to be a slave until he proved himself free. Since he was expressly denied by the new law the right of speaking on his own behalf, and of a jury trial, he had to rely upon the uncertain justice of the marshal and the intervention of white friends. "The Union is not worth a curse as long as distinction exists between negroes and horses," a Representative from Louisiana had declared in Congress in 1850. He had gotten his way.

One of the first slaveowners to claim a fugitive in Pennsylvania under the new law secured the arrest of a colored woman, Euphemia Williams, who had run away twenty-two years before. He claimed also her six children, all born in

Pennsylvania. There was great excitement, and the judge decided, whether out of prudence, humanitarianism, or the legal facts of the case, that she was not the slave the Marylander was seeking. But for every Negro so freed many were carried over the border.[2] All across Southern Pennsylvania the Negroes quietly began to arm themselves and organize for action.

On the night of September 11, 1851, Edward Gorsuch, a Maryland slaveholder, led five armed men, including a United States marshal, in a hunt for four escaped slaves said to be hiding near Lancaster. It was just breaking daylight when they converged on a little stone house near Christiana. When the marshal hammered on the door, it was opened by a massive Negro, William Parker.[3]

The marshal pushed his way in and started for the narrow staircase. Parker darted up ahead and grabbed a long, five-pronged harpoon.

"Take another step and I'll break your neck," he said.

"I've heard many a nigger talk as big as you, and then have taken him."

"You haven't taken me yet," said the Negro, flinging the harpoon and then grabbing an ax he had hidden on the landing.

The marshal retreated to Gorsuch's side. At this point Parker's wife, who was upstairs with the four fugitives, blew a horn out the window. Within minutes the house was surrounded by a crowd of Negroes armed with guns, scythes, clubs, and corn cutters.

A tall, thin young miller named Castner Hanway, riding by on his horse, stopped to watch. The marshal, learning that a white man was outside, showed him the warrants and demanded his help. The new law "commanded" all citizens to aid in its execution, including the capture of fugitives. It threatened fine and imprisonment to anyone who aided runaways, and made him liable for the value of each escaped slave, which was fixed at $1,000. The marshals were guaranteed $10 if they restored a suspected slave to his owner and only $5 if they discharged him. "The law," quipped Anson Burlingame, "fixed the price of a Carolina Negro at one thousand dollars, and of a Yankee soul at five." [4] Lincoln was to point out that Northerners were under legal obligation to do "a sort of dirty, disagreeable job, which . . . as a general rule, the slave-holders will not perform for one another." [5]

Hanway heard the marshal out, and replied shortly: "I'll do nothing to help the Fugitive Slave Act or any other act." Two Quakers also refused the marshal's order and advised him coldly to get off the place and avoid bloodshed. The three white men then turned away.

What happened after is not too clear from Parker's narrative nor from the trial records. Shots were exchanged; the marshal and his men ran away leaving Gorsuch with only his son and nephew. The latter two were wounded but escaped. Edward Gorsuch, after emptying his gun, went down under four Negroes. When they finally left him, bleeding and unconscious, the women moved in with scythes and corn cutters and hacked him to pieces.

By nightfall every runaway slave from Baltimore County was on his way to Canada, and the hay mows and straw stacks on the Underground Railway were crawling with fugitives. The Christiana riot immediately became a national emergency. This, the first killing resulting from the Fugitive Slave Law, wrathful Southern editors laid squarely at Thaddeus Stevens' door. Maryland's Governor E. Louis Lowe threatened secession.

The Pennsylvania Governor, acting under orders from Secretary of State Daniel Webster, and Attorney General John J. Crittenden, indicted Castner Hanway, the two Quakers, and thirty-eight Negroes for treason against the United States. Hanway at once appealed to Thaddeus Stevens. He accepted the case and conducted it largely by himself through the preliminary hearings. Realizing then that his own antislavery record might hinder his clients, he secured three other lawyers, among them a prominent Democrat, John M. Read, who presented the final argument for the defense in the federal court in Philadelphia.

When the thirty-eight Negroes filed into the court room on the second floor of Independence Hall, they were dressed and barbered exactly alike, each one wearing a red, white, and blue scarf about his neck. Lucretia Mott, the well-known Quaker feminist and antislavery agitator, sat near them, knitting with red, white, and blue yarn.

The prosecution, led by Maryland's Senator Cooper, described Lancaster County as a hotbed of abolitionism, with armed bands of Negroes patrolling the area to recapture runaways from their lawful owners. Stevens countered with evidence that professional kidnappers were invading the county and carrying off free blacks. Hanway and the Quakers, he insisted, had come upon the riot accidentally; there was no "previous combination" to resist the United States Government. Fortunately, the prisoners had been indicted not for defying the Fugitive Slave Law but for "wickedly and traitorously intending to levy war against the United States," an accusation so palpably absurd that Judge Grier took pains to advise the jury that while the prisoners were clearly guilty of aggravated riot and murder, the riot did not "rise to the dignity of treason or levying war."

Having discharged his duty as a judge, Grier went on to complain against abolitionists, calling them "infuriated fanatics and unprincipled demagogues . . . teaching that theft is meritorious, murder excusable and treason a virtue." Lashing indirectly at Thaddeus Stevens and Lucretia Mott, he said: "With the exception of a few individuals of perverted intellect . . . male and female vagrant lecturers and conventions, no party in politics, no sect or religion, or any respectable numbers or character can be found within our borders who have viewed with approbation or looked with any other than feelings of abhorrence upon this disgraceful tragedy. . . . The guilt of this foul murder rests not alone on the deluded individuals who were its immediate perpetrators, but the blood taints with even deeper dye the skirts of those who promulgated doctrines subversive of all morality and all government." [6]

The jury, out twenty minutes, returned with a verdict of not guilty.

The Christiana riot was the bloodiest of a series of protests against the Fugitive Slave Law. In February, 1851, an escaped slave named Shadrach, detained in a court room in Boston, was rescued by a mob of Negroes. Richard H. Dana, Jr., saw him carried down the steps, "his clothes half torn off, and so stupefied by his sudden rescue and the violence of his dragging off that he sat almost dumb," his rescuers moving off "like a black squall, the crowd driving along with them and cheering as they went." [7] The Reverend Theodore Parker wrote in his journal: "This Shadrach is delivered out of his burning, fiery furnace without the smell of fire on his garments. . . . I think it is the most noble deed done in Boston since the destruction of tea in 1773." [8]

The number of rescues was small, but every one was given tumultuous publicity. It is hard to say which converted more people to abolitionism, the stories of rescues or the sadder tales of recapture. Thomas Sims, a Georgia slave, was arrested in Boston on April 3, 1851, and three hundred policemen ushered him to the ship bound for Savannah. He was the first slave to be sent south from Boston by legal process since Revolutionary days. Southerners noted with dismay that his recapture cost his owner fully $5,000. [9]

One index of what the Fugitive Slave Law meant in the North was the 1851 election returns. The Governorship in Massachusetts went to the Radical antislavery Democrat, George S. Boutwell, and the Senatorship to Freesoiler Charles Sumner. Ohio sent Ben Wade to the Senate. These three radicals, along with Thaddeus Stevens, were to be among the chief architects in charge of rebuilding the smashed political structure of the South after the Civil War. It is worth noting at this point, then, that all three went into office on a platform in which the chief plank was indignation.

Boutwell was a self-righteous and pedantic abolitionist, honest and sincere enough to win some respect, but too much of a scold to be effective in a minority. Ben Wade was a compound of New England Puritan, visionary philanthropist, and Western backwoodsman. He created a sensation in Washington shortly after taking his Senate seat. Challenged by a Southern Senator, he broke the antidueling tradition of the Northern Congressmen and accepted. When asked to choose the weapons he named squirrel rifles at twenty paces "with a white paper the size of a dollar pinned over the heart of each combatant." The Southerner hastily withdrew. [10]

Neither Boutwell nor Wade was to leave so ineffaceable a mark on the nation as either Charles Sumner or Thaddeus

Stevens. Sumner was six-feet-four, a handsome, earnest bachelor, whose mop of wavy hair falling over his forehead gave him a perennially boyish look. His friends, who included some of the most influential literary and political figures in England and France, saw him as a gentle, amiable man with an eager mind and disarming unworldliness, clumsy at repartee and uncomfortable with a jest. All agreed that he had courage, learning, and a superior talent at formal oratory.

Men who disliked him found him pedantic, opinionated, and egocentric. George S. Hillard, who criticized him in his letters to Francis Lieber for his "absolute incapacity to bear contradiction or dissent," and his "cool assumption of moral superiority," wrote on December 8, 1854: ". . . he is essentially a man of emotions and sentiments, and . . . it is very easy for him to believe anything to be true that he wishes to. His nature is facile, impressible, and feminine. . . ." [11]

Sumner was no doubt tactless and arrogant, but in speaking out against slavery he saw no necessity for being genteel. "I have been attacked bitterly," he wrote to his brother in 1848, "but I have consoled myself by what John Quincy Adams said to me during the last year of his life: 'No man is abused whose influence is not felt.' "

More than any other man in American history—more even than Thaddeus Stevens—Sumner personified the Puritan in politics. "We are told," he said in attacking the Fugitive Slave Law in the widely proclaimed speech that assured his election, "that the slavery question is settled. Yes, *settled—settled,*—that is the word. *Nothing, sir, can be settled which is not right.* Nothing can be settled which is against freedom."

After the election, Reverend Theodore Parker wrote to him: "You told me once that you were in morals, not in politics. Now I hope you will show me that you are still in morals although in politics. I hope you will be the senator *with a conscience.*" Sumner went into the Senate with the aspiration to be not just *the Senator with a conscience,* but to be the conscience of the whole nation. Unlike Stevens, whose Puritanism had been attenuated by years in the Machiavellian school of Pennsylvania politics, he believed in government by exhortation. "The Senate chamber," he wrote, "is a mighty pulpit from which the truth can be preached." And the remarkable thing is that Sumner's exhortation actually became and continued for years to be an undeniable political force. Massachusetts, turning her back on Daniel Webster, as the symbol of compromise, kept him in the Senate until his death twenty-three years later.

Sumner had begun his war on caste in 1849, when he defended the right of Negro children in Boston to attend white schools. The Massachusetts Supreme Court had decided against him. But in 1855 the legislature reversed the court and prohibited separate schools.[12] The state was moving fast—faster on this issue by over a hundred years than the states in the deep South—but the direction of the national revolution against caste was here resolutely defined, and while often temporarily checked, it was never to be completely reversed.

Although Massachusetts was sprinting ahead, Pennsylvania at this moment was somersaulting backwards. Revolted by the bloody Christiana riot, Lancaster County saw enough votes turn against Thaddeus Stevens so that the same ferment that sent Sumner to the Senate knocked him out of the House. Moreover, it was Pennsylvania rather than Massachusetts that reflected the majority opinion of the United States in 1852. However rapidly the Fugitive Slave Law was making converts to the antislavery cause, it did not yet materially affect the overall election returns. The proslavery New England Democrat, Franklin Pierce, became President, defeating the Mexican War general, Winfield Scott, who as an antislavery Whig had campaigned with a proslavery platform.

Stevens, bitterly pessimistic, believed the country lost to the compromisers and his own political career at an end. He made a brief, informal statement in the House, saying in parting: "It is more than probable that hereafter I shall never meet any member here or anywhere else officially, and I desire to part with no unfriendly feeling toward any." [13]

He was now sixty-one. Looking back on the past four

years, he felt mostly frustration—he had once written to a friend of his "foolish absence in Congress"—and he seems to have returned to his law practice with relief as well as vexation. His practice had not disappeared, since he had frequently left the House to conduct cases before the Pennsylvania Supreme Court—thereby giving the Democratic press a chance to snipe at him—nevertheless it needed rebuilding if his ironworks, perennially losing money, were to be saved. Actually he was as lost to politics as an addict to his drug. But now, as never before since he first tasted the intoxication of this life, he was truly a man without a party.

The Whig organization was shattered beyond repair by the defeat of 1852. Out of its ruins, like an evil spirit released from an ancient corked bottle, emerged a new political apparition. This was the Native American or Know-Nothing Party, which mushroomed briefly into power in 1854. The Native Americans were dedicated to checking the political power of new immigrants, chiefly Irish Catholics. The American Party demanded that immigrants be residents for twenty-one years before receiving voting privileges, and that only the native-born hold public office. This was the kind of demagoguery of which Antimasonry had been compounded, and which in the future would fire the crosses of the Ku Klux Klan. What was new about the American Party was the secrecy shrouding its organization. Every member swore oaths promising never to vote for a Catholic or a foreigner, and vowing to keep all party secrets. Horace Greeley, irritated by his failure to elicit any information for his *Tribune* other than "I know nothing," called it the "Know-Nothing" party, and the name stuck.

A good many Free-Soilers and Conscience Whigs, disgusted with the proslavery trend of national politics, were sucked into its ranks. Sumner was a notable exception. "A party which, beginning in secrecy, interferes with religious belief, and founds a discrimination on the accident of birth, is not the party for us," he said.[14] Seward kept clear, and Lincoln made no secret of his distaste. "I am not a Know-Nothing," he wrote to Joshua F. Speed on August 24, 1855. "That is certain. How could I be? How can any one who abhors the oppression of negroes, be in favor of degrading classes of white people? Our progress in degeneracy appears to me to be pretty rapid. As a nation, we began by declaring that *'all men are created equal.'* We now practically read it 'all men are created equal, *except negroes.'* When the Know-Nothings get control, it will read 'all men are created equal, except negroes *and foreigners and catholics.'* When it comes to this I should prefer emigrating to some country where they make no pretence of loving liberty —to Russia, for instance, where despotism can be taken pure, and without the base alloy of hypocrisy." [15]

Thaddeus Stevens joined the Know-Nothings in 1854, taking the oath of secrecy and participating in the party rituals.[16] Some of his friends found this inexplicable. They were reluctant to believe him guilty of the cheapest kind of political cynicism, grabbing at power in the first party that came along to fill the vacuum created by the Whig collapse. That Stevens, the great foe of Masonry, should have joined an organization steeped in secrecy and intolerance showed that what had become more necessary to him than any set of principles was the sense of belonging and the exhilaration of fighting, and also, perhaps, that one constant ingredient in his hatred of the Masons had been envy. But let it be said that he joined the party late and deserted it the moment a party more consonant with his lifelong principles appeared. He made no speeches against Catholics and foreigners, content to work secretly for the Know-Nothing slate of candidates, a hodgepodge drawn from all party factions.

To everyone's astonishment the party managed to elect nine governors and claimed 104 out of 234 members of the House of Representatives. "Our surprise may be understood," wrote Alexander McClure on the Pennsylvania results, "when I state the fact that when the vote was counted an entire ticket was elected not one of whom was publicly known as a candidate. . . . I confess that I never saw political highjinks played to the limit as it was by the Know-Nothings in 1854. . . . It practically absorbed the Whig Party." [17]

The country was ripe for a third party; mercifully, it was not to be this one. The Native Americans split on the slavery issue into North Americans and South Americans and shortly disappeared inside the Republican and Democratic parties, carrying with them their traditions of bigotry and violence.

The party Thaddeus Stevens had been waiting for so long began when it did largely as a result of a political blunder by Stephen A. Douglas. Early in 1854 the Little Giant, pugnacious leader of the western Democrats, coolly shattered the Compromise of 1850 by persuading Congress to swallow his witches' brew known as the Kansas-Nebraska bill. This provided that the question of slavery in the two new projected states be settled by "squatter" or popular sovereignty, and threw open almost the whole far west as fair game for slaveholders.

At once leading Missourians announced their intention of carrying slavery into Kansas. Already many Southern politicians were claiming New Mexico, and talking about annexing Cuba as an additional slave state. The illegal slave trade —made possible by the fact that ships were fitted out by unscrupulous New York businessmen—was actually increasing and had become a national scandal.[18]

A great many Northerners, uneasily feeling that they had been duped, for the first time began to look at the record. Hitherto optimistic or apathetic, they were troubled to see what an aggressive minority—a minority even in the South —had won over the years by bluff, intimidation, and the deft use of the presidential ambitions of Northern legislators. "If a Southern man aspires to be President," Lincoln would note, "they choke him down instantly, in order that the glittering prize of the presidency may be held up on Southern terms to the greedy eyes of Northern ambition. With this they tempt us and break in upon us." As Thaddeus Stevens put it bitterly: "Somebody has said that in the South they hunt slaves with dogs—in the North with Democrats." [19]

Clergymen, lawyers, journalists, and teachers, joined by some businessmen, now moved decisively into the antislavery ranks, and the cause for the first time became a genuine mass movement, energized not only by indignation and idealism but also by a belated awareness that Northern politics must no longer be played by wholesale default of power. Abolitionism ceased being synonymous with fanaticism, and the Fugitive Slave Law, which had been actively

supported by many in the North who did not approve of it,
now was openly flaunted.

The Republican Party, organized in 1854 in Michigan
and Wisconsin as a party of protest against the extension of
slavery into Kansas, spread with considerable speed. Although the party was slow to take hold in Pennsylvania,
Thaddeus Stevens joined it early in 1855. He was one of
seventeen to attend the first meeting in Lancaster, no other
leading Whig appearing. His year-old flirtation with the
Native Americans over, he carried into the Republican
Party none of their proscriptions but a shrewd awareness of
the strength of their appeal. In the new party he found at
last a political organization that would command his affection and unflagging dedication. And in Thaddeus Stevens
the Republican Party won a gifted political tactician who
could be counted on to pursue the party ideals with a frightening intensity.

The young party quickly attracted able leaders. Within
eighteen months it had acquired, in addition to Stevens,
Salmon P. Chase, Henry Wilson, James G. Blaine, Charles
Francis Adams, Joshua Giddings, Owen Lovejoy, David
Wilmot, Schuyler Colfax, and John Sherman. Significantly,
Lincoln and Seward hesitated longer before officially abandoning the Whig name, though by 1857 Lincoln would
describe the members of the new party as "the best hope of
the nation, and of the world." [20]

The antislavery movement now had an efficient political
weapon. It had, moreover, something equally important,
most of the North's young intellectuals. It had a philosopher
in Ralph Waldo Emerson, it had poets in John Greenleaf
Whittier, William Cullen Bryant, Henry W. Longfellow,
Oliver Wendell Holmes, and Walt Whitman. It had the
nation's most talented newspaper editor in Horace Greeley,
essayists and editors of conspicuous ability in Henry J.
Raymond and James Russell Lowell, and a propagandist of
formidable proportions in Harriet Beecher Stowe. Antislavery literature poured forth now in an irresistible flood
of pamphlets, speeches, poems, and essays. The North's intellectuals, who in normal times would never permit themselves to be organized on behalf of a faith or a cause, had

turned, like Milton, from poetry to polemics. They made a small but mighty phalanx.

One thing was needed to turn the antislavery movement into a dynamic political force—a serious outbreak of Southern violence. Accustomed by the traditions of slave-holding to a fairly steady diet of violence, the South was not long in providing it. Here the tradition of vigilante action, which normally died out as the frontier moved west, was still strong. More than three hundred persons were hanged or burned by mobs in the South between 1840 and 1860, only ten per cent of them Negroes, and the area, as W. J. Cash has pointed out, "had become peculiarly the home of lynching." [21] Some Southern editors openly encouraged the fashion. One in Virginia offered a reward of $50,000 for the head of William H. Seward; another $10,000 for the kidnapping and delivery to Richmond of Joshua R. Giddings, or $5,000 for his head. Southern postmasters publicly burned whatever books they considered dangerous, and their actions were pronounced constitutional by Caleb Cushing, Attorney General under President Pierce. [22]

Violence came at the end of May, 1856, with burning and pillaging in Kansas, and with the beating of Charles Sumner upon the floor of the Senate. The story of the Brooks assault bears retelling briefly here in light of the fact that it transformed Sumner for some years into a cripple, so that he shared for a considerable period something of the same kind of suffering endured by Thaddeus Stevens over a lifetime. In a long speech on May 19 and 20, 1856, Sumner blistered the Democratic administration for its Kansas policy, describing it as "the rape of a virgin territory, compelling it to the hateful embrace of slavery." He singled out particularly the two Democrats he believed most responsible for making Kansas a slave state, Senators Andrew P. Butler of South Carolina and Stephen A. Douglas. Comparing them to Don Quixote and Sancho Panza, he said: "The senator from South Carolina has read many books of chivalry, and believes himself a chivalrous knight, with sentiments of honor and courage. Of course he has chosen a mistress to whom he has made his vows, and who, though ugly to others, is always lovely to him; though polluted in the sight of the world, is chaste in his sight: I mean the harlot Slavery. For her his tongue is always profuse in words."

Douglas made a witty and insulting answer on the floor of the Senate, but Senator Butler was not present to make his own reply. Preston Brooks, a young Congressman from South Carolina, decided to avenge his honor. Arming himself with a heavy gutta-percha cane—the punishing instrument for schoolboys—he confided to two colleagues, Keitt of Virginia and Edmundson of South Carolina, that he was going to teach Sumner a lesson.

What Brooks and his Southern colleagues seem to have particularly loathed in Sumner's speech were not the Latin phrases and moral indignation, which they had heard before, but the sexual allusions. Slavery was a sexual problem as well as a moral, economic, and political problem, but to insinuate such was to violate an ancient and respected Senate taboo. Sumner was a bachelor of forty-five who lived with his mother and maintained a reputation for singular purity in his private life. When he identified slavery as a mistress and harlot, and spoke feelingly of the "rape" of Kansas, he seems to have kindled a special fury among those who held him in contempt as a man.[23]

Brooks waited until the Senate adjourned on May 22, and then entered with Representatives Keitt and Edmundson. Sumner was sitting at his desk writing. "I have read your speech twice over," Brooks said. "It is a libel on South Carolina, and Mr. Butler, who is a relative of mine." Then without warning he raised the heavy cane and struck Sumner on the head with all his strength.

The first blow was paralyzing. Sumner's long legs were caught beneath his desk, which was bolted to the floor. With a mighty effort he wrenched the desk loose and staggered upward. But Brooks continued to batter him until the cane broke in two. Still he kept on with the butt of the cane until the reeling Senator fell senseless and bleeding to the floor.

Several Senators rushed to Sumner's aid, but Keitt intercepted them, brandishing his pistol and shouting: "Let them alone!"

There were cries, "Hit him, Brooks!" "He deserves it!" Senator Toombs of Georgia stood by, openly applauding. "I approved it," he said bluntly, when a Senate committee later questioned him. Senator Slidell said pointedly to the same committee: "I did not think it necessary to express my sympathy or make any advances toward him." [24]

There were two gashes at the back of Sumner's head, both two inches long and so deep that the bones of his skull were laid bare. Lesser wounds and bruises covered his face, arms, shoulders, and hands. Men finally broke past Keitt and raised him from the floor. After a time he regained consciousness and was helped to an anteroom, where the worst of his wounds were hastily stitched.

News of the beating swept over the North like a prairie fire, kindling a rage that would not be extinguished. Southerners recklessly fed the flames. Jefferson Davis, a cabinet member, and Senator Mason, wrote letters of esteem for Brooks; Representative Savage of Tennessee said Sumner "did not get a lick more than he deserved." The *Richmond Examiner* called Sumner "a foul-mouthed poltroon, [who] when caned for cowardly vituperation falls to the floor an inanimate lump of incarnate cowardice." Students of the University of Virginia voted Brooks a gold-headed cane "bearing the device of the human head badly cracked and broken." [25]

The House voted 121 to 95 for Brooks' expulsion, less than the necessary two-thirds. Whereupon Brooks made a speech threatening to "commence a line of conduct which would result in subverting the foundations of the government, and in drenching this hall in blood." Afterward he announced his resignation and marched out of the House, to be met at the entry by several Southern women who rapturously embraced him.[26] He was tried for assault in the Circuit Court of the District and fined $300.

Brooks' constituents sent him back to the House in two weeks, with only six dissenting votes. Seven months later he died unexpectedly of what was called acute inflammation of the larynx and sudden strangulation. Massachusetts diagnosed it less clinically as the fingers of God about his throat.

Sumner's wounds became infected and refused to heal. He suffered from high fever and loss of weight, and for months afterward staggered as he walked. Southern editors meanwhile taunted him with cowardice. "You are aware that the whole South persists in believing that he is afraid to go back to Washington," Francis Lieber wrote to George S. Hillard, December 13, 1856. "If he resigns they will glory in it as a new proof of cowardice." [27]

He returned to the Senate two or three times to cast his vote on key issues. After a day there in February, 1857, he wrote to Theodore Parker: "After a short time the torment to my system became great and a cloud began to gather over my brain. I tottered out, and took to my bed. I long to speak but cannot." [28]

Searching for relief from his shattering headaches, he went abroad, where he fell into the hands of one of the most sadistic quacks in Europe, Dr. Brown-Séquard, whose celebrated "fire cure" consisted of applications of burning agaric cottonwood to the back and neck for five or ten minutes at a time. The treatment brought on Sumner's first heart attack, and resulted in ghastly burns that refused to heal.

"He applies fire to my neck and spine. Fire is fire . . . as I have ample occasion to know," Sumner wrote to a friend from Paris, June 22, 1858. A few months later he wrote: "I am a poor cripple, halting about in torment. It came upon me suddenly. Perhaps it is the result of a cure." [29] Eventually he went on to another physician who tormented him with "dry cupping along the spine."

Between Preston Brooks and European doctors, Sumner was kept an invalid for three and a half years. Massachusetts re-elected him in his absence, and his empty seat in the Senate remained a mute reminder to the nation's lawmakers. When he was abroad Sumner led a fairly active social life despite his illness, as the Southern press continually pointed out. The charge of cowardice continued to be flung at him, and may well have scarred him as severely as the Brooks' beating.

Charles Sumner and Thaddeus Stevens were to become

the joint chief architects of Southern Reconstruction after the Civil War. It will be seen that each in his own fashion had special reasons for wanting to scourge the South. Stevens took no pains to hide his hatred. Sumner on the other hand openly forgave Brooks and insisted that he bore him no malice. He likened him "to a brick that should fall upon my head from a chimney," and called him "the unconscious agent of a malign power." [30] But Sumner's hatred was possibly no less an energizing force than Stevens', though it seems to have been buried so deep that he could deny that it was there at all.

NOTES

1. Letter to Joshua F. Speed, Basler (ed.), *Collected Works,* II:321.

2. Nye, *Fettered Freedom,* p. 209. Nye reports that the *Anti-Slavery Bugle* listed twenty-three kidnappings in 1846, and that after 1850 this number tripled.

3. Parker's account of what happened in the Christiana riot was published in "The Freedman's Story," *Atlantic Monthly,* February–March, 1866.

4. Quoted in Nevins, *Ordeal of the Union,* I:381.

5. Speech at Peoria, October 16, 1854, Basler (ed.), *Collected Works,* II:268.

6. See U. S. Reports, Circuit Court, 3rd. Circuit. *Cases . . . reported by John W. Wallace,* United States v. Hanway, II:140–207; W. U. Hensel, "The Christiana Riot and the Treason Trials of 1851," *Lanc. Co. Hist. Soc. Papers,* 1911, XV:1–134.

7. C. F. Adams, *Richard Henry Dana,* I:182, quoted in Nevins, *Ordeal of the Union,* I:388.

8. February 16, 1851, John Weiss, *Life and Correspondence of Theodore Parker,* I:103.

9. *New York Tribune,* May 10, 1851, cited in Nevins, *Ordeal of the Union,* I:388. Nye, in *Fettered Freedom,* pp. 197–216, counted 81 "important cases" out of several hundred between 1850 and 1860. There are no certain statistics on the number of slaves who escaped annually from the South. The 1850

census listed 1,011 for that year; the 1860 census, 803. Allan Nevins, *Emergence of Lincoln,* App. V, p. 489, has estimated the monetary loss in 1860 as possibly $800,000. Stampp, *The Peculiar Institution,* p. 418, believes to be reasonable the estimate of a Southern judge in 1855 that the South had lost upwards of 60,000 slaves to the North.

10. T. Harry Williams, *Lincoln and the Radicals,* p. 66.

11. Letters of February 10, 1852; November 9, 1850; and December 8, 1854; Lieber Papers, Huntington Library. Hillard was bitterly anti-abolitionist.

12. Charles Sumner to George Sumner, November 15, 1848; Speech at Faneuil Hall, November 6, 1850; Theodore Parker to Charles Sumner, April 26, 1851; Charles Sumner to William Jay, February 19, 1850. All quoted or described in Pierce, *Memoir and Letters of Charles Sumner,* III:185, 212, 229, 250. The school fight is described in III:40–41.

13. *Cong. Globe,* 32 Cong., 2 Session, March 3, 1853, p. 1164.

14. Speech at Faneuil Hall, November 2, 1855. Pierce, *op. cit.,* III:421.

15. August 24, 1855, Basler (ed.), *Collected Works,* II:323.

16. This is attested by several contemporaries. See John W. Forney, *Address on Religious Intolerance and Political Proscription,* p. 47, and *Anecdotes of Public Men,* I:381; *Philadelphia Daily News,* September 30, 1854; *History of the Rise, Progress, and Downfall of Know-Nothingism in Lancaster County,* by Two Expelled Members; Alexander Harris, *op. cit.,* p. 164; and Oscar J. Harvey, *History of Lodge No. 61,* p. 86.

17. McClure, *Old Time Notes of Pennsylvania,* I:198, 209, 215. See also Nevins, *Ordeal of the Union,* II:398.

18. See House Executive Document No. 7, 36 Cong., 2 Session, 648 pages dealing with this subject.

19. A. Lincoln, October 1, 1856, *Complete Works,* Nicolay and Hay (eds.), 1905, II:304. Thaddeus Stevens, Speech at Cooper Institute, New York, September 27, 1860, Stevens Papers.

20. "Fragment on Formation of the Republican Party," February 28, 1857, Basler (ed.), *Collected Works,* II:391. See also William Starr Myers, *The Republican Party;* and Andrew W. Crandall, *Early History of the Republican Party.*

21. Cash, *The Mind of the South,* p. 43.

22. See George W. Julian, *Political Recollections, 1840 to 1872,* p. 173; and John F. Hume, *The Abolitionists* . . . *1830–1864,* p. 13.

23. Hints of this feeling even among Northerners may be seen in the Francis Lieber–George Hillard correspondence in the Huntington Library. For the text of Sumner's Speech, see *Cong. Globe,* 34 Cong., 1 Session, App. pp. 530 ff.

24. For a detailed description of this episode see 34 Cong., 1 Session, House Committee Reports, I: No. 182; also the *New York Herald, New York Tribune,* and *New York Times* for May 23, 1856; and Pierce, *op. cit.,* III:471 ff.

25. Pierce, *ibid.,* III:487, 496.

26. *New York Tribune,* July 15, 1856.

27. Letter from Columbia, South Carolina. Lieber Papers, Huntington Library. The imputation that Sumner was a coward became a favorite Southern theme. Jefferson Davis reiterated it at a private party June 28, 1861, as reported by Mary Boykin Chesnut in her *Diary from Dixie,* pp. 71–72. It is still echoed by pro-Southern historians. See Avery Craven, *The Coming of the Civil War,* p. 367, and George Fort Milton, *The Eve of Conflict, Stephen A. Douglas and the Needless War,* pp. 231–236.

28. Quoted in Nevins, *Ordeal of the Union,* II:445.

29. Letter to N. W. Senior, June 22, 1858, from Paris, and letter to Samuel G. Howe, November 30, 1858, from Nismes, France. Huntington Library.

30. In a conversation with George William Curtis, reported in Pierce, *op. cit.,* III:524.

From Dynamite:
The Story of Class
Violence in America

By LOUIS ADAMIC

THE HOMESTEAD STRIKE

With the rise of the American Federation of Labor, the capitalists were confronted with a hard-boiled organization —and this only a few years after they had rejoiced over the disastrous effect of the Anarchist Trial upon the workers' movement. They began to see that on occasions when labor leaders were unpurchasable labor would have to be dealt with by methods at once more subtle and more brutal than had been employed to subdue the upheavals in the seventies and eighties. They added a new weapon to their war equipment—the injunction. This was an improvement upon the old "conspiracy law," which had made it illegal for workers, in some instances, to strike and picket and generally to advocate their cause.

The first labor injunction case occurred in 1888, in Massachusetts, when a court enjoined the strikers of a spinning mill from "displaying banners with devices as a means of threats and intimidation to prevent persons from entering or continuing in the employment of the plaintiffs." The effect was to deprive the workers—most of them citizens of the United States—of their constitutional rights of freedom of speech, press, and assembly, and of the right even to appear in the street near the employers' property.

Thereafter the injunction was used by the capitalists in many big industrial battles, often very effectively, along with the lockout, the blacklist, bullets, police clubs, spying, and propaganda. The courts were almost without qualification on the side of big money and against labor.

Of course, from the capitalist point of view, the injunction was not unjustified. A strike was after all an insurrection against the existing system, and under the circumstances it was not illogical for the chief beneficiaries thereof to abrogate the civil law. During the interval of armistice in the struggle between the classes civil law might pretend to referee in class and individual relationships, but a strike was war—referred to as *war* by both sides—and an injunction was an act of war.

On the other hand, the injunction—which meant that labor leaders were arrested and held as "prisoners of war" as soon as they began a strong movement against the employers—stirred in the working class more and more bitterness. Labor began to lose its illusions about the justice of the country's legal system. Labor's impulse to violence—to dynamite, arson, and assassination—became stronger after each injunction, after the failure of each peaceable effort to better its conditions.

II

The eight-hour agitation was resumed soon after the appearance of the A. F. of L. Gompers and his colleagues were not enthusiastic about it. The idea was too radical for them, and the anarchist affair was still fresh in the public mind. But as soon as industrial conditions improved slightly, in the late eighties, there came a grumbling demand from the rank and file of the unions for a shorter workday.

At the convention in 1888, the A. F. of L. officially decided to declare a general strike on May 1, 1890, demanding the eight-hour system for all industries represented in the organization. The decision was greeted eagerly by the mass of workers; but at the next convention the leaders became terrified by the idea. They felt that the consequences of the probable failure of the strike would be much too disastrous to risk such an action and so they decided instead to have just one union—the Carpenters—strike on the appointed day. The Carpenters were well organized; theirs was a highly skilled trade and they had a large fund in the treasury. The strike was called, and within a few weeks they won the eight-hour demand in over one hundred cities and towns.

Encouraged by the Carpenters' success, the Mine Workers announced their intention to walk out on May 1, 1891, but on the eve of the strike the leaders suddenly realized that the union was in no position to do so, and ordered the men to stay on the job. The leaders' fear of failure was justified, for in the mines there was a multitude of unorganized immigrant labor available for scabbing, while the Miners' strike fund was too meager to fight a long battle. The intention to strike had been a mistake; the calling-off of the strike demoralized the entire eight-hour agitation, and it was years before the movement regained any vigor.

For a time Gompers breathed easily. He had been compelled to endorse the eight-hour agitation of the rank and file of the unions, but in his heart and mind he opposed it. The idea was too radical; it endangered his conservative policies, to say nothing of his position as president of the A. F. of L. He was not a militant man, nor an impulsive fighter, but a plotter, a politician, a compromiser. He fought openly only when there was nothing else to do.

III

But there was no real peace; indeed, the war was just beginning in earnest.

In 1892 there burst out the fury of the so-called Homestead Strike, which really was a lockout, involving on the one hand the Iron and Steel Workers, who, with a membership of nearly 25,000, were one of the strongest unions in the country, and on the other the Carnegie Steel Company. Three years previously the union had been recognized by the company; indeed, had entered with it into a three-year contract, at the expiration of which Carnegie wanted the men to take a reduction of wages. The union declined these terms and on July 1, before they could declare a strike, the workers were suddenly locked out.

Before that occurred, however, Andrew Carnegie, already famous as a major prophet of American "democracy," anticipating violence, had hurriedly turned the command over to the company's superintendent, Henry C. Frick, a frank and brutal union-hater, and departed for Europe.

Frick immediately indicated by his action that he meant war to the bitter end. He erected a wire fence three miles long and fifteen feet high around the works and called upon the Pinkerton Detective Agency to send him three hundred gunmen.

The locked-out men heard that the Pinkertons were coming, and they watched for their arrival. They knew that the gunmen would be armed and prepared themselves to meet them on their own terms.

On the night of July 5, a boatload of "Pinkertons" attempted to land in Homestead. A battle followed, in which ten men were killed and three times that number wounded. At the end the workers got the better of the gunmen, captured the entire three hundred, minus the few who were killed, held them "prisoners of war" for twenty-four hours, and finally ran them, disarmed, out of town.

Incensed, Frick then called upon the Governor of the State of Pennsylvania for the militia and within a few days the little mill town of 12,000 was an armed camp.

The soldiers stayed till the end of November, when the strike officially ended in the utter defeat of the workers. The union's treasury was empty; winter was coming on, and the men's families were cold and hungry. In desperation, they returned to work as non-unionists.

IV

But Frick did not win the battle unscathed. There was then in the United States a young anarchist, Alexander Berkman, an admirer of the late Louis Lingg and lover of Emma Goldman, who, on hearing of the gun-fight between the steel men and the Pinkertons, hastened to Homestead and there burst into Frick's office. (I take the details from Berkman's *Memoirs*.)

"Mistah Frick is engaged," said the negro porter to whom Berkman had handed his card. "He can't see you now, suh."

Berkman sauntered out of the reception-room; then,

quickly retracing his steps, passed through a gate separating
the clerks from the callers, brushed aside the appalled porter, and stepped into a room where a moment before he
had glimpsed a black-bearded, well-knit man sitting by a
long table.

There were two other men at the table, obviously holding
a conference with Frick.

"Frick—" began Berkman; then the look of terror in
Frick's face struck him speechless. "He understands," Berkman thought to himself. "Perhaps he wears armor," he reflected and, pulling out his revolver, aimed at his head.

Frick clutched with both hands the arm of his chair
and averted his terror-stricken face. Berkman fired. Frick
dropped to his knees, his head against the arm of the chair.
"Is he dead?" wondered Berkman. Then some one leaped
upon him from behind and crushed him to the floor. Others
piled up on him and held him down. Then they picked
him up, and he saw that Frick was not dead. Blood oozed
from a wound in his neck. His black beard was streaked
with red.

For an instant the young and as yet inexperienced terrorist had a "strange feeling, as of shame"; then he was
annoyed with himself for entertaining an emotion "so un-
worthy of a revolutionist."

The police came and hustled him to prison.

"I've lost my glasses," Berkman complained to the
officers.

"You'll be damned lucky if you don't lose your head,"
snapped a policeman.

Berkman was sentenced to twenty-two years in prison.
He served fifteen. His act was considered a crime, but behind it—as behind most of the other violent incidents in
the class war—was a motive of social revenge, a blind attempt on the part of a social idealist to help the desperate
workers on strike by removing the powerful tyrant who opposed them.

VIOLENCE IN THE WEST

Almost simultaneously with the uprisings in the East and
Middle West, there were violent labor upheavals in the West.

The Homestead Strike of 1892 was not yet over when the miners in the Coeur d'Alene region in Idaho struck against repeated wage cuts. But the strike was as good as lost when it started. The men were badly organized, lacking effective leadership and adequate strike funds.

The mine operators hired scabs. There were battles. Men were killed by the militia. Some one blew up a quartz mill, and the strikers drove the scabs out of the district. The companies, deeming the state militia inadequate to deal with the situation, had the Governor of Idaho appeal to the President of the United States. Presently Coeur d'Alene was under martial law, with regular troops guarding the property, while the employers brought in more strikebreakers.

The failure of the strike had immediate tragic results for the workers, but it led, eventually, to the organization of the Western Federation of Miners, which in the next decade developed into the most aggressive, violent, and revolutionary labor body in the United States and became, years later, the backbone of the I. W. W. or wobbly movement.

II

In the second half of the nineties an intense situation developed in the mining regions of Idaho, Colorado, and Montana.

By 1896 the Western Federation of Miners was already a powerful outfit. Its leaders were real miners, radicals, fighters, with more "guts" than was good for them, among them Bill Haywood, a product of the West, one of the most interesting characters that has sprung up in the American labor movement. They believed in violence—an eye for an eye!—and made little secret of it. The leaders themselves engaged in fist and gun fights with the scabs and the militia. They carried guns and on a number of occasions shot it out with the enemy. They did time in jails and military "bullpens," along with thousands—literally thousands—of their fellow union members.

For years after the disturbance at Coeur d'Alene, Idaho was the scene of endless outbreaks. Regular soldiers patrolled the mining districts. The State government, it appears, was too weak to deal with the situation. Almost every month some mine or mill was dynamited. Men were shot dead at night and in the day time. Pitched battles occurred between members of the W. F. of M. and non-union men, resulting in hundreds of casualties.

By May, 1897, the feeling had become so intense that President Boyce of the W. F. of M. urged every local union in Idaho and Colorado to organize a rifle corps, "so that in two years we can hear the inspiring music of the martial tread of 25,000 armed men in the ranks of labor."

One strike was scarcely over when another began.

The war reached a sort of climax in the spring of 1899, when the $250,000 mill of the Bunker Hill Company was destroyed by the miners with dynamite. Frank Steunenberg was then Governor of Idaho. He had been elected on the Populist ticket, with the support of labor, and had been up to that time in hearty sympathy with labor organizations, having himself been a member of the printers' union. Called upon by the mine owners for redress, he now promptly responded by asking President McKinley for Federal troops and declaring Shoshone County in a state of "insurrection and rebellion."

The President ordered several companies of Negro soldiers from Brownsville, Texas. Striking miners were rounded up by the thousands and put into specially erected bull-pens. There were white troops available hundreds of miles closer than Brownsville, Texas, and Bill Haywood is justified in writing as he does in his autobiography:

> We always believed that the government officials thought it would further incite the miners if black soldiers were placed as guards over white prisoners. It did raise a storm of indignation, not so much against the colored soldiers as against those responsible for bringing any soldiers into the mining region.
>
> One of the officers, a dirty white scoundrel, sent letters to the wives and sisters of the men in the bull-pen, asking them to entertain the soldiers, saying that they would "receive consideration." The hell-hound was not concerned about the men under him, his action was intended to add insult to the other injuries already inflicted upon the helpless prisoners. It was an insult in any case to ask the miners' families to

have anything to do with soldiers, and it was a deliberate attempt to add race prejudice to the situation.

III

The miners blamed Steunenberg for nearly everything that happened in the mining country in the late nineties. After leaving office a prosperous man, which he was not before election, he became a sheep-rancher on a large scale and for six years devoted himself also to other business interests.

Then, on December 30, 1905, he opened the gate of his home at Caldwell. It was his last act. To the gate was tied a piece of fish-line, one end of which was attached to a bomb, which instantly tore him limb from limb.

An eye for an eye! "Dynamite . . . that's the stuff!"

Violence—
THE CHICAGO MASSACRE (1936)

By MARY HEATON VORSE

The workers had won at Jones & Laughlin, but there was trouble ahead. What Philip Murray called an "unholy alliance" had been formed by the Independents of Little Steel. Youngstown Sheet and Tube, which had been negotiating for a long time, now joined Inland Steel, and Republic, in saying it would make a verbal agreement but would sign no contract.

Meantime, Republic fired seventy-five workers, and closed the plant in Massillon where organization was strong. The S. W. O. C.* charged unfair labor practices and appealed to the N. L. R. B. In May, the S. W. O. C. organizers met in Pittsburgh and voted to leave a strike call to the discretion of Philip Murray. In Massillon the workers took a strike vote without waiting to hear from Pittsburgh. There was considerable strike pressure in Youngstown. On May 26, the strike with Little Steel was called. It was spread through seven states and a dozen cities and involved 83,000 men. On May 30, the Chicago massacre occurred.

To the majority of employers, Tom Girdler of Republic Steel is a hero. He defied the Steel Workers Organizing Committee. He defied the National Labor Relations Act. Because of this eighteen men are dead. Let us first look at the way in which they died. Ten were shot to death at the Memorial Day Massacre in front of the Republic Mills in Chicago.

* Steel Workers Organizing Committee.

Let the dead walk before you, and acquaint yourselves with their names. There is Earl Handley, dead of hemorrhage because his wounds were not treated. Workers got him into a car and the police dragged him out and he bled to death.

Otis Jones had his spinal cord severed by a bullet in the back.

Kenneth Reed bled to death in a patrol wagon. A bullet had sliced through his back and into his abdomen.

Joe Rothmund was shot far down in his back. It was over the case of Joe Rothmund that Officer Higgins perjured himself before the La Follette Committee. On the stand Higgins said that Officer Oakes, lying down with Rothmund's knee about to hit him, shot in self-defense. He had testified differently before the investigators in Chicago, as they showed when they were brought to the stand. And the inquest proved that Rothmund was shot from a distance—shot in the back.

But perjury is common in the high Senate Caucus room. Perjury is the fabric of the officers' defense. Go on with the roll call of the dead:

Lee Tisdale died of blood poisoning from a wound.

Anthony Tagliori also died from a bullet in the back.

Hilding Anderson died of peritonitis.

Alfred Causey was shot four times and he died.

Leon Francisco was another who was shot in the back.

Sam Popovitch was not shot but his skull was battered to pieces by police clubs as he ran, an old man, bald, trying in vain to shield himself. The police ran after him and they beat him when he was down. You can see him in the Paramount film for yourself, a little scared old figure flying from the flailing clubs.

But these folks are not all the dead. There are others to be added to this procession of workers with their mashed heads, dead of blood poisoning, dead of wounds in the back, dead of peritonitis.

George Bogavitch of Youngstown belongs with these Chicago workers.

James Eperjessi, also of Youngstown, was killed there by deputies on Saturday night, June 19.

George Mike belongs with this long list of dead. He was a

world war veteran, so wounded and gassed in the war that he was unable to work. He was selling tickets in front of the mill for a C. I. O. dance, and his skull was mashed by a long distance gas cartridge fired by another ex-service man. He was not even a striker. He had come from Aliquippa to Beaver Falls to sell tickets for a social occasion.

Chris Lopez, beaten to death, was said to have died of heart disease.

Fulgencio Calzada of Massillon was shot in the back of the head on the night of July 11, when the deputies fired into a crowd.

Nick Vadios was shot through the abdomen and mortally wounded by these deputies.

A man in Cleveland was killed on the picket line when the troops tried to open the mills.

Seventeen are dead and ten more are seriously wounded. The number of minor wounds in the steel area goes far above one hundred and fifty. These are the treated hospital cases. The record of the smaller wounds, the gassings, will never be known.

Witnesses have come to Washington to the La Follette Civil Liberties Committee to tell how all this happened and how these men were wounded in the Memorial Day Massacre. There are workers, a doctor, a minister, a lawyer, a social worker. Irrefutable evidence of an unprovoked slaughter. We can reconstruct what happened that Memorial Day Sunday from these numerous witnesses.

The right of peaceful picketing had been denied the workers. The reduced picket line had been driven far behind the railway track. Attempts to picket had been broken up by the police.

The strike began on the 26th; Wednesday, Thursday, Friday, the picket lines were driven away by the police. There were clubbings and arrests. On Sunday, May 30, the workers assembled at "Sam's Place." The big map of the La Follette Civil Liberties Committee showed Sam's Place far off from the mills, separated by a waste field and a railway track. At Sam's Place the meeting was peaceful. Various disinterested spectators testified that the people had come with their families as to a celebration. The women were dressed in their Sunday clothes. Fathers and mothers brought their children.

Leo Krzycki, a well-known organizer for the Amalgamated Clothing Workers, was one of the principal speakers. He joked with the crowd. A statement from the Mayor affirming the workers' rights for peaceful picketing was read. Some of the women sang. A vote was taken that the meeting should then proceed across the fields and picket the Republic Mill for the purpose of affirming the workers' rights to picket in accordance with the Mayor's decision.

The audience started out strolling rather than marching, by groups of twos and threes, groups of women marching together, women who laughed and chatted and talked among themselves, as Mrs. Lupe Marshall, the social worker from Hull House, testified.

Probably no group of people ever strolled more casually toward death and wounds. Some of the strikers deployed across the fields, apparently to see what was happening. There is a story of a man's carrying a branch of a tree. Mrs. Lupe Marshall says that she heard someone cry sharply to a worker who picked up a stone, "Dump that, we don't want any of that." There were no guns. The crowd did not even carry clubs. The police, on the other hand, were armed with revolvers, clubs, and tear gas as well as with hatchet handles such as the mill guards carry and which were furnished by the mills.

The testimony showed that the police had been eating in the mills and a platoon of fifty policemen was seen walking out of the mills that morning. The testimony goes to show that this was a planned attack; that the police came out with the intention of shooting down the workers and then arresting them wholesale. The police had planned to make this peaceful picket line seem like a Red plot to capture the mills. The brave policemen were to have warded off the revolution. But their plan failed. There were too many witnesses and too many cameramen.

So the two groups met: the unarmed workers with their two American flags leading them, and the police ready and waiting for the attack. In the Paramount Newsreel which was shown in the high Senate Caucus room you could see the leader of the strikers in the picture arguing peacefully with the police. He is earnest, emphatic, unthreatening. The testimony is that they asked for their rights of peaceful picketing; they begged the police to let them through; that the Mayor had said they had a right to picket. The police testified that they used insulting language and they cried out that they wanted to occupy the factory and that they shot to prevent greater bloodshed in the factory. It is strange that the police defense was so overdone and stupid and that their lawyers should not have advised them better, considering that every steel worker and every thoughtful person in America knows that occupying the factory was not in any worker's mind. Another officer added a touch of the grotesque to the macabre testimony.

"They came along smoking cigarettes like they were doped. I supposed they were smoking marijuana. They seemed to be chanting a long, monotonous chant which seemed to go 'C. I. O., C. I. O.' "

"Is that what smoking marijuana does to one?" Senator La Follette asked with sarcasm.

The pickets argued with the police.

Suddenly there were shots. Some stones flew through the air. In a moment a heap of people were piled up within a few feet of the police line. This happened so quickly that you could hardly believe your own eyes, but there are stills that also tell the story, and some of these are worse than the Paramount film. There is a terrible picture of Mrs. Lupe Marshall with her hand slightly outstretched, as in a gesture, talking to a policeman (who, she records, called her a foul name), and as she talks, unconscious of what has happened, behind her is a piled heap of the wounded. There is another picture: Lupe Marshall has turned and sees the wounded. In another picture, she bends over them, and in this scene there is a frightful picture of a policeman with his club raised up for a shattering blow. The stills proceed. Now the workers are in full flight, hands upraised. They face the murderous gunfire, the flailing clubs, the clouds of gas. But for sheer horror, the testimony of the bystanders of what happened on the way to the hospital, of what happened at the hospital, was more terrible.

The story of Mrs. Lupe Marshall is a shocking record. She is a social worker, and the mother of three children, fifteen, eight, and four. She is also a distinguished linguist and was helping put on a play at Hull House that very night. She did not put it on because she was arrested.

Tiny Mrs. Marshall weighs ninety-two pounds and is four feet, eleven inches high. You can see her being beaten and see that she has her head broken open by a club. You can see her in the photographs and the Paramount film trying to minister to fallen workers and you can see a policeman twice her size, towering over her and twisting her around viciously as he arrests her and shoves her into the patrol wagon.

Piled on top of each other in this patrol wagon were sixteen dying and seriously wounded. They lay every which way, on top of each other. They couldn't stand, they couldn't sit, they were falling over each other. The blood dripped upon the floor of the wagon.

Lupe Marshall tried to help them. She tried to lift them off each other and straighten out their wounded arms and legs. She pillowed one man's bloody head in her lap. He made a gesture that he wanted to smoke. She reached in his pockets to try to find his cigarettes but they were soaked in blood. Then he said.

"Never mind, you're a good kid," then he shivered, straightened out and died with his head in her lap.

They bounced, rattling, through Chicago streets. She did not know where they went. They seemed to go from place to place. The men were groaning and blood was oozing around her and the dead man lay with his head in her lap. Then at last they got to the hospital.

What happened in the hospital was almost worse than all the rest. The hospital was overwhelmed with the dead and the wounded! There were calls outside for volunteers to help the doctors *but the police tried to keep the volunteers from helping.*

There was a little wounded boy and Lupe tried to help the doctor with him, but the police drove her away. She came back and the police drove her away again. When at last her turn came to have her wounded head dressed she felt very sick from the beating and the gas and the sights she had seen. The nurses wheeled her tenderly upstairs in a wheel chair. She went in the toilet and a policeman followed her there. He grabbed her, saying, "I guess you can walk all right," and dragged her down the stairs into the patrol wagon, to the jail. There they searched her. "What's that in her purse?"

"Communist literature, of course," replied the matron. The "Communist literature" was a handbill with an announcement of a meeting and an advertisement of a post-office auction sale. But every one of the scores arrested that day was booked as a Communist.

This stroll across the fields from Sam's Place had to be made into a dark Red plot paid for by "Moscow Gold."

Harry N. Harper, the blinded man, was booked as a Communist. Groping, he had been led in and out of the meetings by his young and pretty wife. Perhaps his testimony was the most horrifying. His voice came out hollow and deep as though he himself had retreated far into the shadows. He told his story slowly, as though each word cost him a painful effort. From time to time Senator La Follette helped him with suggestions.

Harper was a steel worker, a boilermaker and welder employed by Interlake Iron. With his wife he had gone to visit his mother that bright Sunday. They had planned to go to the country. But his mother was ill and she was crying, for Harry Harper's brothers worked at Republic Steel. One was striking and the other was in the mill and she was afraid he was being kept there by force. Disturbed by his mother's grief, Harry Harper, the boilermaker bound on a holiday, went to Sam's Place, encountered the line of marchers, walked up to the head of it, and begged the officer to let him go to the mill to look for his brother because his mother was sick.

He found himself surrounded by hostile faces. They cursed him. *"They seemed,"* he said, *"to be intoxicated with something I can't explain."*

There was a blast of a whistle and then hell broke loose.

"Seems as if they were going down, as if you'd taken a scythe."

He was struck on the left side of his head and the blood was running in his mouth. There was a blinding pain in his eye. He fled, blinded by pain and blood. He fell in a ditch. Another man lay groaning beside him.

"The man said, 'Help me, buddy.' I said, 'I am helpless myself.' " A gas bomb like a green ball of fire was sputtering beside him. It went off, affecting his other eye. He said, "A terrible trembling feeling came over me and I went back groping. I lost the vision of my right eye too. I called for help."

You could get a picture of him, his eye beaten out, blood running into his mouth, stumbling and groping and crying for help. He told, too, of his terrible ride in the patrol wagon. He could hear men groaning. He could hear officers saying, "Some of them are breathing yet, but we'll take the others to the morgue," and he knew men were dead or dying beside him. And when he groaned, they said, "Shut up, you damn so-and-so, you got what's coming to you."

He said, and his sightless face did not turn toward the police officers sitting in their uneasy indifference,

"Among those officers there were many of them brought up in my faith, for I am a Catholic, I went to parochial school and I attended Sunday School and Mass faithfully. I think they have forgotten what we all learned there, 'Thou shalt not kill!' "

There is plenty of other testimony, that for instance of the lawyer, Frank W. McCulloch, Social Relations Secretary of the Council of Social Action of the Congregational Church. The meeting at Sam's Place to him was a friendly holiday crowd asserting their rights to organize under the N. L. R. B. He saw a policeman seventy feet away from the marchers empty a gun and reach for another clip.

The Reverend Charles B. Fiske, a Congregational minister, a minister concerned about civil liberties, had gone down as an impartial observer. He heard the shots, saw the people give way and he took pictures, as he thought, of the whole flight. He took pictures of men being beaten on the ground. In the end he was arrested and thrown into jail and kept incommunicado for nineteen hours and his pictures were taken from him.

There was Meyer Levin's testimony. He is a writer and an editor of *Esquire*. He heard the outbreak of the shooting. He watched workers being shot down and he carried a bleeding child. He was kept by police out of the Burnside Hospital where volunteers had been called for.

Dr. Lawrence Jacques held a mannequin in his hand high up so the crowd could see. He jabbed at this with a pick as he showed where the wounds were made by police bullets in the Chicago Memorial Day Massacre. Behind the two investigating Senators of the Civil Liberties Committee, Robert La Follette and Senator Thomas (Utah), were four charts. The chart showing a man's back is peppered with red spots. Each one of these means a gunshot wound. The doctor dropped the doll and moved to the charts. The charts of side views showed scattered wounds. On the chart showing the front view of a man there are no red spots. The dead and wounded were shot in the back as they ran.

The familiar story of the murder of workers was spread out before the people of this country. It was read into the record of the Senate Civil Liberties Committee, before a distinguished Washington audience of five hundred. It is an old story—perjury and Red framing. You can see the dead and wounded dragged like sacks over the ground. You can hear of wounded workers dragged from cars to bleed to death, wounded workers snatched from the hospitals.

It is nothing new. The use of the police by the mills to shoot steel workers asking for their constitutional rights is an old story. The shooting of workers in steel began in Homestead in 1892 and has gone on steadily ever since. In the steel strike of 1919, twenty-one people were killed, including Fannie Sellins who was shot by gunmen as she bent over some children to protect them. They killed steel workers in Ambridge in 1933.

The number of United Mine Workers dead in its long fight for organization is uncounted. The mines of West Virginia are drenched with the blood of workers. The Ludlow massacres are fresh in everyone's mind. Textile workers were killed in 1929 at Marion and at Honea Path, North Carolina, in 1934. The purpose of the killings is always the same. It is to crush the workers' lawful right to organize.

It is new that there should be a hearing at all, that the story should be accessible to the public. Here people could see how it's done. For once this familiar perjury was brought out by the photographs and by impartial testimony.

What is new is that gathered into one room should be unassailable and impartial witnesses—lawyers, social workers, doctors, ministers—who corroborate and fill out the story. What is new is that this massacre should be documented with hundreds of pictures and climaxed with a Paramount film. Wholesale murder, planned beforehand. . . . Well, who can doubt the collaboration of the mills?

In our estimate of this police brutality, let us not be mistaken. It is part of a country-wide plan, headed by Little Steel, to take from labor its recent gains and to confuse the general public with propaganda to give the impression that labor is violent and the C. I. O. irresponsible. In this hearing the country can see plainly what this plot is and recognize it as part of a vast frame-up against the workers.

Public and Private Violence: 1919

By ARTHUR WASKOW

When John dos Passos sought a date upon which to center *U.S.A.*, his trilogy about intense social conflict and a crisis in American values, he chose 1919.[1] The choice was no mistake. In the development of American attitudes toward the public and private use of violence in dealing with intense social conflicts, 1919 was a critical year. It was particularly critical as the year in which Americans began to cope with racial upheavals of a new kind.

In the wake of the greatest war that had ever scourged the West, upheavals were perhaps to be expected. As Hannah Arendt has written, "The magnitude of the violence let loose in the First World War might indeed have been enough to cause revolutions in its aftermath even without any revolutionary tradition and even if no revolution had ever occurred before."[2] Although in the United States there was no single revolutionary attack upon the basic structure of society or the state, there were a number of intense clashes of power between various social groups. Some of these conflicts exploded into outright violence, in the form of head-on local riots; others remained non-violent but nonetheless intense confrontations.

The authorities whose job it was to cope with such clashes of power were deeply ambivalent. The choices before them, real though never faced in such terms, were these: Should they support one side in these conflicts between different economic and racial groups? Should they stand aside and allow the conflicts to be resolved according to the relative strength of the parties? When actual violence broke out in these conflicts, ought they to play a role that would be different from the role they should play so long as the conflicts were being fought out by non-violent means?

The proper role of the state in dealing with internal conflict and violence was not, in 1919, an issue to be faced by American political authorities alone, but by the authorities of other nations as well. Max Weber was treating it as a general problem of the postwar world rather than as a special problem of the American state, when he remarked in 1918: "Today the relation between the state and violence is an especially intimate one." He explained that "a state is a human community that (successfully) claims the *monopoly of the legitimate use of physical force* within a given territory." [3] By Weber's definition, it should be noted, the police forces of a state are using violence—legitimate violence—whenever they use physical force to arrest private citizens. Violence, in other words, is not synonymous with brutality; legitimate violence, as expressed in an arrest by authority of the state, may be used brutally or courteously. The state may also use violence either neutrally as between different social groups, or with a bias against one or another social group. To be an act of "state," the violence must simply be carried out by the one institution that within a given territory is agreed to be the only legitimate user of violence. . . .

The failure to establish an American "state" with a monopoly of legitimate violence can be seen at two levels of American society. At one level, there had been a long-standing reluctance to proscribe private violence. That reluctance was expressed early in American history by assertions of "the right of revolution" in a number of state constitutions and by the Second Amendment to the Federal Constitution, which specified "the right of the people to keep and bear arms." The political logic of the Second Amendment was followed through most of American history by treating religious riots,[4] vigiliante hangings,[5] labor dynamitings, private businessmen's armies,[6] and southern lynching parties[7] all as half-accepted aspects of American life. Not only the right to keep and bear arms, but the right to use them was accorded private citizens carrying on their political quarrels. As for larger aggregations of citizens, it was not until after the Civil War that Americans agreed that the various component states of the Union could not legitimately make war on each other; and even then, long after the Civil War, industrial empires and labor unions made war on each other, often with impunity. Thus, until the First World War the United States still seemed to be following the logic of the Second Amendment, denying to any institution the monopoly of legitimate violence that would have made it what Weber could recognize as a "state."

On a second level as well, the United States avoided centralization of the public use of violence in the European mode to which Weber was accustomed. Through most of American history, the "European" way of institutionalizing public violence in a large standing army had been most deeply feared. The tradition of the Farewell Address, in which Washington had warned that "overgrown military establishments" were "inauspicious to liberty," [8] had been not merely applauded in rhetoric but obeyed in action. The standing army had been kept small, and only during the overwhelming crisis of the Civil War had a mass army been created, then to be soon disbanded.

The First World War, however, again called into question the relationship of the United States, state, and local governments to the use of violence by private persons or institutions. The use of conscription and the creation of a mass army for the first time since the Civil War had emphasized for the United States, as the war itself had done in other countries, what Weber called the "intimate relation" between the state and violence. This relation was intensified by the fears of revolution that haunted many Americans from 1917 on, stimulating them to demand controls over private groups that might advocate or use violence.

By 1919, then, American society was again facing a series of major issues concerning the public and private use of violence, although these issues were only half articulated. Should the old pattern of semi-acquiescence in private violence be allowed to continue, or should European norms of "the state" with a monopoly of legitimate violence be applied in America? Should the political authorities go even further than controlling private violence, and intervene in intense conflicts even when the parties in conflict did not resort to violence?

These questions most frequently arose in connection with the intense labor disputes of 1919 and the upsurge in labor radicalism. What Selig Perlman and Philip Taft called the period of "post-war militancy" [9] among laboring men forced many localities, states, and the federal government to reassess their role as monopolists of legitimate violence.

In February, the city of Seattle experienced a general strike. The striking workers, by Mayor Ole Hanson's own account, never offered to use violence against business, non-striking workmen, or the government. But, the mayor warned, "Revolution . . . doesn't need violence." He pointed to the unions' announcement that *"Labor will preserve order"* as an indication of the revolutionary intent of the strikers to take over the government, and he threatened to shoot the first man who tried to do so.[10]

In line with these pronouncements, Hanson met the strike with preparations to use state-legitimated violence. He spent $50,000 on the hiring of special police.[11] He arranged for United States soldiers to aid police in keeping order and to guard a newspaper that published despite the strike. Finally, he threatened to impose martial law to end the strike unless it were called off voluntarily.[12]

After the Seattle workers had returned to their jobs, the state's power to use legitimate violence was directed against "radicals," even though they had not taken any part in calling or running the strike. Members of the Industrial Workers of the World (IWW) were arrested, the Socialist Party's offices were raided and its candidate for City Council arrested, and a labor-owned printing plant was closed down by the police.[13] Thus the Seattle affair indicated the readiness of at least some local officials to have "the state" use its own physical force against even the specter, let alone the actuality, of the use of private violence by organized labor.

This motif of state action to suppress radicalism can be followed through the year. Aliens who were members of the IWW in Seattle were hurriedly deported from the state, and many of them from the country, by the federal government.[14] The Immigration Bureau and the Department of Justice joined hands to hunt down radicals, both aliens and American citizens, and to deport or jail them. In November, some 300 members of the Union of Russian Workers were arrested on suspicion of anarchism and sedition; and the technique of mass raiding reached its climax just after New Year's Day, when thousands of presumed radicals were arrested and held incommunicado by order of Attorney-General A. Mitchell Palmer.[15] These attacks on radical persons and organizations were justified by the fear that such groups were contemplating private revolutionary violence, so that public use of violence was necessary to assert the state's monopoly of legitimate force.

On the local level, the fear of private violence from radical labor organizations sometimes led the state to co-opt, in effect, some private groups as arms of the state itself in the permissible use of violence. Thus in Centralia, Washington, on November 11, 1919, an IWW union hall was attacked by ex-soldiers parading in commemoration of Armistice Day. "Wobblies" barricaded within opened fire on the attackers, killed four of them, and wounded four. It was the Wobblies who were jailed, and that night the police allowed one of them to be taken from his jail cell and lynched. Seven others were convicted of second-degree murder.[16] In effect, the ex-soldiers had been treated by the officials of Centralia as if they were still in the armed forces, with the authority to use violence against private groups that might be contemplating the use of violence. Thus the men who had defended the IWW hall against attack had been treated as if they had killed policemen or soldiers while resisting arrest. . . .

In thirty-seven different cities across the country, attempts to form police unions troubled city governments, whose officials claimed to fear that a police union might turn the symbols of legitimate violence to the use of particular private interests. An effort to unionize the police of Washington, D.C., brought opposition from the President and the

Secretary of War, who together with local officials prepared to use the Army to replace the police if necessary, and ordered policemen to quit the union.[17] In Boston, the police union's leaders were suspended from the force and the policemen went on strike September 9. Street rowdyism and mob attacks on property followed, and were stopped only when state troops took over the police powers. All strikers were dismissed, and Calvin Coolidge, then the governor of Massachusetts, made clear that private interference with the public police powers would not be tolerated.[18] President Woodrow Wilson added his belief that "any association of the police force . . . such as will endanger the public peace" should not be permitted.[19] Thus the new American emphasis upon state control of the use of violence was strengthened.

In two other instances, state police power was used to suppress labor union activity that was thought to threaten the social order, even though the unions did not use violence. These occasions were the great strikes in steel, which began September 23, 1919, and in coal, which began November 1.

In the steel strike, Pennsylvania state troopers dispersed groups of strikers from the streets and forbade the holding of union meetings. The fear that the strike leaders were revolutionists was used in justifying attempts to suppress the strike.[20] When violence did break out between steel-union men and strikebreakers in Gary, Indiana, the state's National Guard was dispatched to keep order and then was followed by federal troops when the strikers held a parade against the militia's orders. The federal troops imposed martial law and limited picketing.[21]

The coal miners were faced with a federal court order to halt their strike, an order based on the war powers of the federal government and on the President's warning that a strike would interfere with American aid to the Allied Powers during the continued legal state of war.[22] Federal troops moved into the coal fields in Utah, Washington, New Mexico, Oklahoma, and Pennsylvania in accordance with the federal government's attempts to end the strike.[23] In Kansas, the governor first recruited strikebreakers and then gave them military protection to reopen the mines.[24]

In almost all of these cases, as in most of those in which force was used against radicals, the state's legitimate violence was being used or threatened not against the actual outbreak of private violence but against the possibility that some private group might begin to use violence. In the postwar atmosphere of 1919, under the pressures of fear of radical social upheaval and in the consciousness that it actually possessed enough armed forces to effect its will, the federal government acted not only to monopolize violence but to use its monopoly to take one side in conflicts that had not yet become violent.

Although the threat of attacks on the social order by labor organizations frightened officials most, less actual violence occurred during 1919 in connection with struggles between labor and capital than in connection with conflicts between Negroes and whites.

In many parts of the United States, the semi-private use of violence by whites to control Negroes had long been permitted by the state in the form of lynchings which, though formally illegal, were rarely punished.[25] In addition, there occurred on several occasions what Gunnar Myrdal has called a "terrorization or massacre." [26] Such events were "mass lynchings," analogous to the Eastern European "pogrom," in which a large number of whites attacked a large number of Negroes and the state did little or nothing to interfere.

Myrdal has distinguished such a pogrom against Negroes from a true riot, which he said was "not a one-way punishment but a two-way battle." In a riot, he explains:

> The Negroes may be hopelessly outnumbered and beaten, but they fight back. There is danger to the white man participating in the riot as there usually is not when he engages in other forms of violence against Negroes.[27]

This distinction between a "pogrom" and a "riot" is not intended to suggest that all occasions on which racial mob violence occurs can be easily assigned to one or the other category. The two words, rather, express "ideal types" which are useful in discussing phenomena that in reality exist on a continuum, not in two neat packages.

The kind of continuum involved in the one-sidedness or two-sidedness of mass racial violence can be seen by looking at several instances. One almost pure example of a "pogrom" was the New York "draft riots" of 1863, in which hundreds of Negroes were killed and many of their homes and businesses burned by Irish-Americans who were enraged at being conscripted to fight in a war to free Negroes while the Negroes stayed at home.[28] An example of a mostly one-sided affray in which a few Negroes did fight back was the Atlanta eruption of 1906. Ten Negroes were killed, but so were two whites. The general impact of the riot was more one-sided than these figures would indicate, however, since many Negroes had their houses looted and burned, and many of them afterward sold their property and left the city.[29]

In all American history, perhaps the event that most nearly approximated the "ideal type" of a riot was the Chicago riot of 1919, in which twenty-three Negroes and fifteen whites were killed, and many observers noted the wholehearted commitment of the Negro community to "fighting back" when attacked. Other racial confrontations that occurred in 1919 were not quite so clearly "riots" as the Chicago affair, but many of them were far closer to the "riot" end of the continuum than previous racial violence in the United States had been.

This group of riots was, however, only one index to an atmosphere that permeated the Negro community in America after the First World War. Indeed, the propensity of Negroes in 1919 to challenge the assumption of their own subordination startled America and constitutes one major reason to study the explosion of race riots that characterized 1919. For the 1919 riots gave birth to "the new Negro"— the first generation of Negroes to win that appellation— and signaled the first new departure since Emancipation in the history of Negroes' efforts to end their subordination.

The 1919 race riots merit study not only for their importance as a turning point in race relations, but also because they confronted the holders of office with the necessity of dealing with actual private violence on a large scale. The complex arrangement of local, state, and federal responsibilities for police action to control public and private violence, an arrangement that had emerged from the Civil War and the industrial upheavals of the 1890's, stood in the balance. For not since the Civil War had the federal government had at its disposal as large an army as it did during and just after the First World War, and perhaps not since the Civil War itself had it been confronted with the occurrence of mass violence of such great size in so many places across the country. In 1919 the new American "state" that had emerged from the First World War was forced to decide whether to enforce its monopoly of violence or instead to allow private violence full sway. Although federal officials were not conscious of making a momentous choice of the future role of "state" power in America and did not theorize about their choice, their actions did in fact embody a decision.

NOTES

1. The second volume of the trilogy is simply titled *Nineteen Nineteen*. John dos Passos, *U.S.A.*, p. i.

2. Hannah Arendt, *On Revolution*, p. 9.

3. Hans Gerth and C. Wright Mills, *From Max Weber: Essays in Sociology*, p. 78. This remark was made by Weber in a speech given in 1918 and published as "Politik als Beruf" in 1919. *Ibid.*, n. p. 77.

4. Ray A. Billington, *The Protestant Crusade*.

5. John W. Caughey, *Their Majesties the Mob*.

6. Samuel Yellen, *American Labor Struggles;* John A. Fitch, *The Causes of Industrial Unrest;* Louis Adamic, *Dynamite;* Robert V. Bruce, *1877: Year of Violence*.

7. Arthur Raper, *The Tragedy of Lynching*.

8. Henry S. Commager (ed.), *Documents of American History*, p. 171.

9. John R. Commons *et al.*, *History of Labor in the United States, 1896–1932,* Vol. IV, *Labor Movements,* by Selig Perlman and Philip Taft, p. 433.

10. Wilfrid H. Crook, *Communism and the General Strike,* p. 21.

11. *Ibid.,* p. 52.

12. *Ibid.,* pp. 56–57.

13. *Ibid.,* pp. 57–58.

14. William Preston, Jr., *Aliens and Dissenters,* pp. 198–206.

15. *Ibid.,* pp. 207–220; Zechariah Chafee, *Free Speech in the United States,* pp. 196–240.

16. Commons *et al.,* IV, pp. 427–28; Adamic, pp. 298–305.

17. Louis Brownlow, *A Passion for Anonymity,* pp. 83–89.

18. Commons *et al.,* pp. 446–47.

19. Brownlow, p. 88.

20. George Soule, *Prosperity Decade,* p. 194; Adamic, pp. 288–90; Fitch, pp. 195–96.

21. Commons *et al.,* IV, pp. 466–67.

22. Soule, pp. 195–96.

23. Memo, Office of Army Chief of Staff to Adjutant-General, November 8, 1920, War Department MSS., National Archives.

24. Commons *et al.,* IV, p. 473.

25. Gunnar Myrdal, *An American Dilemma,* pp. 558–66.

26. *Ibid.,* p. 566.

27. *Ibid.*

28. John Hope Franklin, *From Slavery to Freedom,* p. 275; Samuel E. Morison and Henry S. Commager, *Growth of the American Republic,* I, p. 706.

29. Franklin, p. 433; Myrdal, p. 567.

THE LOS ANGELES
RIOT OF 1943

By CAREY McWILLIAMS

On Thursday evening, June 3, 1943, the Alpine Club—
made up of youngsters of Mexican descent—held a meeting
in a police substation in Los Angeles. Usually these meetings
were held in a nearby public school but, since the school
was closed, the boys had accepted the invitation of a police
captain to meet in the substation. The principal business of
the meeting, conducted in the presence of the police captain,
consisted in a discussion of how gang-strife could best be
avoided in the neighborhood. After the meeting had adjourned, the boys were taken in squad cars to the street
corner nearest the neighborhood in which most of them
lived. The squad cars were scarcely out of sight, when the
boys were assaulted, not by a rival "gang" or "club," but
by hoodlum elements in the neighborhood. Of one thing the
boys were sure: their assailants were not of Mexican descent.

Earlier the same evening a group of eleven sailors, on
leave from their station in Los Angeles, were walking along
the 1700 block on North Main Street in the center of one
of the city's worst slum areas. The surrounding neighborhood is predominantly Mexican. On one side of the street
the dirty brick front of a large brewery hides from view a
collection of ramshackle Mexican homes. The other side of
the street consists of a series of small bars, boarded-up store
fronts, and small shops. The area is well off the beaten paths
and few servicemen found their way this far north on Main
Street. As they were walking along the street, so they later

stated, the sailors were set upon by a gang of Mexican boys. One of the sailors was badly hurt; the others suffered minor cuts and bruises. According to their story, the sailors were outnumbered about three to one.

When the attack was reported to the nearest substation, the police adopted a curious attitude. Instead of attempting to find and arrest the assailants, fourteen police remained at the station after their regular duty was over for the night. Then, under the command of a detective lieutenant, the "Vengeance Squad," as they called themselves, set out "to clean up" the gang that had attacked the sailors. But— miracle of miracles!—when they arrived at the scene of the attack they could find no one to arrest—not a single Mexican—on their favorite charge of "suspicion of assault." In itself this curious inability to find anyone to arrest—so strikingly at variance with what usually happened on raids of this sort—raises an inference that a larger strategy was involved. For the raid accomplished nothing except to get the names of the raiding officers in the newspapers and to whip up the anger of the community against the Mexican population, which may, perhaps, have been the reason for the raid. . . .

Thus began the so-called "Zoot-Suit Race Riots" which were to last, in one form or another, for a week in Los Angeles.

·1·   THE TAXICAB BRIGADE

Taking the police raid as an official cue—a signal for action—about two hundred sailors decided to take the law into their own hands on the following night. Coming down into the center of Los Angeles from the Naval Armory in Chavez Ravine (near the "Chinatown" area), they hired a fleet of twenty taxicabs. Once assembled, the "task force" proceeded to cruise straight through the center of town en route to the east side of Los Angeles where the bulk of the Mexicans reside. Soon the sailors in the lead-car sighted a Mexican boy in a zoot-suit walking along the street. The "task force" immediately stopped and, in a few moments, the boy was lying on the pavement, badly beaten and bleeding. The sailors then piled back into the cabs and the caravan resumed its way until the next zoot-suiter was sighted, whereupon the same procedure was repeated. In these attacks, of course, the odds were pretty uneven: two hundred sailors to one Mexican boy. Four times this same treatment was meted out and four "gangsters"—two seventeen-year-old youngsters, one nineteen, and one twenty-three—were left lying on the pavement for the ambulances to pick up.

It is indeed curious that in a city like Los Angeles, which boasts that it has more police cars equipped with two-way radios than any other city in the world (Los Angeles *Times*, September 2, 1947), the police were apparently unable to intercept a caravan of twenty taxicabs, loaded with two hundred uniformed, yelling, bawdy sailors, as it cruised through the downtown and east-side sections of the city. At one point the police did happen to cross the trail of the caravan and the officers were apparently somewhat embarrassed over the meeting. For only nine of the sailors were taken into custody and the rest were permitted to continue on their merry way. No charges, however, were ever preferred against the nine.

Their evening's entertainment over, the sailors returned to the foot of Chavez Ravine. There they were met by the police and the Shore Patrol. The Shore Patrol took seventeen of the sailors into custody and sent the rest up the ravine to the Naval Armory. The petty officer who had led the expedition, and who was not among those arrested, gave the police a frank statement of things to come. "We're out to do what the police have failed to do," he said; "we're going to clean up this situation. . . . Tonight [by then it was the morning of June fifth] the sailors may have the marines along."

The next day the Los Angeles press pushed the war news from the front page as it proceeded to play up the pavement war in Los Angeles in screaming headlines. "Wild Night in L.A.—Sailor-Zooter Clash" was the headline in the *Daily News*. "Sailor Task Force Hits L.A. Zooters" bellowed the *Herald-Express*. A suburban newspaper gleefully reported that "zoot-suited roughnecks fled to cover before a task force of twenty taxicabs." None of these stories, however, reported the slightest resistance, up to this point, on the part of the Mexicans.

True to their promise, the sailors were joined that night, June fifth, by scores of soldiers and marines. Squads of servicemen, arms linked, paraded through downtown Los Angeles four abreast, stopping anyone wearing zoot-suits and ordering these individuals to put away their "drapes" by the following night or suffer the consequences. Aside from a few half-hearted admonitions, the police made no effort whatever to interfere with these heralds of disorder. However, twenty-seven Mexican boys, gathered on a street corner, were arrested and jailed that evening. While these boys were being booked "on suspicion" of various offenses, a mob of several hundred servicemen roamed the downtown section of a great city threatening members of the Mexican minority without hindrance or interference from the police, the Shore Patrol, or the Military Police.

On this same evening, a squad of sailors invaded a bar on the east side and carefully examined the clothes of the patrons. Two zoot-suit customers, drinking beer at a table, were peremptorily ordered to remove their clothes. One of them was beaten and his clothes were torn from his back when he refused to comply with the order. The other—they were both Mexicans—doffed his "drapes" which were promptly ripped to shreds. Similar occurrences in several parts of the city that evening were sufficiently alarming to have warranted some precautionary measures or to have justified an "out-of-bounds" order. All that the police officials did, however, was to call up some additional reserves and announce that any Mexicans involved in the rioting would be promptly arrested. That there had been no counterattacks by the Mexicans up to this point apparently did not enter into the police officers' appraisal of the situation. One thing must be said for the Los Angeles police: it is above all consistent. When it is wrong, it is consistently wrong; when it makes a mistake, it will be repeated.

By the night of June sixth, the police had worked out a simple formula for action. Knowing that wherever the sailors went there would be trouble, the police simply followed the sailors at a conveniently spaced interval. Six carloads of sailors cruised down Brooklyn Avenue that evening. At Ramona Boulevard, they stopped and beat up eight teen-age Mexicans. Failing to find any Mexican zoot-suiters in a bar on Indiana Street, they were so annoyed that they proceeded to wreck the establishment. In due course, the police made a leisurely appearance at the scene of the wreckage but could find no one to arrest. Carefully following the sailors, the police arrested eleven boys who had been beaten up on Carmelita Street; six more victims were arrested a few blocks further on, seven at Ford Boulevard, six at Gifford Street—and so on straight through the Mexican east-side settlements. Behind them came the police, stopping at the same street corners "to mop up" by arresting the injured victims of the mob. By morning, some forty-four Mexican boys, all severely beaten, were under arrest.

·2·   **OPERATION "DIXIE"**

The stage was now set for the really serious rioting of June seventh and eighth. Having featured the preliminary rioting as an offensive launched by sailors, soldiers, and marines, the press now whipped public opinion into a frenzy by dire warnings that Mexican zoot-suiters planned mass retaliations. To insure a riot, the precise street corners were named at which retaliatory action was expected and the time of the anticipated action was carefully specified. In effect these stories announced a riot and invited public participation. "Zooters Planning to Attack More Servicemen," headlined the *Daily News*; "Would jab broken bottlenecks in the faces of their victims . . . Beating sailors' brains out with hammers also on the program." Concerned for the safety of the Army, the Navy, and the Marine Corps, the *Herald-Express* warned that "Zooters . . . would mass 500 strong."

By way of explaining the action of the police throughout the subsequent rioting, it should be pointed out that, in June, 1943, the police were on a bad spot. A man by the name of Beebe, arrested on a drunk charge, had been kicked to death in the Central Jail by police officers. Through the excellent work of an alert police commissioner, the case had finally been broken and, at the time of the riots, a police officer by the name of Compton Dixon was on trial in the courts. While charges of police brutality had been bandied about for years, this was the first time that a seemingly airtight case had been prepared. Shortly after the riots, a Hollywood police captain told a motion picture director that the police had touched off the riots "in order to give Dixie (Dixon) a break." By staging a fake demonstration of the alleged necessity for harsh police methods, it was hoped that the jury would acquit Dixon. As a matter of fact, the jury did disagree and on July 2, 1943, the charges against Dixon were dismissed.

On Monday evening, June seventh, thousands of *Angelenos*, in response to twelve hours' advance notice in the press, turned out for a mass lynching. Marching through the streets of downtown Los Angeles, a mob of several thousand soldiers, sailors, and civilians, proceeded to beat up every zoot-suiter they could find. Pushing its way into the important motion picture theaters, the mob ordered the management to turn on the house lights and then ranged up and down the aisles dragging Mexicans out of their seats. Street cars were halted while Mexicans, and some Filipinos and Negroes, were jerked out of their seats, pushed into the streets, and beaten with sadistic frenzy. If the victims wore zoot-suits, they were stripped of their clothing and left naked or half-naked on the streets, bleeding and bruised. Proceeding down Main Street from First to Twelfth, the mob stopped on the edge of the Negro district. Learning that the Negroes planned a warm reception for them, the mobsters turned back and marched through the Mexican eastside spreading panic and terror.

Here is one of the numerous eye-witness accounts written by Al Waxman, editor of *The Eastside Journal*:

> At Twelfth and Central I came upon a scene that will long live in my memory. Police were swinging clubs and servicemen were fighting with civilians. Wholesale arrests were being made by the officers.
>
> Four boys came out of a pool hall. They were wearing the zoot-suits that have become the symbol of a fighting flag. Police ordered them into arrest cars. One refused. He asked: "Why am I being arrested?" The police officer answered with three swift blows of the night-stick across the boy's head and he went down. As he sprawled, he was kicked in the

face. Police had difficulty loading his body into the vehicle because he was one-legged and wore a wooden limb. Maybe the officer didn't know he was attacking a cripple.

At the next corner a Mexican mother cried out, "Don't take my boy, he did nothing. He's only fifteen years old. Don't take him." She was struck across the jaw with a night-stick and almost dropped the two and a half year old baby that was clinging in her arms. . . .

Rushing back to the east side to make sure that things were quiet here, I came upon a band of servicemen making a systematic tour of East First Street. They had just come out of a cocktail bar where four men were nursing bruises. Three autos loaded with Los Angeles policemen were on the scene but the soldiers were not molested.

Farther down the street the men stopped a streetcar forcing the motorman to open the door and proceeded to inspect the clothing of the male passengers. "We're looking for zoot-suits to burn," they shouted. Again the police did not interfere. . . . Half a block away . . . I pleaded with the men of the local police substation to put a stop to these activities. "It is a matter for the military police," they said.

Throughout the night the Mexican communities were in the wildest possible turmoil. Scores of Mexican mothers were trying to locate their youngsters and several hundred Mexicans milled around each of the police substations and the Central Jail trying to get word of missing members of their families. Boys came into the police stations saying: "Charge me with vagrancy or anything, but don't send me out there!" pointing to the streets where other boys, as young as twelve and thirteen years of age, were being beaten and stripped of their clothes. From affidavits which I helped prepare at the time, I should say that not more than half of the victims were actually wearing zoot-suits. A Negro defense worker, wearing a defense-plant identification badge on his work-clothes, was taken from a street car and one of his eyes was gouged out with a knife. Huge half-page photographs, showing Mexican boys stripped of their clothes, cowering on the pavements, often bleeding profusely, surrounded by jeering mobs of men and women, appeared in all the Los Angeles newspapers. As Al Waxman most truthfully reported, blood had been "spilled on the streets of the city."

At midnight on June seventh, the military authorities decided that the local police were completely unable or unwilling to handle the situation, despite the fact that a thousand reserve officers had been called up. The entire downtown area of Los Angeles was then declared "out of bounds" for military personnel. This order immediately slowed down the pace of the rioting. The moment the Military Police and the Shore Patrol went into action, the rioting quieted down. On June eighth the city officials brought their heads up out of the sand, took a look around, and began issuing statements. The district attorney, Fred N. Howser, announced that the "situation is getting entirely out of hand," while Mayor Fletcher Bowron thought that "sooner or later it will blow over." The chief of police, taking a count of the Mexicans in jail, cheerfully proclaimed that "the situation has now cleared up." All agreed, however, that it was quite "a situation."

Unfortunately, "the situation" had not cleared up; nor did it blow over. It began to spread to the suburbs where the rioting continued for two more days. When it finally stopped, the Eagle Rock *Advertiser* mournfully editorialized: "It is too bad the servicemen were called off before they were able to complete the job. . . . Most of the citizens of the city have been delighted with what has been going on." County Supervisor Roger Jessup told the newsmen: "All that is needed to end lawlessness is more of the same action as is being exercised by the servicemen!" While the district attorney of Ventura, an outlying county, jumped on the bandwagon with a statement to the effect that "zoot-suits are an open indication of subversive character." This was also the opinion of the Los Angeles City Council which adopted a resolution making the wearing of zoot-suits a misdemeanor! On June eleventh, hundreds of handbills were distributed to students and posted on bulletin boards in a high school attended by many Negroes and Mexicans which read: "Big Sale. Second-Hand Zoot Suits. Slightly Damaged. Apply at Nearest U.S. Naval Station. While they last we have your Size."

·3·   **WHEN THE DEVIL IS SICK . . .**

Egging on the mob to attack Mexicans in the most indiscriminate manner, the press developed a fine technique in reporting the riots. "44 Zooters Jailed in Attacks on Sailors" was the chief headline in the *Daily News* of June seventh; "Zoot Suit Chiefs Girding for War on Navy" was the headline in the same paper on the following day. The moralistic tone of this reporting is illustrated by a smug headline in the Los Angeles *Times* of June seventh: "Zoot Suiters Learn Lesson in Fight with Servicemen." The riots, according to the same paper, were having "a cleansing effect." An editorial in the *Herald-Express* said that the riots "promise to rid the community of . . . those zoot-suited miscreants." While Mr. Manchester Boddy, in a signed editorial in the *Daily News* of June ninth excitedly announced that "the time for temporizing is past. . . . The time has come to serve notice that the City of Los Angeles will no longer be terrorized by a relatively small handful of morons parading as zoot-suit hoodlums. To delay action *now* means to court disaster later on." As though there had been any "temporizing," in this sense, for the prior two years!

But once the Navy had declared the downtown section of Los Angeles "out of bounds," once the Mexican ambassador in Washington had addressed a formal inquiry to Secretary of State Hull, and once official Washington began to advise the local minions of the press of the utterly disastrous international effects of the riots, in short when the local press realized the consequences of its own lawless action, a great thunderous cry for "unity," and "peace," and "order" went forth. One after the other, the editors began to disclaim all responsibility for the riots which, two days before, had been hailed for their "salutary" and "cleansing" effect.

Thus on June eleventh the Los Angeles *Times,* in a pious mood, wrote:

> . . . at the outset, zoot-suiters were limited to no specific race; they were Anglo-Saxon, Latin and Negro. The fact that

later on their numbers seemed to be predominantly Latin was in itself no indictment of that race at all. No responsible person at any time condemned Latin-Americans as such.

Feeling a twinge of conscience, Mr. Boddy wrote that "only a ridiculously small percentage of the local Mexican population is involved in the so-called gang demonstrations. Every true Californian has an affection for his fellow citizens of Mexican ancestry that is as deep rooted as the Mexican culture that influences our way of living, our architecture, our music, our language, and even our food." This belated discovery of the Spanish-Mexican cultural heritage of California was, needless to say, rather ironic in view of the fact that the ink was not yet dry on Mr. Boddy's earlier editorial in which he had castigated the Mexican minority as "morons." To appreciate the ironic aspects of "the situation," the same newspaper that had been baiting Mexicans for nearly two years now began to extol them.

As might have been expected, this post-mortem mood of penitence and contrition survived just long enough for some of the international repercussions of the riots to quiet down. Within a year, the press and the police were back in the same old groove. On July 16, 1944, the Los Angeles *Times* gave front-page prominence to a curious story under the heading: "Youthful Gang Secrets Exposed." Indicating no source, identifying no spokesman, the story went on to say that "authorities of the Superior Court" had unearthed a dreadful "situation" among juvenile delinquents. Juveniles were using narcotics, marihuana, and smoking "reefers." Compelled to accept drug addiction, "unwilling neophytes" were dragooned into committing robberies and other crimes. Young girls were tattooed with various "secret cabalistic symbols" of gang membership. The high pompadours affected by the *cholitas,* it was said, were used to conceal knives and other "weapons." Two theories were advanced in the story by way of "explaining" the existence of these dangerous gangs: first, that "subversive groups" in Los Angeles had organized them; and, second, that "the gangs are the result of mollycoddling of racial groups." In view of the record, one is moved to inquire, what mollycoddling? by the police? by the juvenile authorities? by the courts?

Backing up the news story, an editorial appeared in the *Times* on July eighteenth entitled: "It's Not a Nice Job But It Has To Be Done." Lashing out at "any maudlin and misguided sympathy for the 'poor juveniles,'" the editorial went on to say that "stern punishment is what is needed; stern and sure punishment. The police and the Sheriff's men *should be given every encouragement* to go after these young gangsters.". . .

The zoot-suit riots in Los Angeles were the spark that touched off a chain-reaction of riots across the country in midsummer 1943. Similar "zoot-suit" disturbances were reported in San Diego on June ninth; in Philadelphia on June tenth; in Chicago on June fifteenth; and in Evansville, Indiana, on June twenty-seventh. Between June sixteenth and August first, large-scale race riots occurred in Beaumont, Texas, in Detroit, and in Harlem. The Detroit riots of June 20–21 were the most disastrous riots in a quarter of a century. The swift, crazy violence of the Harlem riot resulted, in a few hours' time, in property damage totalling nearly a million dollars. The rapid succession of these violent and destructive riots seriously interfered with the war effort and had the most adverse international repercussions. The spark that ignited these explosions occurred in *El Pueblo de Nuestra Señora La Reina de Los Angeles de Porciuncula,* founded by Felipe de Neve in 1781, settled by Mexican *pobladores.*

None of these disturbances had more serious international consequences than the zoot-suit riots. On April 20, 1943, President Roosevelt had held his historic meeting with President Camacho on the soil of Mexico. At the time the riots occurred, Mexico was our ally in the war against Germany, Italy, and Japan. Large-scale shipments of Mexican nationals had just begun to arrive in the United States to relieve the critical manpower shortage. "Our two countries," President Roosevelt had said, "owe their independence to the fact that your ancestors and mine held the same truths to be worth fighting for and dying for. Hidalgo and Júarez were men of the same stamp as Washington and Jefferson." President Camacho, replying to this toast, had said that "the negative memories" of the past were forgotten in the accord of today. And then in the largest city in the old Spanish borderland had come this explosion of hatred and prejudice against Spanish-speaking people.

In response to a request from the Mexican ambassador, Secretary of State Hull had asked Mayor Fletcher Bowron for an official explanation. With a perfectly straight face, the mayor replied that the riots were devoid of any element of prejudice against persons of Mexican descent! The same edition of the newspapers that carried this statement also carried another statement by the mayor under a headline which read: "Mayor Pledges 2-Fisted Action, No Wrist Slap"—a reference to police action contemplated against the Mexican minority. On June ninth Mr. Churchill Murray, local representative of the coordinator of Inter-American Affairs, wired Mr. Rockefeller that the riots were "nonracial." "The frequency of Mexican names among the victims," he said, "was without actual significance." If all this were true, asked Dan G. Acosta in a letter to the Los Angeles press, "Why are we consistently called hoodlums? Why is mob action encouraged by the newspapers? Why did the city police stand around saying very nonchalantly that they could not intervene and even hurrahed the soldiers for their 'brave' action? Not until these questions are answered, will the Mexican population feel at ease."

What the riots did, of course, was to expose the rotten foundations upon which the City of Los Angeles had built a papier-mâché façade of "Inter-American Good Will" made up of fine-sounding Cinco de Mayo proclamations. During the riots, the press, the police, the officialdom, and the dominant control groups of Los Angeles were caught with the bombs of prejudice in their hands. One year before the riots occurred, they had been warned of the danger of an explosion. The riots were not an unexpected rupture in Anglo-Hispano relations but the logical end-product of a hundred years of neglect and discrimination.

The riots left a residue of resentment and hatred in the minds and hearts of thousands of young Mexican-Americans in Los Angeles. During the rioting, one Los Angeles newspaper had published a story to the effect that the *cholitas* and *pachucas* were merely cheap prostitutes, infected with venereal disease and addicted to the use of marihuana. Eighteen Mexican-American girls promptly replied in a letter which the metropolitan press refused to publish: "The girls in this meeting room consist of young girls who graduated from high school as honor students, of girls who are now working in defense plants because we want to help win the war, and of girls who have brothers, cousins, relatives and sweethearts in all branches of the American armed forces. We have not been able to have our side of the story told." The letter, with a picture of the girls, was published in Al Waxman's *Eastside Journal* on June 16, 1943. Still another group of Mexican-American girls— real *pachucas* these—bitterly protested the story in another letter which the metropolitan press did not publish. These girls insisted that they should be examined, as a group, by an officially appointed board of physicians so that they could prove that they were virgins. Long after the riots, I have seen Mexican-American boys pull creased and wrinkled newspaper clippings from their wallets and exhibit this slanderous story with the greatest indignation. Four years have now passed since the riots, but the blood has not yet been washed from the pavements of Los Angeles.

INVASION AND COUNTERATTACK

By CHARLES ABRAMS

The movement of southern Negroes to the cities provided the first major test since the Oriental influx of how the challenge to American neighborhoods would be met. From 1920, when the European immigration trailed off, to 1930, which signaled the end of the boom years, 615,000 Negroes left the South. Georgia, South Carolina, and Mississippi lost the bulk. They headed mainly east, concentrating in the big cities. Others moved to the Middle West, notably Chicago and St. Louis. Once the trek had started there was no substantial letup, even during the depression years. Chicago alone received no less than 43,000 between 1920 and 1930.[1]

The Negro at first headed toward already established Negro areas. He had less difficulty doing this in cities which were already punctuated with Negro districts. But soon expansion into new sections became inevitable and once-stabilized white belts began to feel the pressure as the Negro spread outward from his bulging ghetto. Sometimes he moved into all-white slums, sometimes into more costly neighborhoods. He was able to do this by doubling up and sharing the cost, because of the rise of a small professional class able to pay for better housing, because of the tendency of unionization to establish equal pay, or because of the presence of more than one breadwinner in the family.

The whites met the problem in a number of ways:

Some elected to stay put. This occurred where the Negro migration was small and no major challenge felt.

Some elected to escape the whole business by moving to new territory. The suburb was the city's sub-frontier and wider rings of new land were within time distance, thanks to the automobile and fast commuters' trains. The exodus made some of the vacated space available to the Negro.

The reaction of others, however, was to stay and fight it out with legal devices. The introduction of zoning made it possible to ban Negroes by the simple addition of a new prohibition of occupancy by black human beings. When racial zoning was struck down by the courts and the racial covenant succeeded it, application of the covenant proved more difficult in the older neighborhoods. The opposition then often resorted to the third means—force, one of the oldest devices for keeping minorities in their place and one of the most effective.

In the South, where intimidation had been the established procedure to protect the social structure, there was no absence of leaders to organize the required resistance to unauthorized Negro movements. As long as the necessary subordination patterns remained undisturbed, however, southerners took no action. The Negroes in turn were not disposed to move where they were not wanted. But sometimes the Negro's necessity overcame his caution, and the white man's temper ran ahead of his senses. The records of the period show the results.

In 1929, shots were fired into a Negro house in Memphis, and the house burned down.[2] A riot in Phillips County, Arkansas, resulted in the killing of 25 to 50 persons in 1919. There was also a riot in East St. Louis, Illinois, during World War I which took the lives of 39 Negroes and 8 whites. In Houston, in 1917, 17 whites were killed, 13 Negroes hanged, 41 imprisoned for life.[3] There were bombings or riots in Louisville, Kansas City, and Baltimore.

Violence had been less common in the North which had once espoused the Negro's cause and even welcomed him. Nevertheless, in 1924, Negroes were forced to give up their homes in Garfield Heights, Ohio, because "they had no right to buy such a nice place."[4] In 1931, after a cross-burning in Pittsburgh, organized threats were made to withdraw financial support from the Y.M.C.A. and the Community Chest if these organizations did not force two Negro doctors and a Y.M.C.A. secretary to move from their recently bought homes. Thereafter, a mob of 3000 whites attacked a new home built by a Negro post office employee.[5]

There were explosions in westward areas, too. A Negro's house was torn down in Denver in 1926.[6] In fact there were 26 riots in American cities in 1919 alone, the most notorious of which was a Chicago outburst which took the lives of 15 whites and 23 Negroes, besides injuring more than 500 persons. This outbreak had been preceded by a concerted campaign marked by organized meetings, circulars, and antiracial propaganda led by a property owners' organization which was said to have been responsible for the bombing of 58 Negro homes in a period of less than four years.[7]

Despite the violence, however, the Negro established his foothold in the cities. By 1940 there were 4,000,000 Negroes in the North, and it was only a prelude to a greater march in the years to follow. Housing, however, remained the big problem. In Chicago, where there were now 240,000 Negroes, a seven-room flat on East 56th Street, which thirty years before had been rented to middle-class whites at $27.50 a month, had been broken up into four one- and two-room apartments occupied by three to seven persons each. A single bathroom served the seven families. The Black Belt now stretched southward from the central business section for seven and a half miles. Eighty per cent of the city's property was said to be covered by restrictive covenants, and property owners' associations were actively organizing opposition against Negroes. Population density was 70,000 to the square mile, compared to 34,000 for whites.

In Cleveland, Negroes in 1940 were 9.6 per cent of the population; Columbus 11.7, Dallas 17.1, Detroit 9.2, Gary 18.3, Houston 22.4, Indianapolis 13.2, Los Angeles 4.2, New York 6.1, Philadelphia 13, Youngstown 8.7.

The early war boom years 1940–1942 saw no great movement of Negroes but when the bars to Negro employment were relaxed they migrated to the war centers in droves. Some 750,000 Negroes moved across state lines into new industrial centers. The Detroit area alone gained

80,000. A larger group moved to the West Coast cities, and between 1940 and 1944, Los Angeles, Portland, Vancouver, Seattle, San Diego, and the San Francisco area acquired 121,000, a gain of 113 per cent. The Los Angeles metropolitan area gained 59,000. Simultaneously, a northward move saw 80,000 going to Chicago alone.

As the labor shortage sharpened, an inflow of Mexicans began across the Rio Grande. The number of Mexicans recruited for agricultural work leaped to 120,000 in 1946. Later they came faster. The Puerto Rican migration was stepped up simultaneously. More Islanders were seen in the New York subways and the streets of Harlem, Brooklyn, and the Bronx.

Racial tensions accompanied the migrations: the usual rumors of "rape" or the general feeling that the servile Negro servant was now becoming insolent. There were stories of impending attacks by Negroes in mass—"We've got to kill them before they kill us." There were also some fiery crosses burned as far north as Newark, New Jersey. In Missouri a group of 200 farmers in an all-white community seized some Negro tenants on a farm, forced them into trucks, and drove them out. The superintendent of the high school was forced to flee the building when 100 senior students threatened him because his father was the first landowner to bring Negroes into the community. A series of anti-Negro demonstrations in southeastern Missouri communities followed. When enforcement officers were threatened for protecting the employees, the FBI stepped in to investigate.[8] The most serious incidents during the war were in Detroit, where rioting erupted in 1942 and 1943. On the whole, however, racial tensions during the migrations were held in check by the patriotic fervor of the war period and its emergent considerations. The enemy's emphasis on race purity and its extermination of "impure" races sublimated confused emotions at home. Some Negro-white neighborhoods exhibited heroic cooperation and boasted a patriotic tolerance. The rumors of race riots, though plentiful, never grew to serious proportions.[9]

Toward the end of hostilities and the relaxation of war controls, the tensions blew into the open. The first serious disturbances in the South followed the rise of the Columbians, whose aim was to prevent Negroes from moving into homes formerly occupied by whites. Donning uniforms with special insignia and openly advocating dictatorship, the Columbians proposed to solve the Negro problem by deporting every Negro. A race riot in Columbia, Tennessee, in February, 1946, culminated in the shooting of four officers and two white civilians and the maiming of dozens of Negroes. It was the climax of a series of assaults upon Negroes in the streets and even in their homes. Others were falsely charged by white ruffians with stealing. In Monroe, Georgia, two Negroes and their wives were assassinated.

A report on November 4, 1946, to *The New York Times* on the Columbians in Atlanta read: "Throughout the South are heard predictions that the housing problem may succeed the overcrowded buses of the wartime period as the greatest potential for inter-racial quarrels and, perhaps, violence."

The rumors were not unfounded. A wave of violence swept through the country from the South to the North, from East to West. A Negro's home was burned in Redwood City, a suburb of San Francisco, in December, 1946. In Chicago, in the same month, a hundred policemen swinging nightsticks battled a mob that had hurled rocks at a truck moving a Negro veteran's belongings into a housing project. The crowd stoned police cars as well and only when the police charged into the crowd did the barrage stop.[10]

BIRMINGHAM "CREATED BY THE LORD"

The wave hit Birmingham, Alabama, where Negroes comprised 43 per cent of the population. A series of zoning laws had been enacted and re-enacted despite invalidation by the courts. A Negro's home which had been the object of three court suits involving the ordinances was blasted by dynamite. Thereafter, tensions rose and on March 26, 1949, three more Negro homes were dynamited.[11] Two months later the City Commission voted a "buffer zone" between white and Negro sections on the west side of town, consisting of a 50-foot strip running six blocks north from a housing project to a highway. The zone was for "commercial construction only."[12] At a federal court hearing on the law,

the mayor testified, "There would be bloodshed and tragedy.
. . . There are some things that go beyond the written law
. . . things created by the people and the Lord." [13]

Threats continued to be made to Negro residents. The
K.K.K. was active. There were assaults and attempts to
lure Negro leaders into traps where they could be man-
handled. One night seven Birmingham police officers and
detectives swooped down without warrant on a Negro home.
They said they had heard that white people were living
there with the Negro family.[14] On August 13, 1949, two
midnight blasts rocked Negro houses zoned for whites only.
The explosions were heard over most of Birmingham. When
they occurred, several Negroes, on guard in anticipation of
the attack, fired at a speeding automobile from which the
bombs had been thrown. The shots missed. The police commissioner charged the Negroes as "partly to blame for the
incident for not informing police." [15]

In April, 1950, a blast ripped through the home of a
Negro minister in Birmingham. It was the second dynamit-
ing of the house in less than a year. It was followed in nine
days by another blast at the home of a Negro dentist,
causing $11,000 damage.[16] In December, 1950, the home
of a Negro woman who had led a court fight against the
city zoning law was dynamited. The heavy explosion was
set off shortly before midnight and was heard for several
miles. The bomb apparently was placed or thrown on a
screened porch. The contractor who had completed the
house only a month before estimated damage tentatively
at about $8000. It was the fifth bombing of a Negro house
since the spring of 1949. Three were blasted then and another the April before.[17]

In May, 1951, the two homes which had been the targets
of the dynamiters for three years were finally burned to the
ground.[18]

ELSEWHERE

Nor were the Birmingham outbreaks an isolated affair.
Chicago had a wave of riots after World War II, plus hundreds of minor incidents. Bombings were occurring simultaneously in other areas and in 1950–1951 there were

bombings in Nashville, Wake Forest (North Carolina), Miami, Dallas, Rome (Georgia), and Crossville, Phenix City, and Cottonwood, Alabama.

In Chattanooga, in May, 1950, a Negro home in a previously white section was bombed for the second time, almost killing two children. In Nashville, after cross-burnings, a bomb was hurled from a passing automobile which shook houses in a six-block radius. In March, 1951, several sticks of dynamite were exploded in the backyard of a house recently sold to Negroes, touching off a whole wave of dynamitings in the area. In seventeen months preceding August 11, 1951, Negro homes were the target of 13 dynamitings in Dallas.

Considerable violence occurred elsewhere that the press never reported. These sample news items will give a running idea of what was happening from 1949 through 1952:

GEORGIA ACTS TO ENFORCE HOUSING SEGREGATION

Georgia is moving to halt sales of white neighborhood homes to Negroes, a practice that has brought sporadic violence to the South. . . . Saturday night, dynamite ripped a home in a white section of Atlanta. Negroes had just purchased the house. —New York *World-Telegram,* March 9, 1949.

NEGRO'S LICENSE REVOKED IN SALE OF "WHITE" HOMES

Georgia today took away the license of a Negro real estate dealer who sold homes in a white neighborhood to Negroes.— *The New York Times,* March 24, 1949.

WASHINGTON MEMO

. . . A Negro family moved into a home in a "white neighborhood" over the weekend; within a few hours the house had been stoned, a trash fire was discovered in the backyard and a "citizen's meeting" protesting the advent of the Negroes had been held. Reports of Klan activity in the area are current.— *New York Post,* April 6, 1949.

BIG CROSS BURNED

Nashville, Tenn.—A fifteen-foot cross was burned last night near the site of a proposed Negro housing unit in a section of town predominantly occupied by white persons.—New York *Sun,* April 7, 1949.

NEGRO DOCTOR'S WIFE BLAMES PREJUDICE IN BOMBING OF HOUSE

Warren, O.—A homemade dynamite bomb which heavily damaged a Negro doctor's incompleted $50,000 home was set off in spite motivated by race prejudice, the doctor's wife told police today.—Chicago *Tribune,* April 8, 1949.

BRONX HOME STONED IN NIGHT AFTER TALK OF SALE TO NEGRO

New York Post, June 17, 1949.

NEGRO HOUSING HALTED; HOMES AT NASHVILLE BLAST SCENE NOW SLATED FOR WHITES

Plans have been abandoned for a Negro housing project in an area here that has been the scene of a cross burning and an explosion.—*The New York Times,* January 7, 1950.

BLASTS DAMAGE CAROLINA HOMES

Richmond (Va.) *Times-Dispatch,* April 7, 1952.

POLICE ALERTED AS WHITES THREATEN NEGRO NEIGHBORS

. . . A group of spokesmen suggested . . . "If you leave this neighborhood you will live longer and be happier."—Houston *Chronicle,* June 17, 1952.

RACIAL ECHO IN BLASTING OF HOUSE

An explosion here early Sunday morning blasted the front of an empty house about to be occupied by a Negro family. Police said the house is in a predominantly white neighborhood.— Atlanta *Constitution,* June 18, 1951.

NEGRO HOME BUILT NEAR WHITE AREA IN DALLAS BOMBED

The bombing was the twelfth in the area in recent months.— St. Louis *Post-Dispatch,* July 12, 1951.

THREATENED NEGRO GUARDED ON COAST

Since Gary moved in the neighbors have been protesting his presence. Last night a stone crashed through the kitchen window and at 4:30 A.M. today another rock was hurled against the house. A reinforced guard of sheriff's deputies was thrown around Gary's home.—*The New York Times* dispatch from Richmond, California, March 18, 1952.

Los Angeles (UP)—Two home-made bombs were exploded yesterday outside the home of William Bailey, a Negro science teacher, and a residence, across the street, occupied by white persons. No one was injured but both buildings were damaged extensively.—*The New York Times,* March 17, 1952.

CHICAGO MOB FIRES HOUSE ON "NEGRO" RUMOR *Chicago* (UP)—A mob of about 4,000 persons attempted to burn a two-family house last night after they heard rumors that Negroes planned to move into the building.—*New York Post,* July 2, 1952.

An article in the *New South* for June–July, 1952, published by the Southern Regional Council at Atlanta, sums up the violence in the South for an 18-month period as follows:

Since January 1, 1951 more than 40 bombings have been perpetrated in the South by terrorists and vandals, and many more have been attempted . . . most of these depredations have grown out of racial and religious tensions. . . . Not a single case of bombing growing out of racial and religious tensions has resulted in conviction of the perpetrators.[19]

A group of homeowners originally from Georgia and Arkansas spearheaded a mob scene in Contra Costa County in the San Francisco Bay area. Despite urgent appeals law enforcement was represented only by two policemen in a parked car who made no effort to disperse the crowd. A riot was avoided by the firm intervention of the California Attorney-General.[20] There were a series of bombings of Negro homes in Houston, in August, 1953.[21] A Negro was shot at in Madison, Wisconsin, and on September 30, his home vandalized.

Organized opposition in a Cleveland neighborhood brought tension and vandalism for almost two weeks. The sale of a home to a Negro was protested by organized meetings of hundreds of owners. Intervention by the mayor, the Community Relations Committee, churches, and civic officials brought the situation under control.[22] In 1953 there was arson, violence or bomb-throwing in Kansas City, Atlanta, Chicago and East St. Louis, Cleveland, Indianapolis, Long Island, and Los Angeles County.[23]

Bombings continued in 1954. In Sacramento, California, dynamite blew a hole in the cement porch of a Negro couple while they were sleeping. Chicago continued seething. The

Supreme Court decision barring school segregation un-
leashed new antagonisms in Southern communities. Three
successive explosions rocked Norfolk County, Virginia, between August 24 and September 11, causing extensive
damage.

On June 27, in Louisville, Kentucky, where 17 percent of
the population is Negro, a bomb shattered the wall of a
house belonging to Andrew E. Wade IV. The house had
been bought for the Wades through a Mr. and Mrs. Carl
Braden, a white couple who were their friends. The explosion had been preceded by cross-burning, rock-throwing,
and gunfire. The prosecutor started an investigation. Instead
of finding the hoodlums responsible for the outrages, he
raided the Braden home and the homes of their friends.
Literature characterized as "Communistic" was seized. With
a passion for irrelevancy, a grand jury then indicted the
Bradens and three of their friends for advocating sedition.
Another friend of the Wades was indicted for causing the
explosion. The jury's finding was simple. The conflict over
homes in Louisville was not between whites and blacks but
between whites, blacks, and Reds. It was all found to be a
Communist plot. "It is very significant," said the jury know-
ingly, "that the case seems to follow the pattern used by the
Communist party in this country to create trouble between
the respective races . . . and then causing incidents such
as this." [24] In December, Braden was convicted, the jury
recommending a 15-year jail term.

Yet in the face of violence, slurs, and threats, the Negro
continued pushing his way into the cities. He was there to
stay. Racial covenants and mob action made things harder,
but they could not force him back to the cotton and tobacco
fields. He was establishing his new base. He was completing
the migration he had put off while European immigrants had
poured in. It was one of the momentous efforts of a subordinate race to rise to its place in the American sun. If it
was met by resistance, prosecutions, terror, and violence,
and left traumatic marks on the body politic, they were the
price for the gains that were being achieved.

NOTES

1. R. A. Schermerhorn, *These Our People,* Boston, D. C. Heath and Company, 1949, p. 134. From 1930 to 1940, the Negro population of the Southeast and Southwest dropped from 6,395,-000 to 6,289,000, while urban Negro population jumped from 2,966,000 to 3,616,000.

2. Monroe W. Work (ed.), *The Negro Yearbook,* Tuskegee, Alabama, Negro Yearbook Publishing Company, 1931.

3. Gunnar Mydral, *An American Dilemma,* New York, Harper and Brothers, 1944, p. 567.

4. *The Crisis,* Vol. 29, No. 1, November, 1924, p. 20.

5. *Negro Housing,* President's Conference on Home Building and Home Ownership, Vol. VI, Washington, 1932, pp. 46–47.

6. *Ibid.*

7. *The Negro in Chicago,* The Chicago Commission on Race Relations, University of Chicago Press, 1922, p. 122.

8. *The New York Times,* January 15, 1944; New York *Herald Tribune,* January 16 and 18, 1944; New York *World-Telegram,* January 17, 1944.

9. James A. Dombrowski, "The Southern Conference for Human Welfare," *Common Ground,* Summer, 1946, pp. 14–25; also Florence Murray, "The Negro and Civil Liberties During World War II," *Social Forces,* Vol. 24, No. 2, December, 1945, p. 212.

10. *The New York Times,* December 10, 1946.

11. Washington *Times Herald,* March 26, 1949.

12. *The New York Times,* June 1, 1949.

13. *New York Post,* December 14, 1949.

14. *New York Post,* June 10, 1949.

15. New York *Herald Tribune,* August 14, 1949.

16. Atlanta *Constitution,* April 24, 1950.

17. Atlanta *Journal,* December 22, 1950.

18. *New York Post,* May 7, 1951.

19. "Blighted Housing and Bomb Violence," pp. 1–2.

20. Letter from Edward Howden, Executive Director, Council for Civic Unity of San Francisco, August 8, 1952.

21. Houston *Post,* August 31, 1953.

22. *Memorandum on Housing Situation, Lee-Harvard Area,* Confidential Report, The Community Relations Committee, Cleveland, Ohio, July 23, 1953.

23. *Civil Rights in the United States 1953. A Balance Sheet of Group Relations,* New York, American Jewish Congress and the National Association for the Advancement of Colored People, 1954.

24. *The New York Times,* October 10, 1954.

PART

THREE

VIOLENCE
IN THE
SIXTIES

Introduction

Although the forms may have changed, none of the violence discussed in the historical part of this book has ceased. The Indians still have their rights violated, and are poor and hungry. Vigilante groups are prospering, such as Newark's North Ward Citizens Committee. Students, priests, and others burn draft cards and napalm draft records, and sabotage is committed against the military. Racist institutional violence, covert and overt, not unlike slavery for many blacks, still exists. Synagogues are now burned and bombed as Catholic churches were more than a hundred years ago. Poor working conditions, for coal miners and others, are still more often the rule than the exception for both organized and unorganized workers. Anarchists tried to bomb the Statue of Liberty in 1967. Labor violence fluctuates, but most often goes unreported in the mass media. Race rebellions are a common occurrence and homes of blacks are still bombed when they try to live in white neighborhoods. One major difference is that today more domestic violence involves more young people than in the past. The articles in Part Three by Steve Lerner, David Horowitz, and Eldridge Cleaver are accounts written right after or during a violent event, and are often quite different from those written many months or years after the violence.

Part Three treats a brief span of American history— only eight years. It is organized to show the major sources or impulses that create and help to escalate violence. Many overlapping demands now converge in two major foci of revolt, dissent, and protest: race, and the combination of the war in Vietnam (and war generally) and politics. As in Part Two, this section is organized to show the continuity, the escalation of violent control and revolt during the 1960's. There are articles about youth related to violence, the civil rights, civil liberties, and black power movements, protest against the war, rebellions in the cities, violence on campus, hunger, unemployment, poverty, mental illness, sabotage, and Chicago. As in Part Two, we will discuss here a number of important events that cannot be represented by separate essays due to space limitations, and then will introduce the chapters in Part Three.

The press often stops reporting violence when it seems to be unimportant, isolated, or bleeding itself out. As Garver pointed out in Part One, because violence in most sectors of American life has become institutionalized, it has become unnoticeable, woven into everyday life. Violence often gets media attention only when there is a mass support such as Selma, or when someone of fame looks into violence, with the press following. In 1968 a violent strike at the Masonite Corporation in Laurel, Mississippi, drew no national coverage and was only reported by the Southern Conference Educational Fund in their small newspaper, *The Southern Patriot,* in October of that year:

> The company split many of the black workers from the mass of white strikers by a new system of playing one group against the other. Masonite 'Klan-baited' the local by spreading reports that it was run by Ku Klux Klansmen, and other unions gave little support.
>
> After nine months of struggle, which saw five men killed, the international union placed Local 5–443 under trusteeship. The international officers then signed a contract with the company which the strikers called a 'sweetheart deal.' The strikers said they learned that Masonite had threatened the international union with a $3,000,000 suit if it didn't put the local in trusteeship.
>
> Nineteen hundred men were thrown out of work. It looked as if the local was finished, but the strikers pulled themselves together and looked for ways to fight back.

Masonite is the only real industry in Laurel, a small Mississippi town. The workers were denied use of their union hall, and charges have been filed with the National Labor Relations Board. The case is in court, and the men and their families are hungry and cold. The company continues to split black and white workers, while substantial rumors have it that the Defense Department is buying large quantities of Masonite for use in Vietnam.

Violence against migratory workers has continued since they were first imported into California in the mid-nineteenth century. In the past few years violence has flared even more often since Cesar Chavez and his National Farm Workers Association have begun organizing the poorly paid migrants, made up primarily of Mexican-Americans in California, but including many Negro families in states such as Florida and Texas. The grape-growing industry has met the strikers with scabs, and more. In 1966 Andrew Kopkind reported in *The New Republic* that "Some growers went down the margin of their fields with spraying machines, shooting insecticide and fertilizer at the pickets. More commonly, foremen would race along the roadside in tractors, swirling up dust to choke the strikers. Some put farm machinery between the workers and the pickets or followed the pickets with machine motors racketing at full throttle to drown out their calls." All the strikers want is a minimum wage and decent living conditions, and to organize in order to receive benefits such as medical care. Even Robert Kennedy visited Chavez and his men in Delano, but the strike has now been going on for four years and only a few big growers have agreed to organized labor. Others fight it violently. Most businessmen and industrialists, policemen and sheriff's deputies are on the side of the growers; they ignore workers or are quick to clamp down on them.

The *Washington Post* reported on October 11, 1968, that since 1964 the federal government, specifically the Defense Department, has increased its purchase of grapes sixfold, from 113 tons in 1964 to 667 tons in 1968. The television news on Thanksgiving eve, 1968, showed servicemen in Vietnam eating fresh California grapes. As in the past, the government takes sides with the growers. Despite strikes and national boycotts, farm workers remain poor, sick, hungry —their lives tragically violated.

Most Americans didn't even think about the continual

violence directed against those involved in the SNCC sit-ins, CORE Freedom Rides, the grape strikes, nationwide boycotts and sympathy demonstrations, antiwar protest, and demands for university reform. Hundreds of young people were continually attacked and arrested by the police and their deputies long before Watts exploded. Most Americans today have forgotten Martin Luther King's Montgomery bus boycott and his description of "The Violence of Desperate Men" in *Stride Toward Freedom*. One commentator pointed out that "not until Negro demonstrations resulted in violence did the national government begin to work seriously on civil rights legislation." Now that we are nearing the end of another decade, it is too sadly obvious that most of this legislation has not stopped violation of personhood or prevented more overt violence, and not only because it has not been enforced, but because the legislation has not usually gotten to the roots of the problems.

Americans seem to be able to ignore violence and brutality except when some event is extremely massive or symbolic (such as the murder of a President), and then they have an orgy. In a recent book, *Violence: America in the Sixties,* Arthur Schlesinger, Jr., mentions the murders of John and Robert Kennedy and Martin Luther King, but neglects other equally important murders: Bobby Hutton was killed by the Oakland police; Elijah Bennett was murdered for jaywalking in Washington; Schwerner, Chaney, and Goodman were murdered by the police and friends of the police in Mississippi*; Viola Liuzzo and Jonathan Daniels were murdered in Alabama; four little girls died when a Birmingham church was bombed; and Medgar Evers was shot in cold blood.

Schlesinger argues that "obviously most Americans are decent and God-fearing people," insisting that Americans are appalled by murder and violence. He insists that it is only the police who are violent. Although he has a chapter on history and is known as an historian, he neglects even an outline of major violence in American history. He believes that if there were less violence on television, there would be less violence in reality, unlike Bruno Bettelheim,

* See William Bradford Huie, *Three Lives for Mississippi*, New York, Trident Press, 1965.

who insists that the amount of violence shouldn't be our major concern, but rather we should try to understand that violence and learn to cope with it. Schlesinger argues that America is a civil and responsible society, and that we must be collectively responsible but not collectively guilty.

It is difficult to focus on the civility he is referring to, unless he means talk about law and order. And how can a nation, a people, have collective responsibility without also assuming collective guilt? What Schlesinger fails to understand is that it is the respectable citizens who allow and encourage brutality, murder, and violence. Violence is most obvious in a policeman's club, which Schlesinger recognizes, but he fails to see institutional violence that operates quietly and systematically every day. Murder and bombings are only part of the experiences shared by civil rights workers; even more important are the hunger, poverty, brutality, and cruelty that the poor must suffer daily in both the North and South. Professor Schlesinger neglects all this. The United States Commission on Civil Rights said in its 1965 report:

> During 1963 and 1964 substantial racial violence occurred in . . . Mississippi. The local authorities—sheriffs and police —were ineffective in controlling this violence or apprehending the persons responsible. The testimony of these officials at the Commission's hearings and the records which they produced in response to subpoena disclosed investigations that ranged from nonexistent to perfunctory. Records and testimony also indicate that in some instances officials treated civil rights workers not as victims but as suspects. Hostility to Negroes was also demonstrated by harassing arrests of civil rights workers engaged in lawful activities, and by law enforcement officials' publicized membership in organizations committed to white supremacy and the preservation of segregation.

Little wonder that civil rights workers no longer believe in nonviolence.

In the North violence has been less overt, less publicized, but equally institutionalized: until 1965 white colleges asked all applicants for information on race and for photographs; in 1968 both black men and black women made about fifty percent less than their white peers; and today the real rate of unemployment and underemployment of black people runs from twenty-five to seventy-five percent in most large cities and in many rural areas. Michael Harrington and Gabriel Kolko document these figures, and others, in their respective books, *The Other America* and *Wealth and Power in America*. Ralph Nader, writing in *The New York Review of Books*,* points out:

> The current assault on the health and safety of the public from so many dangerous industrial products, by-products, and goods has resulted in violence that dwarfs the issue of crime in the streets. (During the last three years, about 260 people have died in riots in American cities; but every two days, 300 people are killed and 20,000 injured while driving on the highways.) What the consumer movement is beginning to say—and must say much more strongly if it is to grow—is that business crime and corporate intransigence are the really urgent menace to law and order in America.

Three major reports were issued in 1968 about hunger in America, and a major television program was devoted to hunger. The House Committee on Agriculture was so outraged by the reports and programs that it issued two reports saying that hunger is not an issue in America except in a few small areas. Denying institutionalized hunger, they claimed that so much food is distributed free that hunger, starvation, and suffering just don't exist—and where hunger is located, it can be cured by education. The other three reports involved careful documentation by medical doctors and skilled investigators. The most important, *Hunger U.S.A.*, is now available in a Beacon paperback. The introductory comment in that book by Robert F. Kennedy is a good summary:

> Last week, the Citizens Board of Inquiry—a distinguished group of private citizens—released their findings on the scope of hunger and malnutrition in the U.S. They found across this country what some public officials suspected, but which too many ignored or denied: that in the wealthiest nation in the history of the world, millions of men, women and children are slowly starving.

* November 21, 1968.

They found that American babies die in infancy, because their mothers cannot nurse them, and cannot buy the milk to keep them alive.

They found that thousands of American children are anemic and listless, their physical growth stunted because they lack adequate protein.

They found that scurvy and rickets, surely diseases of an alien past, cripple American children who never drink citrus juice, and who rarely drink milk.

They found that American children in large numbers suffer from hookworms and roundworms, parasitic infections that drain what strength these children have.

They found that hundreds of thousands of school children cannot learn their lessons, because they go to school without breakfast, have no money for lunch, and return to a supper without meat or green vegetable.

And they found that countless old people in America exist almost entirely on liquids, because they cannot buy or find a decent meal.

Like other forms of violence, hunger cannot be dealt with until Americans understand to what extent it exists, and what may be institutionally done about it. Hunger will not go away with Christmas baskets.

The Christian Science Monitor reported in June, 1968, that violence dominates prime television time. The number of murders and killings each hour on television is phenomenal, and most occur during hours when children are watching. The television industry doesn't know what to substitute for violence. Stanley Kauffman comments that "metaphorical murder in the Madison Avenue meeting-room and the stomping in a deserted park are both as American as cherry pie. The acceptance of disguised brutalities has helped the acceptance of overt violence—homicidal violence—as an ingrained part of American life. Not all of us would use such violence but not many of us are really shocked by it any more." *Violence has been normalized:* we should not be surprised that it appears so often on television, and in all the media, including films and books.

A review of *In Cold Blood* and *Bonnie and Clyde* by Frank Conroy, in *The New York Review of Books,** in-

* July 11, 1968.

dicates that violence has become more important than sex in movies and books.

> *Bonnie and Clyde* is an action picture about criminals, a hip variation of an old form in which violence has a specific symbolic meaning—the irreversible separation of the criminal from society, and his special morality. . . . violence is paced with the meticulousness one usually associates with music, and relates throughout to other themes in the movie—escape, speed, innocence, ignorance, loneliness. Moreover, the violence is not, however much there is of it, an end in itself but is put to use to dramatize the helplessness of a pair of weak young people rushing toward an early death. It is not, therefore, salacious. However shocking the famous scene in which Bonnie and Clyde are machine-gunned to death may be, it is certainly not gratuitous. Indeed, the excessive violence of their deaths is entirely appropriate literally and symbolically: the police hysterically keep shooting, because they are attempting to destroy a myth, while the audience witnesses some artful images (the pear exploding in the air, the dead bodies, animated by the force of the impacting bullets) which convincingly reinforce our sense of morality and of the fragility of the pair. Death simply *arrives,* with more strength than anyone can imagine, and the corpses jump like puppets.

An article in *Trans-Action* in January, 1969, reports on violence to the human body that is mortifyingly brutal. Not only are prisoners used by other prisoners for sexual gratification, but a large drug firm operates a laboratory in the Holmsburg Prison in Philadelphia in which prisoners are used as human guinea pigs. Often the pay for these services, high for prison work, is used to buy homosexual partnership. Many people believe that law and order (justice is not needed for people in prison) come naturally in a prison, because it is a total institution. Prisons do protect us from so-called criminals who are caught, but the violence and mental torture they suffer in prison will be reflected once they are free.

The *Trans-Action* article by Alan J. Davis found that "sexual assaults in the Philadelphia prison system are epidemic. . . ." And he has no reason to believe that Philadelphia prisons are atypical. Homosexual rape is common; the least hardened criminals suffer the most. In the same article, the following excerpt by a prisoner describes an incident that took place in the prison, but similar assaults take place each day in sheriffs' vans taking prisoners from one prison to another and to court.

He went over and was talking to this kid and slapped him in the face with a belt. He was saying come on back with us and the kid kept saying I don't want to. After being slapped with the belt he walked back with Cheyenne and another colored fellow named Horse. They were walking him back into E Dorm. They were telling him to put his hand down and stop crying so the guard will not know what is going on. I looked up a couple of times. They had the kid on the floor. About 12 fellows took turns with him. This went on for two hours.

After this he came back to his bed and he was crying and he stated that 'they all took turns on me.' He laid there for about 20 minutes and Cheyenne came over to the kid's bed and pulled his pants down and got on top of him and raped him again. When he got done Horse did it again and then about four or five others got on him. While one of the guys was on him, raping him, Horse came over and said, 'Open your mouth and suck on this and don't bite it." He then put his penis in his mouth and made him suck on it. The kid was hollering that he was gagging and Horse stated, 'you better not bite on it or I will kick your teeth out . . .'

This could quite easily happen to a relative or friend, and will until these and other forms of prison violence are ended and prisons are made fit for human habitation. Another report indicates other ramifications of imprisonment: beatings, lashings, bludgeonings, murders, slave labor, degradation, inadequate housing and dining and medical facilities, isolation, filthy living conditions, spoiled food, and long hours of unendurable work without any rehabilitation. This investigation by the Southern Regional Council in 1968 found electrical torture machines in frequent use and bodies of prisoners in unmarked graves. The report concludes:

The most indifferent researcher could fill volumes with reports of individual atrocities, and they would amount to a terrifying condemnation, indeed. . . . But no legislative or executive fiat could effectively end this inhumanity because it is inherent in the system. Self-supporting prison systems must, in the end, become slave camps. Slavery is the partner of the lash. The wielder of the lash is brutalized along with the victim, and brutes will sometimes kill.

Another expert on prisons comments: "Maybe we should be honest with ourselves; if what we want is vengeance, we've got pretty good models going right now. If we want to make streets and our property safer, we had better redefine what those places with their walls and guns are required to do." Prison is terrible enough in itself. Extra savagery is not needed.

Many Americans have found that burning draft cards and other unique forms of communication are necessary to make clear their opposition to the war in Vietnam, and the reaction to them is almost always covert or overt violence. Not only are they subject to prison, but their sentences are sometimes vindictive, and this knowledge creates an atmosphere of fear to express what one really believes. Many men who oppose the war are silent, and their silence is immoral, a disservice to their nation and to themselves. Some of the most violent men sit in judgment of war resisters and dissenters within the armed services. They deal out sentences that include four years and a dishonorable discharge; two years at hard labor; three years at hard labor plus a dishonorable discharge. In the last case the jury panel deliberated ten minutes and passed sentence.

One of the most well-known cases was the trial of Captain Levy, a military doctor who refused to train Special Forces medical aidmen going to Vietnam, because he believed the war to be wrong, illegal, immoral. He was sentenced to three years of hard labor at Leavenworth, Kansas, for refusing to train those medics and for inspiring "disaffection" among enlisted men. He commented that "The whole point, of course, is castration—to rob soldiers and prisoners of their manhood and their identity, their pride. Sex deprivation in prisons is the most blatant tactic for that, and if they can take away your manhood, they can do anything with you they want." This process involves short haircuts; prison uniform; scrutinized reading material; only five correspondents and visitors; censored letters; censored subscriptions to magazines; lights on when you want to sleep. We must wonder how many lives are ruined, crushed, because of a steady diet of violence in prisons.

Most outrage about violence is after the fact, and the so-called respectable leaders who cry out often find little support among the mass of the people, who for many reasons are pleased by violence as long as it does not touch their lives. American history is filled with the reports of commissions that looked into violence. The commissioners themselves are becoming much more conservative, according to Allan Silver, who compares the Kerner Commission in 1967 with the Commission on Industrial Relations in 1915. He begins his essay in *Urban Riots: Violence and Social Change* with an excerpt from the Kerner Commission report:

> "Those few who would destroy civil order and the rule of law strike at the freedom of every citizen. They must know that the community cannot and will not tolerate coercion and mob action." It is instructive to contrast this statement with the majority report in . . . 1915, which was largely carried by labor union representatives: "Through history where a people or group have been arbitrarily denied rights which they conceived to be theirs, reaction has been inevitable. Violence is a natural form of protest against injustice."

The kind of personal and public lives that commissioners lead will always be an indication of the kind of report they issue. Thus it is not difficult to predict that President Johnson's Violence Commission will produce a very, very conservative report, and that it will be severely criticized by Harvard sociologist Gary Marx. The latter, in a speech before the American Political Science Association in 1968, criticized the report made by the Kerner Commission for its "failure to deal with variation in types of disorders, to catch the sense in which a riot is an emergent process, and to refine and document the importance of current racism, as well as its failure to systematically relate types and levels of causality." I would add that the Kerner Commission failed to suggest significant specific remunerative proposals, but that didn't seem to matter in the end, because the President refused to endorse its report. Marx also mentioned "the report's omission of almost any mention of the Vietnamese war and the general connection between war and civil disorder." He believes this is important because

> Wars abroad have been strongly related to violent internal conflicts at home. More than two-thirds of all race riots in the fifty-year period from 1913 to 1963 occurred during (or immediately before or after) war periods. Or put another way, approximately three-quarters of the race riots occurred in one-quarter of the years devoted to wars.

In northern New Mexico most people avoid strangers, keep guns and dogs at their bedsides, and are generally fearful. This is that part of America where between 1880 and the 1930's Spanish-Americans lost nearly six million acres of land; that injustice led to a depressed region filled with hunger, unemployment, and disease that still exists. Because of this constant violent oppression, the old Mexican land war is being renewed. Clark Knowlton points out that there is a recurrent cycle*:

> The fires of discontent have always burned in the northern mountains. The anger flares up in an epidemic of fence cutting, barn and ranch-house burnings, and warnings to the Anglo-American ranchers and politicians to vacate Spanish-American lands. Cries for law and order bring out troops and the National Guard. Numerous Spanish-Americans are repressed, their leaders are exiled, assassinated or imprisoned. The flames die down and the Anglo-Americans forget. However, the names and exploits of past Spanish-American leaders are kept alive in the stories and chronicles told and sung in the village bars. A new Spanish-American generation appears: new causes of protest arise; new protest organizations develop. The cycle starts all over again.

Today the protest is led by Reies Lopez Tijerina, who is head of an organization called the Alliance of Free City States (the Alianza). As Knowlton reports, their message is simple:

* "The New Mexican Land War," *The Nation*, June 17, 1968.

You have been robbed of your lands, your water rights, your grazing rights, your language and your culture by the Anglo-Americans. No one is interested in helping you. Join us. Together, we will get the land back—preferably through the courts or Congress, but one way or another we will get it back.

It is not untraditional that the state of New Mexico has reacted with violence and repression, but Knowlton points out that in order for this to end, "New Mexico must experience a serious outbreak of rural and urban terror before the authorities learn that repression and jailing are not the answer to Spanish-American problems." He is rightfully angry at the wholesale violation of human and civil rights that the American government does nothing to protect. Alianza members are trying all kinds of tactics to get their land back. So are American Indians in growing numbers. Knowlton points out that unless human and civil rights are restored, guerrilla warfare is very possible. And not only in New Mexico!

Twenty thousand Americans are killed every year by guns; since 1900 more than 800,000 Americans have been killed by firearms, but only 600,000 Americans have died in all our wars from the Revolution to Asia. *The Nation* reports* that the number of guns purchased in the months King and Robert Kennedy were assassinated doubled from the previous year in that month. They estimate that in California alone there are more than 20,000,000 guns, or one for every resident. "In the period from 1963 to 1967, the annual sale of rifles increased from 875,000 to 1,882,000; shotgun sales from 603,000 to 1,515,000; handgun sales from 596,000, to 1,182,000." *The Nation* believes there are three kinds of arms buyers: private citizens, the police, and paramilitary or vigilante organizations. "What the reports of the new private arms race indicate is that, as a people, we are obsessed not so much with violence, as with security. And we seem to believe that security can be bought." The editors of *The Nation* continue:

We exhibit the same obsession with security in our foreign policy. We are a nation armed to the teeth—not because we

* December 2, 1968.

have a lust for violence but because we believe that a fantastic overkill capability will protect us from violence. The danger in all this is that an obsession with security can and does set the stage for violence, because it derives from fear and stimulates fear in others.

Writing in *The New Republic* in 1966 about Charles Whitman, the student who stood on top of a tower at the University of Texas and shot sixteen of his classmates, Robert Coles insists:

> We were once again proven a savage, uncontrollable, unpredictable, gun-ridden and murderous people, with our pilots showering upon Asians the same brutal iron a Texas youth blasted down on his classmates in Austin.
> We cannot prevent insanity in adults or violence and delinquent urges in many children by curbing guns, but we can certainly make the translation of crazy or vicious impulses into pulled triggers less likely and less possible. It is as simple as that, though many politicians refuse out of fear to let it be as simple as that.

In 1969 America is finding it easier to substitute instant and long-term technological violence for power because of the revolution in the development of weaponry for the suppression of international and domestic conflict. New forms of technological violence are substituted for power by the military, the police, and a growing number of citizens.

Federal Laboratories manufactures a gas they call CS, which "causes intense irritation of all moist skin areas, a burning sensation, and severe chest pain," and is especially dangerous to people with heart trouble, lung disorders, and emphysema. Furthermore, according to the *Hartford* (Connecticut) *Courier,** the company has sold large amounts of CS gas grenades to the city of Hartford, and most probably to other cities. *CBW: Chemical and Biological Warfare,* a recent book edited by Steven Rose, a biochemist, warns that there is a new emphasis, world-wide, being placed on chemical and biological weapons despite the lack of information

* November 23, 1968.

about their long- and short-term effects on people and their environments.

Much of the violence discussed in Part Three involves young people demanding change. Almost every nonviolent protest was counteracted with violence. In light of these facts, it should not be surprising that in the early 1960's the desire for a kind of "pure" nonviolence, based on Jesus, King, Thoreau, and Gandhi, did not significantly create change and end terrible injustices that were and still are often violent. Although black people can now buy a cup of coffee almost anywhere, they are still poor and hungry, and black infants have a much higher infant mortality rate than whites.

Students began to understand that their nonviolent protest did not create institutional changes. Nonviolence began to wane as a way of creating protest and change. The creation of the Black Panther party in Alabama to run candidates in the 1964 election was an indication of the need for political power. By 1965, after the constant violence of the Mississippi Summer Project, and after the Meredith march in Mississippi during which Stokely Carmichael coined the term black power, it was obvious that civil rights and civil liberties groups were moving from protest to resistance, what Staughton Lynd calls nonviolent obstructive civil disobedience. Keniston, Lynd, and Cleaver deal with this change in their respective articles.

Young people, and many others, began to clearly perceive a growing violence in the world around them, especially in the response of police and troops in the ghetto and in Vietnam. But many understood that it was not only the police who were brutes, as Newton Garver pointed out. In 1964 Paul Jacobs wrote in *Dissent:* "Those who participate in such ugly physical violence are not the only brutes. Violent redneck resistance to civil rights for Negroes is one mark of the brute; the polite businessmen who sneer at the suggestion that they should contribute a tiny percentage of their profits to help the poor are brutes too, dressed up in dinner jackets."

Part Three begins with a short discussion by Kenneth

Keniston, written in 1968, but also meaningful to those who are now nearly thirty and who were activists in civil rights and peace activities in the early sixties. (How sad that most of them have retired from action politics.) Keniston teaches in the department of psychiatry at the Yale Medical School and has published two important books on youth, *The Uncommitted* and *Young Radicals: Notes on Committed Youth.*

"Violence: Sadism and Cataclysm" is taken from an article in *The American Scholar,* based on the latter book. Keniston explains that young radicals are able to understand and confront violence, in large part because they have grown up in a violent world. What is often obscured and overlooked by those who write about young blacks in the early sixties is the fact that most of them, from the day of conception, have lived in a society saturated with violence, poverty, bad schools, little shelter, hunger, and unemployment. A series of articles by Robert Coles near the end of Part Three will deal with some of these forms of violence.

Staughton Lynd, radical scholar, political activist, former Yale professor, and co-director of the Mississippi Summer Project in 1964, is the author of many books, including *Class Conflict* and *Slavery and the U.S. Constitution.* He is also the co-author of *The Other Side,* written with Tom Hayden about their travels to North Vietnam. In the following article, "A Radical Speaks in Defense of SNCC," Lynd traces critical changes in SNCC and the movement, and why they occurred. He differentiates between riot, rebellion, and the right of revolution by discussing remarks by Stokely Carmichael and H. Rap Brown, explaining changes in SNCC from 1962 to 1967, when he wrote the article. Lynd explains why the Mississippi Project was an important turning point, by bringing out the point of view of Bob Moses, who relates the similarities of violent policies in America and in Vietnam.

Eldridge Cleaver wrote "Requiem for Nonviolence" just after Martin Luther King's murder in Memphis. Cleaver, who spent many years in prison, ran for President of the United States on the Peace and Freedom ticket in 1968. He is, in exile, minister of information for the Black Panther party, and author of the best seller, *Soul on Ice.* He explains, very succinctly, why nonviolence is no longer meaningful.

The year 1960 was not only the beginning of the Southern student movement. The 1950's are often referred to as the silent fifties, but it was the fifties that gave rise to students at San Francisco State and Berkeley who were moving into the forefront of politics and social action in 1960. Students around the nation were supporting the student movement in the South with "boycott Woolworth" picket lines. In the San Francisco Bay area there were protests against the brutality of capital punishment; at Berkeley, against mandatory ROTC training; but the major event occurred near the end of the spring term in 1960, when nonviolent protest against the witch-hunting of HUAC hearings at the San Francisco City Hall was met with massive police brutality and violence.

David Horowitz and Fred Haines wrote about Black Friday. Their selection is from Horowitz's book, *Student*, published in 1962. Haines is a reporter and commentator for the listener-supported Pacifica Foundation radio stations in Berkeley, Los Angeles, and New York City. At the time of Black Friday, Horowitz was a teaching assistant and militant student leader at Berkeley. Since leaving Berkeley, he has worked for Bertrand Russell in London, has written about foreign policy and the cold war, was the editor of *Containment and Revolution* and the author of *Free World Colossus*, and is now on the staff of *Ramparts*. "Black Friday" is a description of what happened on one day at the San Francisco City Hall when, as Malvina Reynolds wrote in her folk song, "they washed them down the city hall rotunda." The stupid remarks made by the FBI and HUAC, trying to show the public that the demonstration was inspired by Communists, helped make the student movement grow, and nonviolent demonstrations around the nation evolved from Black Friday.

Since the first sit-in and Black Friday, there have been hundreds of demonstrations and political actions around the nation in the 1960's. We can only consider a few here. One of the most violent was a national protest involving more than 100,000 people who came to the Pentagon on Saturday, October 21, 1967, to protest the war in Vietnam. Nonviolent protesters were met with violence, intimidation, and repression by more than 2,000 troops and 400 U.S. marshals.

There was severe dishonesty on the part of the media in failing to report great amounts of violence and brutality directed against the nonviolent protesters. The *Washington Post* called the protest ugly, but said, "It is doubtful whether yesterday's protesters could account for more than a few small niches on a Gallup or Harris poll." Like many others, the *Post* missed the point and the action. The Committee of the Professions published an advertisement in *The New York Times* a month later* that conveyed the real horror and meaning of the demonstration against the war: the rule rather than the exception seemed to be, meet demonstrations with all the power and violence that the police and the military can muster with the flowing support of the state and the people. Of course this violent policy of suppression and control only warned those who disagreed with the war and other American policies to "be ready" next time. After the Pentagon, the movement had no choice but to move from protest to resistance and confrontation politics.

In 1967 and 1968 many university students began expressing their anger with the closed corporations the universities had become.† Students didn't like the fused relationships between those institutions and big business, the government, and the military. They were also angry about the lack of relevant courses and the general meaninglessness of college life; and black students, especially in predominantly white colleges, were protesting the lack of courses which dealt with black history and culture.

That there are students demanding change, even revolution, is not a new phenomenon in America, or in the world, as Mervin B. Freedman points out in his article about San Francisco State College.‡ Freedman is a professor of psy-

---

* December 3, 1967.

† See James Ridgeway, *The Closed Corporation: American Universities in Crisis*, New York, Random House, Inc., 1968.

‡ Readers interested in comparing the San Francisco State scene with Columbia University will want to look at the *Report of the Cox Commission*, New York, Vintage Books, 1968; and Jerry L. Avorn, Robert Friedman, and members of the *Columbia Daily Spectator* staff, *Up Against the Ivy Wall: A History of the Columbia Crisis*, New York, Atheneum Publishers, 1968.

chology and former chairman of that department at San Francisco State. He wrote "Urban Campus Prototype" before the teachers union went on strike, and it was originally published in *The Nation*.* Freedman was holding his classes off-campus, as were many teachers at State, when his article was published, but he was not an active participant in the picket lines. He has written before about students, including *The College Experience,* published in 1967.

There is great parallel between student rebellion and big-city revolts. Both groups are demanding participation in decisions that affect their lives, and both are deeply concerned about their civil rights and liberties. Simply put, many students and many blacks want to control their own lives. On the other hand, most blacks in ghettos and most college students are afraid to participate, afraid to get involved, afraid that their already shaky existence will topple. Bennett Kremen wrote in *The Nation*† about a bus ride in Harlem as a rebellion was starting:

> The man leaped through the door and called out: "Get her out of here; they're flingin' bottles at the cops." The driver threw a wild left turn, racing the bus three blocks off course.
> "Ladies and gentlemen," he announced. "This is no longer the Lenox Number Three—the scenic route." No one smiled until faces loosened with relief as the flashing red lights quickly receded behind us. And again, by seeing this with my own eyes and not relying on the inadvertent distortions of the media, I was enlightened. For I realized that the mayhem that goes on in the ghettos is what gets glaringly dramatized, while the feelings and actions of most Negroes, like those that surrounded me on the bus, are often ignored —not by design, perhaps, but because of limitation of time on television and of space in the papers. Thus the image of the crazed black man, heedless of death and with murder in his heart, gets priority on television screens and feeds already believing minds of white America.

Ever since Watts, many black people have found a kind of instant politics in riots and rebellion, but it is clear that the cause of the riots is institutional racism and all that this

* January, 1969.
† April 22, 1968.

involves. Most of what has been written about these rebellions has been, at best, inaccurate, and for the most part, blatantly dishonest and untrue. There are some exceptions: books by Tom Hayden and Robert Conot, and articles by Kenneth Clark, Tommy Tomlinson, and J. H. O'Dell.

O'Dell's article, "The July Rebellions and the 'Military State,'" is reprinted here from *Freedomways*,* a quarterly review of the Negro freedom movement. Mr. O'Dell has been associate managing editor of *Freedomways* for five years and was formerly director of Voter Registration and Political Education for the late Dr. Martin Luther King's Southern Christian Leadership Conference. He has also lectured on Afro-American history on CBS television. O'Dell first places big-city rebellions in historical perspective, and secondly, discusses the meaning of racism and its relationship to those rebellions. He then looks at poor blacks and the Vietnam war. He sees war being waged against the domestic colonies black people live in, describes how the larger society maintains those colonies, and how those in the colonies must act if they wish to become free men.

As violence committed by the state against the people grows, the people search past nonviolence and resistance, toward sabotage. The Catonsville Nine, a group of priests and Catholic laymen, destroyed draft records in Maryland, and a similar group did the same in Milwaukee. Andrew Kopkind, a former reporter for *Time* and *The New Republic*, at present a regular contributor to *The New York Review of Books* and the *New Statesman,* and an editor of *Hard Times* (formerly *Mayday*), reports on sabotage across the land as a reaction to a government that is unable to understand violence at home and in Asia. Kopkind points out that sabotage, rather than guns or nonviolence, seems to be the only form of communication when all else has failed.

Robert Coles writes about violence (during the last four years) that is covert and institutionalized, yet frequently avoided, often because it is too cruel and brutal to face. There are selections from four articles that deal with the

---

* Fourth Quarter, 1967.

violence inherent in welfare, poverty, unemployment, migratory work, and mental hospitals. More than a third of the nation is poor, but what is most important is that the policies of big business and government keep people poor. Coles is concerned with both poor individuals and the violent institutionalization of poverty. He is a research psychiatrist at Harvard, an expert on mental and physical problems of children, contributing editor to *The New Republic,* a civil rights worker, and a prolific writer of many articles and a brilliant book, *Children of Crisis: A Study of Courage and Fear.*

An article in *The New York Times* on September 15, 1968, was headlined, "Pentagon Gaining a Key Role on Domestic Violence." The troops sent to Chicago were trained by the Pentagon, which has a large center for the study and control of big-city riots. The Pentagon claims they will only move in when local and state law-enforcement agencies are "unable to control." Nothing is mentioned about protection. The Pentagon is now training police. Former Attorney-General Ramsey Clark commented that "of all violence, police violence in excess of authority is the most dangerous. For who will protect the public when the police violate the law?" He made that speech in September of 1968, and three months later the Walker Report, published for the National Commission on the Causes and Prevention of Violence, claimed that Chicago police rioted.

Chicago and the Democratic convention have already disappeared from the minds of too many Americans despite the Walker Report and the hundreds of articles written about that event, often described as the beginning of a police state. Right after the convention Arthur Miller wrote in *The New York Times Magazine*:

> Had there never been a riot on Michigan Avenue the meeting in the amphitheater would still have been the closest thing to a session of the All-Union Soviet that ever took place outside of Russia. And it was not merely the heavy-handed discipline imposed from above but the passionate consent from below that makes the comparison apt.

The first article about Chicago is by Steve Lerner, who writes an excellent narrative of the events during the Democratic convention in 1968. Lerner is a reporter for *The Village Voice,* which originally published his account. One of the major organizers of the confrontation in Chicago was Tom Hayden, former president of Students for a Democratic Society, organizer in the slums of Newark, and author of the best book on big-city rebellions, *Rebellion in Newark: Official Violence and Ghetto Response.* The final article in Part Three, and the second about Chicago, is a review by Tom Hayden of the events in Chicago and a critique of the Walker Report.

All of the articles in Part Three continually mention violence and brutality committed by the police, but as Monsignor Paul Hanley Furfey argues in *The Respectable Murders:*

> It is an infinitely tragic fact that the greatest crimes in history are committed with the cooperation or at least with the passive consent of the solid citizens who constitute the stable backbone of the community. . . . the great evils, the persecutions, the unjust wars of conquest, the mass slaughters of the innocent, the exploitations of whole social classes—these crimes are committed by the organized community under the leadership of respectable citizens.

Respectable citizens most often speak out after the fact; yet even more tragic, murder, unsafe working conditions, brutality, cruelty, and poverty quickly recede from our minds. Speaking out after the fact becomes violence, too.

VIOLENCE: SADISM AND CATACLYSM

By KENNETH KENISTON

Those who are today in their early twenties were born near the end of World War II, the most violent and barbarous war in world history. The lasting imprint of that war can be summarized in the names of three towns: Auschwitz, Hiroshima and Nuremberg. *Auschwitz* points to the possibility of a "civilized" nation embarking on a systematized, well-organized and scientific plan of exterminating an entire people. *Hiroshima* demonstrates how "clean," easy and impersonal cataclysm could be to those who perpetrate it, and how demonic, sadistic and brutal to those who experience it. And *Nuremberg* summarizes the principle that men have an accountability above obedience to national policy, a responsibility to conscience more primary even than fidelity to national law. These three lessons are the matrix for the growth of post-modern youth.

The terror of violence that has hung over all men and women since the Second World War has especially shaped the outlooks of today's youth. In the first memories of a group of young radicals, for example, one finds the following recollections: a dim recall of the end of World War II; childhood terror of the atomic bomb; witnessing the aftermath of a violent riot in the United States; being frightened by a picture of a tank riding over rubble; being violently jealous at the birth of a younger brother; taking part in "gruesome" fights in the schoolyard. Such memories mean many things, but in them, violence-in-the-world finds echo and counterpart in the violence of inner feelings. The term "violence" suggests both of these possibilities: the *psychological* violence of sadism, exploitation and aggression, and the *historical* violence of war, cataclysm and holocaust. In the lives of most of this generation, the threats of inner and outer violence are fused, each activating, exciting and potentiating the other. To summarize a complex thesis into a few words: *the issue of violence is to this generation what the issue of sex was to the Victorian world.*

Stated differently, what is most deeply repressed, rejected, feared, controlled and projected onto others by the post-modern generation is no longer their own sexuality. Sex, for most of this generation, is much freer, more open, less guilt- and anxiety-ridden. But violence, whether in one's self or in others, has assumed new prominence as the prime source of inner and outer terror. That this should be so in the modern world is readily understandable. Over all of us hangs the continual threat of a technological violence more meaningless, absurd, total and unpremeditated than any ever imagined before. Individual life always resonates with historical change; history is not merely the backdrop for development, but its ground. To be grounded in the history of the past two decades is to have stood upon, to have experienced both directly and vicariously, violent upheaval, violent world-wide revolution, and the unrelenting possibility of world-wide destruction. To have been alive and aware in America during the past decade has been to be exposed to the assassination of a President and the televised murder of his murderer, to the well-publicized slaughter of Americans by their fellow countrymen, and to the recent violence in our cities. To have been a middle-class child in the past two decades is to have watched daily the violence of television, both as it reports the bloodshed and turmoil of the American and non-American world, and as it skillfully elaborates and externalizes in repetitive dramas the potential for violence within each of us.

It therefore requires no assumption of an increase in biological aggression to account for the salience of the issue of violence for post-modern youth. The capacity for rage, spite and aggression is part of our endowment as human beings: it is a constant potential of human nature. But during the past two decades—indeed, starting before the Second World War—we have witnessed violence and imagined violence on a scale more frightening than ever before. Like the angry child who fears that his rage will itself destroy those around him, we have become vastly more sensitive to and fearful of our inner angers, for we live in a world where even the mildest irritation, multiplied a billionfold by modern technology, might destroy all civilization. The fact of violent upheaval and the possibility of cataclysm has been literally brought into our living rooms during the past twenty years: it has been interwoven with the development of a whole generation.

It should not surprise us, then, that the issue of violence is a focal concern for those of contemporary youth with the greatest historical consciousness. The hippie slogan "Make love, not war" expresses their sentiment, albeit in a form that the "realist" of previous generations might deem sentimental or romantic. Although few young radicals would agree with the wording of this statement, the underlying sentiment corresponds to their basic psychological orientation. For them, as for many others of their generation, the primary task is to develop new psychological, political and international controls on violence. Indeed, many of the dilemmas of today's young radicals seem related to extraordinarily zealous efforts to avoid any action or relationship in which inner or outer violence might be evoked. Distaste for violence animates the profound revulsion many of today's youth feel toward the war in Southeast Asia, just as it underlies a similar revulsion against the exploitation or control of man by man. The same psychological nonviolence is related to young radicals' avoidance of traditional leadership lest it lead to domination, to their emphasis on person-to-person participation and "confrontation," and even to their unwillingness to "play the media" in an attempt to gain political effectiveness. Even the search for forms of mass political action that avoid physical violence—a preference severely tested and somewhat undermined by the events of recent months—points to a considerable distaste for the direct expression of aggression.

I do not mean to suggest that post-modern youth contains a disproportionate number of tight-lipped pacifists or rage-filled deniers of their own inner angers. On the contrary, among today's youth, exuberance, passionateness and zest are the rule rather than the exception. Nor are hippies and young radicals incapable of anger, rage and resentment— especially when their principles are violated. But for many of these young men and women, the experiences of early life and the experience of the postwar world are joined in a special sensitivity to the issue of violence, whether in themselves or in others. This confluence of psychological and historical forces helps explain the intensity of their search for new forms of social organization and political action that avoid manipulation, domination and control, just as it contributes to their widespread opposition to warfare of all kinds.

Yet the position of psychologically nonviolent youth in a violent world is difficult and paradoxical. On the one hand, he seeks to minimize violence, but on the other, his efforts often elicit violence from others. At the same time that he attempts to work to actualize his vision of a peaceful world, he must confront more directly and continually than do his peers the fact that the world is neither peaceful nor just. The frustration and discouragement of his work repetitively reawaken his anger, which must forever be rechanneled into peaceful paths. Since he continually confronts destructiveness and exploitation in the world, his own inevitable potential for destructiveness and exploitiveness inevitably arouses in him great guilt. The young men and women who make up the New Left in America, like other post-modern youth, have far less difficulty in living with their sexual natures than did their parents; but what they continue to find difficult to live with, what they still repress, avoid and counteract is their own potential for violence. It remains to be seen whether, in the movement toward "resistance" and disruption of today's young radicals, their psychological nonviolence will continue to be reflected in their actions.

In pointing to the psychological dimension of the issue of violence, I do not mean to attribute causal primacy either to the experiences of early life or to their residues in adulthood. My thesis is rather that for those of this generation with the greatest historical awareness, the psychological and historical possibility of violence have come to potentiate each other. To repeat: witnessing the acting out of violence on a scale more gigantic than ever before, or imaginatively participating in the possibility of world-wide holocaust activates the fear of one's own violence; heightened awareness of one's inner potential for rage, anger or destructiveness increases sensitivity to the possibility of violence in the world.

This same process of historical potentiation of inner violence has occurred, I believe, throughout the modern world, and brings with it not only the intensified efforts to curb violence we see in this small segment of post-modern youth, but other more frightening possibilities. Post-modern youth, to an unusual degree, remain open to and aware of their own angers and aggressions, and this awareness creates in them a sufficient understanding of inner violence to enable them to control it in themselves and oppose it in others. Most men and women, young or old, possess less insight: their inner sadism is projected onto others, whom they thereafter loathe or abjectly serve; or, more disastrously, historically heightened inner violence is translated into outer aggression and murderousness, sanctioned by self-righteousness.

Thus, if the issue of violence plagues post-modern youth, it is not because these young men and women are more deeply rage-filled than most. On the contrary, it is because such young men and women have confronted this issue more squarely in themselves and in the world than have any but a handful of their fellows. If they have not yet found solutions, they have at least faced an issue so dangerous that most of us find it too painful even to acknowledge, and they have done so, most remarkably, without identifying with what they oppose. Their still-incomplete lives pose for us all the question on which our survival as individuals and as a world depends: Can we create formulations and forms to control historical and psychological violence before their fusion destroys us all?

A RADICAL SPEAKS IN DEFENSE OF SNCC

By STAUGHTON LYND

In the eyes of spokesmen for the *ancien régime,* the emergent revolutionary reordering of society appears as chaos. "The Old Left," said *Time* magazine, April 28 [1967] "had a program for the future; the New Left's program is mostly a cry of rage. . . . They have no program and they do not want one." Similarly the recent disturbances in Newark and Detroit seemed to most Americans chaotic happenings appropriately characterized by adjectives such as "irrational," "senseless," "indiscriminate." The rioters themselves were perceived as a faceless mask. Their program was assumed to be nonexistent.

A principal reason why American society is cracking into a house divided is the inability of those who govern it to deal with the political philosophy implicit in the actions of insurgent Americans. Their domestic blindness is also their blindness toward the world at large: they assume that only a society based on private property can be free, that orderly government requires a system of representation, that it is commonsensically obvious for speech to be free but action limited by the will of the majority. When populations in and out of the United States begin to put societies together on different assumptions, those who presume to articulate the American purpose see these alternative orderings merely as subversive to the only ordering imaginable to them.

Herein lies the importance of whether the urban disturbances are called "riots" or "rebellions." The difference between a riot and a rebellion is that a rebellion is assumed to have goals. The physical incidents of riot and rebellion are very similar. An eyewitness would perceive much the same events in either case: people running through the streets; orators haranguing spontaneous assemblages; the precinct police station stoned or the home of the distributor of stamps sacked; tea dumped into the harbor or television sets taken from certain stores; finally shooting, mostly by uniformed representatives of constituted authority, and bodies on the sidewalks.

Yet one such occurrence will be called a riot, defined by the dictionary as "disorderly behavior," because the eyewitness fails to see an ordering of action by intended goals. A similar happening, no different in its externals, may go into history as a rebellion—"open renunciation of the authority of the government to which one owes obedience"—if those who write the history empathize with the motives of the protagonists.

This is why black radicals insist on the term rebellion or revolt ("a casting off of allegiance; . . . a movement or expression of vigorous dissent or refusal to accept") rather than the term riot. They perceive order in the disorders. As Tom Hayden, staff member of the Newark Community Union Project and a founder of Students for a Democratic Society, has observed, those who rioted in Newark regarded what they did as a more rational relating of means to ends than anything available from the channels of decision-making customary in quiet times.

It may help us to approach an understanding of the political philosophy of the American resistance to existing authority if we attempt to relate it to the theory of revolution found in Locke, the Declaration of Independence and Abraham Lincoln's first Inaugural Address.

THE RIGHT OF REVOLUTION?

"This country," President Lincoln said when he took over a country on the eve of dissolution, "belongs to the people who inhabit it. Whenever they shall grow weary of the existing government, they can exercise their constitutional right of amending it, or their revolutionary right to dismember or overthrow it."

The harshest critic of Stokely Carmichael will have to recognize some kinship between Lincoln's affirmation and Carmichael's statement, reported last October by the United Press, that "there is a higher law than the law of the government. That's the law of conscience." Clearly President and peripatetic agitator agree that government cannot be the ultimate arbiter of right and wrong. And well they might, for that way, surely we would all concur, lies Eichmann.

Nor can anyone deny that in his statement on the occasion of his arrest, July 26, 1967, H. Rap Brown employed precisely the logic of the preamble to the Declaration of Independence:

> I am charged with inciting black people to commit an offense by way of protest against the law, a law which neither I nor any of my people have any say in preparing. . . .
> I consider myself neither morally nor legally bound to obey laws made by a body in which I have no representation. That the will of the people is the basis of the authority of government is a principle universally acknowledged as sacred throughout the civilized world and constitutes the basic foundation of this country. It should be equally understandable that we, as black people, should adopt the attitude that we are neither morally nor legally bound to obey laws which were not made with our consent and which seek to oppress us.

This dignified statement was made the same day that Martin Luther King, Roy Wilkins, A. Philip Randolph and Whitney Young issued a joint public declaration so far abandoning the First Amendment that it urged that advocacy of riot or arson be punished as equivalent to the commission of those acts themselves.

There is one important difference between the political philosophy of the Declaration and that of Carmichael and Brown. In classical democratic theory, the right of revolution belonged only to majorities. This was one of the reasons that a bourgeois gentleman like Locke could justify revolution with such confidence.

"Nor let anyone say," he wrote, "that mischief can arise . . . as often as it shall please a busy head or turbulent spirit to desire the alteration of the government. It is true such men may stir whenever they please, but it will be only to their own just ruin and perdition; for till the mischief be grown general, and the ill designs of the rulers become visible, or their attempts sensible to the greater part, the people who are more disposed to suffer than right themselves by resistance are not apt to stir " Locke's majoritarian theory of revolution might appear to cut the theoretical ground from under the activists of the New Left in general, and of SNCC (the Student Nonviolent Coordinating Committee) in particular.

Yet a dispassionate observer might rebut as follows. In the first place, SNCC is not, for the moment at least, attempting to overthrow the government of the United States. The rioters have not gone downtown. What they want is control of those neighborhoods in which they constitute a majority. They ask, not that city hall move over and make room for them, but that city hall and especially city hall's policemen stay out of where they are. Rap Brown's argument that men cannot be bound by laws to which they have not given their consent would fit this situation perfectly, provided it could be shown that such consent had not, in fact, been forthcoming. In the Deep South the prima facie case that whites have imposed on blacks a "law and order" expressive only of the wants of whites is overwhelming.

In the second place, it is hardly the fault of Afro-Americans that they constitute a minority in the United States. We white folks brought them here, and one of the persistent considerations in the minds of those who did the importing was to get enough black laborers to do their work for them, but not so many that the laborers might successfully revolt. What is the Afro-American supposed to do? It seems to him that his oppression is of that pervasiveness and degree which Locke said justified revolution on the part of those oppressed. Should he then not rebel because his numbers are few? That counsel hardly fits with the tradition of white revolutionaries who sought liberty or death. Whether or not he would concede the kinship, that is the tradition to which Rap Brown belongs, as he stated when arrested.

The fact of the matter is that men who feel as Brown feels find themselves precisely in the position of the revolutionary guerrilla. Having rejected, not merely this or that law, but the entire structure of authority in the country in which they happened to be born, they are nevertheless powerless at present to overthrow the government which they reject. Their perspective must therefore be to live for an indefinite future under the nominal authority of a government to which they no longer feel legally or morally bound.

This political philosophy of noncooperation is, after all, not so different from that to which many white Americans have felt themselves pushed by war crimes in Vietnam. A number of American professors, including Noam Chomsky of the Massachusetts Institute of Technology, have drafted "A Call to Resist Illegitimate Authority" which proceeds on the same premises as those of H. Rap Brown. The principles of the Nuremburg Tribunal constitute, for the signers of this call, "commitments to other countries and to Mankind (which) would claim our allegiance even if Congress should declare war." (Just so SNCC, following Malcolm X, now speaks of universal "human rights" rather than of the "civil rights" defined by American law.) Consciously or unconsciously borrowing a turn of phrase from the preamble to the Declaration of Independence, the call terms resistance to collusion with the war and the encouragement of others to so resist "a legal right and a moral duty." Brown ends his statement with the words, "Each time black human-rights workers are refused protection by the government, that is anarchy. Each time a police officer shoots and kills a black teenager, that is urban crime. We see America for what it is, and we recognize our course of action." The call ends similarly: "Now is the time to resist."

EMERGENCE OF A MOVEMENT

It may still be said that a justification of revolution akin to Jefferson's does not quite add up to a vision of the future.

True enough, in part that vision is implicit in the actions of SNCC and SDS (Students for a Democratic Society) organizers rather than fully articulated. For example, "the Movement" prefers to make its decisions by consensus, not by delegating decision-making authority to representatives. Again, in contrast to the sharp distinction in liberal democratic theory between thought and action, the Movement places a high premium on "putting your body where your mouth is," which is to say, acting on what you believe. It should be easy enough for any moderately sympathetic listener to extrapolate these clues into a sketch of future institutions.

Yet such extrapolation is hardly necessary. The Port Huron statement, a statement of aims by SDS in 1962, remains an accurate declaration of what both SDS and SNCC might do if they had power. The Port Huron statement lists a plethora of recommended programs which, if controversial, can hardly be considered irrational.

Participatory democracy represented a corollary to SNCC's 1960 statement of purpose, which affirmed the need for "a social order of justice permeated by love" and took its stand on "the moral nature of human existence." So, too, in every phase of its history, SNCC workers have sought, in the words of the Port Huron statement, "to encourage independence in men."

The evident common ground, despite all differences in experience, between the SNCC and SDS statements of purpose makes rational the hope that what will ultimately emerge is an American radical movement led by black people but with participants both white and black. Stokely Carmichael wrote as recently as 1966 that the society SNCC seeks to build "is not a capitalist society. It is a society in which the spirit of community and humanistic love prevail." We may yet see white and black together striving for that society.

What has changed since 1962 is not ends but means. One sees this in the increasing toughness of slogans. "Love" and "participatory democracy" have given way to "black power," "we won't go," "resist," "not with my life, you don't." Nevertheless, each of these phrases seeks to articulate the underlying thought that persons now excluded from our society's decision-making—which means almost all Americans, but especially the young, the poor and those of dark skin—should assume control over their destinies. Even in 1962, as the Port Huron statement noted, the civil rights movement had "come to an impasse." That impasse and our society's failure to overcome it explain why the hopeful and innocent dreams of five years ago have metamorphosed into the hard-bitten strategies of today.

THE ROAD TO REVOLUTION

Like any other guerrilla, the Afro-American in rebellion will seek allies where he can find them. Experience, and more particularly experience (as he has perceived it) of betrayal by white and black respectable Americans, leads him to seek such allies in the Third World overseas.

This perspective did not spring full-grown from the brows of Stokely Carmichael and Fidel Castro. It is not the invention of outside agitators. Those who wish it did not exist ought to recall how they acted at the Democratic party convention in 1964, what their response was to Julian Bond's unseating by the legislature of Georgia, how quickly and publicly they protested (or failed to protest) the arrests of H. Rap Brown.

Some of us watched Robert Parris Moses, the principal SNCC leader in the Negro voter-registration drive in Mississippi, as experience took him step by step from an initial orientation to the use of electoral machinery and the cultivation of white allies toward embittered black nationalism. The turning point in Bob's development, so far as this outsider has been able to understand it, was when, on a visit to Africa in 1965, he saw a magazine published by the United States Information Agency. A center spread in the magazine showed pictures of Moses and Mrs. Fannie Lou Hamer, the Mississippi civil rights worker, over some such caption as, "Bob Moses and Mrs. Hamer leading delegates of the Mississippi Freedom Democratic party to their seats at the Democratic party convention." Bob felt not only that the magazine had lied in stating that the M.F.D.P. delegates had been seated, but that it had used him, and those who had died in Mississippi as a result of his activity, to convey to the rest of the world that democracy still existed in a country which could produce Bob Moses. This experience blended with accounts of Central Intelligence Agency machinations, as in Ghana, which Bob visited shortly before the deposition of Nkrumah. Robert Moses, gentlest of men, returned to the United States convinced that no infamy or perfidy was beyond the capacities of this country.

Others traveled the same road. As recently as the summer of 1964, this writer, then directing "freedom schools" for the Mississippi Summer Project, insisted that discussion of foreign policy be excluded from the curriculum of the schools because SNCC had no position on foreign policy. The trauma of the Democratic party convention, followed by the bombing of North Vietnam a half a year later, set in motion a change. The April, 1965, demonstration in Washington against the war in Vietnam, organized by Students for a Democratic Society, had its District of Columbia headquarters in the SNCC office. In July, 1965, Negroes in McComb, Mississippi, where Moses had started voter registration in 1961, issued the following statement on the occasion of the death in Vietnam of John D. Shaw, twenty-three years old, who had participated in thte 1961 demonstrations and sit-ins:

Here are five reasons why Negroes should not be in any war fighting for America:

1) No Mississippi Negro should be fighting in Vietnam for the white man's freedom, until all the Negro people are free in Mississippi.

2) Negro boys should not honor the draft in Mississippi. Mothers should encourage their sons not to go.

3) We will gain respect and dignity as a race only by forcing the United States government and the Mississippi government to come with guns, dogs and trucks to take our sons away to fight and be killed protecting Mississippi, Alabama, Georgia, and Louisiana.

4) No one has a right to ask us to risk our lives and kill other colored people in Santo Domingo and Vietnam so that the white American can get richer. We will be looked upon as traitors by all the colored people of the world if the Negro people continue to fight and die without a cause.

5) Last week a white soldier from New Jersey was discharged from the Army because he refused to fight in Vietnam and went on a hunger strike. Negro boys can do the same thing. We can write and ask our sons if they know what they are fighting for. If he answers 'freedom,' tell him that's what we are fighting for here in Mississippi. And if he says 'democracy,' tell him the truth—we don't know anything

about communism, socialism and all that, but we do know that Negroes have caught hell here under this American democracy.

In midsummer, 1965, the thrust of the McComb statement still ran at cross-purposes to SNCC's desire to win liberal white support for its effort to challenge the seating of the regular Democratic party congressmen from Mississippi. The Washington, D.C., office of the Mississippi Freedom Democratic party repudiated the McComb statement. But with the defeat of the congressional challenge a few weeks later, no inhibition remained to the expression of SNCC dissent to American foreign policy. The SNCC staff joined unanimously at Christmastime, 1965, in a statement which expressed sympathy and support for those "unwilling to respond to the military draft." For the first time SNCC conceptualized what it had been doing for the past five years as a "black people's struggle for liberation and self-determination."

This then laid the basis for a comparison of the murder of SNCC field secretaries unprotected by federal power to the murder of people in Vietnam: "In each case, the U.S. government bears a great part of the responsibility for these deaths." Just as, in the perception of SNCC staff members, "elections in this country, in the North as well as the South, are not free," so overseas, "the ability and even the desire of the U.S. government to guarantee free elections" were questionable. And therefore the conclusion: "We maintain that our country's cry of 'preserve freedom in the world' is a hypocritical mask behind which it squashes liberation movements which are not bound and refuse to be bound by expediency of U.S. cold war policy."

At the time, white Southern liberals, such as the late Lillian Smith and the editors of the *Atlanta Constitution,* wondered aloud what outside agitator had drafted the SNCC statement. Theirs was a dangerous misconception. How genuinely the SNCC statement spoke for rank-and-file Negro sentiment was suggested the next year when an American Friends Service Committee employee, in conversation with Mrs. Ida Mae Lawrence, a leader of the embattled black plantation workers of the Mississippi delta, uncovered the following poem which she had written:

Vietnam: A Poem

We say we love our country
We say other people love their
country
We said that all men are brothers
What would we call the war
in Vietnam
Would we call that brotherly love
Does the word freedom have a meaning
Why do the history books say
America is the
Land of Liberty a Free Country.
Then why do all mens Negro and White fight
the Vietnam and Korea why cant we be Americans
as North and South regardless of
color
What does we have again
the Vietnams?
Why are we fighting them?
Who are really the enemy?
Are Vietnam the enemy or we
Americans enemies to ourselves.
If we are the same as Vietnams
Why should we fight them?
They are poor too.
They wants freedom.
They wants to redster to vote.
Maybe the people in the Vietnam
can't redster to vote
Just like us.

Thus, in its political philosophy concerning illegitimate authority both at home and abroad, SNCC stems directly from long-standing American tradition. The most eloquent white position paper on "the black rebellion" was that issued by SDS. It simply reprinted the preamble to the Declaration of Independence.

SNCC's present advocacy of violence is also altogether in the American grain. It ill becomes white Americans to rebuke SNCC for repudiating that "passive obedience" which the leaders of the American Revolution themselves so much scorned.

Our intention, declared Brown on July 26, is to respond to "counterrevolutionary violence with revolutionary violence, an eye for an eye, a tooth for a tooth, and a life for a life." Is this sentiment essentially different from the import of Locke's question: "If the innocent honest man must quietly quit all he has, for peace's sake, to him who will lay violent hands upon it, I desire it may be considered what a kind of peace there will be in the world, which consists only in violence and rapine, and which is to be maintained only for the benefit of robbers and oppressors. Who would not think it an admirable peace betwixt the mighty and the mean when the lamb without resistance yielded his throat to be torn by the imperious wolf?" And when Stokely Carmichael hints, purportedly, at the assassination of President Johnson, must not those words be catalogued along with Patrick Henry's "Caesar had his Brutus, Charles the First his Cromwell, and George the Third (here Henry was interrupted by cries of 'treason!') may profit by their example"?

Nevertheless, I do not wish to close with a defense of violence, be it George Washington's or H. Rap Brown's. For the political philosophy of those intense young men and women regarded by the American establishment as purveyors of chaos and anarchy appears to me sparked, above all, by compassion. Until we let them down, they struggled to create a "beloved community," a "band of brothers standing in a circle of love," in the face of Southern sheriffs and police dogs. Do we think them different persons now? If so, we are mistaken. There comes to my mind SNCC poet laureate Charlie Cobb, and especially "Charlie's Poem," read at the Berkeley teach-in of May, 1965, when SNCC was halfway between freedom summer and black power. Here is the concluding section:

> so cry not just
> for jackson or reeb
> schwerner, goodman
> or chaney
> or lee

cry for all mothers
with shovels
digging at hovels
looking for their dead

cry for all the blood spilled
of all the people killed
in the Standard Procedure
of the country
which is not ours
but belongs
to those who run it
and can't be seen
but are very few
who
listen to each other
and not to us
cause we don't know
what it takes
that makes
Standard Procedures

now I must say
about these guys who uniform us
in lots of ways
and make us each
the enemy of the other
the world around

that what we've been taught
we should get
is theirs

and not for everybody to get
and what they do
is teach us
to beat
everybody down
who's trying to get
what they already got
and what everybody can't get

So we throw away
our lives
and take instead
their things

and the things they have
are like
missiles & guns
money & cars
slots & walls

we take these things
and use them to
kill and hurt
be AFRAID
and be Unhappy
and to lose life

but to mostly kill

cause we want to die
cause deep down
we know
WE are life
and we have been taught
that's bad
and must be destroyed
(our life)

cause that's a threat
to
missiles & guns
money & cars
slots & walls
cause life can be ours
to be planted and grown
in 2 Billion ways
we can each call our own.

I don't know where Charlie Cobb is now. It doesn't matter; I think I know where we are driving him. In my mind's eye I see him clearly, standing against a brick wall somewhere, blazing away at us from the gun in his hands, with tears of compassion and hatred streaming down his face.

REQUIEM FOR NONVIOLENCE

By ELDRIDGE CLEAVER

The murder of Dr. Martin Luther King came as a surprise—and surprisingly it also came as a shock. Many people, particularly those in the black community who long ago abandoned nonviolence and opted to implement the slogan of Malcolm X—"black liberation by any means necessary"—have been expecting to hear of Dr. King's death for a long time. Many even became tired of waiting. But that Dr. King would have to die was a certainty. For here was a man who refused to abandon the philosophy and the principle of nonviolence in face of a hostile and racist nation which has made it indisputably clear that it has no intention and no desire to grant a redress of the grievances of the black colonial subjects who are held in bondage.

To black militants, Dr. King represented a stubborn and persistent stumbling block in the path of the methods that had to be implemented to bring about a revolution in the present situation. And so, therefore, much hatred, much venom and much criticism was focused upon Dr. King by the black militants. And the contradiction in which he was caught up cast him in the role of one who was hated and held in contempt, both by the whites in America who did not want to free black people, and by black people who recognized the attitude of white America and who wanted to be rid of the self-deceiving doctrine of nonviolence. Still, black militants were willing to sit back and watch, and allow Dr. King to play out his role. And his role has now been played out.

The assassin's bullet not only killed Dr. King, it killed a period of history. It killed a hope, and it killed a dream.

That white America could produce the assassin of Dr. Martin Luther King is looked upon by black people—and not just those identified as black militants—as a final repudiation by white America of any hope of reconciliation, of any hope of change by peaceful and nonviolent means. So that it becomes clear that the only way for black people in this country to get the things that they want—and the things that they have a right to and that they deserve—is to meet fire with fire.

In the last few months, while Dr. King was trying to build support for his projected poor people's march on Washington, he already resembled something of a dead man. Of a dead symbol, one might say more correctly. Hated on both sides, denounced on both sides—yet he persisted. And now his blood has been spilled. The death of Dr. King signals the end of an era and the beginning of a terrible and bloody chapter that may remain unwritten, because there may be no scribe left to capture on paper the holocaust to come.

That there is a holocaust coming I have no doubt at all. I have been talking to people around the country by telephone—people intimately involved in the black liberation struggle—and their reaction to Dr. King's murder has been unanimous: the war has begun. The violent phase of the black liberation struggle is here, and it will spread. From that shot, from that blood, America will be painted red. Dead bodies will litter the streets and the scenes will be reminiscent of the disgusting, terrifying, nightmarish news reports coming out of Algeria during the height of the general violence right before the final breakdown of the French colonial regime.

America has said "no" to the black man's demand for liberation, and this "no" is unacceptable to black people. They are going to strike back, they are going to reply to the escalation of this racist government, this racist society. They are going to escalate their retaliation. And the responsibility for all this blood, for all this death, for all this suffering . . . well, it's beyond the stage of assigning blame. Black people are no longer interested in adjudicating the situation, in negotiating the situation, in arbitrating the situation. Their only interest now is in being able to summon up whatever it will take to wreak the havoc upon Babylon that will force Babylon to let the black people go. For all other avenues have been closed.

The assassin's bullet which struck down Dr. King closed a door that to the majority of black people seemed closed long ago. To many of us it was clear that that door was never open. But we were willing to allow those who wanted to bang upon that door for entry, we were willing to sit back and let them do this. Indeed, we had no other choice. But now all black people in America have become Black Panthers in spirit. There will, of course, be those who stand up before the masses and echo the eloquent pleas of Dr. King for a continuation of the nonviolent tactic. They will be listened to by many, but from another perspective. They will look back upon Dr. King and upon his successors with somewhat the emotions one feels when one looks upon the corpse of a loved one. But it is all dead now. It's all dead now. Now there is the gun and the bomb, dynamite and the knife, and they will be used liberally in America. America will bleed. America will suffer.

And it is strange to see how, with each significant shot that is fired, time is speeded up. How the dreadful days that we all somehow knew were coming seem to cascade down upon us immediately, and the dreadful hours that we thought were years away are immediately upon us, immediately before us. And all eternity is gone, blown away, washed away in the blood of martyrs.

Is the death of Dr. King a sad day for America? No. It is a day consistent with what America demands by its actions. The death of Dr. King was not a tragedy for America. America should be happy that Dr. King is dead, because America worked so hard to bring it about. And now all the hypocritical, vicious madmen who pollute the government of this country and who befoul the police agencies of this country, all of the hypocritical public announcements following the death of Dr. King are being repudiated and held in contempt, not only by black people but by millions of white people who know that had these same treacherous political gangsters made the moves that clearly lay within their power to make, Dr. King would not be dead, nonviolence would prevail and the terror would not be upon us. These people, the police departments, the legislatures, the government, the Democratic party, the Republican party, those commonly referred to as the establishment or the power structure, they can be looked upon as immediate targets and symbols of blame.

But it has been said that a people or a country gets the leaders and the government that it deserves. And here we have at the death of Dr. King a President by the name of Lyndon Baines Johnson who has the audacity to stand before this nation and mourn Dr. King and to praise his leadership and the nonviolence he espoused, while he has the blood of hundreds of thousands of people and the slaughtered conscience of America upon his hands. If any one man could be singled out as bearing responsibility for bringing about the bloodshed and violence to come, it would be Lyndon Baines Johnson. But not just Lyndon Baines Johnson. All of the greedy, profit-seeking businessmen in America, all of the conniving, unscrupulous labor leaders of America, all of the unspeakable bootlickers, the big businessmen of the civil rights movement and the average man on the street who feels hatred instilled in his heart by this vicious and disgusting system—the blame is everywhere and nowhere.

Washington, D.C., is burning. My only thought at that is I hope Stokely Carmichael survives Washington. Chicago is burning, Detroit is burning and there is fire and the sound of guns from one end of Babylon to the other.

Last night I heard Lyndon Baines Johnson admonishing his people, admonishing black people to turn away from vicious and disgusting system—the blame is everywhere and of all the corn pone that he spouted forth one thing struck me and I felt insulted by it. He was ringing changes on a famous statement made by Malcolm X in his speech, "The Ballot or the Bullet." Malcolm X had prophesied that if the ballot did not prevail in gaining black people their liberation, then the bullet would be made to prevail. And Lyndon Johnson said last night that he was going to prove to the nation and to the American people that the ballot and not the bullet would prevail. Coming from him, it was a pure insult.

Those of us in the Black Panther party who have been reading events and looking to the future have said that this will be the Year of the Panther, that this will be the Year of the Black Panther. And now everything that I can see leaves no doubt of that. And now there is Stokely Carmichael, Rap Brown, and above all there is Huey P. Newton. Malcolm X prophesied the coming of the gun, and Huey Newton picked up the gun, and now there is gun against gun. Malcolm X gunned down. Martin Luther King gunned down.

I am trying to put a few words on tape because I was asked to do so by the editor of this magazine, to try to give my thoughts on what the assassination of Dr. King means for the future, what is likely to follow and who is likely to emerge as a new or a prevailing leader of black people. It is hard to put words on this tape because words are no longer relevant. Action is all that counts now. And maybe America will understand that. I doubt it. I think that America is incapable of understanding *anything* relevant to human rights. I think that America has already committed suicide and we who now thrash within its dead body are also dead in part and parcel of the corpse. America is truly a disgusting burden upon this planet. A burden upon all humanity. And if we here in America . . .*

* Cleaver dictated this article about forty-eight hours after the assassination of Martin Luther King. He was interrupted in midsentence by a phone call. Cleaver immediately left to cross San Francisco Bay and go to Oakland where, as an official of the Black Panther Party, he was helping to keep things cool while other cities in America were burning. Within a few more hours, Cleaver himself was in jail.

BLACK FRIDAY

By DAVID HOROWITZ AND FRED HAINES

The spring term began with the excitement of the Chessman case, but that was soon superseded by compelling events of national and international scope. The campaigns for the presidential nominations began gathering momentum, winds of a new summit meeting between Eisenhower and Khrushchev were growing stronger, and suddenly, in April, accounts of students demonstrations in Turkey and Korea were making the headlines. One photograph, in particular, of Korean students being hosed by government police, appeared on the front page of *The Daily Californian,* as an un-noted portent of the future.

On April 26, the papers reported that the House Committee on Un-American Activities had issued subpoenas for hearings to be held May 10–12 (subsequently changed to May 12–14) in City Hall, San Francisco. At the University of California campus in Berkeley, a meeting was called by a 25-year-old teaching student assistant in economics to discuss possible action to protest the appearance of this Committee which had done such unwarranted damage to innocent members of the community the year before.

An account of this meeting was printed on the front page of *The Daily Californian,* informing the students that an ad hoc Students for Civil Liberties organization had been formed by the participants and that plans for a petition campaign, a picket, and a rally in Union Square, San Francisco, on the opening day of the hearings had been made. The petition was an immediate success, gaining 1,000 signatures in three days, while similar petitions against the Committee were circulated and signed by 300 members of the faculty at the University of California and 165 members of the faculty at San Francisco State.

Meanwhile, the news that Douglas Wachter, an 18-year-old sophomore at the University, had been subpoenaed, served to arouse a considerable amount of campus interest. An interview with Wachter was accompanied by a series of editorials disapproving of the Committee's tactics, and urging students to make themselves familiar with the Committee's actions.

On Thursday morning, May 12, an unofficial student picket circled City Hall (the official picket was not scheduled to begin until after the noon rally). Members of this line distributed to newcomers the following instructions printed by the Students for Civil Liberties:

> The purpose of the picket line is to protest the invasion by the HUAC of privacy of individual belief and its free expression, and to gain support from the public for the abolition of this Committee. We strive to achieve respect for the dignity of man. Thus, we must act in accordance with this ideal if we want others to respect it. All persons who participate in this line are expected to show good-will and to be polite, calm, and reasonable to everyone, including police, hecklers, the public and other picketers. Do not show anger and do not use abusive language; do not respond to hoots, jeers, or derogatory language. Do not debate with the public. Questions about the group and its activities, especially from the press should be directed to monitors, who are wearing white arm-bands initialed with a black 'M'. Monitors are in charge of maintaining the order of the picket line, and you are expected to carefully follow their directions. If you cannot abide by the decisions of the monitors or if you cannot remain non-violent in character and in deed, please withdraw quietly from the line. All who wish to demonstrate against the HUAC are welcome to join the line. Remember, your conduct must reflect the ideals for which we are demonstrating.

Meanwhile, several hundred other students had lined up with the general public to be admitted to the hearing room. Just before the hearings began over 150 people carrying special white cards were allowed to enter the hearing room ahead of those who had been standing in line. When these people had gone in, about 75 of those standing in line were admitted.

During the noon hour, when the Committee was in recess, the students held their rally in Union Square. State Assemblymen Philip Burton and John A. O'Connell, and Canon Richard Byfield of Grace Cathedral spoke against the Committee along with two student speakers. The crowd, which numbered 1,000, then proceeded to City Hall to join the picket.

Inside the City Hall trouble was brewing. Only a few of the 75 students (who were not white-card holders) were allowed to re-enter the hearing room. This new restriction increased the resentment of those who had been standing in line all morning and chants of "Let us in! Let us in!" went up. Inside the chamber some of the students joined in the chants and then some of the witnesses themselves began to chant "Open the door! Open the door!" On orders from the Committee, police charged the witnesses and began dragging them from the room. The white-card holders pummeled them as they were drawn away and shouted "Get the bastards out! Send them back to Russia!"

The students began to sing "The Star-Spangled Banner." The white-card holders remained seated, shouted, and hissed. Outside, Sheriff Matthew Carberry appeared in plain clothes and called for quiet. Immediately there was silence. The Sheriff requested the students to leave or at least maintain quiet so that the courts could function. Although not all of the students left, those who remained acquiesced and were quiet.

The newspapers carried the story of this incident on their front pages, playing it up as a "riot," much to the dismay of the students. Beside a picture of Archie Brown being ejected were phrases like "Riotous demonstrators disrupted . . . A wild, uproarious scene . . . 200 student partisans massed in the corridor outside were working themselves into a frenzy . . ." With these words, the whole object of the picket which had walked peacefully around the hall the entire day was defeated.

The student leaders were well aware that even though

no picket had been planned for the next day (Friday), the newspaper stories had insured that an even larger crowd would inevitably line up outside the chamber door seeking admittance. They therefore decided that a picket should be held and an attempt made to convince those inside the City Hall to give up their protest against the white cards and come out. They also decided to contact the police and ask them to make waiting lines outside the room so that the crowd would be more controllable. The police told them that it was a public building and they couldn't tell people what to do.

On Friday morning the white-card holders again walked by the line into the Committee room, and this time only 20 of the several hundred students in the line were allowed to go in. Resentment, naturally, was high and for the rest of the morning the crowd chanted and sang songs in the City Hall rotunda, just outside the room where they had vainly sought admittance.

The following account of what went on inside the rotunda was written by Fred Haines, KPFA reporter who recorded the actual events for his station:

"Shortly before the noon recess I was standing on the police side of the barricade recording the chanting of the students who were by now jammed into the limited space in the rotunda. Sheriff Matthew Carberry came up to the barricade from the police side and asked for attention. The conversation which ensued was not an easy one for the Sheriff. He had been asked, he said, by the presiding judge of one of the Superior Courts, which was convened on the floor above, to quiet the demonstration—the previous afternoon the court had been adjourned because of the noise— and he told them that they were placing themselves subject to arrest by continuing to demonstrate although they could remain in the building if they were quiet. He assured them that a 'representative group—sufficient number' of students would be admitted for the afternoon session. He told them to return at two o'clock—the hearings reconvened at one. He offered to discuss the matter in his office, next week. And he promised to be 'available all day,' and in the building.

"An assistant of some sort kept valiantly trying to get the Sheriff away to take care of some kind of business, but not

before the following exchange with one of the student
leaders took place. The young man told the Sheriff that they
would discontinue the demonstration for the noon hour.

" 'We will cooperate,' he said, 'and if they cooperate
with us at two, and let us in—on equal-come basis—then
at two o'clock, you'll hear from us again, at two o'clock.
Sheriff, is that right? We shall cooperate with you. Until
two o'clock. And if you keep your promise, and let everybody go into that hall, on a first-come, first-served basis,
we'll cooperate. But if we're kept out of here, if we're kept
out of here. . .'

" 'I have nothing to do with admissions,' the Sheriff inter-
jected. 'I told you that.'

" 'I know that, I'm sorry. If, at that time, we find out
that all law enforcement agencies, including the Committee,
which says it is a law enforcement agency, will allow people
to go into that hall on a free and democratic basis—that is,
first-come, first-served—*we* will cooperate with the law
enforcement agencies. However, I would suggest to the
group . . .'

"Sheriff Carberry broke in, saying, 'I promise you full cooperation.'

"And the young man continued, '. . . if the law enforcement agencies, either true, or'—gesturing toward the Supervisors' Chambers—'*not* so true, do not cooperate with us,
that we do organize, that we do use our free assembly, our
right to petition. We do it orderly, but we do it loudly. Are
you with me?' he finished, turning into the crowd.

"They were. No further demonstrations occurred during
the noon hour, and many of the crowd left the building, as
I did, for lunch.

"I returned shortly before one, filled with misgivings. Inside the building again, I found that the group of students
had nearly doubled; they had jammed the tiny rotunda
and had overflowed onto the wide mezzanine landing that
lay seven steps below it on the opposite side from the
Supervisors' Chambers. Still others straggled down the imposing flight of granite steps that led all the way down to
the main floor of the building.

"Halfway up the stairs I met one of the Cal students who
had organized the picket line outside the building. 'I'm

afraid there's going to be trouble,' he told me. 'We can't find anybody to talk to . . .'

" 'Is Carberry here?' I asked.

" 'His office says he's out to lunch and won't be back until two. We've been trying to get someone from the Mayor's office all morning, but he went to lunch in Burlingame . . .'

" 'Isn't there anyone else in charge?' I asked.

" 'Mike McGuire,' he said, 'he's an inspector for the red squad.'

"Another student broke in to ask who McGuire was, and I described him briefly. 'That's what I thought,' he said. 'We've been asking the cops who's in charge and they said McGuire. So we asked this guy if he was McGuire and he wouldn't tell us. I suggested there might be trouble because all these people expect to get in and he just flipped. He shouted, "Are you threatening me? Get the hell out of here!" And I thought he was going to hit me.'

" 'We're going to try to get as many of them inside as possible with white cards,' the picket monitor said. 'We'll send four people in for each one we've got, and then one guy can come back out with the pass and we'll send in four more. We're trying to talk people into getting out of the building and on to the picket line where they belong, too. Other than that I don't know what to do.'

"Exercising my press privilege, I took a station immediately behind the center barricade on the police side. The word went through the crowd to form a line, and, with a few exceptions, they managed to get into a rough approximation of a line, four abreast. The 'Friends of the Committee' gathered just to the right of this line, among them a number of the demonstrators who had somehow acquired the privileged white cards. As I watched, McGuire opened a way through the center barricade and began to admit the white-card holders one at a time; for a moment the waiting crowd paused, and then an angry roar went up. Those in the rear, who were half-way down the stairs and couldn't see what was going on, began to edge forward, and in the resulting crush began to press the flimsy sawhorse barricade toward me and the police officers, who leaped forward to hold it. Angry cries of 'Hold it! Stop pushing!' came from those in front; the barricade held and the police pushed it back to its original position. 'Let's wait and see what they're going to do!' someone called out.

"The barricade back and the crowd quiet, McGuire suddenly noticed that the white-card holders, who were still filing through, included in their number some students. He lunged forward and grabbed one of them roughly. The student wrenched himself free, shouting angrily. 'I've got a white card!' McGuire, taken aback, let go and seized another by the lapels of his packet, this young man thrust a 35-mm camera in McGuire's face and tripped the shutter. Again McGuire let go, and several students managed to slip into the Chambers.

"Then an officer came out of the chambers and announced loudly, "Room for five more!' The response from the crowd was immediate, loud, and angry. 'Nobody go in!' some called out, but five people did manage to get in, although with some difficulty because of the crush in the suddenly explosive crowd.

"Another officer came out of the chambers, spoke to McGuire, and several more were admitted. One of them, a girl who had been standing at the opposite end of the barricade from the entry, chatting with one of the uniformed officers, was led by this officer the length of the sawhorse to the opening, and the crowd obeyed his order to move back from the barricade to let her pass.

"Already the singing was beginning again, raggedly at first, but with greater volume as more and more took up the song. There was only one last move: the picket monitors and others began passing the word to sit down on the floor. Here and there individuals began to sit down, then groups, until finally the whole central part of the crowd was seated. Only two girls remained standing by the flanking pillars in front of the central barricade; I could see all the way across the rotunda to those standing by the seven shallow stairs that led to the landing behind them.

"Four or five minutes had passed since the doors were closed on the expectant crowd, and the crisis was safely over. I supposed the police might begin wholesale arrests shortly, but the possible eruption of violence had been neatly averted, with the vast majority of the crowd safely self-immobilized on the floor.

"Moments later, an attorney who was representing two of the witnesses made his way across the rotunda and arrived behind the barricades just in time to see McGuire opening one of the hydrants. He ran to the officer, shouting, 'You can't do this to these kids.' McGuire shrugged him off. An officer behind the center barricade picked up the nozzle of one of the fire hoses which had been unrolled from the floor and pointed it at several students sitting just beyond the barricade. 'You want some of this?' he shouted. 'Well, you're going to get it!' One of the young men waved at him and kept on singing. A trickle dripped from a nozzle, a spurt, bubbly with air—and then the hose stiffened with the full pressure of the water, which blasted into the group of seated demonstrators.

"The rotunda seemed to erupt. The singing broke up into one gigantic, horrified scream. People fled past me as I ran forward, trying to see what was going on; a huge sheet of spray, glancing off one of the granite pillars, flashed through the air in front of me, and I retreated. It was impossible to comprehend everything that was going on. Those who stood up within ten feet or so of the hose were simply knocked down again by the force of the water, tumbling head over heels on their still-seated friends. Others stood, found no place to run, their way blocked by bodies, and so sat down again. Some huddled together for protection. A second tongue of water licked out in a long arch over the barricades, and through the spray and confusion I saw that McGuire himself was manning the nozzle.

"Everything happened too fast to get more than a vague, overall impression of struggling bodies and the two silvery whiplashes of water exploding against back and heads and faces—and a crazy-quilt of disconnected impressions: John Burke, with whom I was slightly acquainted, stepping gingerly through the water flowing across the treacherously slippery floor, he trying to change the plates in his press camera and I trying to flip the cartridge in my tape recorder —both of us nodding politely as we pass. Another acquaintance, an ex-RAF pilot in the U.S. on a Commonwealth

Scholarship, who had attended the hearings with an idea of writing on them for the *Manchester Guardian,* twisting under the blast of the water, his elegantly-tailored suit matted against his back and his hair splayed out in a sodden halo around his head. A lawyer, in the building on other business, who ran out, angrily protesting the hosing, hit full in the face with a blast from the hose. A newsman near me yelling, 'Where's our photographer?' over and over again. A demonstrator trying to shield the heads of two girls with his soggy suede jacket while a stream of water battered against the base of his skull for what seemed minutes on end. A girl, so expressionless she might have been daydreaming, standing at the pillar next to the barricade and watching a stream of water pour out past her; no place to go, nowhere to hide, unable to move, she waits . . . the officer sees her, brings the hose behind her, and rakes it up her body— slowly—from heels to head at a range of about two feet. Three, four, then five of the demonstrators clawing their way toward the barricade in an insane attempt to rush the police —but they stop two or three yards away, turning their backs to the water blast, and, linking arms, they try to build a human wall to shield the others.

"It couldn't have lasted long, but it seemed forever. It was impossible to grasp; it couldn't be happening. It seemed more like a bad surrealist film than an actual occurrence, and it was so absurd I couldn't even think about it. I re-threaded the cartridge in my tape machine and began recording, automatically and somewhat dazedly, an account of what I was seeing.

"Throughout the hosing you were relatively safe if you stayed in the wings of the rotunda, the area between the massive main pillars and the elevators, and I did, cradling the tape machine in my arms against the spray. Every time I tried to move in closer to the scene I would be driven back by the flying water. In the opposite wing I could see other onlookers, newsmen and passers-by, gazing out on the scene like tourists. As the final touch of lunacy I discovered afterward that I had replaced the microphone plug—which kept falling out as I fumbled with the cartridge—in the machine upside down, and I spent the first couple of minutes babbling into a dead mike.

"And the two streams of water faltered, fell away, and, after a moment, stopped completely. I waded out into the rotunda to see what was going on. Nothing. It was all over. All seemed almost still and silent. Somewhere in the crowd of sodden, bedraggled students a single voice began to sing, 'We shall not, we shall not be moved . . .' Another voice took it up, and another, and presently all were singing, filling the rotunda with a sound that was almost jubilant. There was some sort of activity behind the barricades, but it seemed to be just aimless milling about. I noticed that there were a lot more police officers than I had thought. In addition to the dozen or so who'd been on duty there all day, there were another twenty clad in the helmets, jackets, and jackboots of the motorcycle troops.

"For the first time I had a moment to think, to take stock of the situation. How incredibly stupid and aimless it was: during the past few minutes they'd dumped thousands of gallons of water inside a public building, causing several thousand dollars worth of damage (not counting whatever human injury there had been). And they had accomplished nothing. Perhaps 50 people out of 200 or so had fled, but they surely could have achieved the same end if they had quietly and matter-of-factly begun placing people under arrest—and now they had 150 people wet, angry, and injured, most of whom were rooted to the spot and determined to make as much noise as ever before. But my thoughts were conditioned by the assumption that the police had given up the attempt to dislodge the demonstration.

"The center barricade was shoved to one side, and Inspector McGuire began to line up the motorcycle officers in the breach. Now, I thought, they'll do what any sensible person would have tried first—they'll begin arresting them. But once again I was wrong. There was a shout of 'Let's go!' and the phalanx of officers lumbered forward into the crowd of seated demonstrators, clubs swinging wildly. Once again the refrain of 'We Shall Not Be Moved' broke up, disintegrating into a terrified shriek. The students were hauled to their feet, knocked down again, pushed over each other, kicked, and clubbed in the onslaught. A girl was hauled to her feet and thrown back to the floor on her face.

Another demonstrator rolled in the water on the floor in pain. An ex-Army officer who considered himself only a spectator was struck across the arm, and when he tried to retreat toward the elevators he was seized and thrown violently into the crowd of demonstrators, the officer yelling, 'Get back there where you belong, you Commie!' Some of the students were thrown back toward the doors of the Supervisors' Chambers, where other officers seized them and slapped them around or beat them; one of these was held completely off the floor by several officers while another beat him across the legs with his nightstick. When the attorney who had tried to stop McGuire from turning on the hoses again attempted to intervene, he was grabbed by both arms and an officer threatened to strike him; when he protested that he had to represent clients, he was thrown against the doors and then pushed through. (Inside he came across all three of San Francisco's police commissioners, none of whom seemed at all perturbed about the melee outside. One answered the attorney's protests by telling him, 'You run the Communist party—we'll run the police.')

"Another student who had been beaten behind the barricades was thrown bodily back over the sawhorses into the lake of bloody water running on the granite floor. Yet another, a student who had managed to avoid being hosed by watching from the wings, was seized by his arms, lifted off his feet, and held dangling while a third motorcycle trooper struck him repeatedly in the stomach with his club; when he finally lost consciousness he was thrown across the rapidly clearing rotunda and down the seven steps at the rear to the part of the mezzanine which served as a landing between the rotunda and the great granite staircase that fell by 37 steps to the floor below. He lay there bleeding and unconscious in the water. Closer to where I stood in the wings one of the injured demonstrators was trying to get to his feet when he was kneed by a motorcycle officer who charged into him full tilt, knocking the boy sprawling across the floor. Half falling, half skidding, he tumbled some thirty feet across the floor, past my feet, and down the steps to the first landing where he lay groaning and clutching his stomach.

"I'd had enough. I too retreated to the landing for fear I would be attacked as well.

"Although many had fled, there were still some 50 or 60 people gathered on the landing. Most of those who still hoped to escape, either by going around the mezzanine or risking the descent of the stairs which were flowing with water like an indoor waterfall, had their way cut off by police officers, who forced them to return to the landing. One student had made the main floor already but was intercepted by a police officer who seized him roughly; a girl nearby who tried to intervene was struck in the face by the officer's club. Another had slipped and fallen on the stairs, and an officer below shouted at him, telling him to get back up to the landing, which he did.

"Most of the demonstrators on the landing had again resumed their seated position at the frantic urging of some who apparently feared the result of a mass exit down that hazardous staircase. Here and there the young people clustered around those who were hurt, trying to give them some aid.

"The moments that followed were curiously quiet, another of those strange lulls which were so absurd they seemed almost hallucinatory. Several feet away from me a girl bent over one of the injured boys sobbing hysterically and pleading with any policeman who came within earshot to get an ambulance. Up in the rotunda one of the plain-clothesmen stood quietly rocking on his heels and toes in the water, one hand behind his back, the other holding a toothpick, with which he introspectively poked at his teeth, looking for all the world like a man waiting for a bus. Erwin Goldsmith, who had been inside with Dale Minor taping the hearings for KPFA, finally managed to get out of the Chambers and he stood beside me for a moment as I recorded a description of the scene. When I finished he pointed to an elaborate, wrought-iron electric light stand close by. 'Don't touch that thing,' he said. 'In this water it'll fry you.' We didn't say anything else—there didn't seem to be much to say. I realized for the first time that my shoes, socks, and pant legs were soaked through from the two or three inches of water that was now pouring down the stairs and over the edge of the landing. Nearby a young girl leaned against a pillar staring at nothing in particular; when I looked a second time she was still staring, only this time I noticed she was softly crying.

"Minutes passed, and still nothing happened. The police had brought the barricades forward and lined them along the top of the seven steps to the rotunda, but, for the moment, that was the only action they took. The students had begun to sing and chant again, chanting 'Mr. Willis, we're still here!' again and again. Looking across the wide chasm which lay beyond the landing, I saw that hundreds of people had gathered quietly on the mezzanine and floors above to watch what took place.

"Then the hoses started again—again with no conceivable reason. The students were seated, unable to offer any violence if they wanted to, and none would have been permitted to leave (many had tried). This time few of the demonstrators seemed to mind as much. Most resignedly squatted under jackets or whatever protection they could muster, with their backs to the hoses. Some, in a foolish attempt at bravery, tried to face the hoses and hold their picket signs aloft for all to see, but half a minute of hosing in the face could either cure them of the first notion or drown them, and the water blasted the poster paint lettering right off the signs, and then the signs off the sticks. Again some of the young men went to the fore to form a human wall against the water, and through it all they continued to sing.

"I marveled at the casual gratuity of it all. If there was no reason for turning the hoses on the first time, there was even less now. Why? What good did it do? These officers who directed the pounding streams of water at the young peoples' heads for no reason at all—weren't they good men, who loved their wives and children the way most men do, men who were, like other men, sometimes charitable and generous and upright and even, perhaps, tender? How could they have been brought to such a pitch of fear and hatred that they could engage in this gratuitous cruelty without compunction, without pity?

"As abruptly as the hoses had been turned on they were again turned off. The students rose to their feet and faced the barricades as they sang 'The Star-Spangled Banner' with both dignity and pride. One of them had raised his fist over his head in defiance, thought better of it, and changed the gesture into the famous 'V-for-Victory' sign of World War II. Others noticed it and followed suit until the dripping crowd seemed to blossom out with the sign. But I saw why the hoses had been turned off: on the main floor below, two squads of motorcycle troopers reappeared (I hadn't noticed they'd left the rotunda above), marching in single file up the stairs. The singers were still faced toward the rotunda when the officers arrived at the head of the stairs, and as they finished the final chorus of the National Anthem, the police began clearing a pathway through the crowd and the students courteously moved aside for them.

"Their intention was to remove the 50 or 60 remaining demonstrators from the building. There were six large elevators thirty feet away from the stairhead, and more elsewhere on the floor, but the police chose a different method: they began throwing the demonstrators down the stairs one by one. They were gentler at first, two officers trying to slide a demonstrator down a step or so at a time, but one trooper started a dangerous precedent by grabbing a young Negro by the ankles and pulling him down the stairs on his back, with his head and spine striking every step. Then other officers began grabbing the young people by any convenient part of the clothing or body and half hauling, half throwing them down the long staircase. Those who linked arms were clubbed apart and taken down like the others. One girl was dragged part way down by her hair, another was thrown down over half the length of the stairway in one long tumble. Almost all were thoroughly stunned, in a state of shock, paralyzed, or unconscious by the time they reached the bottom; later, many were unable to tell me how they had gotten out of the building.

"Some of the officers seemed to find great amusement in the debacle, and called encouragement to each other: 'Step on him! Break his legs!' Others were clearly appalled and pleaded with the students to walk down and avoid injury. One girl who had attempted to leave before the second hosing but had been refused passage by the police stood near me, apart from the demonstrators, weeping hysterically until an older officer in a regular uniform took her by the arm and led her down the stairs holding on to the banister. Most of them, however, were afraid to walk down; some who had tried had been knocked down before they reached the bottom, and one young man had been knocked down and his hand clubbed on the balustrade until he let go to be pushed down the stairs. By and large it was safer to keep sitting and let yourself be dragged down.

"At the bottom of the stairs the demonstrators were picked up by other policemen, including some of the plainclothesmen (one of whom was wearing a palm sap) who were marching those who were still conscious through a corridor of spectators. Those who were unconscious were dragged out by the collar, some with their hands still jammed tightly in their pockets. But no resistance was tolerated. Those who tried to sit down again on the main floor were handcuffed and jerked to their feet by the bracelets. One student who was struggling in the grip of six motorcycle troopers was bashed on the head with a nightstick to quiet him. One girl, her arm twisted so tightly behind her back by the officer who was escorting her from the building that she was doubled over, fainted, and another girl who came to help was smacked across the teeth with a club.

"I saw one case of student violence: a tiny blonde girl, perhaps five feet three inches tall, furiously attacked a trooper who was roughly handling her girlfriend. He easily fended her off, but she did succeed in socking him once or twice. (She was never arrested.)

"Meanwhile, only a handful of demonstrators awaited removal at the head of the stairs. A girl pleaded hysterically with them to get up and leave. 'What do you think this is accomplishing?' she demanded. 'Let's not have any more people hurt.' After a moment of indecision, the last defenders of the right to attend a public hearing of a government body straggled to their feet and gingerly made their way down the stairs and out of the building to the taunts and jeers of the spectators. Some of these had edged their way out on the landing from the mezzanine in order to see what was going on near the door. They seemed almost unanimously in favor of the police, some of them even gloating over specific acts of brutality they had seen. 'What about Hungary?' they called, and 'If you wanna fight, why not go fight in Tibet?' I felt sick. Hate, suspicion, ignorance and fear ruled the day.

"But inside the building the show was over. It seemed fairly safe by now, but just in case I held my press card out in front of me and clutched the balustrade tightly on my way down. I shouted 'Press!' at any officer who glanced at me, just in case.

"The next day, Saturday, as was to be expected, the picket swelled to a considerable size, while several thousand people gathered to watch from across the street. Toward the end of the day, a crowd gathered in front of the City Hall (the police had closed the inside of the building) chanting and shouting at intervals. Four individuals were arrested for offering various provocations to the police, but the presence of the mounted officers made any danger of mob action remote. The majority of the students remained on the picket line as they had two days before.

"Some weeks later, the charges against 62 of the 63 defendants arrested on Friday (4 others were arrested on Saturday) were dropped. At this time, 58 of the students issued a statement which said:

"We appreciate Judge Axelrod's courage which has insured the triumph of justice and good sense. The defendants have been vindicated. Encouraged by the court's action, we shall continue our opposition to the HUAC. It is now doubly clear that public protests against it are in accord with American justice.

"The House Committee denies the rights to which we as defendants were entitled before the courts: namely, to be fully represented by counsel, to know the evidence on which charges are based, and to cross-examine accusers. In denying these rights, the House Committee denies due process of law. It smears because it cannot prove, holding up to public attack people who are not allowed to defend themselves. We oppose this. We opposed it when the committee conducted its hearings in San Francisco on May 12, 13, and 14. We acted as citizens aware of our duty to protest any violation of individual rights.

"Nobody incited us, nobody misguided us. We were led only by our convictions, and we still stand firmly by them.

"We shall continue our opposition to the committee. We

thank those who have had the courage to stand with us, and invite the community of which we are a part to join us.

"From our efforts to abolish the committee, we shall not be moved."

PENTAGON: WAR AND PROTEST

COMMITTEE OF THE PROFESSIONS

More than 100,000 Americans demonstrated in Washington on Saturday, October 21 [1967] against the war in Vietnam. Most did not plan to commit acts of civil disobedience, although it was known that some intended to. The events at the Pentagon at the end of the demonstration make these things clear:

·I· OUR GOVERNMENT'S RESPONSE TO OPPOSITION IS ALARMING.

Persons who commit acts of civil disobedience are liable to fines and imprisonment under the law. Historically, Americans have taken such steps reluctantly, but at certain times large numbers of citizens have felt they had no other choice. Thoreau is the inspiring symbol of an individual act of conscience.

Those who choose civil disobedience today to protest the war in Vietnam are responding to their conscience and are prepared to accept the legal consequences. Yet, as opposition to the war moves increasing numbers of Americans—particularly young Americans—to civil disobedience, the Government's response is physical assault. Just as draft protesters and student opponents of campus recruiting by the C.I.A. and Dow Chemical (maker of napalm) have been clubbed mercilessly by the police from California to New England, so in Washington, young people attempting a sit-in at the Pentagon, as well as bystanders, were clubbed and gassed by Federal marshals and paratroopers with fixed bayonets.

This violent response to non-violent protest has only one purpose: INTIMIDATION *and* REPRESSION—*not the restoration of law and order.*

·2· GOVERNMENT OFFICIALS LIE TO THE AMERICAN PEOPLE.

The authorities might have been expected to justify their violence with some reasoned explanation. On the contrary. The Defense Department denied the troops had used tear gas, while the President commended the Federal marshals and soldiers for what he called admirable restraint in the face of provocation.

Numerous witnesses and victims of the clubs and tear gas know the Government is lying. Comparable are Washington's lies that the effort of the Vietnamese people to be rid of domestic oppression and foreign invasion is Communist aggression, and that we are fighting to defend ourselves against Communist China. The credibility gap yawns wider.

·3· AMERICAN NEWSPAPERS LIE TO THE AMERICAN PEOPLE.

Countless newsmen and TV cameramen at the Pentagon witnessed the brutality; some even were gassed. Yet these same reporters wrote—and their newspapers printed without contradiction—statements that the Government forces used no gas: that it was the demonstrators who did. This is contemptible journalism.

Small wonder that the news media—with few honorable exceptions—still help the Government maintain the myth that we are in Vietnam in the name of democracy, a myth belied by our support of a series of unrepresentative Saigon regimes.

·4· BRAINWASHING IS ACCEPTED GOVERNMENT POLICY.

Governor Romney's charge that he and the American people have been "brainwashed" about the war brought scorn and amusement, but it merits serious investigation. The Pentagon demonstration is a case in point:

Clubs and tear gas are used against unarmed demonstrators as if this were a perfectly appropriate reaction. Having taken such action, the Government denies the action took place. Eyewitness reporters, many of them victims, blandly record the denial. In this situation, can the American people continue to credit the statements of government and the press interpretation of major international events and issues? Are those who use it for minor ends less likely to use duplicity for major ends?

A recent Gallup poll reported that the war in Vietnam is now opposed by 46% of all Americans. This is double the number of a year ago. What would the percentage be if there had been no "brainwashing," no distortion of facts, no suppression of news? Here, obviously, is the reason for the official policy of violence.

The issue in Vietnam is not only what is happening to the people of that tragic land. It is also what is happening to the American people.

Today is a proving time. Increasing numbers of Americans have decided that the draft and the war in Vietnam are immoral, that they must act according to their conscience to terminate those policies. Their courage merits respect.

In times past the abolitionists and suffragettes committed countless illegal acts to support beliefs now generally accepted as fundamental to democracy. More recently, thousands of black and white Americans have violated segregationist laws and have seen history vindicate their judgment.

We owe many of the meaningful changes in our society to the courage and dedication of such individuals, who risk personal security because of moral principles.

The true American patriots—the winter soldiers—are those who are now opposing U.S. policy in the face of growing misrepresentation and intimidation.

EYEWITNESS REPORTS

As I started to look for my daughters—Elizabeth, 20, and Susan, 17—in the crowd at the Pentagon Mall, I became aware that some of the seated people were singing softly. Others were quietly talking to each other. Suddenly one of the soldiers began to shuffle his feet forward, pressing hard upon one individual seated in front of him, and quickly two or three troopers grabbed the man and pulled him behind their line. I distinctly saw the marshals and soldiers clubbing an individual on his head and shoulders and back as he squirmed on the ground trying to avoid the clubs. . . . I called to the girls to come back where I was. A well-dressed man near Liz shouted at me, "Go away. You're putting us in great danger." It is obvious that these people had one objective. To sit there as quietly and peacefully as possible, to give the military no excuse for attacking them. . . . I was appalled by what I had seen. I can swear under oath that during the entire time I was on the Pentagon Mall there was not one announcement by the military telling the protesters they were in a restricted area or that they were off limits. . . . I do not believe that our top government officials are evil. But I believe they no longer feel the obligation to protect and respect the rights of dissenters. . . . As a father, I darn well know that young people are not always right. But I fear their disillusionment more than their disobedience.

ALBERT H. GAYNES, *businessman, Hastings on Hudson, New York*

One soldier spilled the water from his canteen on the ground in order to add to the discomfort of the female demonstrator at his feet. She cursed at him—understandably, I think— and shifted her body. She lost her balance and her shoulder hit the rifle at the soldier's side. He raised the rifle, and with its butt, came down hard on the girl's leg. The girl tried to move back but was not fast enough to avoid the billyclub of a soldier in the second row of troops. At least four times that soldier hit her with all his force, then as she lay covering her head with her arms, thrust his club swordlike between her hands into her face. Two more troops came up and began dragging the girl toward the Pentagon. . . . She twisted her body so we could see her face. But there was no face there: all we saw were some raw skin and blood. We couldn't see even if she was crying—her eyes had filled with the blood pouring down her head. She vomited, and that too was blood. Then they rushed her away.

> HARVEY MAYES, *English Dept., Hunter College, New York*

. . . After about 6:00 p.m. and until well into the morning of Sunday there were many beatings and arrests in the area where I spent the night. Not a single one was for acts of civil disobedience or violence. We sat in an area in which we were told we were legal until midnight Sunday. . . . The number of people wounded has been said to be 47, but that is the number of the *arrested* wounded. I personally saw many young people with bloodied heads, and one young man lying unconscious for about two hours. . . . Not once did the troops or marshals announce that we had to move from where we were, or that we were violating any kind of law whatsoever. The worst moment came between 11 and midnight, when the troops and marshals pushed forward in a wedge to cut our group in two. Clubs and rifle butts were flailing everywhere. The troops attacked a group of young people, boys and girls, who were sitting quietly, who were unarmed, who were not breaking any law. They were attacked by armed soldiers. . . . I have seen violence in the South and in World War II, but I have never seen anything as brutal as that attack.

> DOUGLAS F. DOWD, *Prof. of Economics, Cornell University, New York*

The Washington Sunday *Star* of Oct. 22 blamed 200–300 war resisters for an outbreak of violence at 10:30 p.m. What occurred, which many of the troops saw and opposed, was an attack by a group of U.S. marshals who, without provocation or warning, used clubs and rifles to beat quietly sitting protesters. In spite of this attack, which was loudly condemned by some, good rapport was established between many of the war protesters, MPs and a few U.S. marshals.

In a private conversation a marshal stated that most of them had been made marshals for the occasion at low pay.

> WILLIAM C. DAVIDON, *Assoc. Prof. of Physics,*
> *Haverford College, Pennsylvania*

The troops tear-gassed us at least twice, and only the self-discipline of the marchers prevented a riot. Later, on the steps, the resisters were quiet and orderly.

> ANTHONY HEILBUT, *English Dept., Washington*
> *Square College, New York University*

Late Saturday night we heard General O'Mally's radio denial that the gas had been used. We heard and saw this claim supported for several days by some of the very newsmen we must have seen running from the gas with handkerchiefs to their faces. . . . A priest talked quietly to the troops. He explained again and again that we love our country and that this was why we couldn't stand aside while she committed such grievous wrongs. He implored the soldiers to be more gentle as they dragged each demonstrator away. The man was in his fifties or sixties. When the soldiers finally decided to arrest him, he was afforded a particularly brutal treatment. Needless to say, this priest made no attempt to resist. He was grabbed by four MPs who pulled at his hair as he was yanked off the ground and who bobbled him up and down against the asphalt as they prepared to drag him off and who placed their feet under him and kicked at his spine. Finally, they dragged him away.

> KARSTEN J. *and* PAULA STRUHL, *respectively,*
> *Philosophy Depts., Long Island University and*
> *Hunter College, New York*

The young people's sense of seriousness is what impressed one most while standing on the Pentagon steps at midnight. The seriousness inspired a calm—even a cheerfulness—which withstood the provocation of clubs, rifles, curses and kicks. Camaraderie, dedication, understanding, good humor —these, not violence, are the words which properly describe the mood of those shivering youngsters. The boys and girls I talked with had not previously been involved in protest actions; indeed, had never given any thought to civil disobedience.

Louis Kampf, *Assoc. Prof. of Humanities, Massachusetts Institute of Technology*

Several weeks prior to the march we contacted officials in the D.C. Health Department and, on behalf of the Medical Committee for Human Rights, offered the services of a group of physicians to set up or help staff emergency first-aid stations for the Mobilization. Assurances were given that plans had already been made. A similar offer was made to medical officials in the Military District of Washington, under whose jurisdiction came the responsibility for medical facilities at the Pentagon grounds. They rejected our offer. . . . The facilities at the Pentagon were dangerously inadequate. During the afternoon a U.S. marshal arbitrarily moved the Red Cross unit to an area inaccessible to everyone except those who were later arrested. . . . By late afternoon it became obvious that there were many people who needed immediate medical attention and a volunteer group of physicians decided to set up an emergency first-aid station. No equipment, water, lights or readily available ambulance facilities were provided, and we were repeatedly refused medical supplies by the military authorities. From 5 to 9 that Saturday evening we treated about 40 people, using some equipment carried in from facilities several miles from the Pentagon. Included among the injured were many severe lacerations, several fractures, many tear-gas injuries and three cases of asthma. Some of the cases were of such severity that, after preliminary evaluation, they had to be taken to nearby hospitals. It must be said that it is very fortunate that no one died. . . .

Sidney M. Wolfe, M.D., Arthur Frank, M.D., *and* Jesse Roth, M.D.

The news media gave a distorted account of the mood of the demonstrators. I was struck by its seriousness and the relative absence of singing and chanting. . . . For the most part the soldiers acted with restraint, as they should have.

However, there were instances of unnecessary force which might be traced to the reports that sergeants and officers consistently referred to the demonstrators as "the enemy," thus creating a battle-like atmosphere. The Pentagon denials concerning the use of tear gas are just one more example of the untrustworthiness of any statements concerning the war issued out of the Executive Branch.

NEIL FABRICANT, lawyer, New York City

On Saturday, Oct. 21, at about 5 o'clock, I witnessed two groups of soldiers being sent into a massive crowd gathered below the Mall entrance to the Pentagon. They behaved with restraint. They were immediately surrounded by the crowd. There was no apparent shoving by the demonstrators. Then, suddenly, from the side, came several U.S. marshals, then a dozen. Over the shrubbery they went, freely swinging their clubs, apparently trying to free the troops. In my opinion their action clearly provoked the crowd. Certainly the marshals brought unnecessary bloodshed.

THE REV. THOMAS LEE HAYES, *Executive Director, Episcopal Peace Fellowship, New York*

We saw gas masks on soldiers' faces, gas sprayed at the crowd, people with streaming eyes overcome with retching. . . . In the 14 hours we were with the main body of some 1,500 demonstrators on the Mall, we neither saw nor heard of any act of violence to the troops or U.S. marshals. On the other hand, we saw and suffered from violence at the hands —and feet—of marshals and Army officers. And their violence was systematic and deliberate, a fundamental part of their strategy. They wanted us gone, but they did not want to arrest 2,000 people, nor did they want to drive all of us out with gas or clubs or guns. And so they had to frighten us, wear us down, pick off leaders, keep us unsettled. . . . For most of Saturday night, unprovoked arrests were accompanied by great violence. People were pulled away with no warning, clubbed and kicked in the sight of their friends; women and sleeping demonstrators were favorite targets. Those who held on to the sleeping were beaten and also dragged away. . . . Other harassments were stupidly petty.

At about 5:30 in the morning, a sergeant walked along the line, emptying canteens of water on our backs.

> PAUL LAUTER *and* FLORENCE HOWE, *respectively Assoc. Prof., Antioch College, and Ass't Prof., Goucher College*

By sundown, 2,000 demonstrators had gained forbidden territory on the closest parking terrace, but they were hemmed in by three ranks of troops. . . . The 6,000 troops (National Guardsmen, airborne infantrymen, military police, armed Federal marshals) had very little to do during the night. . . . Those on the front steps stood stiffly at attention. . . . Only the few dozen soldiers in the front lines, pressed against the shivering sit-ins, saw any action, and even that was sporadic. One or two detachments had thrown tear gas (the Pentagon denied it, but reporters and demonstrators saw the soldiers in the act). Early in the morning, some of the soldiers relieved their obvious boredom by kicking seated demonstrators or jamming rifle butts into their spines.

> ANDREW KOPKIND, *writer, New Statesman*

The confrontation above the steps of the Pentagon was a nonviolent vigil. It was for the most part orderly in spite of repeated provocations by the administration police. We earnestly and lovingly attempted to appeal to that bit of God in each of the men who were forced to treat us as their enemy. . . . I was surrounded by MPs and marshals. I had gone limp. I continued to talk of love and continued to appeal to their humanity. The reply was "Okay, lover boy." I was prodded and beaten on the body. A marshal began beating on the soles of my feet. Sticks were jabbed in the soft parts of my body. Two night sticks were clamped on my throat and two marshals lifted me up. I couldn't breathe or speak. They threw me back on the ground, twisted my arms behind my back and handcuffed me and carried me for a minute by the handcuffs. Camera lights went on. A marshal said to carry me by arms and legs. I non-cooperated all the way to Occoquan [workhouse], was dropped, kicked, etc. All the time I was being carried I tried to appeal to the humanity of my persecutors. . . . I trust in the power of the Spirit and know it will sustain me through my trials.

JERRY D. COFFIN, *Philadelphia*

The soldiers began to push two young men at the head of the crowd at about 10:30 p.m. A Federal marshal burst through the line of troops and began to savagely beat the two young men as a prelude to their arrest. Time after time his club smashed down upon the heads and backs of his two victims. The soldiers joined in, brutally and repeatedly brought their rifle butts down upon the bodies of the demonstrators. The two young men were literally being beaten to death. I was dazed by disbelief. . . . I reached out and tried to drag the victims back into the protection of the crowd. The Federal marshal's club immediately thrust down upon my hand, this being repeated half a dozen times. A soldier added his rifle butt to the assault.

CLIFF FORSTADT, *student, Chairman, Judicial Board, Hunter College, New York*

The only violence I saw was that practiced against the demonstrators by Federal marshals and troops. This violence was selective and tactical, not widespread. . . . Some persons—frequently girls—were kicked and clubbed repeatedly and very severely. I believe this was done tactically, to shock and discourage the crowd from staying on. But it was clear that several of the officers, and particularly the marshals, enjoyed doing it. . . . If any complaints or angry shouts came from the crowd, they were directed at the officers and marshals responsible for the brutality. Widespread sympathy for the soldiers was expressed throughout the 12 hours that I was present.

ALLAN BRICK, PH.D., *Lutherville, Maryland*

I was one of the volunteer attorneys helping the people at Occaquon Workhouse to which demonstrators were taken following their arrest. Although most of the people arrested were charged simply with violating a regulation about where they could go (equivalent to a park rule about keeping off the grass), there was a substantial number of people bearing bruises and otherwise showing the effects of having been beaten and these people were usually charged with assault, apparently to justify the beatings inflicted upon them.

JEREMIAH GUTMAN, *lawyer, New York*

The most brutal acts that I myself saw occurred Saturday night around 10 p.m. on an access road leading to the Pentagon, guarded by about 15 deputy U.S. marshals. The marshals ran at a dozen or so demonstrators sitting on the road with linked arms, clubbing them severely on the legs, face and head, and shouting at them. There were no cars approaching. I was yelling at the marshals to stop their clubbing and to get medical help for a protester whose face was dripping blood when a marshal came directly at me shouting, "Get that big fat one." I was the first person thrown into the waiting paddy wagon.

JAY SCHULMAN, *Ass't Prof., School of Industrial and Labor Relations, Cornell University*

My main fear was claustrophobia and trampling. About 8 p.m. they started grabbing people—dragging them off and arresting them. Quite soon I was next to the troop lines and all of a sudden I heard that tear gas was being used. . . . The troops suddenly went crazy. It seemed they were kicking at us, tugging at the people . . . and all of a sudden it was just a sprawl of bodies. . . . I was on top of several people. I was very exposed and this was the time I started getting hit on the head. . . . So for some reason or other I headed for the troops, through their legs. I think I remember getting through three rows of troops—it seemed like that—then I passed out.

CHRISTIE HUIDEKOPER, *art student, New York City*

A Federal marshal came down the line and spoke quickly to several MPs in front of me. Then suddenly those MPs moved forward, kicking at me. At the same time a Federal marshal began striking me on the head. I brought my knees up to my chest, covered my head with my arms, and tucked my head down. As I did this the marshal stabbed at me with his billy club and succeeded in hitting me in the genitals. Then I was grabbed by the legs and dragged to a van about 150 yards distant. Another marshal, saying "Watch out for the press, watch out for the press," picked me up by the shoulders, and I was thrown into the van.

JOHN MARK BLOWEN, *Philadelphia*

Urban Campus Prototype

By MERVIN B. FREEDMAN

San Francisco

I teach at San Francisco State College. Along with several dozen faculty members and students, I stand at a fifth-floor window and watch a noontime rally of strikers and their supporters. After an hour or so of speeches, the crowd displays a certain agitation. Police begin to appear on the scene. They march and countermarch in squads and platoons. Eventually skirmishing and some open fighting develop. Several dozen strikers and bystanders are clubbed and hauled off in paddy wagons. Some policemen are injured, mostly by rocks and other missiles. The warfare lasts for about an hour. An uneasy calm then settles on the campus, and at noon the next day almost the same scene is repeated, like a regularly scheduled public spectacle.*

As I watch these terrifying events, various images come to mind—the Hapsburgs or Romanovs looking down from the palace windows through the snows of Vienna and St. Petersburg at the cavalry clashing with students and workers. From time to time the military quality of the scene below suggests that I have assumed the vantage point of some nineteenth-century general, Napoleon at Austerlitz, perhaps, surveying a battle from a hill through a spyglass. Since I was raised in Ocean Hill in Brooklyn and served in World War II for three and a half years as an enlisted man, before

* See David Swanston, "San Francisco State: How to Wreck a Campus," *The Nation*, January 8, 1968.

I was commissioned a second lieutenant, identifications with emperors and generals are not particularly congenial. The most apposite image to come to mind is Oswald Spengler's —the Roman soldier grimly going about his business (in my case, teaching my classes off-campus) while his world crumbles. But I am not a very good Roman soldier, either. I have too many doubts. So I go about in a whirl, torn by contradictory impulses.

Only the theater of the absurd can do justice to some of the scenes at ground level. I stand in a crowd of strikers who are about to hold a rally. The crowd is San Francisco —pretty blondes dressed like Sacagawea, chic black girls with natural hair, assorted Oriental and brown-skinned young people conservatively dressed, and dignified black adults, goateed black young men, bearded and long-haired white young men, clergymen with clerical collars, gray-haired white adults. I recognize some people—students, faculty members, prominent San Francisco politicians. Who are the others—strikers, supporters, onlookers, townspeople, police spies? Who knows? Suddenly a voice booms out from loudspeakers: "This is Acting President Hayakawa." He is standing on the roof of the Administration Building a hundred yards away. A great chorus of boos goes up from the crowd. President Hayakawa proceeds to pontificate over the loudspeakers in donnish tones. (The remoteness of leader from public somehow reminds me of Mussolini haranguing his vassals from the balcony of the Palazzo Venezia.) Meanwhile the crowd at the strike rally takes up a chant, "Fuck Hayakawa" (although most of the older adults do not join in). The president terminates his remarks by wishing his audience a Merry Christmas. The crowd responds to this seasonal civility with hoots of derision and paroxysms of laughter. My companion throughout this scene, a young assistant professor, Yale A.B. and Stanford Ph.D., has been rendered almost catatonic. Finally he blurts out, "This is too much."

The situation of San Francisco State College baffles description and analysis. The Black Students Union and the Third World Liberation Front (composed of other minorities, for example, Orientals and Mexican-Americans) have called for a strike. Their demands, centered on more support and autonomy for black and other nonwhite students, faculty and programs, range from stipulations that most students, administrators and faculty consider reasonable to those that seem extreme and very difficult to meet—the demand, for example, that the college admit *all* nonwhite students who apply for the fall semester of 1969–70. Spokesmen for the Black Students Union and the Third World Liberation Front state that they will not compromise their demands. Certain activities disruptive of academic procedures have been carried out. Classrooms have been invaded, bomb threats have been phoned in, small explosive devices have been set off, fires have been started, etc. Serious injuries have been few and damage relatively slight, but it is certain that the climate is troubled and alarmed. Many classes now meet off-campus in dormitories, homes, churches and the like. A union of faculty members, an affiliate of the American Federation of Teachers, is attempting to obtain wider union support for a faculty strike. The split between faculty members and the board of trustees of the state colleges has been growing for a long time; now one of the faculty demands is that the trustees, who have been as adamant as the striking students in their refusal to negotiate, enter into discussion with strikers, both faculty and student.

At dinner parties I am harassed by the question, "What is the solution?" By now I have a reply ready. There is, I say, no solution in the present focus. The problem of San Francisco State College is the problem of all urban campuses, and it is the basic problem of American urban society generally. Can whites, blacks, browns, reds, yellows, adults, youth, hippies, straights, revolutionaries, conservatives live together in sufficient harmony to maintain some orderly processes of society? The answer is not yet final, but the data at hand are not encouraging. Some years back I used to make predictions about complex social events, but I lack such confidence now. I offer the reader three alternatives:

1) The disorders on campuses are but transitory phenomena which will end soon.

2) During the next decade the San Francisco State situation will become the norm for urban college campuses and for cities generally. Disorder, explosions, fires, guerrilla warfare, strikes will be common events. At the end of this time a more just, humane and peaceable society will emerge.

3) Out of recurrent tension and disorder will issue a Fascist state. College campuses and society generally will increasingly resemble South Africa.

San Francisco State is unique in some respects. It has suffered in recent years from an absence of leadership because of rapid turnover of presidents. The California state college bureaucracy is rigid and cumbersome. Militants in San Francisco are very militant, and conservatives in California, followers of Ronald Reagan or Max Rafferty, are very primitive. But the problems of San Francisco State are basically the problems of any urban campus, and the future of American higher education is increasingly the large, urban, commuter campus. No simple procedures are available for avoiding repetitions of the calamities at San Francisco State all over the country. The close interplay now seen in every big city between society at large and the urban campus is evident in the San Francisco State scene. The governor of California, the mayor of San Francisco, various state assemblymen and senators, clergymen, leaders of the black, Oriental and Mexican-American communities, and the San Francisco Labor Council have all entered the fight. Von Clausewitz's dictum may be applied to the student strike—it is simply a more militant form of political action.

The urban campus reflects the conflicts of urban society —nonwhite or non-Anglo militancy, alienated middle-class youth, repressive public opinion and public officials, heavy-handed police procedures, drugs, and the like. And as with society at large, the system of academic government is not adequate to the task. Jeffersonian-style democracy and checks and balances cannot cope with the pace and the complexity of mass technological society. The traditional campus community also belongs to another age, the nineteenth century. In static times a system can carry an inadequate leader. When traditional procedures break down, the qualities of the leader assume crucial importance. The United States could accommodate Calvin Coolidge in the 1920's; Columbia University could do likewise with Nicholas Murray Butler. Such indulgences are no longer possible. The president of an urban college must grasp, make evident, and somehow cope with a bewildering variety of issues, for many or for most of which there are no precedents. He is thus sailing stormy and uncharted waters.

The president of an urban campus must attempt to fashion a viable institution of a student body that is a very mixed bag. The interests of student groups are diverse and often conflicting—jocks versus radicals, upper-middle-class students with educational goals centered on personal development versus lower-middle-class students who are concerned with rising out of their parents' occupational status, minority groups versus more established groups, and sometimes one minority group against another. The governing of most private universities and colleges, where the student body is relatively homogeneous, is a far easier task.

The traditional concept of a campus community is based on the premise that people know one another and share many experiences and concerns. On a fragmented, urban, commuter campus this is hardly the case. The president frequently finds himself discussing an explosive issue with a group of students whom he has not met before. For all he knows, some of these young people may not be students. Should an ex-student be considered a member of the campus community? How about a resident of the local community who has never been enrolled in the college? Should the president refuse to talk to a young man or woman if it develops that he or she is an "outside agitator"?

Needless to say, public opinion is a force with which college presidents must reckon. In California Ronald Reagan, Max Rafferty, and such figures stalk the land, ever alert for signs of sexual immorality, pornography, drugs and radical or unpatriotic sentiments and behavior on campuses. Public support for their views is considerable. In the California gubernatorial election of 1966, Ronald Reagan campaigned very successfully against radicals and hippies on the Berkeley campus of the University of California. I should estimate that the citizenry of California oppose the strike at San Francisco State by a margin well above three to one. In response to this public opinion the trustees of the state college system and the regents of the university system have infringed upon certain faculty prerogatives—for example, in the Eldridge Cleaver case. In a time of George Wallaces and

Max Raffertys it may seem ludicrous to suggest that college presidents must educate public officials and citizens at large on the basic issues of intellectual and academic freedom. But they must nevertheless try.

Students and trustees, legislators and public opinion are by no means the limit of the president's concern. When a campus is in turmoil one hears comparatively little about the faculty. This is a serious oversight, as any president knows. A faculty can immobilize a campus as effectively as any other group. One hundred students can bring in the police and cancel classes. Fifteen faculty members can block almost any program by talking it to death.

For the past nine months, I have been studying faculty attitudes toward student militancy and campus unrest. It may be said that faculty members are like other Americans at this time. They are somewhat demoralized, weary of conflict, and they are shifting perceptibly to the right in the face of radical challenge. Most campuses have a small group of faculty whose views resemble Hearst editorials circa 1938 and another minority which supports student dissidence. The majority of faculty members on an urban campus are liberals. Robert Kennedy and Eugene McCarthy were their candidates. They want a fast compromise solution to Vietnam. They want justice along with law and order. But at the gut level of daily action, things are not so easy. Respectable professional men bristle when confronted by obscene language, outlandish dress and bad manners. Black militants may frighten them. Differences in personal style can obscure areas of agreement and avenues of potentially profitable exploration.

Faculty members are lords of small empires and masters of orderly schedules. A teacher meets classes on Monday, Wednesday and Friday, researches and writes on Tuesday and Thursday. Forty-two lectures on the United States, 1865–1914, are to be delivered in the spring semester. The symphony orchestra will give a concert on December 1, 2, and 3, and the Drama Department's performance of *Heartbreak House* takes place on November 10 and 11. Interruptions are resented. One faculty member said to me: "If the college wants to schedule a convocation on Vietnam, let them do it nights or weekends. The convocation took two days out of my teaching. I can't afford to miss two days, considering all the material I have to cover." Roger Heyns, chancellor of the University of California at Berkeley, has made the point that the faculty presumes a college campus to be an institution that almost by definition is to be free of tension. A president must make the faculty see the unreality of such a view in these turbulent times.

The president's domestic complexities are not confined to students, faculty or academic administrators. He must give heed to campus police, secretaries, dormitory residents, business officers and other nonacademic staff. They are an important and neglected element of the community. When three black students meet, a campus police officer suspects that they are up to no good. Secretaries may quake when approached by a black man whose appearance is not respectably middle-class. Hippy garb and grooming can be comparable sources of difficulty. These nonacademic contacts can contribute considerably to campus tension.

The financing of higher education for lower-class blacks and other American minority groups is receiving considerable attention at this time. An even more critical issue than finances is the question of what to do with such students once they arrive on campus. College presidents might begin to educate their constituencies concerning some of the implications of black studies. Militant blacks and their allies have thrown light on the hypocritical underpinnings of the "land of the free and the home of the brave"—the slaughter of Indians, the unjust wars, slavery. They have helped to arrest the march of technology and scientism that a decade ago seemed destined to kill the humanistic spirit. They have greatly contributed to the realization that white, middle-class America does not necessarily walk hand in hand with God. And now they are taking on meritocracy, as exemplified by grades and degrees. They demand that colleges contribute to the development of students rather than that students be tailored to the abstract demands of professions, industry and the like.

Such fundamental issues must be explained and placed within a framework of rational discussion. It may be that the conflicts besetting the urban campus cannot be solved by reason, but the president must live by the faith that rational debate is still useful. These are revolutionary times, and most middle-aged liberals are ten or fifteen years behind the times. They would have made good college presidents in 1955. They are of the alcohol rather than the drug generation.

In order to talk to dissident students today a president must know where "they are at." He must grasp their sense of outrage and their spirit of anarchy, and recognize the ground on which they justify confrontation and violence. He must appreciate the appeal of antithought. He must be able to talk to students in a language that is not dead. The manners, style and language of rebellion are powerfully evocative. The worst of sins among dissident youth is not to feel. And tired old liberal rhetoric can smother feeling like a blanket. See what it did to Hubert Humphrey's standing with radical youth.

None of this is to suggest that presidents abandon faith in democracy and the meliorative possibilities of the college. They must attempt to draw dissident students into that framework. But the tragic view is in order. They may not be successful in so influencing their students, and it may be that reform of the American system of higher education demands confrontation, that meliorative procedures will not work.

At all events the time for playing it cool is past. I suggest that presidents eschew the role of behind-the-scenes diplomat and administrator and return to the nineteenth-century concept of president as teacher and orator. Heaven knows, their constituencies have much to learn. They might begin by pointing out to rebellious students that while a revolution evokes an extraordinary sense of freedom and possibility, evocation of a mood is not a political end in itself. History indicates that revolutions cannot be expected to conform to plan, but some coherent vision of the post-revolutionary scene is nevertheless necessary. French students took over the Sorbonne and then did not know what to do with it. They thereby lost much support from the French citizenry. Exegesis of the true state of affairs in the governing of colleges and universities is badly needed. Abuse of the trustees is often misplaced. To be sure, trustees can wield power in tyrannical fashion. More often, however, policy is determined by the faculty. The view of Columbia University as a medieval fief ruled by President Kirk and the trustees is myopic. Rather, President Kirk and his trustees maintained a very loose hegemony over a series of duchies and baronies, the various departments, schools and colleges, most of which enjoyed considerable independence. Above all, a president must find suitable ways for students to participate in the operation of the institution. Only then will students assume true responsibility. Given the nature of campus government, which has grown by accretion, this is no easy task.

A president must hold up to his faculty and his non-academic staff the picture of rigidity and intolerance in which all of us share. The times are too perilous to afford these luxuries. This is not to suggest that faculty members should abandon standards, but some openness and humility are in order. The president might remind a faculty member who is disturbed by disruptions of his class that in five years most of his students are not likely to remember his name, much less what they learned in the laboratory of Botany 1A on April 17. Above all, a president must exhort his faculty and staff to function in their professional environment as any mature citizen must live in our turbulent society—that is, tolerating much confusion and ambiguity. The faculty can ill afford short fuses and snap judgments. Some faculty members are quick to label almost all student protest and dissent an SDS plot to revolutionize American society. Such facile judgments needlessly polarize factions.

These days the chances are that the president who abandons the role of playing it cool and stands forth to exert moral force will be punished. The president of a complex urban institution faces an almost impossible task under the best of circumstances, and statistics show that they do not last long in their jobs. Like baseball managers they come and go, but unlike baseball managers their reasons for going are rarely publicized. A president who is fired for publicly standing by principle, whose firing therefore means something, is infinitely to be preferred to the president who goes out with a whimper, because he cannot do the near impossible—that is, hold the urban campus together. Certain elements of the public may enjoy the spectacle of a Socrates receiving his just rewards. A president, however, may inspire and unite his own constituency, his students and his faculty, by a display of moral leadership, a commodity which is usually in short supply and which appears to be critically lacking in the United States at this time. Perhaps some foundation could assume the burden of aiding financially those true teachers among college presidents who lose their jobs by taking unambiguous stands on matters of intellectual and academic principle. Foundations have been known to do less rewarding things with their moneys.

THE JULY REBELLIONS AND THE "MILITARY STATE"

By J. H. O'DELL

There is a currently popular American folksong whose lyrics speak philosophically concerning time and the turn of the seasons.

What was earlier in this decade described as our summers of discontent now turns into seasons of growing popular revolt against the conditions of life in America. The war in Vietnam continues as does the determined popular resistance to the war by large sections of the American people. The Military Establishment grows more brutal and arrogant, at home and abroad. The freedom-consciousness of the black ghettos becomes more articulate in act as well as in word, as one of the major institutions of racism (the ghetto condition) comes under assault. This is part of the cutting edge of an emerging new Resistance Movement. The month of July [1967] proved the premier month as thirty-seven cities, stretching across the continent from East Harlem to San Bernardino, California, and as far South as Riviera Beach, Florida, were shaken by revolts of varying magnitude, large and small.

These events call attention, in a dramatic way, to the fact that in the midst of its much-boasted affluence, the self-styled Great Society, like its predecessors, Rome and the Third Reich, has fallen upon bad times.

The defenders of the *ancien régime* respond with characteristic venom. "Get those niggers . . . get those niggers" is the police yell in Newark and Plainfield, New Jersey, as they fan out to occupy the ghetto. "The gooks are still in there . . . burn down as much as possible" echo similar voices on television, coming from Lien Ho and Bon Son, Vietnam, on the other side of the world, an area also being "pacified" American style. The language of insult even comes from the lips of the Texan who has been called America's accidental President, as he describes the leaders of the ghetto revolts. His audience is a convention of chiefs of police and he is asking for support for his "safe streets" legislation.

The language of insult is accompanied by the language of confusion as the American people are given a definition of these events in the ghetto as "riots." This is the term repeated over and over again by the news media and the most prominent leaders of white American opinion.

For all practical purposes, to understand these events and what they mean, it is necessary to clear up the problem of definitions. This is particularly necessary because language is used by the oppressor, often very effectively, to keep freedom fighters on the defensive. American society has a long history of charging its black victims with "guilt" by cleverly using the language as a weapon. In this, as in so many other ways, the United States shows how very much it is a part of the Western world.

When one reads the history of the Negro people in the United States, especially the long slavery period, one reads of Nat Turner's *rebellion*, or of Denmark Vesey's *revolt* and of the more than two hundred other slave *revolts*. These were violent efforts by men, individually or collectively, to throw off the chains of slavery exploitation. And if, in the course of events, they set fire to a plantation or took some food from the slaveholders' warehouse, freedom-loving mankind the world over hailed this as quite naturally in the spirit of liberty. Only the slavemasters and their allies regarded such events as "riots" and the men struggling to throw off the yoke of slavery as "hoodlums."

More than a century before these freedom revolts by African slaves under the rule of the American Republic, a series of similar events had shaken British rule in the colony of Virginia. In 1676 the governor's plantation was stripped of its crops and domestic animals, and a militia was organized among the planters, farmers and white indentured servants to back up their demands for lower taxes, and an end to corruption and favoritism in the government. This was known as Bacon's Rebellion, named after Nathaniel Bacon, its leader, who died in jail while twenty-nine of his compatriots were hanged by the British authorities, and dozens of others jailed and fined.

The Royal Commission appointed by the Crown to "investigate these disturbances" was sharply divided in its opinion between those who argued that "the unrest is just the work of a few rabble who could be put down by a [military] force of 200 men" and the more conciliatory commissioners who contended "the unrest is widespread because of real grievances . . . which should be investigated."

Each of these events, in its own time-setting, was a landmark in the development of greater political consciousness among the aggrieved population.

THE NATURE OF THE CURRENT REVOLTS

In the slavery period of our American experience, the main institution of confinement is the plantation. In the post-slavery period, especially since the First World War, the main institution of confinement for the black population in the United States is the ghetto.

The Negro ghetto has been described often and elaborately. It is an enclave within the larger American urban setting, whose inhabitants pay high rents for slum houses or buy second-hand houses at inflated real estate prices; an area of run-down schools, overcrowded and poorly staffed, with a curriculum which is designed to give the child an inferior education, and consequently handicap him in the competition for college or a good job later in life. The ghetto family pays marked-up prices for poor-quality food and other merchandise—with the weighted scale in the meat market and the padded credit accounts in the furniture store everyday forms of robbery. It is a population preyed upon by petty hustlers and charlatans and a variety of other social parasites who wouldn't be allowed to "operate" in other communities. It is a population occupied by a police force acting as overseers on this urban plantation.

By way of definition, the functional role of the ghetto, as an institutionalized form of racism, is to facilitate the special exploitation of the black population, through the mechanisms we have described. As such, the ghetto is merely an updated, modified version of the nineteenth-century slave quarters, in the American system of exploitation. And the revolts against the conditions in the ghetto today are linked by history to the revolts against slavery in the past. Such terms as "riots" and "hoodlums" have no place in any honest, objective appraisal of these events.

The central continuing fact of American economic and social history over the past three and a half centuries is the special exploitation and robbery of the Negro community. As a corollary to this reality, the central theme in the life and history of the Afro-American population is one continuous struggle to free itself from this agonizing situation. The recent rebellions in Newark, Detroit, and revolts elsewhere over the past four years are but the latest examples highlighting this truth.

No useful purpose is served by Negro civil rights leaders straining to disassociate themselves from the forces of the ghetto rebellion. Whitney Young's cautious statement that "the vast majority of Negroes are exercising patience, restraint and loyalty" is as irrelevant to understanding the freedom movement today as it is reassuring to the white power structure for whom such statements are obviously intended.

What is new, and therefore very relevant, is the fact of a growing number of youthful black men and women who are no longer patient but fed up; no longer restrained but ready to "go for broke"; and are indeed loyal, to *themselves* and their people because they are convinced the country is not loyal to them.

Disappointed in the civil rights movement and its leaders, to whom they looked for *their* emancipation, too, disillusioned, they have begun to act on their own. They didn't create the ghetto slums, but as the victims they are making the ghettos of American the new battleground. They are confronting the whole fabric of exploitation in the ghetto at the level that they see it functioning: the absentee-owned stores, and the property of the absentee slumlords, and the police occupation force representing the state power of the colonial regime.

If, as some people say, these revolts "have nothing to do with civil rights," it is only because the very concept "civil rights" is too narrow to deal with the basic economic and political problems facing the black population today. If the method of resistance is no longer exclusively nonviolent, it is because violence is the language of America and they, the colonized, wish to be heard. If they are not making their appeal by way of moral argumentation, it is because they have concluded, *from the record,* that the leadership of this nation is basically immoral in its dealing with non-white people, the world over. So their manifesto is in the deed rather than the rhetoric, and in this course of action they are making the title of James Baldwin's famous essay, "The Fire Next Time," a prophetic reality.

Unlike the violence which has characterized American life and history, the violence of the ghetto rebellion is not motivated by greed and inhumanity. It is a form of resistance to deprivation and a protest against being ignored by the Affluent Society.

In their confiscation of food and useful merchandise from stores whose owners have been looting their pockets for years, they are showing their contempt for the "property rights" of all the petty exploiters, and regard this as a way of "getting even."

In their combative defiance of the armed forces of the regime, and risking life and limb in the contest, they are giving their answer to current popular notions among "sociologists" concerning the "emasculation of the Negro male."

Like millions of their countrymen, Negro Americans increasingly understand that a government which is currently spending 75 billion dollars a year on war and outerspace efforts to put a man on the moon has no intention of providing adequate funds to end joblessness, slum conditions and correct educational deprivation in the ghettos. In spite of the official deceptive propaganda to the country, racist wars abroad are not in the least likely to serve the cause of multiracial democracy at home. If anything, racist wars abroad make the forces of domestic racism more arrogant, and the colonized nationalities in America (Afro-American, Spanish-speaking and Indian), all of whom are the victims of racism, have an instinctive understanding of this.

So, certain of the colonized are acting upon their own definitions for they are convinced ours is a struggle for survival in a hostile, racist society. One does not have to be a die-hard advocate of violence or anarchy to recognize the validity of a social rebellion by the oppressed which takes a violent form. Riots have little to do with freedom; revolts or rebellions against oppression have everything to do with freedom.

All reasonable people prefer to see social change and social emancipation effected in as peaceful and constructive a manner as possible. We are reminded that Detroit had the largest nonviolent civil rights march in the history of any one city in America. In June, 1963, 125,000 people—including thousands from the ghetto—marched for Freedom Now! led by Martin Luther King and Walter Reuther. This was two months before the march on Washington. I remember in 1959 how hundreds of people came from the Newark ghetto to the nation's capital for the national March for Integrated Schools, which brought 25,000 people to Washington, led by Jackie Robinson, A. Philip Randolph and others. Today Newark has thousands of black children on split shifts in overcrowded, run-down schools, as do most ghettos across the country. As is well known there are more completely segregated schools in the Northern urban centers today than there were when the Supreme Court's decision on public education was declared in 1954, while the South has desegregated only about twenty-five percent of its school districts during this period.

For more than a decade, through law suits and a variety of nonviolent direct actions against segregation, the many organizations of the freedom movement forced the nation to look at segregation and the daily humiliations that institution imposed upon Negro Americans.* Since 1964, in

* It is not true, as Eric Hoffer suggests, that the nonviolent movement for civil rights was (or is) a movement of "middle-class Negroes." It

flash-seasons of violent direct action, the dispossessed in the ghettos are forcing the country to look at their condition as a particular class (the most painfully exploited) among Negro Americans. This is the same struggle for human dignity appearing in different forms.

The revolts against the ghetto condition are centered among the youth and the poorest sections of the working class, those whose economic circumstances today are very similar to the condition of the majority of the American working class during the Great Depression.

In a lengthy article in *The New York Times Magazine,* Bayard Rustin makes a quite different appraisal, in the following:*

> Daniel Patrick Moynihan is correct in locating the riots in the "lower class," or in the words of another controversial man, Karl Marx, in the "lumpenproletariat" or "slum proletariat." Lower class does not mean working class; the distinction is often overlooked in a middle-class culture that tends to lump the two together.
>
> The distinction is important. The working class is employed. It has a relation to the production of goods and services; much of it is organized in unions. It enjoys a measure of cohesion, discipline and stability lacking in the lower class. The latter is unemployed or marginally employed. It is relatively unorganized, incohesive, unstable. It contains the petty criminal and antisocial elements.

Further on in the article, Rustin coins the phrase "black slum proletariat" to describe his lower class or lumpenproletariat.

Of course one does not have to be an especially keen observer of society to recognize that the working class has many gradations within it, ranging from the poorest-paid, unskilled and semiskilled workers to the higher-paid skilled workers, who are usually able to secure more steady employment than the unskilled for rather obvious reasons. In an industrial society of rapidly advancing technology, the job experience of the unskilled is likely to include more

---

embraced all social classes in Negro life, because all classes are affected, in varying degrees, by the reality of segregation and racial discrimination.
  * "The Way Out of the Ghetto," August 13, 1967.

part-time work ("marginal employment") and longer periods of unemployment than that of the skilled worker.

However, they are all part of the working class because
their class position is not determined by which one has a
job and which is unemployed.

The auto worker in Detroit who operates a tool and die
machine and the farm laborer in Arkansas or Texas who
picks vegetables are both part of the working class because
neither owns the means of production (land, factory and
machines) and each sells his labor power for wages. The
Rustin-Moynihan thesis is mistaken because it sets up a
quite artificial division between employed and unemployed
workers by suggesting that only the employed are part of
the working class, the rest being lower class or lumpenproletariat.

Unemployment and marginal employment (part-time employment) make up a big part of the job experience of
millions of black workers in America. This reality is linked
to the whole history of institutionalized racism in America.
The sharecropper or tenant farmer who is pushed off the
land by the rapid changes in technology in agriculture may
settle with his family in Charleston, Savannah, or New
York. He will live in the ghetto slums because that is the
only kind of social environment a racist society has designed for him and his family. He will begin to look for
work as a common laborer on a construction gang or down
on the waterfront, or he may join a group of migrant workers headed for the truck farms of New Jersey, upstate New
York or Florida.

In any of these, as longshoreman, construction worker or
migrant worker, his employment is likely to be "marginal"
at best, due to many factors, including the seasonal character of some work, or lack of seniority required for steady
employment in such industries as the maritime. However
as (part-time) longshoreman, construction worker or farm
laborer, that he is part of the working class of America
should be obvious.

The working class within the ghetto, which is predominantly Negro, and the working class which lives outside
the ghetto and is multiethnic, are component parts of the
same class. Marx used the phrase lumpenproletariat to de-

scribe what he called "declassed elements": rejects from the working class; parasites who live on the lower depths of society and who are basically not concerned with employment because they have found other ways to live. Marx's emphasis was on the *parasitism* of this group, as distinct from the working class.

There are such antisocial elements in the ghettos, and in the course of a revolt they may "get into the act," because they *are* petty parasites. The liquor store is often their target on such occasions. However, to attribute the ghetto revolts to the activity of this group, "locating the riots in the lumpenproletariat" as Rustin proposes, is to be grossly out of touch with everyday life in the ghetto.

Joblessness, police brutality and the lack of recreational facilities are among the things deeply resented by the youth, the middle-aged, the unemployed and the employed alike. The revolt is to be "located" in their resentment.

One wonders whether or not there is a relationship between Bayard Rustin's analysis of what he calls "the riots" and his call for the police to "stop the riots by whatever force is necessary," a sentiment which fortunately did not find its way into the text of the statement* issued by the four national civil rights leaders on the same day.

WHO RIOTED?

In taking into account the significance of these events, one would be remiss not to recognize there was an element of rioting in this whole picture. The trigger-happy, panicky, ruthless conduct of many police and national guardsmen was on the scale of a riot. Apartment buildings "suspected of hiding snipers" were sprayed with machine-gun bullets. In some areas a point was made of systematically damaging Negro-owned businesses which had been left untouched by the uprising. In Plainfield the occupation troops conducted Nazi-type, house-to-house raids upon the ghetto neighborhoods, under the pretense of "looking for guns." This was in clear violation of the Constitutional protection against illegal search and seizure. They also sprayed a kind of nerve gas on the streets of the ghetto which temporarily

* *The New York Times,* July 27, 1967.

paralyzes whomever it contacts. In Detroit more than six thousand political prisoners were taken and there are reports that part of Belle Isle recreation park was converted into a temporary concentration camp. This was a grim replay of similar scenes occurring in the South a few years ago when state fairgrounds were converted into concentration camps and public school buses were used to transport children to jail. We must add to these examples the wanton assassination by policemen of three unarmed black men in the Algiers Motel in Detroit during the week of the revolt.

The police, state troopers and national guardsmen literally rioted as they occupied the ghettos last summer, just as they had done in Watts, San Francisco, and elsewhere since 1964. The long list of civilian dead and injured in the ghetto is testimony to this fact.

This riotous conduct by the armed forces of the state, directed against the local civilian population, is in the classic style of colonial rule and is, today, the most overt expression of the growing fascist pattern developing in the United States.

THE COLONIAL WAR AT HOME

The arrogant display of military force at the local level is supplemented by a court system whose decisions regarding bail are often merely a convenient way of making the colonized hostages of the state. When a court sets bail at from 10,000 to 200,000 dollars for an everyday wage earner, or a youth whose family is on welfare, or an unemployed worker, that amounts to a declaration by the state that these "citizens" are really hostages of the state.

The state power at the local level is expanding its arsenal of weapons and troop reserves all in the name of "riot control." In New York City a Tactical Patrol Force (TPF), organized in 1959 with 75 troops, now reportedly has 650. This is an elite corps, sent into combat against the youth in the Puerto Rican ghetto (*El Barrio*) in East Harlem for four nights last summer. A similar type TP unit had been used to keep the Negro ghetto in East Side Detroit under surveillance during the previous summer (1966), even though there had been no violent eruptions in that city.

Place	Number of Political Prisoners Taken	Date
Albany, Georgia	700	December, 1961
Birmingham, Alabama	3,200	June, 1963
Selma and Central Alabama	3,000	January–March, 1965
Watts	3,952	August, 1965
Detroit	6,670	July, 1967

The city councils in both Newark and Tampa (Florida) have given approval to spend tens of thousands of dollars for "emergency shipments" of new weapons. These, and other examples which could be cited, are a further extension of the pattern of domestic military build-up for which Jackson, Mississippi, received some attention when its city council bought an armored tank for use against nonviolent civil rights demonstrations a few years ago.

The general enlargement of the arsenal of weapons is accompanied by an active build-up in the size of the police forces, often way out of proportion to any civilian public-safety requirements. Why, for instance, does liberal New York City, with a population two and a half times larger than Los Angeles, have a police force six times larger than Los Angeles?* There is also the matter of the kind of conservative ideology cultivated among the police, especially in the cities with large Negro or Spanish-speaking populations. This is not a monolithic picture. There are undoubtedly many decent men on the various police forces—men who have a good relationship with the poeple in the communities and are a credit to their profession. We are concerned here with general patterns of governmental power which are developing in our country. The kind of racist campaign conducted by the Patrolmen's Benevolent Association to defeat the Civilian Review Board in New York, and the brutal beatings given peace marchers by the Los Angeles police (June 23) during demonstrations against the war in Vietnam while President Johnson was speaking at a fund-raising banquet there—these are significant cases in point.

Despite certain concessions to civil rights and a number

* See *The New York Times*, July 20, 1967.

of important court decisions favorable to the defense of civil liberties, militarism and the military presence are rapidly becoming the main features of governmental power in American life. Whether expressed in the form of armed tactical units occupying the ghettos, a police mobilization to brutalize peace marchers, or a massive military build-up in Southeast Asia, the economic, political and psychological ascendancy of militarism is a primary factor shaping the character of national life in our country today. In its ultimate expression, this development represents a serious, totalitarian threat to Constitutional liberties.

There are times when the contemporary spirit of a nation's institutions creeps through in the most unexpected places. At the world's fair in Montreal, Expo 67, the male guides at the United States pavilion were dressed in the uniform of various branches of the armed forces. The spirit of militarism is abroad in the land, stretching its corpselike influence over the fabric of the Republic. This, at once, reflects and contributes to the fact that governmental conduct has sunk to the lowest level of barbarity, public deception and dehumanization of any period since the blood bath which overthrew Reconstruction in the last century.

Frederick Douglass, in commenting on the passage of the Fugitive Slave Act and its impact, once said: "the Mason and Dixon's line has been obliterated; New York has become as Virginia and the power [of slavery] . . . remains no longer a mere state institution but is now an institution of the whole U.S. . . . coextensive with the Star-Spangled Banner. . . ."

As in 1852, once again it is true today. The line between Mississippi and Michigan, between Birmingham and Newark, is rapidly being obliterated as the rise of the Military Establishment takes on a special meaning. Policemanship as a style of government is no longer confined to the Southern way of life but is now becoming institutionalized on a national level. And the line between foreign and domestic policy is fading out as well, as militarism and the military presence become "coextensive with the Star-Spangled Banner."

The escalation of the war in Vietnam and the escalation of the military budget (which is one of the hidden purposes behind all such military adventures), quite aside from the senseless death toll and dishonor it has brought the nation, have had as a net result the *escalation of the economic and political power of the Military Establishment*. This escalation, like the war itself, has taken place at a geometric rate of acceleration during the four years of the Johnson presidency.

The economic power of the military is in that lion's share of the national budget, earmarked under the euphemism "defense." This military budget has been increased from 35 billion dollars in 1963 to 70.3 billion dollars in the current fiscal year of 1967–68. This does not include appropriations for the space program. As a point of reference and comparison, the military budget of the United States is twenty percent larger than the military budget of Britain, the Soviet Union, France and China *combined,* even though the total population of these four countries adds up to five times the population of our country.*

The political power of the military resides in the neo-Confederate chairmen of key committees in Congress, as well as in key personalities in the executive branch of the government. In addition to Secretary of State Dean Rusk of Georgia and General William Westmoreland of South Carolina, commander of United States forces in Vietnam, the following are included:

Name	*State*	*Chairman*
Richard Russell	Georgia	Senate Armed Services Committee
L. Mendel Rivers	South Carolina	House Armed Services Committee
John Stennis	Mississippi	Senate Preparedness Sub-Committee
F. Edward Hébert (From Leander Perez's Dixiecrat machine)	Louisiana	House Preparedness Sub-Committee
John McClellan	Arkansas	Senate Committees Investigating the "Riots"
James Eastland	Mississippi	
Russell Long	Louisiana	(Senate Democratic Whip)

* See "The Military Balance, 1966–67," published by the Institute for Strategic Studies, London, pp. 8–27.

These are the kingpins of the new Confederacy through whom the hawks in the Pentagon exercise their influence. Since his days as Senate Majority Leader, Lyndon Johnson has been the high priest among them.

The manpower resources of the Military Establishment rest directly in the draft system, but also indirectly in the labor of the three and a half million workers* whose pay checks derive from employment in the factories and offices of those companies contracted to engage in the production, transportation and stockpiling of military hardware, napalm and other weapons of mass destruction.

It is the combination of manpower recruited in the labor market, at relatively high wages, to manufacture military weapons, and the manpower guaranteed by the "forced labor" of the draft system which constitutes the manpower pool made available to the Military Establishment. Serious defections in either of these areas of manpower resource, by large numbers of people refusing as a matter of conscience to cooperate with militarism, would be a major contribution toward keeping alive the tradition of civilian-controlled government in our country.

Sensitive to this, the draft has been hurriedly renewed for four years by Congress. The railroad workers strike, the first in twenty years, has been broken by the government, with the public rationale that "one thousand boxcars of ammunition must be sent to Vietnam each week." Such is the atmosphere created that auto workers, on strike against the Ford Motor Company (Secretary of Defense McNamara's home base), are told by their leaders to cross their own picket lines in order to guarantee shipments of truck parts needed by the military for Vietnam.

We are reminded that Mussolini and Italian Fascism came to power under the slogan of "getting the trains running on time."

In his important book, *The Accidental President*, the political analyst Robert Sherrill makes the following observation:

> It was during his [Johnson's] years as the most powerful man in Congress that the permanent diplomatic and military estab-

---

* Estimated by economist Victor Perlo in his book, *Militarism and Industry*.

lishment . . . were given the funds and the freedom by Congress to gain the overwhelming influence that they still have today and *which it is not likely will be taken from them in normal fashion.* * (Emphasis mine, J.H.O.)

THE NEW RESISTANCE MOVEMENT

The road which leads from the Indian massacres of the last century to the Pentagon and another from the oppressive slave plantation to the ghetto are major conjunctive highways running through the very center of American life and history. In turn, they shape the mainstream contours of American national development. The idea that there is no warlike tradition of militarism in America is, of course, one of the most cherished of national myths. Popular belief in this mythology serves as an opiate and a blinder for United States colonialism, past and present. There is, indeed, no goose-stepping tradition of the Hitler Germany kind in America, but that is a matter of national style.

In the present period in the evolution of the American social system, the structured Military Establishment with its staggering financial resources in the public treasury, its ideology of barbarism and its manipulative control over the lives of millions, especially the youth, represents the main social cancer in the body politic of the nation. It is an historically evolved deformity which, at once, aggravates and brings into visible focus all the other social contradictions underlying the American way of life. The contradiction between squandered wealth and dehumanizing poverty; the contradiction between a congenital racism and feeble efforts at becoming a democracy; the contradiction between a tradition of civilian-controlled government, academic and other institutions, on the one hand, and the institutional power requirements of the military-industrial complex on the other —all of these are exacerbated by the escalation of the power of the military in the affairs of the nation today. Any leadership—whether in civil rights, peace, labor, church or the academic community—which ignores this reality and the

---

* Robert Sherrill, *The Accidental President,* New York, Grossman Publishers, Inc., p. 16.

dangers inherent in it is a leadership which is already obsolete.

The most hopeful development on the national scene in this period is the fact that this reality is being confronted by a growing mood of *resistance* among large sections of American people. The revolts against the ghetto condition are but one form of this. The peace coalition represented by the National Mobilization to End the War in Vietnam, with its new emphasis on direct action, expressed in the movement slogan "Confront the Warmakers," is another form, as are the college and university campus demonstrations against military recruitment and military research. In addition there is the growing subculture which has been called hippy. Despite certain hang-ups which limit the effectiveness of their example, the hippies are engaged in a creative, irreverent assault upon all of the hypocritical, moribund, antihuman values and mores of the present social order. Therefore, they too are an important component of the emerging new Resistance Movement.

This movement for an end to the tyranny of racism-militarism and for a revolution in American values is a vital stream of humanist consciousness in American life. It also marks a nodal point, a qualitative change, in the deepening sense of "alienation" felt by a cross section of the American people. Cutting across racial, class and ethnic lines, this sense of alienation from the present governmental structure is a rapidly growing phenomenon embracing a few million. The Resistance Movement is the *organized* expression of this much larger phenomenon, and is just in the beginning stages of its development. Yet the nationwide visibility it is getting as a result of its varied activities is also beginning to awaken the ranks of organized labor, that decisive social force still tragically handicapped by a conservative bureaucracy in the AFL-CIO.

The basic objective of the Resistance Movement is to mobilize and build a massive, organized grass-roots opposition among the American people, capable of bringing to a halt and reversing the current trend toward a military state in our country. The style is confrontation—on many levels —with the military machinery, its economy and its ideology. The program is to rescue human life from this juggernaut and redirect the nation toward a course of genuine social progress. The immediate focus is upon ending the military intervention in Vietnam. Vietnam, more than any other issue in this century, symbolizes the dangerous shift of decision-making, institutional power into the hands of the military. It also epitomizes (in such acts as the burning of villages, the bombings of schools and hospitals, the mutilation of bodies for "souvenirs," etc.) the continued erosion and dehumanization of the American national character.

For all freedom fighters, therefore, the watchword is RESISTANCE! Unyielding resistance and the building of a movement for all seasons. Whether in the streets of the ghettos, on the college campuses, at the Pentagon or elsewhere, the movement of confrontation-resistance is the vehicle for asserting a new social morality in America; a civilized morality which asserts the primary value of *human life* and its right to survive as the basis for liberty and the pursuit of happiness.

JOURNEY INTO THE MIND OF THE LOWER DEPTHS

By ROBERT COLES, M.D.

Dickens observed that the poor are frequently ungrateful for small favors, and a source of continuing frustration. His observations still hold. The Peace Corps has so far succeeded in its aim of doing specific jobs abroad in a spirit of alliance rather than hauteur. Roads have been built, classrooms taught. We have begun asking ourselves if we might not enter our own backward counties and boroughs in the same spirit. We still have millions of voteless, jobless Negroes and more millions of migrant workers whose lives and times are remarkably similar to what Steinbeck described twenty-five years ago; even more millions of hillbillies and sharecroppers. We have whole states spotted with decay, and we have Indian reservations and city slums.

A phrase like "social dynamite" used by Dr. Conant indicates that our problems are becoming threatening enough to frighten our most responsible leaders. We get increasingly nervous before our unemployed or delinquent youth or our Negro youth demanding their rights as never before. The rising involvement of the young in those stagnant pools of our national life is obvious. For the first time they are the majority of our unemployed, and we hear of their predominance in crime and racial conflict. They lead the Negro in protest against customs long endured by their elders, and Southern jails are full of high school students. I have seen ten-year-olds go to jail, and twelve-year-olds sit in at lunch counters.

Freud remarked that "we shall probably discover that the poor are even less ready to part with their neuroses than the rich, because the life that awaits them when they recover has no attraction." There is much which is beyond our grasp as psychiatrists and middle-class citizens in a society that is still segregated socially and racially. We have delinquency, a word which includes everything from minor vandalism and thievery to unspeakable violence; unemployment, a word which fails to convey its victims' feelings of uselessness, rejection, and dangerous boredom under a vast sky of continually unspent time; racial segregation and religious prejudice, that are for those affected a constant reminder of disfigurement or blemish. In the darkest and most forgotten lowlands of our national life, there is the final anonymity of mere survival, where food and shelter themselves are in constant question.

The exiled become just what they are told they are and so they believe their worthlessness. And there is today an odd outrage to Freud by those who caricature the purposes of psychoanalysis by substituting for "why bother?" remarks like "what's your unresolved problem that you bother?" The problem is that of understanding the world the poor and the outcast inhabit, the world of their lives and feelings, and equally understanding what our attitudes toward them are, what our world is willing and unwilling to do for them. It is their lives meeting ours which causes the crisis.

The poor live and act differently. In Palm Beach County in Florida I have been studying migrant agricultural workers and their children. Thousands of these families pick fruit and vegetables during Florida's warm winter, then continue "up the coast" to New Jersey or New York. It is a story of sharecroppers and hillbillies, white and Negro, dispossessed of their meager land and now wandering in an exploitive bondage of disease, malnutrition and ignorance, working side by side in a relative absence of prejudice which only utter but shared squalor can ensure.

I visited a child guidance clinic in that county, and its roster of patients in psychotherapy contained not one migrant child. To accuse this clinic—it is a good one, well equipped and staffed—is to ignore what happens in many similar clinics all over the land: the caseload comes heavily from middle-class families; the rich purchase private care and the poor rarely appear. "I only goes to the hospital when I thinks I'll die." She has eleven children. One is, I suspect, retarded and epileptic. The older children, in their early teens, are what we describe as promiscuous or pre-delinquent, and we could add a few more psychiatric terms which describe defective consciences, poor capacity to deal with impulses, faulty organization of thinking and of emotional resources. This is just about universal for the population of migrant camps. What we call wayward is part of the life of the backward.

This life of the backward will have to be significantly changed for these people to change. Even with social and economic improvements it will take time. Some would offer urban renewal or rural electrification, with a sprinkling of surplus food, and become quickly dismayed, then outraged by the persistence of suspicious, untidy and wanton ways in the recipients. Our best writers avoid this trap. Agee with Alabama sharecroppers, Dan Wakefield with Puerto Ricans in New York, Oscar Lewis studying poor Mexicans—these sensitive observers emerged from their work with descriptions of human beings, struggling to live, resisting or submitting to disease, seeking and receiving love, expressing pleasure and pain, giving way to hate and wild indulgence, offering kindness and tenderness.

I recall small American children on farms eating thickly fried gruel or potatoes out of pans on the floor, not at tables, not with knives and forks. They attract a doctor's eye with their vitamin deficiencies, infectious and parasitic diseases, stunted growth; the teacher's eye of my wife because they are badly, vaguely, intermittently taught, and often not due to any lack of trying on the part of those few who teach them. I recall the casual familiarity of some Negro children I know with their city slum world of alcohol, narcotics, rats, lice, disease and crime. Negro children or the children of nomadic farm hands care for one another, tend rather than compete. Their mother is the pivot of their life, with men often around yet not necessarily filling the role of father. The children may dimly perceive that one child is not "all there," but this means its protection. When they get older, that is ten or twelve, it is "natural" for them to smoke and drink and have plenty of sex—sex is one of the few pleasures costing nothing.

These children are free of the maze of restrictions and exhortations that hedges middle-class children, but others arise. In place of school phobias, obsessions, compulsions, anxieties tied to sexual inhibitions or restrictive toilet training, there are promiscuity, pilfering and then stealing, gang formations and violence, hurt and hurtfulness not dreamed but lived and practiced.

Their glimpses of the other world are on television, and through the "boss man" or the racist mob or the clerk at the unemployment office or relief station—*their* packages of food, checks, authority and power, with all its questioning welfare workers, patrolling cops, collecting slum landlords, traveling salesmen anxious for money and just as anxious not to enter their flats and shacks. If strangers come, young and kindly people, white or black, and want to "help" them, teach their children or feed and clothe them, or assist them in organizing or registering to vote, the first response, a measure of their sense of worthlessness, is to question why they would want to do that.

A dismal camp for migrant workers received a group of intelligent, well-intentioned college men and women bent on a summer's good deed. I doubt if they knew that many of the people were constantly frightened by their presence and by friendly acts such as going to homes with gifts or offering rides. A wave of "relief" on the part of the migrants followed their departure. I am not arguing nonintervention here; quite the contrary, what I am saying is that the customs and fears of people, the solid and formidable resistance of their condition, must be considered if they are to be offered help. "They come breezing through," I heard a gang leader in a Northern city say. He was asking for help and hoping that if it came it would be effective, not "gone with the wind" of a fickle breeze.

VIOLENCE IN GHETTO CHILDREN

By ROBERT COLES, M.D.

AN IMPOSSIBLE SITUATION

I often find welfare workers, as well as the police, present in the pictures ghetto children draw. They stand near the police like dogs, caricatures of themselves, with huge piercing eyes, ears that seem as twisted as they are oversized, and mouths either noticeably absent or present as thin lines enclosing prominent and decidedly pointed and ragged teeth. To ghetto children, as to their parents, the welfare worker is the policeman's handmaiden, and together they come, as one child put it, "to keep us in line, or send us away."

I have listened to public welfare workers and their "clients" talk, and I recognize the impossible situation they both face, the worker often as insulted as the family he visits by the rules and regulations they must contend with and find a way around. I often compare the relationship between the workers and their clients with one that develops in psychotherapy as powerful forces for a while pull both doctor and patient backward in time toward those early years when parents check up on children, trying to keep them on the right side of a "line" that constantly puzzles the child and perhaps also the parent more than she or he realizes.

One welfare worker recently summarized the situation for me:

They behave like evasive kids, always trying to avoid getting caught for this or that. And me, I'm like a child myself, only an older one, always trying to take care of my poor brothers and sisters, but also trying to get them in trouble or find them in trouble so I can squeal on them.

No wonder I encounter anger, frustration, and violence in ghetto children. Everywhere things go wrong: the lights don't work; the stairs are treacherous; rats constantly appear, and they are not timid; uniformed men patrol the streets, certain that trouble will appear; teachers work in schools they are ashamed to call their own, at work they judge hopeless, under a bureaucratic system that stifles them, that is, if they are still alive; jobs are few, and "welfare" is the essence of the economy.

Yet—and I am writing this article chiefly to say so— the ghetto does not kill its young children. That perhaps comes later, at age twelve or fourteen, when idleness becomes a way of life, when jobs are nowhere to be had. For a while, during the first decade of their existence, ghetto children huddle together, learn about the world they have inherited, and go on to explore it, master its facts, accept its fate, and burn from day to day their inner energy and life, able for a while to ignore the alien outside world.

I find in these children a vitality, an exuberance, that reminds me often of the fatally ill I once treated in hospital wards: for a long time they appear flushed with life, even beautiful, only to die. I remember hearing from a distinguished physician who supervised a few of us who were interns: "They're fighting the battle of tuberculosis, and they're going to lose, but not without a brilliant flash of energy. It's a shame we can't intervene, right at the critical moment, and help them win."

He, of course, had the faith that some day medicine would intervene—with one or another saving treatment. Ghetto people have no such confidence, and I am afraid that I, at least today, share their outlook.

STRIPPED BARE AT THE FOLLIES: A REVIEW

By ROBERT COLES, M.D.

After a showing of *Titicut Follies* the mind does not dwell on the hospital's ancient and even laughable physical plant, or its pitiable social atmosphere. What sticks, what really hurts, is the sight of human life made cheap and betrayed. We see men needlessly stripped bare, insulted, herded about callously, mocked, taunted. We see them ignored or locked interminably in cells. We hear the craziness in the air, the sudden outbursts, the quieter but stronger undertow of irrational noise that any doctor who has worked under such circumstances can take only for so long. But more significantly, we see the "professionals," the doctors and workers who hold the fort in the Bridgewaters of this nation, and they are all over. We see a psychiatrist interviewing a new patient. We see another one and his staff as they question another patient and then discuss him upside down. In sum, we see ourselves. Even the most callous and cynical politician has a right to become uneasy and fearful when he sees the most respected, educated and "rational" members of *his* world, his middle-class, professional world, behave as they do in this film.

"Why do you do this when you have a good wife?" asks the doctor of a youth driven to molest children. The questions pour out, one after another—crudely put, monotonously asked; the young man is told that he is sick, sick, sick. His frightened, searching face contrasts with the doctor's boredom, his weariness, his vulgarity, his lack of interest in the man he yet feels free to interrogate (feels he has the right and knows he has the power to interrogate). Then there is the staff meeting where another heartbreaking encounter takes place. A young man feels himself driven mad by the hospital and pleads for a return to a regular jail. Again the questions shoot out at him and in a few minutes shred him to bits. He is given a label, a diagnosis. The faces, the professional faces, smile ever so faintly. They are satisfied. He can go. It is cruel of Mr. Wiseman to have done that to us—all of us who pin names on people in order to brush them aside. . . .

Titicut Follies is a brilliant work of art, and as such it will not go unnoticed, despite the opposition to it. We are asked not to be outraged at others—a cheap and easily spent kind of emotion—but to look at ourselves, the rich and strong ones whose agents hurt the weak and maimed in the name of—what? Our freedom. Our security. Our civilization. Were men's "rights" violated, or do places like Bridgewater strip men of everything, their "rights," their dignity, their humanity? Does a man like Frederick Wiseman have the obligation to say, tell or show what he saw, or is the state entitled to its privacy? If so, how can we move the state to correct its wrongs, to end its evasion or corruption, or worse? (A series of newspaper stories over the years have had only a limited effect.) . . . our Bridgewater state hospitals still stand; and the human beings in them bother us only rarely, when a film like this one comes along or a particularly scandalous story . . . breaks into the news. Anyway, we can even shut out those bothersome events. The inmates of Bridgewater know that, know the limits of our concern. When we see them, that knowledge of theirs, never stated but apparent, unnerves us. For a second *our* privacy is invaded, *we* are stripped bare. Then we compose ourselves and become angry. The rest is easy and perhaps has been best described by T. S. Eliot:

> We demand a committee, a representative committee, a committee of investigation. Resign Resign Resign.

APPALACHIA: HUNGER IN THE HOLLOWS

By ROBERT COLES, M.D.

. . . By turns angry, sad, wry, ironic, resigned or stubbornly determined, he is glad to speak his mind and let me know that like a lot of people from all over the country, he feels cheated this year. So we talk, hour after hour, and I hear his disenchantment—in a way like mine, but also less wordy, less abstract, more concrete, more tied to the particulars of everyday life. He is forty-one, the father of nine children. He was once a mine worker, but lost his job along with many others about fifteen years ago. Now strip mines tear away at the beautiful mountains and leave a legacy of polluted streams, recurrent landslides, destroyed homes and farms and wildlife. "But they get the coal they want, with machines and not our broken backs." He says that angrily, and I'm not the first doctor to whom he has recited the story. Nor is he the first hurt and ailing man I've met in West Virginia or Kentucky.

Even before he was laid off there was trouble, the beginning of serious trouble: "I had a bad cough all the time, like you do when you work down in the mines. After a while you stop thinking about it. You cough like you breathe, on and off all day. Then the cough got real bad and I saw a couple of doctors, company doctors. They gave me medicine to keep the cough down, and I stopped worrying. You can't be a coal miner and worry about what it looks like inside, in your lungs. Then I got hurt, my back. That happens a lot, too—and you either can go back to work or not. I wanted to go back, and I was lucky because I could. I'd still have trouble, but like with the cough, I could keep going. I took some pills when it got bad, but most of the time I showed up first thing in the morning and stuck it out to the end. And I miss those days. Time went fast, and there was money around, enough to pay the bills and live real decentlike and feel like a man, like somebody who was doing at least something with his life.

"Then they mechanized, and they started strip-mining all over with those machines, and we were through, me and all my friends. And ever since it's been the same. We're lucky to be alive each day, that's how I'd put it all together. I've been trying and trying to get on assistance [relief], but they just won't do it, they won't let me by. The doctors, they say I might have some trouble with my lungs and my back, but I was working when I got fired, and I could work now, so far as they're concerned. Hell, you don't have to be a full-fledged cripple to be on assistance, but it's politics, and if I was on the sheriff's good side, that would be fine—I'd have been collecting a check for years; but I'm not, because I got fresh way back and asked them to send the bus up the hollow to pick up my kids. They freeze in the winter walking those two miles to that bus and standing waiting for it. (They don't have the right clothes. We just can't pay for them.) When the courthouse gang heard that, they decided I was real fresh, a real wise guy. So they said if I was so ungrateful for all that was being done for me—and me not working—then I'd learn to regret it. And I'll tell you, I have."

But he is a proud man. Like hundreds of thousands all over those lovely Appalachian mountains, he can find no work, is refused any relief by the county officials, who have near absolute power in the region, and still somehow survives. He grows vegetables. He has a few chickens, and they lay eggs. He goes up the mountains and finds herbs, which he can sell "because they like to cook with them over in the East." And he is always on the lookout for a job, any job, for any length of time: "I can't stand sitting around and doing nothing. You get to hate it. You get to hate yourself. You get to hate everyone around you. I hate my kids growing up like this, seeing me without work. The oldest one, he wants to go to Ohio or Chicago or someplace like that, and get a job in a factory and make some money and then come back here. If I was in better health, I'd have done it a long time ago. That's the only answer these days, go to the city for a while and try to make a few bucks. But you hear it's lousy there, 'lousier than you can ever believe' is the way I hear them say. So they stay for as long as they have to, and then, believe me, they come back here to die. Yes sir. No one born here wants to leave. The tourists say it's pretty, but we *know* it is."

He may be from the oldest American stock, "here from the beginning," but right now he and his family are in this kind of fix: from odd jobs and an occasional gift sent by a brother (who *did* go to Ohio, to Cincinnati and then Dayton), about 750 dollars comes in, and that is all, all the money this family of eleven American citizens receives. They grow some food and they cook and preserve some of it for the winter, but they cannot plant nearly enough (on an acre or two of land up along a steep hill) to keep a supply of tomatoes or beans or cucumbers throughout the long winter and spring. Of course to keep them from literally starving to death, the rich and powerful American government offers its food stamps, which require even now, after all the inquiries and hearings and struggles of the last year, an expenditure of twenty-two dollars at a minimum every month—for a family of eleven that can go for weeks without money. Recently the Congress voted an emergency bill that would allow even that minimum to be waived in cases where there is simply no cash to be had. And here is how it all goes, life and largesse and emergency largesse in the Great Society: "Sometimes we can just raise the money, so we can buy the food stamps, and get about a hundred dollars' worth of food for the month. But we are eleven of us, and it's as expensive to buy food here as any place else. By the third week we're down to nothing, and I'm desperate. They take up collections at the church, and we go borrowing, and with your kin you don't starve to death, no sir. But it's not very good either, I have to admit. For breakfast there's not much I can give the kids. In the winter I have to warm them up. I just have to. So I give them tea, real piping hot. Sometimes they have oatmeal, if there is some, and some biscuits, hot biscuits. Then for supper it depends—if the chickens have left us a few eggs, and if I have some preserves left. The worst time is around January, thereabouts. There's no work. There's no garden. There's nothing but those stamps, if we can raise the money. Then we'll go without supper sometimes, and breakfast, too. Then it's tea and cornbread and oatmeal if we're lucky."

How about the emergency funds that Congress voted, presumably so that no American would starve? It so happens that this family, and dozens of others like it I know, failed to learn about that bit of legislative news. They don't read the *Congressional Record* or the *Washington Post*. They don't even read the very fine *Louisville Courier-Journal* or the not-so-fine *Lexington Herald Leader*. They don't have a television set, and for them a trip to town, unless offered by a neighbor, can cost five dollars. So they remain ignorant of the progress in America: "If it hadn't been for the AV [Appalachian Volunteer] who comes here, we'd never have known about the new program, the stamps you're supposed to get if you don't have money to buy them. But it's been more trouble instead of less; it's been a heartache, trying to get them to certify us and tell us we're eligible for the 'emergency provision,' they call it. We would have to pay someone almost as much as the stamps cost to get to their office—they don't know about things like that in Washington—but the AV drove us over to town, and then it was what we know: the same old people in the county courthouse, sending you back and forth, back and forth, and delaying and telling you they have to investigate and things like that. Now either you're going through an emergency or you're not. I have to borrow food at the end of every month, and they know it. I have to go begging at church and with my kinfolk down the creek to pay for those stamps every month, and they know it. I should be on public assistance, and they know it. But they get everything federal that comes through here, every bit, every dollar, no matter what the senators meant to do in Washington. It may say on paper that the money is for us, but the money goes to the county people, the people who get all the money that comes in here. And they don't intend to let anyone in on the gravy who isn't right in their pockets. I remember when I asked them to send that school bus nearer.

They told me, 'You'll live to be sorry you ever asked.' Well, they were right—though from day to day I wonder if I'll live much more, and be sorry about anything. It can't get much worse than it is."

Their home—one like hundreds I have seen, one like many thousands that stand all over the region—can be tactfully described as extremely modest. It is of wood and tar-paper, and stands on cement blocks. The wind blows right through it. There is no central heating, no plumbing. Water comes from a well several miles away. In winter, in the cold, snowy Appalachian winter, a fireplace provides heat, and eleven bodies leave their five beds to huddle near the burning coals. In summer, flies and mosquitoes are undeterred by screens, and a nearby stream has been badly polluted by a strip mine. Yet they all try hard as a family. They sleep close together, rely on one another impressively, and keep a very neat home. An old picture of John Kennedy is on one wall, and beside it a picture of Robert Kennedy talking with some miners: "After he came here, the teacher gave each child who wanted one a copy of the picture. They got a stack of them from the paper."

The teacher is distant kin of theirs and would like to give them all even more, but cannot: "No sir, none of the children get their lunch at school. No sir, they don't. It's up to the principal, who gets the lunches and who doesn't. The well-off kids from town, they bring their money and so they get fed. It don't mean nothing to their parents, a few dollars here or there. But I can't give each of the kids a quarter every day. I don't have it; I don't have one quarter, never mind six of them. So they just sit there, while the others eat. And they're not the only ones, at least I know that. Sometimes a kid will offer them something he doesn't want to eat, and sometimes my kids are too proud to accept, but sometimes they swallow their pride to get some of that soup they have."

That is the way it is, not only for that one family, but for families up and down hollows in several states of these United States. Respectfully, solemnly, one listens, hears the stories, sees evidence of and feels the bravery and courage and honesty and dignity. But one also has to notice the wear and tear on body, on mind, on spirit, that goes with hunger and idleness; and one has to notice the illnesses that are never treated, the feet that lack shoes, and most painful of all, the children. On my most recent visit, late this summer, I asked a little girl of seven what she'd wish to be if she were given a wish: "Well, I don't know," she answered. Then she had a thought: "Maybe a beaver." I didn't have the nerve to ask her why, but her mother wanted to know and asked: "A beaver, child?" For a second or two there was silence, and then the answer came, cheerfully spoken: "Well, they have a good time. They can chew all day long on trees, like they was bubble gum, and they always get to eat, and they can stop by a stream and drink from it anytime they want."

Soon, though, I am heading home. On the plane, from Lexington to New York or from Charleston to Washington, the shame and anger live on for a while. The salesmen are all around, full of plans and ready with cash—which the government allows them to write off as expenses. Often there are some government officials aboard, finished inspecting this or that. In hours I will be safely in the university, where I can remind myself how complicated everything is, and how hard it is to change things, and how much better things go in Appalachia or in migrant camps or in Delano or in George Wallace's Lowndes County than, say, Biafra or certainly North Vietnam.

There are other bits of encouragement, too. I can read that the House Committee on Agriculture, headed by the honorable W. R. Poage from the great state of Texas, and by its own assertion "always concerned about the ability of all Americans to procure adequate food," has done something called a hunger study—by sending a letter to the health officers of 256 counties all over the nation. "Do you have any personal knowledge of any serious hunger in your county occasioned by inability of the individual to either buy food or receive public assistance?" The county officers were asked that, and in a chorus they answered "no." What is more, a Dr. Pollack from the Institute for Defense Analyses (whose purposes are no doubt patriotic) says that those who have observed hunger and malnutrition among thousands of children in every section of the country have been fooled or mistaken: "What the observers are really declaiming is the failure of people to participate in the food-

stamp and commodity programs because of lack of understanding or inadequate educational support of these federal
programs." And of course after extensive hearings by a
Senate subcommittee and in response to strong public
pressure, the Congress did vote those emergency funds so
that, as Mr. Poage said and Dr. Pollack said, penniless
Americans can "procure adequate food." Naturally the
funds go to county officials, and naturally those are the
people (in Mississippi, in Kentucky, in Delano, California)
who are on the side of the poor—or so I can try hard to
believe, provided that I can forget statements like this one,
written by the director of the Big Sandy Area Community
Action Program, with offices in the Johnson County Courthouse, Paintsville, Kentucky: "As you probably know,
Emergency Food and Medical Services Program has a very
limited amount of money. As a result of this, we do not want
our office deluged with people who have been promised aid
and that aid cannot be forthcoming."

So that is that. The man who wrote those words also
noted that he has only one employee "working the entire
Floyd County area," but nearby in Pikesville, a city of
about five thousand people, there are over forty lawyers
working day in and day out—for what? For poor people?
For the poor land that has been torn apart, then abandoned
to itself, to its own ways—to landslides, to trickles of acid
into streams, to huge rocks that fall upon and crush houses?
The answer is yes—if the preposition is changed from "for"
to "with." The lawyers work with the poor, all right: "They
come up to you and they say their mumbo jumbo and before
you know it, you've got to leave your home or you'll go to
jail." The lawyers work with the land, too; they make sure
it is surrendered to strip-mining companies that do what
they say they do to the land: strip it, makes it as poor as the
people left behind after the machines are gone. But as I
constantly hear some mountain people put it, year in and
year out, "next season may be better." They always add a
qualification, though: "if the trickery down in the courthouse stops." Then they laugh bitterly.

Sabotage: "This Is Number One and the Fun Has Just Begun"

By ANDREW KOPKIND

The war began last winter on the Western front, in the rainy season. The guns of February were four Molotov cocktails, thrown at the Naval ROTC building on the Berkeley campus of the University of California. The shots were not heard 'round the world; as it turned out, they were hardly noticed at all beyond the San Francisco Bay area. But war is not always a recognizable object. More often it is a concept in the mind of the beholder, and only an idea links individual acts of violence in a political train of events.

People are used to thinking of wars of nerves, or wars against poverty, or wars of all-against-all. But the new underground war in America is not just a metaphor for political action or social unrest. This campaign has dynamite, fire-bombs, and *plastique*. It is fought on hilltops in California, in the hollows of Appalachia, on scores of college campuses, in black ghettos and downtown shopping districts. The targets are police cars, draft boards, military facilities, power stations and mining equipment. Although no lives have been taken, property damage runs into the millions.

Very slowly the possibility creeps into public consciousness that all the explosions fit some political pattern. Exactly what the outlines are is difficult to discern. The few newspaper accounts of the various "incidents" do not distinguish between the Cuban exiles' bomb project and the others. Rather everything is lumped into a category of "violence," which seems to have arrived for no reason at all, like an aberrant tornado on a summer's day.

But at bottom, the campaign of revolutionary sabotage grows logically from very real conditions. The failure of traditional mediators of change, on the one hand, and the increasing militancy of the forces of change, on the other, provide a framework in which violent action is at least thinkable. The experience of "real" warfare in Vietnam and widespread violence in urban ghettos lends a certain practicality to any plans that might be hatching. There is no need for national coordination, and there is no evidence at all that any exists. Related action springs naturally and spontaneously from similar causes: revolutionary youths in Delaware do not have to get orders from Berkeley to attack their local draft board. News of one incident spreads quickly enough from coast to coast in the radical underground, and the very knowledge that a war is underway gives support and encouragement all around.

The first attack on the Berkeley ROTC building was followed by the burning of a similar center at Stanford. At about the same time, electric power cables strung over the Berkeley hills were cut. Then three giant electric towers in Oakland were blown to the ground, leaving about thirty thousand houses without power and stopping work at the Lawrence Radiation Laboratory at Berkeley. A few days after the tower was destroyed, a University of Colorado dropout student turned himself in to police to publicize his "crime." He said, "I had to do something to stop their machines—so maybe they would listen, so that this war would be stopped."

Other bombers have not been so open; few have been caught, and the police and FBI seem to be going about their investigations in a curiously low-key way. Most of the attacks on police facilities in Oakland and in the Detroit area have been unsolved. Last week police rounded up several suspects in the anti-Castro campaign, but not many of the war protesters or the other "revolutionary" saboteurs have been apprehended.

ROTC buildings and draft boards remain favorite targets.

The Stanford ROTC building attacked last winter was hit again a few months later, and destroyed. On September 18 a Naval ROTC hall at the University of Washington in Seattle was blasted, with damage estimated at 85,000 dollars. Hundreds of students watched the building burn, and a cheering section chanted, "This is number one, and the fun has just begun. Let it burn, let it burn, let it burn." Five days previously a Naval ROTC building at Berkeley was dynamited and an ROTC hall at the University of Delaware was hit by a Molotov cocktail. Last spring an ROTC building at Nashville (Tennessee) Agricultural and Industrial College burned to the ground while the school's students (all black) kept firemen from fighting the fire effectively. In Eugene—hard by the University of Oregon— a series of explosions destroyed the Naval and Marine Corps Training Center in late September. Damage was put at 106,000 dollars; trucks, a personnel carrier, a crane, and a radio tower were destroyed.

Draft boards have been attacked in North Hollywood, California, and Xenia, Ohio (near Antioch College), and Berkeley. In early September a building near Detroit, housing two suburban draft boards, was bombed. Last March an office used by employment recruiters for defense contractors at San Fernando Valley State College (Los Angeles) was fire-bombed. At Stanford the office of President Wallace Sterling was burned by "arsonists." Sterling's collection of rare books and *objets d'art* were destroyed. One police report attributed the fire to a crank. No one talked much about the heavy criticism of Sterling from students who were protesting his involvement with war contracts and research. In Ann Arbor the unmarked office of the local CIA agent was bombed, and permanently closed. Policemen's private automobiles in stationhouse parking lots in Detroit have been blown up or damaged.

Sabotage of strip-mining operations in Appalachia does not fall into exactly the same category as the university-military attacks, but there are some obvious political connections. The new radical movements have been active in Appalachia since the early sixties. The poverty of the "poor whites" and unemployed miners in the region was one of the first major issues for the New Left, even before the Negro civil rights movement took the center stage. President Kennedy capitalized on sympathy for Appalachia's poor in his 1960 campaign, and the Southern mountains became a fashionable hard-core poverty area for welfare bureaucrats and economic development experts. VISTA volunteers and assorted antipoverty organizers roam about the area, but the economic decay continues and the political stranglehold of company-owned local officials is hard to break.

Strip mining is the most distressing external expression of the ills of Appalachia. Coal companies have succeeded in winning legislative rights to destroy surface land to get at mineral deposits, and in the process have laid waste thousands of square miles of farms and wooded hillsides. The landscape is now barren and unreclaimable. Small farmers and rural residents have no power to push conservationist demands against the influence of the companies and their political allies.

But in the past few months the people of Appalachia have asserted a new kind of power for themselves. On August 24, four men invaded a mine office in Middlesboro, Kentucky; they bound up the night watchman and carted him away, and set off the company's own explosives. A million dollars' worth of equipment went up with the dynamite charge. Throughout the summer, the "Appalachian guerrillas" roamed Kentucky counties, blowing up strip-mining equipment where they could find it. State authorities would like to blame out-of-state organizers, but so far most of the activity seems to have been carried on by inside agitators: townspeople, union men, people who have been run out of the hollows by strip-mine landslides. It would be hard to say they don't have enough to be agitated about.

Appalachian sabotage has a parallel in "civic-action" projects in many black communities across the country— not the well-publicized and televised riots, but the nightly bombings and burnings which police and municipal officials would rather not talk about. In Washington there were several nights of looting and street demonstrations last month after a white policeman shot and killed a black man whose crime had been to cross a street against a red light. (The policeman has been indicted for homicide.) Tear gas filled the streets and the mass media were on hand. But when the crisis subsided, public interest disappeared, and still fire-bombs explode on the same streets, and the white-owned stores (those that remain) are being picked off one by one.

The impact of violent action is largely unfelt in the country, primarily because it is not yet conceptualized as revolutionary warfare. The myth of America's commitment to nonviolence is persistent, despite the enormous amount of recent (and historical) evidence to the contrary. Violence is still thought of as a tactic of bearded Central Europeans or untrustworthy Latins. But the new bomb throwers in America have not been landed on offshore islands by enemy submarines. They are home-grown varieties of middle-class students, farmers, ghetto dwellers, and hippies. They work together in small groups, and they are wise not to talk about their plans. Their targets are not people but property— perhaps the only valid object of attack in a superindustrial, technological society.

As a strategy for the radical movement, revolutionary sabotage presents obvious and perhaps overwhelming problems. After all, violence is not naturally legitimate as a form of political action in the United States. In Paris a cabinet minister's wife or son could (and did) hurl *les cocktails Molotov* against police vans and buildings in May, and it was considered fair play in the war game. Here it is still the opposite. Political organizers are afraid that violence without a political base can only be counterproductive, that without a "sea" of support, the revolutionary fish cannot survive.

But it is also possible that violence can legitimize itself. "If you ask people whether they'll support violence, of course they'll shudder and say 'no,'" a radical organizer said recently. "But when violence is happening, when it exists, you don't have to ask any questions."

The more immediate problem is whether revolutionary violence on the left will cause the reaction from the right which now seems so menacing. In California right-wing paramilitary organizations have promulgated a "kill-list" with names of prominent left-wing figures designated as targets. The editors of the Los Angeles *Free Press* (who

claim to be high on the list) are angry with radical pro-
vocateurs of violence who have not considered the need to
protect their friends. "Should we invite Jerry Rubin to Los
Angeles to take up the duty of a defense guard with his toy
M-14 rifle?" the paper asked last week in a cynical editorial.

Despite the warnings, violent revolutionaries are not likely
to keep their bombs defused out of fear of right-wing reaction. Los Angeles is not Weimar—at least not yet—in the
radical perception. "A lot of people do violent things and
they are not suppressed," the radical organizer said, continuing his argument. "Labor guys sabotage company property all the time and nothing happens to the unions—not
as unions. We may very well be suppressed, but it won't be
for what we're doing. It will be for what we think. They
don't need any excuses."

A VISIT TO CHICAGO:
BLOOD, SWEAT, AND TEARS

By STEVE LERNER

At half past midnight last Tuesday, the occupants of Lincoln Park were stormed by the Chicago police. It was not the first day, nor was it to be the last, that the Old City —the Lincoln Park area—had come under attack. During the previous two nights the mayor's ordinance to clear the park by eleven p.m. had been vigorously enforced with nightsticks and tear gas.

Around midnight on Tuesday, some four hundred clergy, concerned local citizens, and other respectable gentry joined the Yippies, members of Students for a Democratic Society, and the National Mobilization Committee to fight for the privilege of remaining in the park. Sporting armbands decorated with a black cross and chanting pacifist hymns, the men of God exhorted their radical congregation to lay down their bricks and join in a nonviolent vigil.

Having foreseen that they could only wage a symbolic war with "little caesar Daley," several enterprising clergy-men brought with them an enormous wooden cross which they erected in the midst of the demonstrators under a streetlamp. Three of them assumed heroic poses around the cross, more reminiscent of the Marines raising the flag over Iwo Jima than any Christlike tableau they may have had in mind.

During the half-hour interlude between the arrival of the clergy and the police attack, a fascinating debate over the relative merits of strict nonviolent versus armed self-defense raged between the clergy and the militants. While the clergy were reminded that their members were "over thirty, the opiate of the people, and totally irrelevant," the younger generation was warned that "by calling the police 'pigs' and fighting with them, you become as bad as they are." Although the conflict was never resolved, everyone more or less decided to do his own thing. By then the demonstrators, some eight hundred strong, began to feel the phalanx of police which encircled the park moving in; even the most militant forgot his quibbles with "the liberal-religious sellout" and began to huddle together around the cross.

When the police announced that the demonstrators had five minutes to move out before the park was cleared, everyone went into his individual kind of panic. One boy sitting near me unwrapped a cheese sandwich and began to stuff it into his face without bothering to chew. A girl standing at the periphery of the circle who had been alone all evening walked up to a helmeted boy with a mustache and ground herself into him. People all over the park were shyly introducing themselves to each other, as if they didn't want to die alone: "My name is Mike Stevenson from Detroit; what got you into this?" I heard someone asking behind me. Others became increasingly involved in the details of survival: rubbing Vaseline on their faces to keep the Mace from burning their skin; buttoning their jackets; wetting their handerchiefs and tying them over their noses and mouths. "If it's gas, remember, breathe through your mouth, don't run, don't pant, and for Christsake don't rub your eyes," someone thoughtfully announced over the speaker. A boy in the center of the circle got up, stepped over his seated friends, and made his way toward the woods. "Don't leave now," several voices called in a panic. The boy explained in embarrassed tones that he was just going to take a leak.

Sitting in a cluster near the main circle, Allen Ginsberg, Jean Genet, William Burroughs, and Terry Southern were taking in the scene. Ginsberg was in his element. As during all moments of tension during the week, he was chanting *OM* in a hoarse whisper, occasionally punctuating the ritual with a tinkle from his finger cymbals. Burroughs, wearing a felt hat, stared vacantly at the cross, his thin lips twitching in a half smile. Genet, small, stocky, baldheaded, with the mug of a saintly convict, rubbed his nose on the sleeve of his leather jacket. I asked him if he was afraid. "No. I know what this is," he replied. "But doesn't knowing make you more afraid," I asked. He shook his head and started to speak when the sky fell on us.

It happened all in an instant. The night which had been filled with darkness and whispers exploded in a fiery scream. Huge tear-gas canisters came crashing through the branches, snapping them, and bursting in the center of the gathering. From where I lay, groveling in the grass, I could see ministers retreating with the cross, carrying it like a fallen comrade. Another volley shook me to my feet. Gas was everywhere. People were running, screaming, tearing through the trees. Something hit the tree next to me, and I was on the ground again. Someone was pulling me to my feet; two boys were lifting a big branch off a girl who lay squirming hysterically. I couldn't see. Someone grabbed onto me and asked me to lead them out of the park. We walked along, hands outstretched, bumping into people and trees, tears streaming from our eyes and mucus smeared across our faces. I flashed First World War doughboys caught in no-man's-land during a mustard-gas attack. I couldn't breathe. I felt sure I was going to die. I heard others choking around me. And then everything cleared.

Standing on the sidewalk at the edge of the park, I looked back at a dozen little fires which lit up the woods, still fogged with gas. The police were advancing in a picket line, swatting at the stragglers and crumpled figures; huge trucks, usually used for cleaning the streets, swept toward us spraying more gas. Kids began ripping up the pavement and hurling snowball-sized chunks at the truck windows. Then they flooded out into the streets, blocking traffic, fighting with plainclothesmen who awaited our exodus from the park, and bombarding hapless patrol cars which sped through the crowds.

The ragged army split up into a series of mobs which roamed through the streets, breaking windows, setting trash cans on fire, and demolishing at least a dozen patrol cars which happened to cruise down the wrong street at the wrong time. Smoke billowed from a house several blocks from me and the fire engines began arriving. A policeman ran from an angry, brick-throwing mob, lost his cap, hesitated, and ran away without it. At the intersection of Clark and Division, four cop cars arrived simultaneously and policemen leapt out shooting in the air. From all four sides the demonstrator let them have it; most of the missiles were overthrown and hit their comrades or store windows on the other side of the street. Diving down into the subway, I found a large group of refugees who had escaped the same way. The tunnel looked like a busy bomb shelter; upstairs the shooting continued.

Everyone knew that Wednesday was going to be the big one. Rumors circulated among the police that a cop had been killed in Tuesday's "white riot." The demonstrators had their own beef: not only had they been gassed and beaten, not only had one of their leaders, Tom Hayden, been arrested twice on trumped-up charges of inciting to riot, disorderly conduct, resisting arrest, and letting the air out of the tires of a police vehicle, but the police had also broken into their community centers up near Lincoln Park.

Finally the demonstrators were also set on marching to the Amphitheater, where what they called the Convention of Death was going through the motions of nominating Hubert. Crossing the bridge from the park in front of the Hilton to the band shell in the middle of Grant Park, demonstrators filed into their seats, listening to the prophetic words of Bob Dylan's "The Times They Are A-Changing." The police had already surrounded the park, the National Guard held all the bridges leading across the railroad tracks to Chicago's downtown Loop area, and helicopters filled the skies like hungry mosquitos.

The mayor had been good enough to circulate an announcement telling the demonstrators that they were welcome to stay at the band shell all day and enjoy themselves, but that no march on the convention would be tolerated. His instructions, however, were apparently too subtle for his henchmen, who saw the demonstrator as the enemy and couldn't wrestle the idea of a truce into their image. Accordingly, when a demonstrator replaced the American flag with revolutionary red, the police became incensed at the unpatriotic slur and moved in to restore decency and the American way of life. (Jerry Rubin, accused of "soliciting to mob action" and out of jail on 35,000 dollars, says that one of the demonstrators who claims to have taken part in the lowering of the American flag was his personal bodyguard assigned to him by the Mobilization. The same young man later turned out to be an undercover agent who had been keeping Rubin under surveillance.)

During the police charge, which was ostensibly aimed at lowering the red banner, the police went considerably out of their way to crack the skull of Rennie Davis, spokesman and leader of the Mobe, along with four or five others who had been sitting on their benches in the open-air auditorium, listening to antiwar speeches by Vietnam veterans and the ever-present Phil Ochs. Medics scrambled over broken benches (later used as ammunition against the police) in a display of greater enthusiasm than efficiency. Within minutes the program continued as if nothing extraordinary had occurred. "The merchants of death are trying to make themselves present in the delivery room of our movement," Carl Oglesby, once chairman of SDS, screamed over the microphones as the police withdrew to the periphery of the crowd. Hayden, furious at the indifference with which people learned that Davis was "stretched out," exhorted the People's Army to break up into small groups and invade the streets of the Loop, "to do what they have to do." Some of the hard heads followed him, but the vast majority of the demonstrators stayed with Ginsberg, who was organizing a nonviolent march to the Amphitheater.

While Genet, Burroughs, and Southern chose to stay with the marchers, Norman Mailer provided brief comic relief when he made his excuses, saying that he would not march because he was writing a long piece about the convention and demonstration, and he couldn't write it from jail. "But you'll all know what I'm full of if I don't show up on the next one," Mailer said, with his characteristic hurumph for emphasis after the last word in the key sentence. Mailer ended by comparing the Chicago demonstrators favorably with those he had written about at the Pentagon march last October.

Once outside the band shell and onto the sidewalk of a highway which runs through the park, the marchers were immediately halted by a line of guardsmen who blocked the route. Seeing a confrontation emerging, hundreds of newsmen rushed to the front of the line to be in on the action. Instead they formed a protective barrier between the troops and the demonstrators, a pattern which was to be repeated frequently during the next two days. After hours of frustrating negotiations which led nowhere, the demonstrators moved in a bloc toward one of the bridges which led back to the Hilton. It, too, was barricaded with troops, as were the next four bridges, where tear gas was used to keep the demonstrators from trying to break through.

Most of us got across the fifth bridge and joined the mule-drawn covered wagons of the poor people's campaign which were headed for the Hilton. Michigan Avenue, for the first time in anyone's memory, clearly belonged to the people. There was a sense of victory and momentum as the mob of some eight to ten thousand people converged on the Hilton. Everyone was still sneezing and spitting from the gas, but they felt high at having outfoxed the police, who had clearly meant to isolate them in the park, or split them up before they got to the Hilton.

A police line across Michigan Avenue on the doorstep of the hotel finally halted the march, and people began to mill around, undecided on the best strategy.

Finally the police solved the problem by taking the initiative. To put it neatly, they decided to clear the street. In the process of allowing for the circulation of vehicular traffic, they sent some three hundred demonstrators to the hospital with split skulls and broken bones. When the charge came, there was a stampede toward the sidelines. People piled into each other, bumped over each other's bodies like coupling dogs. To fall down in the crush was just as terrifying as facing the police. Suddenly I realized my feet weren't touching the ground as the crowd pushed up onto the sidewalk. I was grabbing at the army jacket of the boy in front of me; the girl behind had a stranglehold on my neck and was screaming incoherently in my ear.

Across the street the other half of the crowd was being squashed against the walls of the Hilton. The pressure was so great that a plate glass window shattered. Terrified demonstrators were pulled through the window by a *Life* correspondent, and a sympathetic waitress gave them instructions as to where they could hide. Within minutes police piled into the hotel to protect the clientele by beating the protesters senseless in the plush corridors of the Hilton.

Outside, demonstrators were being peeled off the wall one at a time, sprayed with Mace, beaten, and occasionally arrested. More forays by the police into the park across from the hotel sent people headlong into trees. During one of these maneuvers I watched a medic throw himself over the bloody head of a demonstrator—like a GI clutching a live grenade to his gut. When I saw him emerge from the fracas, the medic's head was in a worse state than the patient's.

By ten p.m. the National Guard had pinned one group in the park in front of the Hilton and pushed the other two groups north and south down Michigan Avenue. A paddy wagon was caught in one of the mobs, and demonstrators started rocking it back and forth in an attempt to overturn it. A busload of police got to them before they succeeded.

Down the side streets groups of fifty to a hundred demonstrators broke off from the main action to disrupt the town. They moved quickly, leaving a trail of overturned garbage and shattered glass in their wake. Chased by police, they would split up and re-form with other groups. One contingent, calling itself the Flower Cong, was particularly well organized and effective. I was following them up State Street when I caught sight of a blond girl, a member of the Resistance, whom I'd talked to earlier in the day. I caught up with her just as the street filled up with cops. We turned to run in opposite directions and I lost sight of her until it was all over. Having seen that the police had blocked both ends of the street, I took refuge in a drugstore with several others. When I came out, she was trying to sit up in the street, blood soaking through her hair, running down her chin and neck, and collecting in her collar. A car stopped and offered to take her to the hospital, so I carried her over and laid her out in the back seat. The car owner wanted to put newspaper under her head so she wouldn't stain the seats.

My hotel was nearby so I decided to go up and get rid of my shirt, which was covered with her blood. At the main entrance I was stopped by a security guard who wouldn't let me in. I showed him my key, but he still refused. After two similar rebuttals I was finally allowed to sneak in the back entrance and up the service elevator. "We don't want you walking around the lobby like that," one of the hotel policemen advised me. Up in my room I turned on the tube just as Daley was being asked by an interviewer if there was any evidence of brutality. Outside my window I could hear screams. I opened the shade and leaned out as the police pinned a bunch of demonstrators against the wall of the hotel. From the window above me someone heaved a roll of toilet paper and screamed "pigs!" When the street cleared, four bodies were lying in the gutter. Daley's voice droned on about how he had received no indication of police brutality.

Later that evening the McCarthy delegates, having lost the football game, as one Flower Cong put it, joined the demonstrators in a dramatic candlelight procession. It was irrational, but I hated them. I hated them for having come to the bloodfest late. I hated them as I hated every necktie in the Hilton. I hated them not because they had tried to win the football game, but because their very presence among the real demonstrators co-opted and made respectable the blood and snot that speckled the streets of Chicago. The earlier crowd, the scruffy-hippie-commie-beatnik agitators, were the ones who had exposed the military backbone of the liberal system. It took blood to prove to the prime-time viewers that civil rights—the right to dissent, the right to assemble, the right to pass freely in the streets, the right to be tried before being clubbed—were all okay as long as you didn't actually try to use them.

The delegates were received with mixed feelings. Outwardly almost everyone welcomed them, even those who earlier had shouted "McCarthy is not enough." They represented a kind of vindication of the demonstration. In addition they lent respectability and a certain amount of protection to protesters who had been kicked around for five long days. But in spite of this there was a feeling among most of those who had been initiated by violence that the support of the delegates would only be tolerated as long as the movement in the streets remained the property of those who had grown and suffered with it.

Wednesday was the bloody catharsis; Thursday was farce. There is a certain credible nature about a policeman's nightstick which inspires a kind of defiant respect. But a tank is hard to take seriously. I know a lot of people who cracked up when they saw the tank sitting in the middle of the street, pawing at the pavement like a lost rhinoceros who has wandered out of the jungle into the city by mistake. Mortars, flamethrowers, machine guns, and bazookas—who are they kidding?

Standing in line, waiting to be arrested in Thursday's march to Dick Gregory's house, I happened to end up next to a very stoned young couple, groping at each other and taunting the troops with their sexual freedom. "Fuck, don't fight," the young man pleaded with the troops as he fondled his woman. A black army medic finally responded with a smile, "Is it true that all you people run around without any clothes on up in Lincoln Park?" Then the jokes were over and they turned on the gas. Four times in all until they had pushed us back to the Hilton. Then another three times in front of the Hilton just in case the TV crews had missed anything.

The absurdity of the police and military overreaction to the demonstrators had been driven home to me earlier in the day when I was stopped by five policemen under the tramway on Wabash Avenue. One of them grabbed me and looked at my press credentials, making some wise-assed remark about the hippie underground press from New York. His buddies laughed and I thought I was going to be let go. "Let's see your underarms, kid," my interrogator said. Earlier in the week I had heard some Yips complaining about a similar request, but I never had figured out why anyone wanted to check their pits. Taking my jacket off, I held my hands over my head thinking that maybe this was the new slang for "reach for the sky." But that wasn't it. They wanted me to take off my shirt, and when I refused, they ripped it under both arms and, by God, they checked my armpits. Satisfied, I guess, that I wasn't carrying either concealed weapons or drugs, they chased me away with a warning. After that nothing sounded too absurd.

Walking past a group of guardsmen who were resting up for their next stint of duty, Abbie Hoffman, a Yip leader, was being razzed about his appearance. Finally, without a blink, Hoffman walked up to one of them and said, "Hey, listen, I'll lay a nickel bag that you guys could whip the cops any day of the week." A pensive look came across the trooper's face.

Hayden
on Walker
on Daley

By TOM HAYDEN

The Chicago confrontation—"the most widely observed riot in history," according to *Life*—is still happening in the American mind. In August the first sharp public debate broke out about what went on and who was to blame; in opinion polls, white youth and blacks tended to side with the demonstrators, while the over-thirty whites strongly defended the police. But within the power centers of those over-thirty whites, a profound argument continues beyond the Chicago controversy, to the issue of how conflict in America shall be managed. At first it seemed that within the establishments, only the mass media and a minority of liberal Democrats were willing to criticize the Chicago police. But with publication of the officially authorized Walker Report, the liberal interpretation has been strengthened and the Daley machine further discredited.

For the most part, militants around the country refused to talk with investigators from Walker's task force, because of a justified suspicion of this latest in a series of official "riot" commissions that never result in political change. In spite of that noncooperation, the report presents a relatively sympathetic and accurate description of what happened in Chicago. Endless incidents of police brutality are documented, with the accurate observation that the most severe violence was not "staged" for television but took place in dark corners of the North Side. New evidence comes to the

surface supporting the protesters' claim that their violence
was defensive and forced by the police. More than three-
fourths of the 192 injuries to policemen were sustained on
August 28, on the fourth day of a struggle in which hundreds of protesters had already been clubbed or arrested.
And contrary to official Chicago propaganda, very few
(twelve at most) policemen were injured by chemical sub-
stances, and some of these certainly were felled by their own
wind-blown tear gas and Mace. The protesters' "weapons"
consisted mainly of rocks and bricks; police arrested nine
demonstrators with knives, two with guns, two with "ma-
chetes," and one with a "bayonet."

But the report blames demonstrators for "mounting
provocation . . . in the form of obscene epithets, and of
rocks, sticks, bathroom tiles and even human feces hurled
at police," although the report's own evidence shows that
epithets were the basic "weapons" hurled. On that point
Walker is the victim of the same bewilderment at protest
as most observers: the fact that we were "obscene" rather
than respectful toward authority clouds the issue of the
cause of obscenity. Though Walker implicitly criticizes
Johnson and Daley, the refusal to grant permits, the
massed military force, and the mad-dog police (who shot
and killed one Yippie on the eve of the convention, and
began their beatings immediately as we arrived), it does not
see that obscenity was a natural response and the least that
the Democratic convention deserved.

But the content of the report itself cannot be understood
apart from the political reasons for its publication. Why
should the general counsel of Montgomery Ward, a prominent member of at least the local ruling class, suddenly
appear as a crusader for the most unpopular cause that
could be chosen in Chicago? Why was it permitted by the
Violence Commissioners, a governmental body surely more
conservative in makeup than the Kerner Commission?
Why was the report released in time to cause embarrassment
to the Chicago Grand Jury and the House Committee on
Un-American Activities, both pro-police groups, currently
"investigating" the demonstrations?

The American establishment is bitterly and perhaps fatally divided about the crisis confronting the country. The

report itself only begins to shed light on this inner struggle. At one point it says Roger Wilkins, director of the Community Relations Service in the Justice Department, met with Daley, "thinking he might serve as a mediator between the demonstrators and the city, but the meeting was not productive." A December 2 *Washington Post* article goes much further: "several conflicts swept the top levels of government on the eve of the convention." Vice-President Humphrey apparently pleaded that the convention be moved; the Justice Department favored negotiating a demonstration permit agreeable to all parties; Daley criticized Justice for taking no action against "outside agitators"; Cyrus Vance argued for—and Ramsey Clark against—the deployment of United States troops to Chicago before trouble broke out. The quarreling did not end with the convention. Now there are conflicts about whether to indict protest leaders for "inciting to riot across state lines."

A primary failure of the Walker Report is the lack of forthright reporting of that conflict, which leads to a completely inadequate set of conclusions. The basic finding —that the police "rioted"—is true enough, but only in part. Obviously when the cops threw demonstrators in the Lincoln Park pond, and when they bloodied priests, they were berserk. But on the whole, the police seemed to be acting rationally. Their behavior was patterned and planned. When they attacked crowds, they moved in formation. They tended to club people deliberately, rather than make mass arrests. They very rarely harmed people in the jails, although they threatened to gas, beat, and kill us there.

The police were following orders. They were not as responsible for what happened in Chicago as were the men who gave the orders. Mayor Daley clearly was involved, but who else? The mayor must have been acting with the confidence that he was supported at higher levels. Government and military officials of all ranks conspired to arrange the convention, and John Criswell, of the Democratic National Committee, was in communication with the President. If Humphrey wanted the convention moved, and if (in Walker's account) Justice Department officials "warned a group of Washington reporters that convention week would be a scene of violence like they had never seen before," why did the administration allow the violence to unfold according to its own predictions?

My own view is that street violence was an inevitable risk the government was willing to take in order to accomplish its goals: ratify the Johnson policy and nominate Humphrey. Those goals required a rigged convention and the likely alienation of most Democratic constituencies, particularly the blacks, the young, and the liberals. The first priority of the convention planners was to scare as many people as possible away from the Chicago demonstrations; it would have been embarrassing to affirm the status quo inside the Amphitheater while hundreds of thousands of people rejected it outside. The second tactic was to portray the protesters as a subhuman, disruptive minority, and the Democrats the party of "law and order." The third priority was to keep control of convention machinery while creating the appearance of debate.

The convention planners executed all three short-term tactics, but in the process lost the strategic main chance. But people were frightened away, perhaps by the hundreds of thousands. The deep strains in Democratic politics and the cracks in the system of social control were intensified, not smoothed. The protesters were identified as hard-core militants whose crime was their style of life. The McCarthy and Kennedy Democrats were kept inside the Amphitheater by the perpetual hope of a peace plank or fresh nominee. The liberals would not confront power to the point of breaking with it. They did not openly criticize convention arrangements before August 25. They (McCarthy, Al Lowenstein) even called off their demonstration plans, leaving the remaining protesters with even less legitimacy. And during the convention itself, not until August 28 did they begin to attack Daley's "gestapo." They waited that long in the hope that Daley and friends would "come around" to support their demands. Thus politicians like Daley were the power base for both "liberals" and "conservatives": the very point about the Democratic party which the protest was attempting to make. Probably the protesters exerted enough negative power of their own to deprive Humphrey of the support needed for victory in November; but the fact that the Walker Report doesn't criticize the decision-makers indicates that real power is still where it was in August, and the Walkers feel responsible to it, whatever it abuses.

If standard reaction forms hold, liberals will express relief and radicals will show disdain for the report. But a deeper critique would be more helpful. The report at least helps to deflect the worst blows against militants at a time when stiffer repression is likely. Daniel Walker deserves praise for his courage in taking on the most vengeful political machine in America; he could have been a "good German," but he chose a nobler role.

But at last it is impossible for a protest movement to rely on liberals to save it from repression when the powerful establishments are really threatened. To admire the courage of Walker and to be grateful for his modest help is not the end of criticism. We can still look forward to the day when the United States doesn't need a Montgomery Ward lawyer to confirm the truths which anyone can see.

The question of what will follow the report seems answered already: nothing new. Police reform is unlikely because the police ultimately protect the interests of the Walkers as well as the Daleys. It was the same in Newark; after the 1967 rebellion, a commission of solid citizens recommended improvement in housing, schools, and education, but would not go beyond their criticism of the police to demand proposals for action. What I wrote in the wake of the Newark rebellion is just as true for the aftermath of Chicago: "Good intentions tend to collapse when faced with the necessity for massive spending and structural change. This political bankruptcy leads directly to the use of military force." If that is true, the Walker Report will join many other reports on liberal shelves, and the Daleys will keep the real machinery going, with the legal tools to indict protest leaders while slapping at a few individual policemen for the liberals' benefit.

What neither the Walkers nor the Daleys seem to understand, however, is the depth and seriousness of the protest they are facing. Neither pacification-without-progress nor brute repression will stop the mounting pressure for real change. Most young people surely do not want the confrontation that is here, much less the confrontation that is coming. Some will hope against hope that there is a way out through a Walker, a Lindsay, another Kennedy. Others will pull back from the repression they fear. But there are enough who will not be satisfied by promises, and enough who will become warriors against repression, to push the struggle on.

For all its sophistication, the Walker task force seems finally as puzzled as Mayor Daley by the new militants. One observer described his puzzlement this way:

"The thing about this crowd was that since it thrived on confrontation, it behaved in a way much different than any crowd I've ever seen. During racial riots, the police would break up the crowd and the crowd would stay broken up. It might regroup in another place but rarely would it head back for direct confrontation.

"This was a most unusual crowd. This time the police would break people's heads but the crowd would not run away. What it would do would be to regroup and surge back to the police and yell more epithets, as much as saying: 'do it again.' "

A most unusual crowd for comfortable people to understand: but if your existence, your way of life, is your "crime," then there can be no compromise, no reports about your executioners, no waiting, only a struggle to stop them immediately and forever.

FOUR

LOOKING
AT
OURSELVES

INTRODUCTION

Now that we have confronted American violence, we
see what an integral part it has played in the development
of the United States historically and in the 1960's. Violence may be intrinsic to human nature in general, a natural human reaction in all societies in the face of danger,
threat, fear, pain, and frustration, but the very fabric, the
roots, of America's history make violence in America
unique. It is unique because every people has a unique
history, and perhaps most important in our history is the
fearful refusal to recognize violence as an issue, as integral to American society, politics, and culture. Comparison is a useful technique, and although it sometimes
distracts, it can help us to face ourselves and our own
history. There might be less violence everywhere if as
individuals and as a nation we would recognize the equality
of all mankind despite the difference in life styles.

It is all too easy to say how difficult it will be to change
America, to minimize violence, to find new forms with
which to express aggression. It is not impossible to remove
some of the causes of violence if we are willing to recognize those causes and deal with them. Either we will have
to deal more directly, more realistically and humanely,
with violence, seeking to modify brutal outbursts of violence
and understanding that it is transitory within an evolutionary process of development; or it is possible that it will
reach such heights that fascism will be the result.

The first essay in Part Four is by Judd Marmor, director

of the Division of Psychiatry at Cedars-Sinai Medical Center in Los Angeles. Dr. Marmor has spoken and written extensively on the problems of individual, American, and world violence. In "Some Psychosocial Aspects of Contemporary Urban Violence," written especially for this volume, he discusses various forms of violent behavior and the relationship of individual, national, and world violence. He distinguishes between underlying roots and trigger mechanisms of violent behavior, and then discusses the reasons for the extensive violence of the sixties. Finally, as one might expect of a psychiatrist, he discusses various possibilities and remedies of both short- and long-term duration for the treatment of violence. He believes, as I do, that if we do not heed his message, we may not have the choice of survival.

The next article is by John Lukacs, known for his historical studies of the cold war and most recently the author of *Historical Consciousness*. In his article, originally published in *Commonweal,** Lukacs differentiates between peaceful people and "pacifists" who want to eliminate all conflict, including violence. He argues that the result of "pacifism" today is war to end all war, or violence to end other violence, which is somewhat similar to the cyclical theory I presented in Part One. Lukacs believes that civilization attempts to limit violence, whereas efforts to eradicate violence lead to savagery; and while violence can be constructive, savagery cannot. Lukacs sees savagery in various aspects of American life: football, the automobile as a vehicle for aimless speed, the drug culture which seeks passive hallucination rather than active imagination. Professor Lukacs argues that the American character is not yet crystallized: it contains both kindness and savagery; but he concludes that if we continue to be impotent in the exercise of our own powers, wealth, and technology, that impotence will lead to despair, fatalism, and savagery.

The final article in the book, "American Violence in Perspective," especially written for this volume, is by sociologist Warner Bloomberg, Jr., a professor of urban affairs and chairman of that department at the University of Wisconsin-

* November 15, 1968.

Milwaukee. Professor Bloomberg is an expert on community organization, a widely respected scholar and a prolific writer, and he is active in university, religious, and community affairs. He is now at work on Volume Three of the *Urban Affairs Annual Review*, and most recently was a contributor to and editor of Volume Two, entitled *Power, Poverty, and Urban Policy*. He has written for *The New Republic, Commentary, Urban Review, Young Children,* and other journals.

Professor Bloomberg is concerned with putting violence in America in perspective as to violence in other cultures and societies, and with trying to understand why Americans are both unique and similar to other peoples. He traces the evolution of violence in American society, and explores the kinky historical arrangement between blacks and whites, indicating how this has evolved into institutional racism. Bloomberg indicates the need to listen to the views of minorities and reformers, and to create institutions that are sensitive to all men, and to a kind of radical reformation that can lead us to a more peaceful nation and world.

SOME PSYCHOSOCIAL ASPECTS OF CONTEMPORARY URBAN VIOLENCE

By JUDD MARMOR, M.D.

Violence is a form of behavior intended to injure or destroy an object that is perceived as an actual or potential source of frustration or danger, or as a symbol thereof. Much controversy has raged for many years over the question of whether violence is rooted in an instinctual aggressive urge that is inherent in the nature of man. Many classical psychoanalysts, following the lead of Sigmund Freud, tend to believe that it is. They hold, moreover, that this urge is of autochthonous, spontaneous origin, requiring some external outlet if it is not to be "turned inward" with resultant psychopathology. According to this theory, all assertive behavior, even that which is creative and adaptive, is a form of aggression, although in such instances the aggression is assumed to be "fused" with positive libidinal drives which enable it to have constructive rather than destructive goals.

Most behavioral scientists, however, are of the opinion that although man, like other mammals, is born with an innate *capacity* for violence or aggressive behavior, whether or not this capacity finds *expression* depends almost always on some external factor rather than on a spontaneous inner urge.[1] To put it more succinctly, the fact that the capacity for violence is innate in man does not mean that the expression of violence is inevitable.

A distinction needs also to be made between violence and conflict. Conflict in one form or another will always be part of the human scene. The modes by which conflict is expressed and pursued, however, are highly variable, responsive to pressures for change, and amenable to controls that can limit the degree of destructiveness involved.

The sources of most violence can be found in man's life situation. Indeed, the fact that in all societies rates of violent behavior can be demonstrated to be clearly correlated with certain types of social patterning (e.g., poverty, urbanization, social class, etc.) is an effective argument against the assumption that human violence arises spontaneously on the basis of biological needs or simple idiosyncratic propensities.[2] Moreover, the common tendency to assume that violent behavior is always correlated with anger or hostility constitutes a considerable oversimplification. In today's world there is at least as great a danger that violence will result from the effects of fear as from hostility. Clinical experience has demonstrated that panic is a potent trigger for violence; and extreme fear of an adversary is just as likely to provoke an aggressive act against him as is hatred of him.

Actually a great deal of contemporary violence takes place without either anger or fear in relation to the intended victims. This kind of violence, sometimes called "instrumental aggression," is in the service of "just doing a job," *à la* Eichmann. Much of modern warfare—the dropping of bombs or napalm on faceless, distant, dehumanized dots, or the firing of shells at invisible enemies beyond the horizon —is of such instrumental nature. Indeed, the ultimate achievement of modern war technology, the mathematically precise triggering of intercontinental missiles with nuclear warheads capable of devastating total continents thousands of miles away, is one in which neither anger nor any other passionate emotion has any functional value at all. Thomas Merton, in an essay ironically entitled "A Devout Meditation in Memory of Adolph Eichmann,"[3] has recently pointed out that one of the most terrifying aspects of international warfare and genocide is that so much of it takes place on the basis of cold, planned, precise, and deliberate action. As he puts it:

We rely on the sane people of the world to preserve it from barbarism, madness, destruction. And now it begins to dawn on us that it is precisely the *sane* ones who are the most dangerous . . . who can without qualm and without nausea aim the missiles and press the buttons that will initiate the great festival of destruction that they, the *sane ones,* have prepared.

However, another kind of social violence, quantitatively less massive and less destructive than that of modern warfare, is assuming more distressing and frightening proportions for contemporary Americans, because it is close at hand and because "enemy" and "victim" are both highly visible. I refer to the violence in our urban ghettos, which has reached climactic proportions in recent mass riots and which has been dramatically brought home to millions of Americans via television.

In considering the sources of this phenomenon, it is useful to distinguish between its basic *underlying roots,* on the one hand, and the *trigger mechanisms* that set it off, on the other. At first glance it would seem to be an obvious truism that the source of much of the contemporary violence in our urban ghettos is rooted in the poverty, poor housing, inadequate education, and generally degrading living conditions with which the residents of these ghettos are confronted. Although no one would deny the relevance of these factors, the question still remains, however, of why these outbursts are taking place now with greater frequency and intensity than in the past. One might point out, for example, that the lot of the Negro under slavery was certainly worse than it is today; or that the lot of poor immigrants at the turn of the century in our urban ghettos, with their sweatshops, twelve-hour day, child labor, etc., was worse than the lot of the poor today. And yet there was not as much violence then in terms of organized mass riots as there is now.

The significant difference between these earlier situations and those of the present lies in what has been called the "revolution of rising expectations." Only when people have been stimulated to hope that their unhappy lot can be changed does it really begin to feel unendurable. As de

Tocqueville, referring to the French Revolution, pointed out:

> A people which has supported without complaint, as if they were not felt, the most oppressive laws, violently throws them off as soon as their weight is lightened. The social order destroyed by a revolution is always better than that which immediately preceded it. . . . The evil which was suffered patiently as inevitable, seems unendurable as soon as the idea of escaping from it is conceived.[4]

What has happened in contemporary America to account for this revolution of rising expectations, and for the sense of unendurable frustration that many of the masses in our urban ghettos, particularly the Negro masses, have begun to feel? It seems to me that there are four major factors that account for this change.

1) The first has been the heightened affirmation of the democratic ideals on which our nation was founded. Two world wars have been fought, presumably to make the world safer for democracy, and a succession of American Presidents has emphatically publicized these aims. The eloquent idealism of John Kennedy, upon his accession to the Presidency, had a profound influence on young people in particular, raising their hopes for the realization of the American dream of equality and security for all. The drive to end discrimination took a new lease on life, and American students who had for a generation been "playing it safe" became politically active again through the medium of the civil rights movement. Despite Kennedy's tragic assassination, these hopes for a "great society" received further impetus during the first year of the Johnson Administration, when new civil rights legislation was pushed through Congress in a way that Kennedy himself had not been able to accomplish. The nation's poverty programs, Operation Headstart, new housing laws, and apparent progress in desegregation of schools and other public places all seemed to hold high promise for new and hitherto unattained levels of American democracy.

2) The second has been the migration of hundreds of thousands of black people from Southern rural communities

to the "promised land" of the Northern cities, where they hoped that they would be able to live with new dignity, and that their children would have opportunities to participate as equals in all the good things of the American way of life.

3) The stimulation of these hopes and expectations has been enormously heightened by the communications explosion growing out of modern technology. There is hardly a house in America today that does not have a radio, and more than ninety percent of all households are now reported to have a television set. This means that the message of democracy is being carried into every community and home in the United States, and can be comprehended even by the totally illiterate. Madison Avenue's visible demonstration via television, magazines, and other mass media of better ways in which to live—with constant, tantalizing offers of beautiful homes, tempting foods, attractive clothes, and luxurious holiday resorts—gives increased tangibility and substance to the great promise, in a manner that had never before been possible.

4) The progressive dissolution of colonial empires (at least in their traditional form) in Africa and Asia after World War II, with the emergence on these continents of many new nations whose representatives are accorded full diplomatic respect in the forums and councils of the United Nations, has lent additional strength and impetus to the expectations of our own black population. It has given them renewed pride in their historic traditions, made them less ashamed of their black skin, and heightened their impatience and resentment at the residual manifestations of discrimination which they continue to encounter in their own country.

Given these four factors and the rising hopes and expectations which they have stimulated, it is inevitable that the steady and inexorable escalation of the war in Vietnam, with its inhibiting effect upon the social welfare programs of our country, has tended to create a sense of mounting frustration in our urban ghettos. Poverty programs have had to be curtailed or eliminated, civil rights advances have ground to a standstill, and the massive financing which is needed to rehabilitate the ghettos is no longer available.

It is in this context that much of what is going on in contemporary America can be understood. The growing disaffection on our college campuses, the rise of the hippy movement with its rejection of conventional middle-class values, and the mounting anger and frustration of our black populations are all related to the factors described above. Hopes have been stimulated and are not being fulfilled. Among blacks the intense frustration they have experienced has led to intense anger at the whites who have failed them, particularly white liberals. This apparently irrational focusing of their anger on those who have tried hardest to help them is not quite so illogical when we realize that these whites are considered instrumental in stimulating their hopes and then failing to carry through.

Other factors must also be considered. Violence is rarely something that takes place totally unilaterally. It is almost always a transaction involving two parties. The mounting anger of the deprived black and the growing insistence of his demand for equality now have stimulated much anxiety, particularly among lower-middle-class whites, who have then responded with counteraggression and renewed prejudice—the so-called white backlash. This, in turn, has intensified black nationalism, and the chasm between the two groups has grown deeper and wider, with greater polarization of feelings and a greater predisposition to violence on both sides.

Moreover, although the negative aspects of violence are quite obvious, the constructive aspects of violent behavior are often lost sight of. Violent behavior on the part of masses of people represents a kind of crude signaling device or communication to the body politic that something is wrong. Thus riots or acts of violence serve as a means of opening channels of communication between the ghettos and the power structure, channels that in many instances have never existed previously. Also, as has been thoroughly documented in some of the descriptions of recent riots, they provide a release mechanism which gives a sense of power and status to people or groups who have felt inadequate or humiliated. This explains the sense of elation among riot participants that has so frequently been observed, particularly in the early phase of the rioting, before the suppressive weight of control measures has had a chance to take effect.

With these underlying factors, what are the triggers that have set off mass outbursts of urban violence? Not surprisingly, most of these riots have taken place at the height of summer, when the unbearable heat in the central-city ghettos has lowered the threshhold of irritability of its inhabitants to dangerous levels. Given the basic setting of chronic anger and frustration and such a lowered threshhold of irritability, any police action which seems unwarranted, inconsiderate, or insulting can become the incendiary fuse, as the recent report of the Lemberg Center for the Study of Violence at Brandeis University has pointed out.[5] An unjust arrest, or rumors of a black person being injured or unfairly handled by law-enforcement agencies or by some whites, can suddenly release the pent-up anger in the group, anger which then spreads by mass contagion to explosive proportions.

The "treatment" of mass urban violence needs to be dealt with at two levels. The immediate, short-term need is to reduce and eliminate such triggering mechanisms as much as possible. This calls for better police relations and communications with the members of the urban ghettos, for greater use and employment of black police officers, for a greater degree of local rule wherever possible, and for the elimination of the kinds of patterns of behavior that intensify the sense of degradation which the members of these ghettos feel. Thus, while one can appreciate the tensions under which white police officers operate within a black urban ghetto, certain actions that traditionally are often taken by them seem psychologically indefensible. For example, the common practice of spread-eagling a black suspect over the hood of his car while he is searched is a "castrating" procedure that arouses deep feelings of humiliation and resentment among black men, whose masculine self-image has already been rendered deeply vulnerable by chronic unemployment and racial discrimination.

On a more fundamental basis, of course, the deep sources of frustrations in our central cities have to be dealt with. Although it might logically be argued that if one could eliminate the expectations of our poor, they would be better off, this is no longer possible in today's world. Hopes brought to life are not easily stifled, and the American commitment to a democratic ideology is now too deeply rooted in our traditions to be eradicated. It therefore becomes a matter of urgent necessity to tackle the basic sources of frustration of our poor so that their hopes can again acquire the potentiality of realization. In today's explosive urban situation, gradualism or tokenism will no longer suffice. To the underprivileged blacks gradualism, through long and bitter experience, has come to mean "never." Only a crash program of massive proportions that will enable them to see results rapidly will have any effect in lessening their level of frustration. Unfortunately the tragedy of present-day America is that so long as the war in Vietnam continues, there is no prospect that such a crash program will be or can be undertaken.

The special relevance of the war to these urgent urban needs becomes highlighted when we realize that conservative estimates place the cost of the war at thirty billion dollars a year. It is hard for any average person to fully comprehend the meanings of this magnitude of expenditure. Recently, in a somewhat different context, Warren Weaver of the Rockefeller Institute undertook to explore what thirty billion dollars could buy for science and education. Writing in *Medical World News* on January 5, 1968, he stated:

> We could give a ten-percent raise in salary, over a ten-year period, to every teacher in the United States, from kindergarten through universities, in both public and private institutions (about $9.8 billion); give $10 million each to 200 of the best smaller colleges ($2 billion); finance seven-year fellowships at $4,000 per person per year for 50,000 new scientists and engineers ($1.4 billion); contribute $200 million each toward the creation of ten new medical schools ($2 billion); build and largely endow complete universities, with medical, engineering, and agricultural faculties for all 53 of the nations which have been added to the United Nations since its original founding ($13.2 billion); create three more permanent Rockefeller Foundations ($1.5 billion); and still have $100 million left over to popularize science.

Perhaps a more relevant example was an estimate that I

encountered a year ago after seeing a heartrending film on the filth, despair, and degradation that characterized a typical urban ghetto area, the Ludlow section of Philadelphia, a section in which even the local residents dared not move around after dusk for fear of being raped, mugged, or otherwise violently assaulted. It was an area characterized by rotting slum tenements, accumulating garbage, and rats that roamed at will. A local civic leader estimated that twenty million dollars was needed to rehabilitate that area and make it a livable place for its inhabitants. Twenty million dollars to clean up one typical urban ghetto: this is an amount approximating six hours' worth of the cost of the Vietnam war! That means that the cost of one year of the Vietnam war could pay for the rehabilitation of fifteen hundred such urban ghettos.

This is not to imply, however, that simply pouring money into the ghettos for improved housing and schools will suffice to solve the problems of the poor in our central cities. Of even higher priority to all our poor—white, black, brown, yellow, and red—is the dignity of full employment at a living wage. Perhaps nothing short of a massive federal work program, and work-training program, along the lines of the Works Progress Administration of the Roosevelt era, will provide that solution, since it seems unlikely that private capital can ever make more than token inroads into this problem.

Finally, there are certain other long-term considerations that are relevant to the prevention of violence in American society. Perhaps the most important of these is the need to alter some of the social institutions and basic values of our present-day culture which subtly tend to glorify violence and, not so subtly, to desensitize people to its manifestations.[6] Our history books glorify wars and generals; the millions of victims of war are treated merely as ciphers, and as Arthur Koestler has so aptly put it, "statistics don't bleed." Our movies, our television stories, our comic books, and our newspapers all "sell" violence in huge doses to our children, our adolescents, and our grownups. War games and toys grow ever more realistic.

The issue here is not whether such marketing of violence "creates" aggression in people. The roots of aggression, as we have seen, are of a deeper sort. Moreover, to argue—as many psychologists and psychiatrists have—that war games and toys and violence in the communications media provide "an outlet for hostility" is completely to miss the essential point. Granting that they are indeed such an outlet, the question is whether this is the kind of outlet that is healthy either for the individual or for society. The insidious fact about such marketing of violence is that it *desensitizes* people to the spectacle of human brutality and killing, and *teaches* them techniques for encompassing such ends. Our society needs institutions that will strengthen the dignity and sanctity of human life, not degrade it. Outlets for hostility do not have to be directed at goals of death and brutality. There are "moral equivalents" of violence, to adapt William James's well-known phrase, that serve such psychological purposes equally well. Cheering for one's side in an athletic contest, or participating in one, is also an outlet for hostility, and a much healthier one socially and individually. There is a crying need in our society to identify the various acculturation processes, subtle and not-so-subtle, that abet patterns of human violence, and to try to modify them. Not only can war no longer be considered a rational political instrument in an age of nuclear weapons; the patterns of socially sanctioned violence and brutality in any form need to be eliminated if man is to survive the challenges that face him in the decades ahead.

NOTES

1. Judd Marmor, "War, Violence and Human Nature," *The Bulletin of the Atomic Scientists,* March, 1964, pp. 19–22.

2. Lewis A. Coser, "Violence and the Social Structure," *Science and Psychoanalysis,* Vol. VI, New York, Grune & Stratton, Inc., 1963, pp. 30–42.

3. Thomas Merton, "A Devout Meditation in Memory of Adolph Eichmann," *Raids on the Unspeakable,* New York, New Directions Publishing Company, 1966.

4. Alexis de Tocqueville, *L'Ancien Régime,* trans. by M. W. Patterson, Oxford, England, Basil Blackwell, 1949, p. 186.

5. *Six-City Study. A Survey of Racial Attitudes in Six Northern Cities: Preliminary Findings*, a report of the Lemberg Center for the Study of Violence, Brandeis University, Waltham, Massachusetts, June, 1967 (mimeographed).

6. Judd Marmor, "Psychological Problems of Warlessness," in A. Larsen (ed.), *A Warless World*, New York, McGraw-Hill Book Company, 1963, pp. 117–130.

AMERICA'S MALADY IS NOT VIOLENCE BUT SAVAGERY

The impotent are often the most savage of all

By JOHN LUKACS

"The worst, the most corrupting lies," Georges Bernanos wrote at the end of the Second World War, "are problems poorly stated." Perhaps this is a particularly American phenomenon. Internationalism versus isolationism; broad-mindedness versus narrow-mindedness; education versus ignorance; abundance versus poverty; freedom versus slavery; progress versus stagnation: who would, who would dare to, espouse the latter in America? But are the latter really the problems? Do not the American problems involve, rather, the quality of the former: what kind of internationalism? what kind of education? what kind of abundance? what kind of freedom?

WAR on poverty! CRUSADE against ignorance! Characteristically American slogans; typically American acts. Their propagation often obscures the decaying reality of the alternatives: internationalism tending to become the recipe for global intervention; broad-mindedness becoming flat-mindedness; education becoming a ritual system; abundance becoming the proliferation of junk; freedom turning into abject loneliness; progress becoming a nightmare. The alternatives become slogans—they *are* slogans; they become institutionalized, they are corrupted, and beneath their verbal formulations lie disillusionment and despair.

Problems poorly stated. So it is with *violence,* which is,

I believe, one of the poorest statements of perhaps the profoundest problem that affects the character of the American people. Indeed, the statement is so poor that even the verbal formulation of the alternative, *nonviolence,* limps: a weak word, a kind of nonword. Perhaps it is a weasel word. Why did the people who brought it into wide currency about twenty years ago in this country not call a spade a spade; why didn't they call the alternative to violence *pacifism,* for that is what it is. (One shouldn't attribute motives, but isn't it possible that around 1950, in the then hot climate of American anti-Communism, of democratic superpatriotism, *pacifism* sounded too subversive a word?)

I have a great admiration for pacifists, because there are so few of them. (Perhaps I should say *peaceful* people, men and women *full of peace,* rather than *pacifists,* for to possess an abundance of peacefulness within oneself is one thing, and to belong to a mass movement, to an ism, is quite another.) To turn the other cheek *is* the most difficult of all human responses; it is even more difficult than the exhortation to love one's enemies, since the latter does not always require an act of will. For, to paraphrase Sydney Smith, no man should claim to be a pacifist unless he is prepared to go the whole lamb. Few are capable of going the whole lamb, including of course this writer. War, conflict, violence; struggle, aggression, revenge—they are part and parcel of human nature. But it is not enough to say this; contrary to the now so fashionable neo-evolutionistic theories, war, violence, aggression, revenge, are not merely animalistic residues within evolving human nature, but the eternal and immutable stains of what was once called original sin.

No doubt these are unfashionable assertions. Let me, instead, argue from the record of history. What civilization can do, what civilization did during the centuries of its relatively best achievements, was to keep war, conflict, violence, within limits. One need not be a reactionary to contemplate with respect certain conditions in the history of conflict within Western civilization before 1914, when even wars were fought within tacitly accepted ground rules—meaning, for example, the definite separation of soldiers from civilians, of combatants from noncombatants, of conditions of peace from conditions of war, the latter practiced by professional armies rather than by entire peoples—and when small municipal forces of a police or of a watch were sufficient to insure tranquility and surety in the great cities of the Western world.

All of this has now changed, in no small measure as a result of Wars to End Wars, of Crusades for World Peace, in which the once limited purposes of wars have been transformed and institutionalized. Fifty years ago Americans were told that the then war would end all wars, and a League of Nations would come about to insure the coming reign of peace forever; after a second world war and the atom bomb, they were told and taught that from then on the alternatives were total war or total peace. Nothing like this happened at all, and the premonitions of certain men such as Churchill and de Gaulle, civilized imperialists or old-fashioned patriots, have proven truer than the ideas propagandized by certain savage pacifists.

For there is a world of difference between attempts to limit and attempts to eradicate violence: the first is the inescapable consequence of civilization, the second may lead straight to savagery. The word *violence,* in any event, means something that is better than *savagery.* At worst, violence suggests a sharp and brutal assertion of life, whereas even at its best savagery is permeated by despair. (The French language allows *une violence d'esprit,* which is a kind of mental leap; *sauvagerie d'esprit,* on the other hand, would mean sheer barbarism.) Blocked by a stuck door in a fire, or by a bent piece of metal in an accident, we use violent force to save life, a kind of action not only enforced by our emotions, but dictated by our intelligence—very different from savage fury, which is principally, and impurely, emotional.

Or consider the basic fact of our existence, greatly obscured as this is nowadays. Man is borne by a woman no longer a virgin, meaning that a natural seal within her flesh (do other living beings possess hymens? I do not know, but somehow I doubt it) must have been pierced by an act of certain violence. Violence may be life-giving, whereas savagery smells of death. The desire to inflict pain is the result of savagery, not of violence, as is the often worse

wish to inflict humiliation. But whereas "violent humiliation"—a limping phrase, at that—suggests the debasement
of the perpetrator as well as the victim, "savage humiliation"
involves the reduction of another person to something non-
human.

Lest my readers think that I am making a Fascist or
conservative argument for violence through euphemisms
about law and order, I must make myself clear: I abhor
not only the beating of a person by a policeman, but even
more his humiliation; I see in the outfits of American
state troopers at times the paraphernalia of something savage, rather than the uniforms of monopolists of legal violence; when I dislike policemen it is not because of the
controlled violence they practice, but because of the controlled contempt that seeps through the edges of their
sealed faces and studied expressions. "Move on, buddy!"
—in these three words there may gleam something worse
than violence, that is, the wish to humiliate, something
savage rather than violent.

This country is threatened by savagery, not violence:
and this is not a play on words. The peoples of this world
are governed by their characters rather than by their institutions; and there is a streak of savagery rather than
violence in the American character. Lately this trait has
reappeared on the surface, too. I write "lately" because
during the last few years a monumental shift has occurred
in the United States, from the former conventions of national optimism in the public rhetoric and professed beliefs
of Americans to the now widespread fashion of pessimism
and cynicism. Note that I am not saying that violence is
not part and parcel of American history, too; but violence
is, curiously enough, often the result of a kind of superficial
optimism, not pessimism. Violence is, after all, the consequence of impatience: it has a purpose, even if a bad one,
whereas behind savagery there lurk purposelessness and
fatalism.

Poe was the first, and probably the greatest, American
seer who recognized this subsoil of savage despair underneath the prosperous and rigid democracy of the Northern tropical republic. Notwithstanding all their democratic,
and occasionally antidemocratic, rhetoric, the Palefaces and

the Redskins who followed Poe through the marches of American art and letters failed to recognize this at all: Whitman's and Vachel Lindsay's preachings stopped short of it; Henry James failed to confront it; Ezra Pound made a stab at it, here and there, because he was *for* it, *Rock-Drill* being a prosodic forerunner of rock-and-roll and of the opiate fogs from the Far East. The controlled violence exalted by such disparate Americans as Theodore Roosevelt and Ernest Hemingway was juvenile and therefore insubstantial. Roosevelt did stand for a kind of nearly mature Athletic Christianity (much preferable, at the time, to Wilson's YMCA world philosophy), while Hemingway's very definition of courage—"grace under pressure"—reflects nothing but mechanical fatalism decked out in a fake outfit of Hispanic baroque.

It took a feverish and nearly burned-out Englishman, D. H. Lawrence, to realize, in the depths of his profound disillusionment with savagery (which he had originally exalted), that there was a savage subsoil of American feeling, a deep-seated enmity to European civilization, discernible even with the vacuous civilizational rhetoric of Franklin. Expressed (or rather, spat out) in fragments in his *Studies in Classic American Literature* (a curiously academic title), Lawrence recognized nearly fifty years ago that beneath the growth of a universal mechanical civilization, beneath urbanized Babbittism, beneath the hot American asphalt and under the frozen concrete, the Indian substance was darkly alive and working; that, as so often in history, the subjugated land was about to conquer its conquerors. . . .

WHITE SAVAGERY

At this point it should appear that my preoccupation with savagery (and my distinction between savagery and violence) does not represent a carefully clothed philosophic attempt at striking at the many savage things—for they are savage things—in which American black people are on occasion indulging themselves nowadays. Whites in America are responsible for these things, but not so much because they treated the blacks savagely (though often they did) as because they allowed the rhetoric and the civilization of the entire country to be infected with a peculiar Northern savagery of which the savagely contemptuous tone of New York life became a representative model. For my argument is not that the descendants of Englishmen and Irishmen and Continental Europeans who had come to this nation retained within themselves too much of the Old World, preserving in their minds and practices Gothic vestiges of feudalism, aristocracy, racialism. The very opposite is true: few of these descendants have remained European; they tore themselves away from the roots of the only traditional civilization they may have had. The demonic savagery that threatens America today is of the making of its nomadic inhabitants, mostly whites.

There are so many illustrations of this condition that a few snapshots ought to suffice. If the Black Panthers are making a cult of savagery, so do the Hell's Angels; and there are reasons to believe that the Panthers imitate the Angels. "What is good for America is good for the world": behind the benevolent facial expression of American internationalism lies the often savage—yes, savage— desire to level the world into one big plain, in the name of justice. Even now this Wilsonian slogan dominates the relationship of Americans to the rest of the world, perpetrated as it first was, not by that bumbling General Motors statesman Charles Wilson, but by the Ideal and Idealist President, Woodrow Wilson.

What appalls me, a European, about American football is its savagery, not its violence: the now Martian outfits of the players; its peculiarly American pattern of savage speeds and jerky long stops; the savagery in the face of Vince Lombardi (perhaps even more than in the punky features of George Wallace), for that is what Midwestern America can do to an Italian face.

Savagery, not violence, marks the appalling features of our automobile civilization: the uprooting of breathing nature; the inhuman spaces of hot, lonely parking lots; the roaring trucks with their garish lights and jeweled rubber chaps. And it is the artificial excitement of savagery, not the violent, impatient desire to hurry time, that makes boys burn and shriek back and forth on our highways at night. Aimless speed: the American predicament. In the late forties and early fifties one often saw carloads of boys, in black hot rods, sitting erect and half-naked, bronzed in the cars, jeering and screaming, with wild music blaring, rocketing off at the stops. The radio music then was still Midwestern and automatic; but the savage rock-drill, the rock-and-roll—consider, for a moment, all of the Nordic primitive savagery compressed within these two words—of the American sixties was already contained within their black repainted cars, mechanical insects, bug-like germs of the then near-future.

Meanwhile the intellectuals have caught on. For the last eight or nine years a hitherto unsurpassed cult of ugliness and of savagery has been abroad in the land, among the hards as well as the softs, often propagated in the name of Consciousness, Self-Realization, Imagination; and whereas this diabolical (for that is what it is) cult of ugliness has spread, like an oil slick, on the surface of Europe, here it draws some of its sickly strength from the marrow.

Consciousness! Imagination! What miseries. . . . Imagination has decayed to a level where it has remained stuck, for years now, at the sickening patterns and even the lettering of the Art Nouveau style of 1900. The sense-hallucinatory practices induced by drugs, too, have nothing to do with the cultivation of imagination, for imagination is nourished by more or less conscious sources from our personal past, whereas hallucination is the very opposite of memory; oriented toward a nonexistent future, it wishes to blot out reality, unlike memory, which is attracted by the deepening of it. Far from representing a deepening of consciousness, hallucination represents a regression to a more primitive form thereof. Dependent on external stimulants, it is fundamentally passive, whereas imagination is fundamentally active. And here I come to a sad important point: that Americans are a fundamentally, *very* fundamentally, passive people. How could they be otherwise? For a long time now they have been taught, and they have come to believe, that human beings are results, products. Behind much of the superficial impressions of restlessness and hyperactivity there lies a deep American sense of passivity, just as behind superficial overoptimism there often lies the sense of despair.

What are the principal sources of this American attitude? They are, I believe, Puritan, democratic, Indian. Puritan, because of a conviction of predestination which from its original religious sources went on, transmuted, into the present overall acceptance of scientism, meaning that a man is *determined* by his hormones, complexes, environment, IQ's, DNA—a Western fatalism, if there ever was one. Democratic, because the ideology of democracy, as de Tocqueville foresaw, threatens civilization less through anarchy and violence than through conformism, through the acceptance of philosophies that cannot and will not recognize human free will, philosophies which even the most successful leaders of a democracy come to share wholly (whence, for example, John Kennedy's enthusiastic espousal, in the foreword of his *Profiles in Courage,* of Hemingway's mechanical and fatalist "definition" of "courage"). Indian, because no matter how much concrete is poured over their dead campsites, the curse on their land remains. They infected the American soul, and the face is the mirror of the soul. I am not only speaking of the now stupid fad of Indian fashions, ranging from the American juvenile cult of hallucinatory inarticulateness to the obscene scenes of fat German trucking executives whooping it up along the black Upper Danube in breechcloths, tents, wigwams; I am looking at the faces of some of our public figures of the sixties: Goldwater the Indian Jew of the Southwest, Bobby Kennedy the Irish Indian Boy.

Kindness and savagery, generosity and suspicion, utopianism and fatalism—these are principal American characteristics, elements of the American national character that has not yet crystallized. Its crystallization was disrupted, slowed down early in this century, at the very time when the place of the American empire in the world was beginning to crystallize. Twice in this century America had come to help save the democracies of Western Europe, no doubt out of mixed motives; but at least one of these motives was the wish of many Americans to save Western Europe from barbarianism. This motive was obscured by slogans and submerged by the hazy, strong desire to make the entire world like America; but perhaps a chastened realization of America's place in the world may be around the corner now. The value of this realization, however, depends on the recognition that America's relationship to Europe is different, that it must be different, from its relationship to the rest of the world, and not only because of political or strategic reasons.

The future of Europe is not its Americanization, all of the superficial servant scribblers notwithstanding. The future of America *is* Americanization, but this may now mean either the increase of savagery or the increase of civilization; and in the event of the latter, Americans must know that Western civilization, no matter what its faults, is essentially, and inescapably, European in its roots. Americans may not recognize this yet, even though they are about to recognize that the era of American omnipotence may be over. And why? Because the working ideas of the New Men, of the American Engineers, who proclaimed not so long ago that history was bunk, brought about the most frustrating and helpless condition in which modern man can find himself, that is, being stuck in an endless traffic jam. For that is what it is, a traffic jam: the cities of the richest power on earth turning into vast slums inhabited by masses of nomads; the most prosperous institutions of industry no longer attracting either the ambitions of greedy youth or the investments of calculating foreigners; the nation with the most gigantic armaments and technology that the world has ever seen now incapable of imposing its will on jungles at home or abroad, impotent in the face of such foreign skirmishes that gunboat statesmanship fifty years ago could handle with ease.

But beware of the preaching of impotence, especially in the United States! The impotent are often the most savage of all. Many of those intellectuals who scream against violence have now become the voyeurs and purveyors of savagery. They are responsible for very, very much. They have been siding with savagery, against civilization. They have gone one worse than the Bourbons after the Restoration: they have forgotten everything and learned nothing. When Mr. Mike Nichols, a now principal culture commis-

sar, says that "Critics are like eunuchs watching a gang-bang.
They must truly be ignored," this is yet another New Man
trotting out yet another of the tatchety clichés of Hem,
the Old Injun of the Ritz; and broadcasting from Hollywood to New York, he has forgotten, too, something else,
which is that one need not be a eunuch to find a gang-bang
revolting.

The Wages of Gang-Bangs is Death. Americans ought
to know this, and preferably learn it not by experience.
For death, no matter whether small or big, comes but once;
and it is irrevocable, no matter the blather of gurus, or of
the Heart Plantation Corporation, now forming.

AMERICAN VIOLENCE IN PERSPECTIVE

By WARNER BLOOMBERG, JR.

There is a peculiar pessimism in much of the expressed concern about violence in the United States today. Some seem to see us moving toward an apocalyptic peak of internal destructiveness, although the objective evidence suggests that, for a nation whose domestic and foreign affairs have been regularly embellished with blood, the present situation is far from maximum. Others, with characteristic American egotism, talk about contemporary turmoil as if we were its originators and main, if not sole, distributors, as if varying degrees of racial-ethnic conflict and student unrest were not epidemic throughout at least the urbanized and industrialized societies of the world. Indeed one might take a little hope from the growing worry over—instead of mere acquiescence in, or even enjoyment of—the chronic elements of violence in American life, especially since those elements themselves show no special increase relative to either our own past or contemporary conditions among most of our societal peers.

Violence is, of course, an intrinsic potential in human nature. It is part of our primate heritage. Yet the aggression of the ape and the baboon has been transformed in human history. Among our evolutionary antecedents, actual violence, apart from the hunt for food, is relatively infrequent. It occurs in struggles for leadership and on the territorial peripheries where bands may momentarily contest for control. It is always brief and seldom results in more than a few individual casualties; the apes and the baboons conduct no holy wars, no campaigns of genocide, no militant expeditions into distant lands. But among humans, as we know so well, violence can be a craft, a consuming and epidemic pathology, and even a national industry.

Where does it come from, this human capacity for immense amounts of violence? This is like asking about the origins of earthquakes and volcanic eruptions. However subterranean their sources, they are not foreign to this earth but are part of its very nature. Psychologically, violence may occur when the need for love is transmuted by cruelty and rejection into rage and hatred. Or it may develop when energies and drives that could be channeled and sublimated into actions to organize and re-create the environment are instead focused by frustrations and fears into efforts to destroy something or someone. Culturally, our capacity to generate unifying systems of belief and humanistic visions of utopia also enables us to produce doctrines of national, racial, or religious superiority which we use to justify the slaughter or subjugation of those with different allegiances, different pigmentation, or different visions of the divine. Technologically, the same skills and tools which we use to build cities, with their centers of art, learning, religion, commerce, and government, we also use to reduce those cities to smoking ruins and crumbling wreckage.

These are not, of course, new insights: Ecclesiastes reminds us that in human existence there is a time for hate as well as for love, for war as well as for peace, for tearing apart as well as for putting together. And in the religious tradition with which I am affiliated, what is called the "evil inclination" is seen as the source of all efforts to modify the world by building structures, engaging in commerce, organizing governments, even painting pictures; the problem is to determine how to make sure that the evil inclination— the tendency to possess, to use, to change—is put to the service of good and useful ends. Thus we mislead ourselves into a fool's errand if we ask how to eliminate violence from human affairs; we can only attempt to minimize the frequency, the duration, and the intensity of its manifestations, seeking constructive expression of our capacities for aggression. But if we try solely to suppress violence once it emerges, then we can be sure that it will appear frequently, be persistent, and reach great heights of destruction.

It is true that there have been some remarkably nonviolent human settlements and societies. One thinks of the Zuni Indians and the Iroquois Nation before Europeans made a violent conquest of this continent. However, there have been very few truly peaceful cities, and this is hardly surprising. Cities have been the bases from which elites launched their campaigns of commercial and military conquest, aggressively reaching out for more power and more material wealth. They have been the centers into which the produce of the peasantry was funneled, often by force. They have been the scene of immense disparities in wealth and well-being, made ever more visible as old barriers to the communication of images and information have disappeared. They have been the setting for all kinds of innovations—technological, organizational, ideological—which disrupt old relationships and customary accommodations to things as they are. In short, nonurban societies may be either unusually peaceful or extremely violent; but the peaceful city is so rare that it almost seems a contradiction in terms. When we find one, it usually turns out to be a decayed and partially fossilized social order that has devolved from an earlier period of more vigorous and violent urbanism.

If, as I have suggested, violence manifests itself as a consequence of cruelty, rejection, frustration, fear, absolutist and imperialistic doctrines, and unconstrained ambitions to control and subjugate, then we would expect the tensions, trepidations, changes of condition and situation, and clashes of ideology that characterize periods of extensive and rapid social change to produce great amounts of violence. If it is also true that our society is in the midst of an evolutionary transition across some sociocultural great divide and has been for most of its history, then we should expect it to be a violent nation, one that might well grow more rather than less violent as it becomes more urban and as the rate of change increases.

This country began, of course, with the disruption of people's lives. Whether colonizers fled tyranny, sought wealth, or were dispatched to this continent as bond servants or penal forced labor, they experienced great psychological stress and often equally violent physical hardships. Their own suffering plus their sense of mission seemed not only to harden them, but also to intensify both their capacity to deal harshly with others and their inner anxieties and fears about the violent and ugly side of their own nature. The witch-hunts in New England were surface manifestations of something much more pervasive in the subterranean levels of the American spirit, a belief in the presence within some of us of a sinister evil which must be exposed and painfully, violently exorcised. It re-emerges in the burning of the homes and shops of actual and alleged "Tories" during the Revolutionary period, the tormenting and exiling of the Mormons, the lynching of Negroes, the harassment and coercion directed against actual and alleged "Reds" and "foreign radicals" during the Palmer and McCarthy periods of political witch-hunting.

To the extent that violence in the United States is some-how distinguishable from the immense amount of turbulence and strife evident within and among so many European nations during this same period of time, it is probably in terms of those elements which are unique to our particular history and which give our version of urban-industrial social strife and external imperialism an especially "American" style or flavor. This is well illustrated by our genocidal campaigns against the Indians, by which we destroyed not only the warrior tribes but also some of the most truly peaceable people who have ever existed, violating again and again the very treaties we had helped to write and sign. Once again we justified our violence by portraying the victims as possessed by evil, as less than human, as in fact the infectious source of the violence we were perpetrating. In a classical psychiatric pattern that is entrenched in the American character, we projected onto others that which we could not confront below the surface of our social order and within our own selves.

Slavery and the Western frontier both contributed to and were characterized by violence "American-style," culminating in the Civil War. The West was eventually pacified (at least as much as the rest of the country), but "race relations" remained an area in which unconstrained and destructive aggression, both physical and psychological, could be perpetrated—at least by whites. We have, of course, repressed until very recently any national memory of the reality of our nation's enslavement of the African, our transformation of him into the Negro, and our imprisonment of that Negro-American in castelike shackles for almost a century after his so-called "emancipation." We have just begun to remind ourselves that the blacks of this nation brought from Africa had rich cultures before they found themselves in the holds of our slave ships: complex languages, intricate religions, powerful myths, great capacities for handicraft. "Cultural genocide" is probably a fair term for the attempt that was systematically made to destroy this original cultural heritage in every generation, though fortunately we did not wholly succeed. Families were disrupted. Literacy, which later we required of all other immigrants, was prevented, often on pain of death. Women were exploited for sexual purposes.

The product of all this was what many psychiatrists, thinking of psychological syndromes, have called the castration of the male. And at the same time the black male had to repress his anger because to become angry at a white man in his presence was to die. Two centuries of this quite predictably produced a surface appearance among many Afro-Americans of apathy and apparent loss of motivation, of lack of self-confidence for risk-taking in many situations —all of it reinforced by systematic exclusion from work roles which in our society mean manhood.

Although we label psychological torture unequivocally as a form of violence when it is perpetrated against American citizens taken as prisoners of war, most of us have failed to recognize it when it has taken an institutionalized form, such as the prejudice and discrimination, incorporated into both law and custom, by which generation after generation of black Americans have been assaulted. We have just begun to understand that the thousands of lynchings were only the more extreme, physical, and individualized manifestations of the institutionalized violence of American racism, and that militant action by blacks has been and continues to be a kind of counterviolence. Thus President Franklin Roosevelt did not establish a Fair Employment Practices

Commission in the United States, even one without teeth, until A. Philip Randolph threatened to march ten thousand Negroes down Pennsylvania Avenue right smack in the middle of World War II. President Truman did not abolish racial segregation in the Army in 1947 because of a sudden insight into the fact that segregation in the armed forces did not quite fit somehow with our claim to being "the world's greatest democracy." He abolished it because A. Philip Randolph threatened to throw a picket line of one thousand black men around the Democratic convention of that year. Congress did not undergo some conversion to humanity when it passed the first major civil rights act. Our representatives acted with the great civil rights march swarming around them in the nation's capitol, with its evident potential for violence. Violence and the threat of violence have been necessary to bring any rapid improvement in the state of the black man in America.

In all societies with puritanical traditions, sex and aggression are often critically linked in the subterranean, surrealistic levels of human perception and motivation. This has been especially evident in the relationships between whites and blacks in the United States, reinforcing tendencies toward overt violence by both, but especially by whites. It is not coincidental that liberalism in the sexual realm and growing emancipation from racist attitudes tend to be displayed by the same segments of the population, especially in the younger generation. Nor is it coincidental that among young people the strongest residues of racism and violent opposition to desegregation seem to be displayed most often by those with "respectable working-class" or "lower-middle-class" backgrounds, groups which tend to be more puritanical, authoritarian, traditionally patriotic, and ethnically parochial than many of those with more education, a longer and more stable experience of affluence, and fewer status anxieties.

Students of race relations have dealt extensively with the psychosexual dimension, and there has been some popularization of such analysis by a few journalists; but there has been less attention paid to the historical connections between this and other dimensions of black-white conflict and violence. What must be further explored is the cumulative development of feelings and images over successive generations.

Early in our history Americans had to rationalize slavery in the face of a growing world-wide condemnation. (The war in Vietnam has presented us with a similar psychological problem today.) Apologists for slavery asserted that the black man from Africa was not quite human; he was portrayed as "the savage from the jungle." And this had important emotional implications for the inner character of the whites, especially in the South—consequences oriented to two mythic self-images generated within the culture of plantation society. The Southern white male was portrayed as chivalrous and highly mannered, but also as lusty, rebel-yelling, sword-wearing, horseback-riding—a dream assembled from notions of the eras of knighthood and chivalry which plantation society was supposed to transform into a reality. But masculine virility and bravado were not matched by a compatible female prototype from, say, that time in England when women sang bawdy ballads, engaged in seductions, had affairs, and in general were often rather lusty wenches. Instead quite a different ideal emerged; that pure, white, chaste, magnolia-scented woman-on-a-pedestal (or woman-on-a-curving-staircase) got built into the emotional substratum.

But across the way on the plantation there lived what the whites perceived as the savage of the jungle, inferior and full of animal lust. So white males, many of them, migrated regularly from the main house through the darkness of the night to the slave quarters, and returned full of guilt and a sense of pollution, and were irresistibly drawn back again and again. And how did the Southern white wife feel about that? What did it mean to her? Yet when she bore children, they were in large part taken care of by one of those black women from across the courtyard. Why? Partly because taking care of children is work, and work should be done by slaves. But perhaps also because little children need warmth and affection—the physical, the "animal" love that the white woman couldn't give but the black woman could.

This rather kinky arrangement went on generation after generation and became introjected into the personality of the Southern white. It generated guilts, fears, and anxieties that in turn were projected onto the Negro captives. Thus that pervasive image of the black man as rapist and murderer externalized from the unconscious of his white master, and the image of the black woman as lustful and sexually desirable. (Nor is this something that died out in America long, long ago: as a youth visiting in the Deep South, I was told by a local white peer that you're not "really a man" until you've "had a nigger woman.") The classic lynching is once again the exorcising of the devil, of the beast, in which a "black savage"—almost inevitably accused of either rape or murder, or attempting such a crime —is seized, beaten, castrated, doused with kerosene, and burned alive.

After the Civil War, Southern whites moved North and West, carrying this syndrome like so many psychological "typhoid Marys." They communicated it to an ever more receptive population in our growing urban areas. For during the decades after the Civil War, an increasing number of white Americans suffered from two forms of severe status anxiety, one resulting from increasing social mobility in a society undergoing rapid change, and the other, even more potent, the status anxiety of the immigrant. Those who came to America in such massive waves during this period were clearly told that they were not Americans; they were polacks, or hunkies, or micks, or kikes, or krauts, but they weren't "real Americans." We have a whole literature, both tragic and comic, portraying the immense status anxiety of these new "hyphenated Americans," an anxiety which persisted beyond their Americanization and which was transmitted to their children and even their grandchildren by those subterranean psychological processes with which we are increasingly familiar.

These people had one certain comfort amidst all their anxiety, all the questioning about who was really an American. They had a bench mark: the black man. He would stay put. He was permanently *not* an American. He was here, but he was permanently an outsider. Compared with him, the white immigrant was more American and higher up the social ladder when he first stepped off the boat. And so people who had never seen a black man learned to hate

Negroes, to accept the Southern imagery of them, and to talk disparagingly of "niggers" in a variety of brogues. Thus was the psychosexual syndrome produced by plantation society fused with a status-anxiety syndrome produced by our unique experience with massive immigration into our society. And this fusion has fueled the potential violence in thousands of situations of contact and conflict between the races, especially in our urban areas.

The normal proclivities for aggressive behavior that are rooted in our primate nature and accentuated by the urban milieu, especially in an era of rapid social change, are thus further strengthened and biased toward violence by some of the unique elements in this nation's history, especially those affecting relationships between the races. It is not surprising that the small, activist cadre of angry white middle-class college students, seeking to mobilize their own somewhat repressed capacities for aggression, have been so enamored of the notion of "the student as nigger" and have taken first the old civil rights movement and subsequently the black power movement as action models for achieving change in academic institutions. It has become clear to them, as it has to most Afro-Americans, that a commitment to nonviolence in a society as predisposed to violence and as inured to it as ours is utterly unrealistic.

Probably only the Negroes, with their cultural emphasis on the suppression of inner anger in the face of the white man, could have generated in the United States a large-scale mass movement committed to nonviolence and held to that commitment by a trained and dedicated leadership. It was bound to fail given this nation's (that is, the white majority's) psychological and institutional preparation to meet such restrained forms of aggression as marches and sit-ins with much less restrained forms of suppression. Nevertheless, the civil rights movement accomplished much. It brought increased momentum to the processes of institutional change; it exposed with essential clarity the immense wellsprings for aggression and the predisposition to violence which characterize the psychological substratum of American culture; and ironically, it provided a necessary stepping stone of both accomplishment and frustration which has enabled a large part of the younger generation of blacks to get past the older Negroes' hang-ups about displaying aggression, even violent forms of it, in dealing with the white majority—that is, it enabled them to become psychologically more like the whites they had to confront.

There is indeed an almost classic pattern emerging which frequently appears during the course of partially blocked social revolutions. Just as the majority of whites today formally delegate to police agencies and the military the use of violence on their behalf, the majority of blacks now informally delegate the same function to the rioters who occasionally and largely spontaneously emerge in urban centers and to the tiny terrorist groups which have been forming, which will probably become more active, and which the black majority will eventually have to help destroy when enough of the goals around which the broader social movement has formed have been achieved. Most black leaders with substantial followings, while no longer eschewing the use of violence, seem to view the cost to the ghetto population of large-scale physical aggression as too high in most cases, given a society so well prepared emotionally and materially to escalate the destruction. They therefore have concentrated on a kind of guerrilla psychological warfare against the white majority, using threats of violence, feelings of guilt among whites, and appeals to international public opinion, especially in the "third world." At the same time they seek to increase their resources for controlled aggression on behalf of the black community's various interests by acquiring more in the way of finances, effective organization, offices vested with relevant authority, and rather loose and tentative "working relationships" with adequately cooperative and compliant whites. In this way new capacities for overt aggression are channeled into less rather than more violent tactics and strategies.

If white student activists continue to emulate the black minority (always with a time lag of six months to a year), we should begin to see a tendency in the majority of radical and reformist students (themselves a small minority of all students) to shift toward a more programmatic approach to reconstructing academic institutions, with a splitting away to some degree of those for whom the link between sexuality and aggression is most intense and who seek a kind of orgiastic experience in confrontations leading to violence. They will continue to promote on-campus protests oriented mainly toward producing climactic moments rather than changes in the system, aided and abetted by a tiny cadre of ideologues whose interpretation of history calls for something close to total destruction of the present academic institution in order to rebuild anything fundamentally better. They are the white student analogues of the most alienated of the militant blacks, those who share in a mythic prophecy of the revolution of the "third world" and who gather their arsenals in preparation for the day of judgment. And both are psychologically closer than they would care to admit to those white adults in such organizations as the Minutemen, who have armed themselves to put down an expected bloody revolution from the left, which is in turn their projective group fantasy.

In the face of these various pressures toward conflict, aggression, and violence in our society, especially in the realm of race relations, pleas for a kind of political pacifism, with educative persuasion somehow replacing the coercive use of power, seem especially irrelevant and even absurd. Whatever it may be time for in the evolution of the American spirit and social order, it is not yet time for that. Indeed the failure of white middle-class liberals to mobilize their potentialities for aggressive strategies and forceful tactics more fully and effectively contributed to the blocking of the civil rights revolution and related reforms, and thus to that frustration of hopes and expectations which brought white-black conflict to a focus in which violence became inevitable. In short, and this should no longer seem so paradoxical, the reformers were not "violent" enough to prevent violence.

Sickened by the Nazi holocaust, by the visible and yet almost incomprehensible slaughterhouse which so much of the world had become during the war, and by the wanton cremation of Hiroshima and Nagasaki (and knowing how utterly American we were when we dropped the bombs), far too many white liberals became enamored of the myth of nonviolence and of a politics of persuasion. At this critical juncture in the emotional development of the reformist elements in our society, their ranks were rent by the reactionary onslaught led by Joseph McCarthy, whose use of psychological violence and political terrorism has seldom been matched in our history. It is a commentary on the state of mind and emotions of so many white liberals and radicals that they took as their hero an admirably adroit and restrainedly indignant attorney whose televised interrogation of the manic senator from Wisconsin introduced his denouement, as if the words (nonviolent, logical, persuasive) somehow did the deed, rather than a growing coalition of vested interests whose respective oxes had been gored in some of McCarthy's wilder moments. Thus, too, their almost worshipful regard for Adlai Stevenson (witty, wordy, gentle, and vacillating in times of crisis with violence on the threshhold); their willingness to lean on the Supreme Court for leverage in bringing about social change, even though it was eminently clear that societies are not in the end reformed by judicial decree (intellectual, logically persuasive, nonviolent), and that the court itself might be brought into peril if used too much in this way; and finally, their compulsive attachment to the old civil rights movement, with its millennial promise that in an aggressive confrontation between rational pacifists (willing even to be beaten and jailed without physical resistance—a typical Negro survival tactic) and those to whom we have officially delegated the acting out of our proclivities for violence, the latter would eventually give in.

But this long period of self-delusion, this feverish dreaming of a pacifist politics in America, is over with at last. It ended for most blacks and for many young whites in the civil rights movement with the bloody encounters on the streets of our cities and with the persistent blocking of reforms for which they willingly endured beatings and sometimes murder. It ended for a great many of their elders on the streets of Chicago during the Democratic party's police-state version of a political convention. There is once again, among the old left as well as among the new, a willingness to face the fact of American violence, and also to realize that it is only our special version of the violence inevitably generated by a rapidly changing urban industrial order. The dream of an essentially pacific human society has not been abandoned, but dreamy strategies and tactics have.

The creation of institutions which secure equality and justice and opportunities for the fruition of the individual human personality still seems to offer the best hope for a social order in which the aggressive potentialities in human nature are harnessed in largest part to constructive endeavors. Neither delusive repression of our present proclivities toward violence nor the violent suppression of frustrated minorities will move us toward such a reconstruction of our social system. Neither will the terrorists and orgiasts, black or white. It will take liberals and radicals, black and white, who are able to use their American capacities for aggression without being caught up in the sexiness of violence, yet who are also prepared to use violence if things must come to that. Our best hope in the present situation seems to be an increasingly forceful politics in behalf of the radical reformation of some of our central institutions, and one in which the pragmatic utilization of aggression takes precedence over doctrinaire compulsions toward confrontation and polarization. Certainly our experience in the realm of race relations tells us how much we must overcome and change, in the subterranean levels of the American character as well as on the surface of its institutional terrain, and how very long it will take—certainly more than one generation—to achieve a social order in which people will be expressing the reality of their lives when they greet each other by saying: "Peace."

INDEX

ABOUT THE EDITOR

THOMAS ROSE is an assistant professor of sociology at Federal City College in Washington, D. C. He has taught also at the University of New Hampshire, Miles College, Marquette University, the College of San Mateo, and *Centro Intercultural de Documentacion* in Cuernavaca, Mexico. Mr. Rose studied at San Francisco State College and has done graduate work at Brandeis University and the University of Wisconsin in Milwaukee, where he took an M.A. in Urban Affairs. He was president of the Milwaukee Students for a Democratic Society. Mr. Rose has published numerous articles in both scholarly and political journals. With James Rodgers, Mr. Rose is writing a history of violence in America.